AMERICA'S
TEST KITCHEN

Also by America's Test Kitchen

Dinner Tonight
The New Vegetarian
The Complete Grilling and Barbecue Cookbook
Cocktails Illustrated
Umma
The Complete Anti-Inflammatory Cookbook
When Southern Women Cook
Food Gifts
America's Test Kitchen 25th Anniversary Cookbook
A Very Chinese Cookbook
Boards

The Sheet Pan
The Skillet
Cook It in Your Dutch Oven
Cook It in Cast Iron
Ultimate Air Fryer Perfection
Kitchen Gear

Baking for Two
Everyday Bread
The Perfect Cookie
The Perfect Pie
The Perfect Cake
The Cook's Illustrated Baking Book

The Science of Good Cooking
Cook's Science
The New Cooking School Cookbook: Fundamentals
The New Cooking School Cookbook: Advanced Fundamentals

Mostly Meatless
Vegan for Everybody
Vegan Cooking for Two
Cooking with Plant-Based Meat
Vegetables Illustrated
How Can It Be Gluten Free Cookbook Collection

The Complete High-Protein Cookbook
The Complete Plant-Based Cookbook
The Complete Beans and Grains Cookbook
The Complete Mediterranean Cookbook
The Complete Cooking for Two Cookbook
The Complete Diabetes Cookbook
The Complete Vegetarian Cookbook
The Complete Autumn and Winter Cookbook
The Complete Summer Cookbook
The Complete Modern Pantry
The Complete Salad Cookbook

The Complete Cook's Country TV Show Cookbook

For a full listing of all our books:
CooksIllustrated.com
AmericasTestKitchen.com

Praise for America's Test Kitchen Titles

"The book is a treasure for its endless kitchen wisdom, heart-filled recipes, and deep-rooted respect for all generations that came before. It showcases home cooking at its best, ranging from sauces, banchan (side dishes), and a slew of kimchi, to gurgling stews, tantalizing meats, and not-too-sweet fare."
Epicurious* on *Umma: a Korean Mom's Kitchen Wisdom & 100 Family Recipes

"This is a one-stop manual for dialing in your home bar. ATK has long been a trusted source for coaxing the best flavor out of ingredients, and this collection is no exception."
Forbes* on *Cocktails Illustrated

"*The Complete Cooking for Two Cookbook*, a perennial bestseller from America's Test Kitchen, makes things much simpler by scaling down over 700 recipes to feed two people . . . Recipes range from rather basic to a little fancy, so this cookbook is a fantastic gift for most couples, regardless of whether they barely know a simmer from a boil or are savvy home cooks.
New York Times* on *The Complete Cooking for Two Cookbook

A Best Cookbook of 2024
LA Times* on *When Southern Women Cook

"This 'very' Chinese cookbook from a father-son duo is a keeper. The book—ATK's first devoted to Chinese cooking—proves that you can teach and entertain in the same volume . . . All in all, it's one of the most charming works I've seen in years, and I already want to get a second copy."
Washington Post* on *A Very Chinese Cookbook

"An exhaustive but approachable primer for those looking for a 'flexible' diet. Chock-full of tips, you can dive into the science of plant-based cooking or just sit back and enjoy the 500 recipes."
Minneapolis Star Tribune* on *The Complete Plant-Based Cookbook

"True to its name, this smart and endlessly enlightening cookbook is about as definitive as it's possible to get in the modern vegetarian realm."
Men's Journal* on *The Complete Vegetarian Cookbook

"A mood board for one's food board is served up in this excellent guide . . . This has instant classic written all over it."
Publishers Weekly* (starred review) on *Boards: Stylish Spreads for Casual Gatherings

"Reassuringly hefty and comprehensive, The Complete Autumn and Winter Cookbook by America's Test Kitchen has you covered with a seemingly endless array of seasonal fare . . . This overstuffed compendium is guaranteed to warm you from the inside out."
NPR on *The Complete Autumn and Winter Cookbook*

"If you're one of the 30 million Americans with diabetes, The Complete Diabetes Cookbook by America's Test Kitchen belongs on your kitchen shelf."
Parade.com on *The Complete Diabetes Cookbook*

"Another flawless entry in the America's Test Kitchen canon, Bowls guides readers of all culinary skill levels in composing one-bowl meals from a variety of cuisines."
BuzzFeed Books on *Bowls*

"*The Perfect Cookie* . . . is, in a word, perfect. This is an important and substantial cookbook . . . If you love cookies, but have been a tad shy to bake on your own, all your fears will be dissipated. This is one book you can use for years with magnificently happy results."
HuffPost on *The Perfect Cookie*

"The book offers an impressive education for curious cake makers, new and experienced alike. A summation of 25 years of cake making at ATK, there are cakes for every taste."
Wall Street Journal* on *The Perfect Cake

The New Cookie

CREATIVE TAKES ON THE CLASSICS YOU LOVE

America's Test Kitchen

Library of Congress CIP data has been applied for.

ISBN 978-1-966027-14-0

America's Test Kitchen
21 Drydock Avenue, Boston, MA 02210

Printed in China
10 9 8 7 6 5 4 3 2 1

Distributed by Penguin Random House Publisher Services

Tel: 800-733-3000

Pictured on front cover: Salted Malted Milk Chocolate Chunk Cookies (page 56), Spritz Cookies (354), Black and White Spiral Sablés (page 209), Blackberry-Thyme Linzer Cookies (page 182), Triple Citrus Gingerbread with White Chocolate (page 86)

Pictured on back cover: Deepest, Darkest, Fudgiest Flourless Brownies (page 308)

Cover and Featured Photography: Kritsada Panichgul

Cover and Featured Food Styling: Christine Tobin

Editorial Director, Books: Adam Kowit

Executive Food Editor: Dan Zuccarello

Deputy Food Editor: Stephanie Pixley

Executive Managing Editor: Debra Hudak

Project Editor: Sacha Madadian

Senior Editors: Camila Chaparro, Joe Gitter, and Sara Mayer

Associate Editor: Claudia Catalano

Test Cooks: Malcolm Jackson and Stephanie Winter

Assistant Culinary Producers, Photography: Hannah Smokelin and Jami Procanik

Additional Culinary Support: Sarah Briscoe, Christina Ferrari, Rachel Michael, Jamie Samuelson-Kopec, and Lee Tan

Kitchen Interns: Canela Almonte, Abby Kolosowsky, Elijah Velasquez

Assistant Editor: Julia Arwine

Creative Director, Editorial: Lindsey Timko Chandler

Book Designer, Interior: Kylie Alexander

VP of Imagery: Casey Stenger

Senior Photography Producer: Meredith Mulcahy

Staff Photographer: Kritsada Panichgul

Additional Photography: Beth Fuller and Steve Klise

Senior Food Stylist: Christine Tobin

Additional Food Styling: Catrine Kelty and Ashley Moore

Prop Stylist: Jeffrey Miller

Project Manager, Books: Kelly Gauthier

Senior Print Production Specialist: Lauren Robbins

Production and Imaging Specialist: Tricia Neumyer

Copy Editor: Cheryl Redmond

Proofreader: Ann-Marie Imbornoni

Additional Proofreading Support: Elizabeth Wray Emery

Indexer: Elizabeth Parson

Chief Executive Officer: Daniel Suratt

Chief Content Officer: Dan Souza

Senior Content Adviser: Jack Bishop

Executive Editorial Directors: Julia Collin Davison and Bridget Lancaster

Senior Director, Book Sales: Emily Logan

CONTENTS

AMERICA'S
TEST KITCHEN

5.3% FRUCTOSE
1.8% FRUCTOSE

Welcome to America's Test Kitchen

This book has been tested, written, and edited by the folks at America's Test Kitchen, where curious home cooks become confident cooks. Located in Boston's Seaport District in the historic Innovation and Design Building, it features 15,000 square feet of kitchen space including multiple photography and video studios. It is the home of *Cook's Illustrated* magazine and is the workday destination for more than 60 test cooks, editors, and cookware specialists. Our mission is to empower and inspire confidence, community, and creativity in the kitchen.

We start the process of testing a recipe with a complete lack of preconceptions, which means that we accept no claim, no technique, and no recipe at face value. We simply assemble as many variations as possible, test a half dozen of the most promising, and taste the results blind. We then construct our own recipe and continue to test it, varying ingredients, techniques, and cooking times until we reach a consensus. As we like to say in the test kitchen, "We make the mistakes so you don't have to." The result is our best version of every recipe. We use the same rigorous approach when we test equipment and taste ingredients.

All of this would not be possible without a belief that good cooking, much like good music, is based on a foundation of objective technique. Some people like spicy foods and others don't, but there is a right way to sauté, there is a best way to cook a pot roast, and there are measurable scientific principles involved in producing perfectly beaten, stable egg whites. Our ultimate goal is to investigate the fundamental principles of cooking to give you the techniques, tools, and ingredients you need to become a better cook. It is as simple as that.

And speaking of the tools we have to make you a better cook: The first is in your hands—a collection of recipes that bring cookie baking into a new era, combining exciting flavors with ATK's bedrock baking techniques. All of these recipes have been tested to perfection in our Boston test kitchen. But there's more to America's Test Kitchen than what you see in this cookbook alone.

We invite you to explore thousands more trusted recipes on our 5-star app and website. You'll also find industry-leading equipment and ingredient reviews, how-to videos, our beloved TV series, and more, all ad-free. And as a special thank-you for purchasing this cookbook, enjoy 50% off your first year of membership—our exclusive Friends & Family offer for readers.

Explore ATK Membership

Scan to learn more and join at your special rate: **cooks.io/ATKCookies**

Be part of the best cooking conversation anywhere

@TestKitchen @AmericasTestKitchen @TestKitchen @AmericasTestKitchen

SMART COOKIE

Introduction

Year after year, since their development in 2009, our Chewy Chocolate Chip Cookies have been one of the most popular recipes in our archives and quite possibly the highest rated recipe we've ever developed. They're distinctly crisp around the edges, chewy in the middle, and imbued with butterscotch flavor—qualities that cookie lovers continue to search for today. And search they do. These handheld treats hold tremendous cultural appeal, with food writers and content creators listing their hot takes on a city's or region's best cookie, and well-known bakeries boasting signature styles that draw long lines.

If the search takes you to the kitchen, we can help you nail the best cookies, chocolate chip among them. Ten years ago we published our aptly titled book *The Perfect Cookie* to do just that. This time we've gone beyond, capturing why cookies are the everlasting *it* dessert.

Cookies' relative simplicity makes them a brilliant canvas for your wildest dessert dreams. Some dream of the biggest, most extravagant bakery-style version of a chocolate chip cookie. For them we have our Salted Malted Milk Chocolate Chunk Cookies, featuring concentric areas of crispy, chewy, and fudgy textures; a deep toffee flavor from malted milk powder; and expansive pools of milk chocolate that complement the malt. Some dream of flavors you may have never imagined in a cookie, like the savory spices that give incomparable warmth to our Garam Masala Molasses Cookies. Some dream of incarnating their favorite fussier desserts as portable cookies. Indulgent Stuffed Red Velvet Cookies fill cocoa-flavored dough with tangy cream cheese frosting. *The New Cookie* explores the flavors of today to make all of these cookie dreams a reality.

In addition to creative inspiration, new cookies require new tricks, and we've incorporated fun ingredients, simple techniques, and helpful tools that we haven't published before. We recommend stocking pantry must-haves like black cocoa powder, which gives our Deepest, Darkest, Fudgiest Flourless Brownies eye roll–inducing dark chocolate flavor and a satisfying black color to match. We regularly grind freeze-dried fruit and add it to doughs, fillings, or toppings for unbelievably concentrated fruit flavor (without the moisture) in cookies like Mango-Lime Meltaways. We freeze balls of rich fillings like Biscoff cookie butter so we can easily wrap dough around them for cookies loaded with a gooey molten center. We pay attention to appearance, making uniform cookie dough portions with cookie scoops and rounding wonky cookies when they come out of the oven with a large cookie cutter.

Of course, we could not publish a cookie cookbook without some of the ATK classics everyone loves. These best-in-class cookies not only capture nostalgic, enduringly craveable flavors and textures; they also display techniques that serve as bedrocks for the new cookies we've developed. Even the most audacious cookies in the book (like Dragon Fruit Mochi–Stuffed Lime Cookies) lean on our years of baking knowledge and often have familiar reference points (we wrap the mochi in a modified Chewy Sugar Cookies dough). The recipes are organized in chapters that represent the full range of cookie textures, satisfying those who spring for chewy, gooey treats they can really sink their teeth into; love delicate and crisp cookies with a cup of tea; or prefer something dense and decadent for dessert.

Each cookie, from the most simple oatmeal to the swirliest meringue, is treated like a standout, showcasing modern flavors, lush textures, or chic exteriors. We hope these very special—but also very attainable—recipes will encourage cookie fans to stop lusting over the cookies you see in media and learn to love making the incredible cookies of your dreams at home.

Supersimple Tips to Make You a Better Cookie Baker

We love cookies because their reward-to-work ratio is so much higher than for many desserts. You don't need to know all the codes of baking to turn out good cookies, but there are some supersimple, immediately implementable habits that will make your everyday cookies taste exceptional.

1 Weigh Ingredients

A digital scale is not negotiable.

This first tip is a little long because we're the most passionate about it: Weigh your ingredients. Inexact measurements yield inferior results. Baking is a science, every recipe is a formula, and the ratios of ingredients are just as important as the role of individual ingredients.

Dry ingredients are particularly challenging to measure by volume with accuracy. Technically, dry measuring cups don't measure ingredients; they measure the amount of space ingredients take up. Those are two different concepts (stay with us). When you fill a cup measure with something light and dry such as flour, that flour isn't the only thing occupying space in the measuring cup; there's air in there, too, and the amount of air mixed in with the flour can vary depending on your measuring style. If you gently spoon the flour into a cup and level it with a butter knife, that's about 120 grams of flour. If you scoop it out of the bag and level it by pressing the cup against the side, that's about 156 grams of flour—a big difference. When you weigh the flour, you'll nail the right amount because the scale won't factor in weightless air.

Not moved by science? Maybe you are by mess. Weighing keeps things clean. Usually, ingredients can go right from the package to the mixing vessel; place the bowl on the scale and tare it between additions. You'll avoid flying flour and sticky sweeteners gluing to measuring cups.

While weighing at all is great, weighing in grams (rather than ounces) ups the accuracy even more, so our recipes provide the gram weight equivalent for most ingredients with a volume of ¼ cup or more.

2 Collect Cookie Scoops

Get the perfect amount of cookie dough every time.

Using a spoon to stuff stiff cookie dough into measuring spoons or cups, forcing the sticky dough out of the measure, and then rolling the amorphous clump between your hands . . . works. But it's certainly not the neatest or most efficient way to portion cookie dough. Our cookie-baking lives changed when we started growing our cookie scoop collection. Choose the tool that matches the volume measure called for in the recipe (see page 40 for more information), scoop, and drop it right on the sheet. The dough comes out rounded, so you don't need to roll it between your hands.

Scooping isn't limited to dough. We like to neatly scoop fillings, such as the warm peanut butter filling for our PB&J Sandwich Cookies (page 173), right onto the cookie before sandwiching. We also use them to form cookie butter centers for our Chewy, Gooey Biscoff Butter Cookies (page 120).

Of course you can also use the scoops for ice cream—even better if the ice cream is being sandwiched by two cookies (see pages 144–147).

3 Get Used to Browning Butter

It gives cookie dough so much more depth.

If you're baking from this book, you're going to brown butter. A lot. The easy extra step turns the simplest cookie—Chewy Chocolate Chip Cookies (page 50), Double Gingersnaps (page 166), or Browned Butter Shortbread (page 201), for example—into the one that stands out at the cookie swap. It makes your bakes taste professional; it makes them taste expensive.

Why is browned butter so special? Browned butter has a deeper flavor than regular melted butter because as the butter is gently cooked, the milk solids separate, caramelize, and take on the flavor of toasted nuts.

4 Choose Chocolate with Care

Chocolate can change the flavor and appearance of cookies.

Chocolate, unsurprisingly, finds its way into a lot of the cookies in this book. What's better than the pull of melted chips when you bite into a warm cookie? But don't just stock up on your favorite snacking chocolate; the type of chocolate you use can have a distinct effect on the cookie.

Chocolate ranges from sweet, mild, and milky to bitter and fruity; you can build a nice round taste by choosing based on the sweetness of the dough or the other ingredients in the cookie. White chocolate adds pockets of richness to our Browned Butter Halva Crunch Cookies (page 112) because it balances the bitter notes of the halva, tahini, and orange. In our Chocolate Chunk Oatmeal Cookies with Pecans and Dried Cherries (page 125), we like how robust bittersweet chocolate stands out from the brown sugar–oat base and complements the dried cherries and buttery pecans.

On pages 24–27, you'll learn that the percentage of cacao in your chunks or chips and even their size can impact the appearance, spread, and texture of your cookies. And chips and bar chocolate melt and set differently—something to think about when chocolate is used as a tasty decoration. Cocoa powder flavors your cookies but the variety of cocoa can also impact their color and lift.

5 Buy Parchment in Sheets

Grab a sheet and go: no cutting, curling, or creasing.

Used to baking around a confetti-cluttered counter of thin parchment trimmings? Parchment sold in sheets fits in a standard rimmed baking sheet without trimming. Does the parchment roll up while you're placing cookies? Precut sheets stay put with no effort. End up with creased or warped cookies? Sheets stay perfectly flat. You may have to mail-order parchment sheets, but the inconvenience pays off with easier baking.

6 Keep Flake Salt Close

It's rare that a sprinkle doesn't make things better.

A finishing sprinkle of flake salt on a cookie is a great idea: It punctuates the flavors, it awakens the palate, and it adds an irresistible little crunch. You may be used to seeing salt with chocolate and caramel, but a sprinkle will make fruit flavors taste more fruity, nuts taste more nutty, and coffee taste more complex.

7 Learn Your Doneness Cues

They're different for every cookie.

To know when a cookie is ready to pull from the oven, you need to know the texture you're trying to achieve. A recipe will provide a time range to follow but it's up to you to use your sight—and sometimes touch—to know the best point at which to pull the batch. If you're going for crunchy cookies, you'll want to bake the cookies until they're adequately dried out; meanwhile, a chewy cookie needs to retain moisture, so it's important not to overbake it. You can learn important doneness cues on page 32.

FLAVOR

Whether you bake a classic chocolate chip cookie (see page 50) or a salted and malted one (see page 56), a chocolate crinkle cookie (see page 336) or an ube one (see page 339), the cookie should package a whole lot of flavor in a few bites. Some of the methods for enhancing flavor in this book are timeless baking tricks, some are new inventions, but all of them create cookies that rival the lineup at the best bakeshops.

Small Cookies, Big Flavor

Timeless Flavor Enhancers

In our pursuit of the best cookie recipes over the years, we've always gone the extra mile to achieve the deepest flavor in our classics. These methods continue to ground our cookie development today. They're sure to level up all of your bakes.

Use Some Brown Sugar

Brown sugar is granulated sugar that's been combined with molasses. Using brown sugar for the sweetener in a recipe is a really easy way to deepen the cookie's flavor. Dark brown sugar, unsurprisingly, has a higher molasses content than light brown sugar.

Sometimes, we use both brown and white sugar in our recipes. That's because the type of sugar you use impacts the texture of a cookie. Brown sugar adds noticeable moisture and is more hygroscopic, so it continues to attract moisture once the cookie is baked and cooled (for more information, see page 37). Using lots of brown sugar is ideal for chewy cookies. Too much brown sugar can compromise a cookie's crisp or crunchy texture, if that's desired.

Brown the Butter

This again. (We said you'd be doing it a lot!) Melted butter provides richness and can contribute to a chewy texture in cookies, but browned butter does all that while giving the cookie a toasted, concentrated flavor.

HOW TO BROWN BUTTER

Our tips for browning butter: Use a light-colored skillet so you can perceive the butter's change in color. Follow the recipe for skillet size and cooking times; both will vary based on the amount of butter you need to brown.

1. Melt butter in skillet over medium-high heat.

2. Continue to cook, swirling skillet and stirring constantly with silicone spatula, until the butter is dark golden brown and has nutty aroma.

3. Unless recipe specifies otherwise, immediately transfer butter to bowl so it doesn't burn.

Add Salt Generously

It's not news that salty goes with sweet. Adequate salt in baked goods makes the flavors sing and every note taste more like itself. Don't be afraid of recipes that add liberal amounts of salt to the dough. Salt also belongs in caramels, frostings, and fillings for cookies. We use table salt in these places because the size of the granules is standard across brands, and it readily dissolves.

Flake salt, like Maldon, is great for a finishing sprinkle. Sprinkle before the cookie bakes and the salt will dissolve a bit; sprinkle after baking (or twice) and, as long as there is something tacky on the surface for it to stick to, the salt will shine and maintain a little crunch. Feel free to experiment with smoked or flavored salts for finishing, too!

Age the Dough

Aging cookie dough refers to chilling it in the refrigerator for a certain amount of time—as little as 30 minutes to as long as three days—before baking. The process ensures superior hydration of the starches, which allows for better browning (browning equals flavor). The flavors also meld during this process. We go in depth on aging cookie dough on page 12.

Bake Adequately

Raw dough tastes, well, raw. Baking brings out flavor in cookies: Sugars caramelize, starches toast, butter browns. Even for chewy cookies that we instruct you to pull from the oven when their centers are still puffy-soft, we recommend baking until the edges brown. For that reason, you'll find that many of our chewy or loaded cookies bake at a higher oven temperature than you might expect—sometimes at 375 degrees, as for our Chewy Chocolate Chip Cookies (page 50) or up to 425 degrees, as for our Loaded White Chocolate–Macadamia Cookies (page 106). This sets and browns the exterior before the chewy or fudgy center dries out. For crispy or crunchy cookies, we often bake at a lower temperature for a longer amount of time to achieve great flavor; this allows the cookie to brown from edge to edge while baking through fully. Our Speculoos with Almonds (page 158) bake at 300 degrees for 30 minutes.

Finish with More Flavor

Anything superficial you add to a cookie after baking is going to stand out. A dusting of sugar or a drizzle of glaze will emphasize the cookie's sweetness. The molasses-tea glaze on our Brown Sugar Milk Tea Cookies (page 78) amplifies the cookie's flavor so you can nail the Taiwanese sugar taste inspiration. The coating of pistachios on our Saffron Sablés with Pistachios (page 210) intensifies the cookies' nuttiness so it stands up to the saffron. A sprinkle of dried rose petals on our Ricotta Rose Cookies (page 392) immediately calls to the perfume within. You can finish cookies however you like, experimenting outside of what's written in our recipes.

Today's Flavors

As we've developed recipes for the book, we've captured a ton of fun flavors—some we've never seen in cookies before. They're inspired by all kinds of foods, our travels, exciting bakeries, and our imaginations—these are the flavors of today, and there's something for everyone.

CHOCOLATY

CARAMELLY

SPICED

HERBAL/FLORAL

NUTTY

FRUITY

CITRUSY

FLAVOR

Freeze-Dried Fruit

Freeze-dried fruit adds the most powerful fruit flavor imaginable to cookies. Unlike fresh fruit, the dehydrated fruit (we often reach for raspberry, strawberry, blueberry, and mango) doesn't introduce unwanted moisture to the baking equation. We grind it to a powder that we mix into cookie dough, stir into glazes for punchy flavor and brilliant color, and use to cover warm cookies from the oven with a brilliant coating. Here are some ways to have fun with this space-age snack.

Flavoring Cookies with Freeze-Dried Fruit

We love the vibrant color and whimsical appearance that a ground freeze-dried fruit finish gives cookies. And the flavor hits you as soon as you take a bite. We finish some cookies with a dusting; others we like coating completely.

DUSTING WITH FRUIT

The easiest way to apply freeze-dried fruit to a finished cookie is to simply dust the baked cookies with ground fruit as you would with confectioners' sugar. We also like the look of dusting a portion of the cookie using a makeshift stencil. For our Simplest Raspberry-Cinnamon Slice-and-Bakes (page 214), we cover the baked cookies with a wire cooling rack and dust with ground freeze-dried raspberries to achieve a checkered effect.

For our Guava-Strawberry Sandwich Cookies (page 348), we create a modern two-tone effect with a piece of card stock. Here we mix the fruit with confectioners' sugar for a snowy consistency and pastel color. You can do this with cookies of different shapes and sizes.

1. **Cover half of row of cookies with sheet of card stock.**

2. **Sift confectioners' sugar through fine-mesh strainer onto exposed cookies.**

3. **Cover sugared half of row of cookies with card stock and sift fruit-sugar mixture onto exposed cookies. Repeat with remaining rows of cookies.**

COATING WITH FRUIT

We also like coating all sides of a cookie with flavor (and color), as for our Sparkling Blueberry-Lavender Shortbread Cookies (page 202). In these cases, we grind the fruit with sugar to help with adhesion. It's important to coat just-baked cookies while they're still hot so that the fruit sticks. If the cookies cool down before you coat them, rewarm them in a 350-degree oven for 2 minutes.

1. Let baked cookies cool for just 5 minutes, then quickly transfer 1 cookie to fruit mixture and toss to coat.

2. Tap cookie gently to remove excess fruit mixture.

3. Transfer cookie to wire rack, repeat with remaining cookies, and let cool completely.

Grinding Freeze-Dried Fruit

Unless we're crushing freeze-dried fruit for a garnish (see page 394), we grind it into a fruity flour before we use it. We don't weigh the fruit to measure it because it's impossibly light; volume is more accurate here. We use a blade grinder, also known as a spice grinder (use a separate grinder from the one you use for coffee!) to grind the fruit chips, in batches if we're working with large amounts of freeze-dried fruit. We sift the powder through a fine-mesh strainer to remove big seeds or clumps before using.

Keeping Away Clumps

Freeze-dried fruit is packaged with silica packets for a reason; the fruit can get sticky in the presence of moisture. If you're working with ground freeze-dried fruit and the weather is humid, it could clump and mar your coating. To fix this, we sift the ground fruit mixture with 1 to 2 tablespoons confectioners' sugar and whisk to combine.

FLAVOR

Taste the Rainbow

There are opportunities to have fun with your fruit and explore a rainbow of colors and flavors. Here we've gone technicolor with our sweetheart thumbprints (see page 230), which pair a fruit-coated butter cookie with a fruity filling. Test cook Stephanie Winter developed the recipe with freeze-dried raspberries and lemon curd, but she also loves freeze-dried corn paired with a blueberry jam filling. (Yes, you can use some freeze-dried veggies too; sometimes they're labeled "dehydrated" instead of freeze-dried.) Here's some more inspiration.

RASPBERRY SUGAR
Strawberry Jelly
Raspberry Jam
Apricot Preserves
PEACH SUGAR
Currant Jelly
Lemon Curd
CARROT SUGAR

FLAVOR

All About Aging Cookie Dough

Refrigerating your cookie dough for a spell before baking "ages" (or rests) the dough. Aging is usually associated with improving fine foods like wine, cheese, and steak; with cookies, a (short) refrigerator rest can also have benefits.

What Is Happening?

For a variety or reasons, often workability, a recipe may call for chilling cookie dough. While aging (resting) and chilling usually go hand in hand (you rest the dough in the fridge, which chills it), there are two different processes happening within the dough.

Chilling firms the butter—important for working with softer doughs or limiting spread in cookies. Meanwhile, the resting period hydrates the starches in the dough so it has less "free liquid" than dough that you mix and bake straight away. Both of these results have benefits.

A cookie that spreads less is thicker and chewier since the middle melts slower in the oven and bakes less than the edges. This way of spreading can also result in wrinkling along the edge of the cookie—a "shar-pei" effect that some bakers enjoy for the texture it adds.

Less free liquid in dough means the dough can brown more. The sugars caramelize, creating crispy cookie edges and deeply complex flavor. The resting period also further impacts spread. Well-hydrated starch gelatinizes more rapidly when baked, so the cookies have less time to spread before their structure becomes rigid.

Ways to Age

Simply cover your bowl of bulk dough tightly with plastic wrap and refrigerate. Then, when it's time to bake, let your dough soften just enough that you are able to scoop it. Alternatively, if you have the space in your refrigerator, you can prescoop the dough onto a parchment paper–lined baking sheet (you don't need space between the dough balls at this point), cover, and refrigerate. At go time, simply transfer the dough balls to freshly lined baking sheets as the recipe specifies. We don't recommend baking on the same sheet that you had in the refrigerator; the cold sheet will inhibit spread and slow the cookies' browning.

When Should You Age Cookies?

We like the effects of aging for chewy cookies, where we crave crispy, browned, caramelized edges and soft chewy centers. The deep, caramelized notes and increased browning you achieve doesn't make much sense for a light, cakey cookie like Black and Pink Cookies (page 380) and certainly isn't meant for bright-white meringues or delicately flavored biscotti. We do not advise chilling cookies that are meant to be crispy or crunchy, because it inhibits the required spread.

If you'd like to implement it, you'lll taste aging more obviously with less intensely flavored cookies. The following are good candidates (do not refrigerate doughs that have baking soda as the sole leavener for more than two days):

Chewy Chocolate Chip Cookies (50), Buckwheat Chocolate Chunk Cookies (54), Salted Malted Milk Chocolate Chunk Cookies (56), Brown Sugar Cookies (76), Maple Sugar Cookies (80), Chewy Oatmeal Cookies (92), Oat Guava Cookies (95), Browned Coconut Butter Cookies (101), Loaded White Chocolate–Macadamia Cookies (106), Peanut Butter Candy and Bacon Cookies (108), S'mores Cookies (114), and Chocolate Chunk Oatmeal Cookies with Pecans and Dried Cherries (125).

Baked Straight Away

- Generous spread
- Relatively even texture across cookie
- Moderate browning

Baked After 30 Minutes in the Fridge

- Moderate spread
- Chewier center than edges
- Increased browning and caramelization

Baked After 24 Hours in the Fridge

- Less spread
- Puffy, fudgy center
- Crispy edges
- Deep browning and caramelization

How Long Should You Age?

You can refrigerate dough for as little as 30 minutes to as long as 72 hours. Is there a sweet spot? We found that increasingly longer refrigeration produces increasingly thicker, chewier cookies that brown and crisp more around the edges—to a point. After 24 hours, the returns diminish: 72-hour cookies are no chewier or more caramelized than 24-hour ones.

FLAVOR

Will It Cookie?

Cookies exist in every culture and most everyone has a memory involving a cookie. Accordingly, many of our recipes have a familiar reference point. We met the challenge of re-creating beloved sweet treats, packaged snacks, and even drinks in cookie form.

ICONIC DESSERTS

Sticky Toffee Date Cookies (page 88)

toffee-drenched like the English pudding

Stuffed Red Velvet Cookies (page 140)

a rich, tangy frosting-stuffed jewel of a cookie instead of a multilayered slice

Banoffee Crunch Bars (page 282)

a caramelly banana cream bar dream

Ginger-Citrus Sweet Potato Pie Bars (page 284)

all the pie, none of the problems (plus streusel!)

Black Forest Brownies (page 310)

a plated brownie with luxe cherries and cream that's more chocolaty than the cake

Chocolate Banana Streusel Cookies (page 383)

a better-than-banana-bread use for ripe fruit

Carrot Cake Cookies (page 384)

a perfect layer of the cream cheese-frosted favorite

EN VOGUE BEVERAGES

Brown Sugar Milk Tea Cookies (page 78)

boba tea lovers, rejoice!

Thai Tea Crisps (page 155)

Thai iced tea cookies with a milky frosting

Gingerbread Eggnog Thumbprints (page 238)

the most holiday holiday cookie

Strawberry Matcha Cream Cheese Blondies (page 330)

more rich and satisfying outside of the cup

Mango Lassi Bars (page 278)

a glass can't contain the cool, creamy, tangy, spiced filling

Chicory Café au Lait Chocolate Bars (page 314)

rich chocolate meets a bitter New Orleans sip

Strawberry Lemonade Coconut Mochi Bars (page 334)

the most vibrant butter mochi you'll ever have

TREASURED SNACKS

Dragon Fruit Mochi-Stuffed Lime Cookies (page 70)

fruity, stretchy mochi encased in a chewy sugar cookie

Crunchy Salty Snack Cookies with Caramel Frosting (page 130)

your favorite snacks—chips, pretzels, and pecans—give cookies crunch

PB&J Sandwich Cookies (page 173)

classic for a reason, between cookies

Salted Caramel Apple Crumb Bars (page 259)

thick, salty caramel-gilded apple bars

Sichuan Peanut Rice Krispie Treats (page 292)

a Rice Krispie treat that's spicy and savory

S'Mores Bars (page 286)

no campfire required

Almond Joy Meringue Kisses (page 362)

a candy bar favorite makes meringue so much better

SHOP-BOUGHT RE-CREATIONS

Double Chocolate Tim Tams (page 175)

the Aussie icon gets even richer

Chocolate-Vanilla Crème Sandwich Cookies (page 170)

Oreos—with double the flavor

Frosted Soft Sugar Cookies (page 386)

eye-catching cookies that satisfy a sweet tooth

Oatmeal Creme Pies (page 96)

soft cookies sandwiching marshmallowy cream—without the wrapper

Iced Espresso Oatmeal Crunchies (page 162)

Archway cookies with an extra shot of flavor

Thin Chocolate-Mint Cookies (page 179)

a way to Girl Scout cookies on the off-season

Levain-Style Chocolate Chip Cookies (page 294)

huge, chunky, and captures the famous bakery's cookie

Chocolate-Marshmallow Sandwich Cookies (page 297)

you'll be over the moon for these generous pies

Giant Coconut-Caramel Shortbread Cookie (page 268)

a Samoa/Caramel deLite, supersized

Going Beyond with Bars

Baked bars are handheld and can be eaten in a few bites, so they definitely belong in the cookie category. Bar cookies as you know them (like Cherry Streusel Bars [page 250]) have layered flavors, tons of textural contrast, and crowd-serving potential. We've developed new ways with every layer.

Streusels like you've never seen! A corn crumble—with incomparable corn flavor from corn flour—is a striking addition to our holiday-appropriate Cranberry-Rosemary Corn Streusel Bars (page 256). Add cocoa to your crumble for rich Chocolate Raspberry Streusel Bars (page 254).

Switched-up shortbread! Short crusts are common in bars for good reason—they're buttery, sturdy, and neutral enough to build on. But there are other bar bases. Our Chicory Café au Lait Chocolate Bars (page 314) have a thin brownie base. A spiced graham cracker crust holds up Ginger-Citrus Sweet Potato Pie Bars (page 284).

This? In a bar? Unforgettable treats result from "what if?" explorations. We put licorice in brownies (see page 306). We dollop blondies with banana jam (see page 326). We fill Rice Krispie treats with Sichuan peanuts and chili flakes (see page 292).

Modernized favorites! If you like Lemon Bars (page 260), you'll love the look and complex taste of Meyer Lemon-Blueberry Reflection Bars (page 262). Miso Magic Bars (page 272) are a savory, seeded upgrade of the sugary bars of childhood.

A humble-looking cookie—is still a cookie. A well-baked cookie will satisfy whether it's perfectly round or a little lumpy. But once you've baked enough cookies, you might want them to look as great as they taste. This could mean making sure each cookie in a batch is exactly the same size, or it could mean giving them an amazing technicolor dreamcoat of freeze-dried fruit. Putting thought into appearance was a fun way to freshen up our recipe collection and make baking cookies exciting.

Lookin' Good, Cookie

Best-Dressed Bakes

The best-looking cookies aren't just the ones with colorful coatings, chocolate drizzles, or fluffy toppings. We see the beauty in the basic sugar cookie because it sports an appealingly golden edge, a perfectly round shape, a shimmery sugar finish, and a landscape of crackling that shows off its inner chewy crumb. Here are the characteristics of visually appealing cookies. Some are fanciful flourishes, most are foundational cookie-making rules that result in the best-looking bakes.

Workable Dough

The appearance of your baked cookies starts in the mixing bowl. You want to fully incorporate the ingredients for cookies—but don't overmix them. Overworked dough can bake up flatter than desired. If you're trying to roll out overworked dough, it will resist, leading to cookies that are too thick or misshapen. Mixing is easy to judge by hand; be sure to follow visual cues for dough readiness when mixing with the more powerful stand mixer or food processor.

The temperature of your dough also impacts baked appearance. Butter will soften in overheated dough, and the dough might stick when you're rolling it, leading to holes or rough surfaces in your rolled cookies. Very warm dough can be difficult to pipe for Spritz Cookies (page 354) and won't hold the ridged shape (very cold dough is also hard to pipe). It can spread too much or too fast. Use the refrigerator as needed as you're working with dough; if at any point a dough you're manipulating feels too soft or sticky, pop it in for 10 minutes or so to make it workable again.

Uniform Size

There are tricks to portioning cookie dough to achieve cookies of all the same size. Cookies that look uniform also bake up more evenly.

For **drop cookies**, we've raved about portion scoops (see page 40). To ensure the last batch looks as good as the first, we recommend that once you've portioned the dough according to the recipe yield, you divvy up any leftover dough among those dough portions rather than make extra cookies. Straggler cookies could bake up inconsistently since you may try to cram them on the sheet pan or bake them on their own. Roll dough portions into balls once you've added the extra dough.

Some of us perfectionists in the test kitchen have another strategy for portioning dough: weighing dough balls so they are identical. We find the weight of our bulk cookie dough (minus the weight of the bowl it's in), divide it by the recipe's yield, and make sure each dough portion weighs that much.

For **slice-and-bake cookies**, uniform size means even thickness. Pre-score your chilled log of dough and use a nice sharp chef's knife, with a blade that's not too thick.

Of course, some cookie dough is **rolled and cut out** with cookie cutters. Be sure to use cutters of the same size for the whole batch to ensure even baking. The recipe will guide you in cookie cutter choice, but you can use any shape or size you want for your own cookies, though you may need to adjust the bake time; look to visual cues to gauge doneness.

Uniform Shape

Shaping your cookies in perfect circles won't make them taste better, but they sure look great, and it's a move worth knowing if you have bakery-worthy cookies in mind. In addition to regulating size, portion scoops regulate **drop cookie** shape by turning out perfect spheres of dough. If you don't use a scoop to portion out dough, you should roll it into balls between your hands.

Even if it goes into the oven perfectly shaped, dough can have a mind of its own when it's baking, with carbon dioxide bubbles or chunks of mix-ins moving around and impacting how the cookie spreads. If you love the idea of perfectly round cookies, there's a way to ensure that look when the cookies come out of the oven. Using a biscuit or cookie cutter more than an inch larger than the size of the cookie, you can make a series of rounding motions to coax the still-warm cookie into the perfect shape before it sets. (Avoid this with ultrafudgy cookies like Triple Chocolate–Cherry Cookies [page 129], or cakey cookies that don't have enough structure.)

ROUNDING COOKIES

1. Place cutter around uneven hot cookie.

2. Use repeated swirling motions around cookie edge to round.

Slice-and-bake cookies need some extra help to keep their round shape. That's because after you shape the log, the dough needs to chill on the flat surface of your refrigerator shelf or a plate. Until the dough gets cold enough to firm up, it will slouch and form a flat bottom. To keep things cylindrical, we like to slice open a used paper towel roll lengthwise and place the dough log in it in the fridge.

You'll want your slice-and-bakes to hold their shape one more time, as you're slicing them and the dough is softening. We rotate the log as we're slicing to keep it as evenly round as we can.

In the world of **brownies and bars**, uniform shape usually means a level top (straight sides are otherwise guaranteed by the walls of your baking pan). Instead of a silicone spatula, we recommend smoothing the top of your batters or fillings with a small offset spatula so you can easily get inside the pan and corners.

SLICING UNIFORM COOKIES

1. Roll piece of dough into log of diameter and length specified in the recipe.

2. Wrap logs tightly in plastic wrap, place in opened paper towel roll, and refrigerate until firm.

3. After letting chilled dough sit on counter to soften slightly, slice dough into rounds, rotating log as you go.

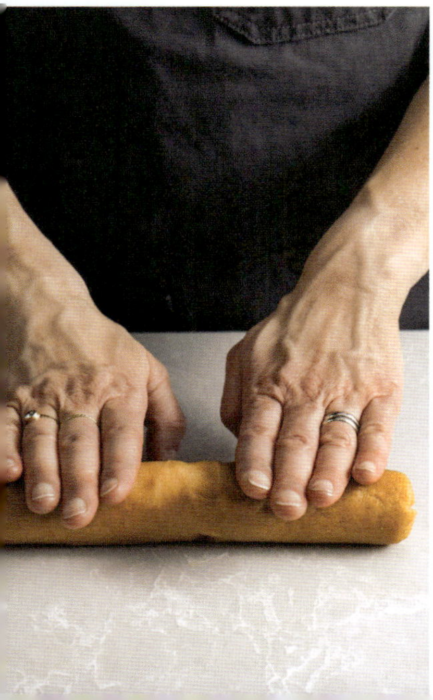

Flat Surfaces

Some cookies are iconic for their relatively flat top, like Chewy Sugar Cookies (page 62) and PB&J Sandwich Cookies (page 173). To discourage doming and encourage spread before the cookies set, we sometimes flatten the dough balls to a specified diameter.

But even cookies that are rolled flat can come out of the oven uneven. If your sheet pan is warped, your cookies will be too—not great if you're trying to glaze cookies evenly or sandwich them together. We have a nifty trick for correcting crooked pans. You can place the baking sheet in a preheated 200-degree oven for 10 minutes to make it malleable. Flip over the baking sheet and, with a mallet, pound the sheet until it's even again.

Another reason for wavy cookies? Conventional parchment paper. We've encouraged you to stock flat sheets (see page 3). We've found that parchment paper's flatness—or lack thereof—could really leave its mark on baked goods. Any wave or fold in the paper leaves behind seams or curved bottoms on the cookies.

A Crackly Top

The way a cookie crackles has little to do with shaping and a lot to do with ingredients, mostly with leavener. Baking powder creates lift that is necessary to a certain degree for many cookies. Baking soda does too, but it can also cause some spread, and the crackly top that is so desirable for cookies like Soft and Garam Masala Molasses Cookies (page 83). How does this work? As long as there's an acidic ingredient in the dough for it to react with, baking soda raises the pH of the dough (baking powder does too but not as high), weakening gluten. The baking soda produces large bubbles of carbon dioxide in the dough that cannot be contained by its weakened structure and the bubbles rise to the top of the cookie and burst, leaving fissures in their wake.

As illustrated below, the effect is dramatic in our Double Gingersnaps (page 166). We use a very liberal amount of baking soda—a full 2 teaspoons—and no baking powder to create a gingersnap with attractive large fissures (here, these allow more moisture to evaporate for the snappiest cookies). Lesser amounts make unremarkable cookies.

Sweets of All Shades

Food coloring has advanced beyond bottles of water-based dye in the spice aisle. You can do so much more (with so much less) food dye.

Food coloring comes in liquid, oil- and water-based gels, powder, and natural forms. Many bakers have moved from **liquid coloring** because the large amount needed to adequately color cookie dough can cause some to taste the dye in their goods. **Gel-based food coloring** is much more concentrated and requires less to achieve the vibrant colors we're looking for in our Peppermint Checkerboards (page 217). This comes in oil- and water-based formulas; you can choose either for doughs or sugar glazes like the one on our Thai Tea Crisps (page 155), but choose oil-based if you're working with chocolate, as for our Sunrise Marshmallow Cookies (page 371), as any addition of water can cause the chocolate to seize.

Some people choose **natural food coloring**. These mostly plant-derived dyes are perfectly fine, but you'll have to use a lot and even then, your baked goods will never become as pigmented as with other dyes. That's OK, as long as you know colors will come out pastel (which can be nice!). The difference in color concentration in these three dyes is illustrated nicely in the glazes above.

In addition to these dyes, powdered food coloring is also available but mostly for professional use, as just the slightest touch creates deep color. It's hard to know how to measure this to incorporate into home-baked goods.

Mix-Ins That Stand Out

When a cookie is fully loaded, we like the mix-ins to stand out visually. Often the dough bakes up around these ingredients and hides them. S'Mores Cookies (page 114) are way more exciting if you can see that there's melty chocolate, chewy marshmallow, and crunchy graham cracker pieces inside. After portioning our cookie dough, we sometimes press extra mix-ins into the top of the dough—a couple nuts, some chunks of chocolate—before putting the cookies in the oven. Chocolate fans love to see what they're going to get, and treats like our Buckwheat Chocolate Chunk Cookies (page 54) look far more indulgent adorned with chocolate chunks. But we avoid hand-placing chocolate chips or morsels on cookies. Polka-dotted cookies look too intentional and, in our opinion, have a mass-produced appearance. Irregular chunks of chocolate work far better.

Finishing with Flair

Finishing cookies with signaling ingredients before or after they bake can really up their interest. Our Browned Butter Halva Crunch Cookies (page 112) have plenty of sesame flavor from halva and tahini, but a roll in sesame seeds beautifies the exterior, adds extra toastiness, and gives you an idea of what you're about to taste. Dunking dough balls in chopped pistachios brightens the otherwise very earthy color of Hojicha Pistachio Cookies (page 91). A sprinkle of Tajín is a clever way to brighten the flavor of Coconut Thumprints with Tamarind Caramel (page 234).

The options for decorating with sprinkles have come a long way. We love the monochrome look of yellow sprinkles on our Lemon Cookie Bars (page 75), but you can order all kinds of sprinkles and little candies to top cookies—from galaxy shapes to nonpareils. Of course, sanding sugar and turbinado sugar, which we use in our Sablés (page 206), are classic ways to add sparkle, as is a sprinkle of trusty flake salt.

For literal sparkle, try edible glitter, which we mix with freeze-dried fruit for our Sparkling Blueberry-Lavender Shortbread Cookies (page 202); a highly sparkling product called Disco Dust comes in disco-ball silver or other shimmering metallic colors. Edible glitter can be found at cake decorating shops, well-stocked craft stores, or online. And of course, we love our freeze-dried fruit, incorporating it into the dough for cookies such as Mango-Lime Meltaways (page 346) for color and flavor throughout, or coating cookies with it when they're warm out of the oven.

Chocolate: Chips, Chunks, and Swirls

Chocolate in cookies carries so much nostalgia, and reliably makes them extra craveable. We use powder, chips, and bars: It's important to know how to work with each.

Types of Cocoa Powder

When we want big chocolate flavor in cookies, we often turn to cocoa powder because it has a higher concentration of cocoa solids than any other forms of chocolate—including unsweetened bar chocolate—so ounce for ounce it tastes more chocolaty.

In addition to flavor, cocoa powder can also impact the cookie's texture and looks. The ubiquitous Hershey's cocoa you might be familiar with is a natural cocoa powder. Dutch-processed cocoa powder goes through a process called Dutching in which an alkalizing agent is added to it. This step darkens the powder's color and mellows its astringent notes, as chocolate is naturally acidic. Below, Chocolate Crinkle Cookies (page 336) made with more-acidic natural cocoa powder are taller, airier, and crumblier because the baking soda in the recipe reacts with the acidity in the cocoa powder. Cookies made with Dutch-processed cocoa powder are more moist and fudgy. If a recipe calls for unsweetened cocoa powder, you can use either natural or Dutch processed. Otherwise, a recipe will specify which type of powder to use.

Cookies Made with Dutch-Processed Cocoa Powder

Cookies Made with Natural Cocoa Powder

Marbling Made with Dutch-Processed Cocoa

Marbling Made with Black Cocoa

Additionally, we love to use black cocoa in this book. Black cocoa has been heavily Dutched so it has really big chocolate flavor and a midnight color. It makes our Chocolate–Vanilla Crème Sandwich Cookies (page 170) look and taste most like their supermarket sisters, and it helped us develop the Deepest, Darkest, Fudgiest Flourless Brownies (page 308). Note that this cocoa has very little fat and therefore lots of starch, so we recommend using it only in recipes that call for it. You can see the color it achieves in our Easiest-Ever Marbled Butter Cookies (page 220) below left.

Chocolate Chips versus Bar Chocolate Chunks

You might think chocolate chips are merely miniature versions of bar chocolate, but that isn't the case. Chocolate chips have a similar cacao percentage but less cocoa butter (i.e., fat) than bar chocolate, which makes them cheaper to produce and more able to maintain their shape when baked. They also generally have more emulsifiers and stabilizers than bar chocolate, which further help them hold their shape. The chocolate chip cookie actually precedes the chocolate chip. Yes—the original Toll House cookie from 1938 called for chopping chocolate and became so famous that in 1941, Nestlé began making the now-ubiquitous teardrop-shape chips.

Chocolate chips are the go-to cookie mix-in, and they distribute chocolate very evenly throughout bites. Chunks that you chop from bar chocolate have more dramatic impact, giving areas of intense chocolate and relief, as well as creating striations within cookie dough. Fèves (thick ovals, like those from Valrhona), disks (thinner round chocolate pieces, like those from Guittard), and callets (smaller chocolate rounds, like those from Callebaut), are all options. You can generally work with what you prefer; however, your choice might have more impact on your result than you think.

CHOPPING BLOCK CHOCOLATE

Callebaut chocolate blocks are easy to find and are a common choice for baking. Chocolate blocks such as these can be challenging to chop into chunks without ending up with a lot of useless flakes.

Here's what we do: We cut the big block into manageable portions with a sharp chef's knife and then further break down those portions into the chunk size of our choice.

GHIRARDELLI
PREMIUM BAKING CHIPS
CALLEBAUT BLOCKS
GUITTARD BAKING WAFERS
NESTLÉ MORSELS
TONY'S CHOCOLONELY
BAR
GHIRARDELLI
BAKING BAR

Chocolate Mix-Ins at Work

When developing batch after batch of new chocolate chipped cookies, we found that chocolate choice impacted not only taste but also appearance. That's because the size of the chocolate combined with the rate at which it melts affects the spread of the cookie, sometimes forcing more spread and even contributing to a greater wrinkling effect along the cookie's edge. We can apply these findings to all of the cookies in the book.

At left you can see cookies baked with chocolate pieces as small as standard Nestlé chips and as large as chunks from a thick block of Callebaut chocolate. If you like to see nostalgic chips, and get some in every bite, you'll like the classic. If you prefer larger chunks that form luscious chocolate puddles and rivers, and result in big, thin, bakery-style cookies, you'll like chopping them from bar chocolate. Based on our experiments, here are some considerations when choosing chocolate for your cookies.

SIZE

Small chocolate chips soften but don't melt (because of their stabilizer content; keep reading), so they don't spread any wider than their initial size. Larger hand-chopped chunks from bar or block chocolate, no matter their melting capabilities, will measure at least as wide in the baked cookie as they did going in—and so they are the best choice if you want a large surface area of chocolate. They also force the spread of the cookies during baking to create thinner rounds that are larger in diameter. Because they can be chopped into odd geometries and can melt into beautiful winding rivers, they can also create areas along the edges of cookies that ripple and wrinkle.

We love this effect in our Salted Malted Milk Chocolate Chunk Cookies (page 56), specifically, and we call for Tony's Chocolonely Milk Chocolate Bars because they're thicker than your average baking bar but not as thick as block chocolate. You can easily chop the thick bar into just the right size chunks to create the effect we were looking for; Callebaut baking blocks (see page 25), for example, can break a bit less predictably and leave shavings throughout the cookie, as is evident in the photo to the left. Standard-size baking bars such as Ghirardelli can't cover as much area as they melt and a have spottier presence.

Chocolate disks, depending on the brand, should fall somewhere in between chips and chunks in how they impact cookie spread and appearance. Guittard Organic Baking Wafers, which are common in grocery stores, are formulated to melt but also mostly hold their shape, so they create thin coins of melted chocolate that are visible from the exterior and don't really impact cookie spread.

CACAO PERCENTAGE

In recipes where you can choose your chocolate type—milk, semisweet, dark—cacao percentage could be a factor in cookie appearance. Chocolate with a lower percentage of cocoa solids *should* melt more and faster than higher-percentage chocolate. In addition, lower-percentage chocolate often contain milk solids (and more of them) and higher amounts of sugar, which lower these chocolates' melting point. However, this can be offset when the chocolates contain a lot of stabilizers. A milk chocolate chip, for example, is still designed to hold its pointy shape. Of course, choose chocolate that you love the taste of; flavor should always come first.

STABILIZERS

Stabilizers such as lecithin, as mentioned, slow chocolate melting and help it keep its shape so you can see the trademark kiss of a chocolate chip in your baked goods. Sometimes we like to use chips for melted chocolate coatings because the stabilizers help the chocolate stay firm and in place when the cookie is at room temperature. Bar chocolate often contains fewer stabilizers (or none at all). This means meltier, less-distinct chocolate shapes in baked cookies made with bar chocolate than with chips. Chocolate disks, fèves, and callets, interestingly, tend to be higher in fat than chocolate chips (so more melting), but their emulsifier and stabilizer content is all over the map—work with what you like.

TEXTURE

Big, bold flavor and gorgeous looks—everyone can get on board with these cookie traits. But opinions divide over a cookie's texture: There are big fans of chewy cookies, defenders of crispy cookies, and those who admire intricate delicacies. We've represented a range of textures in this book, organized by chapter, so you can find what you like. We also love to incorporate different textures into one cookie for interest. Discover how to make cookies that call you to take more and more bites.

Textures That Intrigue

What Cookie Are You?

No matter your cookie preferences, there's a chapter of cookies for you. Find what you love and bake from there first.

1. Chewy and Gooey

You like a classic American cookie, a bendable cookie with a rich core and a crisp edge to grab on to. You're always on the search for The Best (browned butter) chocolate chip cookie, in recipes and in bakeries.

2. Fully Loaded

Cookies aren't a sweet snack; for you, they're a warm, melty main-event dessert. You want a big, indulgent cookie full of fun—and sometimes unexpected—mix-ins (bacon? halva?) and fillings (cookie butter? frosting?) that feels like a once-in-a-while treat.

3. Crisp and Crunchy

Your cookie tastes are refined. You don't want an ooey-gooey chocolate chip cookie; you want a crisp, caramelized one that you can snap in half. You like your cookies with tea and will gladly dunk them, pinkies up.

4. Butter Makes It Better

You like a crumbly cookie with rich flavor and, for you, the ultimate treat might be a tin of European cookies. While you enjoy a simple tea cookie, you're not just a plain Jane. Sometimes you're after a great-tasting shortbread base that you can decorate, flavor, or color to make it your own.

5. Sink Your Teeth In

Easily bored, you believe bars are cookies, too (they are), and like to make them as often as you do others. You want a multilayered cookie with various textures. You'd never eat plain shortbread, but you love it topped with loads of chewy caramel and nuts.

6. Rich and Squidgy

Chocolate people: Welcome to paradise. You prefer a rich brownie or blondie to a round cookie. You don't mind—in fact, you might seek out—a cookie that seems a little underbaked. You crave comfort and like to have dessert on hand at all times.

7. Light and Lovely

You like pretty things, including aesthetically pleasing sweets. You don't *need* dessert but you do like to adorn your coffee saucer with something delicate that looks as beautiful as it tastes. You're inclined to post food photos on Instagram.

8. Soft and Cakey

You might prefer cake to cookies (or enjoy it the same), but you don't have the time to make the larger-format dessert. You prefer fluffy treats to dense, fudgy ones—all the better to pair with swirls of frosting or a dribble of sugar glaze.

TEXTURE

The Way the Cookie Crumbles

Baking recipes are formulas, and any minor change can impact the solution: a cookie's crumb structure. The variables (ingredients) in a given formula can tell you a lot about the cookie's crumb. Below are different cookie textures we often refer to that you can achieve when baking. We've charted how key ingredients work to get you to your desired place. Knowing this will help you figure out if there's a good chance you'll like a cookie by scanning the ingredient list, or with troubleshooting a recipe.

CHEWY

Moist, moderately closed crumb that lightly resists pressure when you take a bite

CRISPY

Short profile with open air spaces; snaps with pressure

SHORT

A tight crumb that's rich, tender, and a little crumbly

CAKEY

An open, lifted crumb that's tender and easy to eat

How Ingredients Impact Cookie Texture

FLOUR	• **All-purpose flour** has a moderate protein content. The protein interacts with liquid to develop gluten, building a cookie with a chewy or substantial crumb. • **Cake flour** has a lower protein content and is good for light or cakey cookies, or even crispy cookies, where you don't want chew.
FAT	• **More butter** makes cookies rich. It coats the flour, hindering gluten development for a tender cookie (or in extreme cases, one that lacks structure and crumbles). • **Less butter** creates a leaner cookie or one with substantial structure. • **Softened butter** is generally creamed with sugar to create a cookie with a light crumb and some lift. Sometimes a reverse-creaming method is used, wherein the softened butter coats the flour particles for a very tender crumb. • **Melted butter** unlocks the water in butter so it can interact with flour for more gluten development, so more chew. Melted butter can also make a looser dough that spreads better. • **Cold butter** can be mixed (or cut) into flour for a workable dough that bakes up short and tender. • **Oil** is mostly unsaturated fat and is liquid at room temperature, so it can make cookies seem more moist. When oil is used in combination with butter, which is mostly saturated fat, it can contribute to a sturdy crystalline structure that requires more force to bite through, for a sensation of chewiness. • **Vegetable shortening** has no water content so it is very tenderizing. It has a higher melting point than butter, so it can keep cookies from spreading. It does not add flavor.
EGGS	• **Egg whites** introduce structure but can also lighten cookie dough, encouraging rise and opening up the crumb. • **Egg yolks** bind dough, add richness to chewy cookies, and discourage crumbliness in thin and crispy cookies.
SUGAR	• **Granulated sugar** adds sweetness with neutral flavor and aids browning and caramelization in cookies, creating crisp edges and crackly tops. • **Brown sugar** imparts caramel notes and provides chew and lasting moisture. • **Confectioners' sugar** is powdery-fine so granules go undetected in cookies, resulting in an ultrafine crumb.
LIQUID	• A bit of milk, buttermilk, or water can loosen a cookie dough so it spreads thin; in larger amounts, the steam created during baking gives cookies cakey lift.
LEAVENER	• **Baking soda** causes dough to rise but it also weakens gluten structure enough to cause more spread and cracks. Moisture can escape from those cracks, resulting in crunchy cookies. The soda also increases flavorful browning. • **Baking powder** produces gas more slowly so the dough rises and sets before gas bubbles can burst, resulting in more cakey lift in cookies.

How Mixing Methods Impact Cookie Texture

The way you mix together your cookie ingredients—in addition to the ingredients themselves—helps determine the crumb structure of cookies. **Creaming** involves beating softened butter and sugar together with a mixer until the butter is pale and fluffy before adding eggs and other liquid ingredients and then the flour. In this method, tiny sugar crystals act like extra beaters, helping to incorporate air into the butter. These tiny air pockets expand during baking, giving cookies like Chocolate Banana Streusel Cookies (page 383) lift and a light crumb. Creaming also prevents cookies that are filled with weighty ingredients, like molasses-rich Garam Masala Molasses Cookies (page 83), from becoming too dense.

We use **reverse creaming** when we want tender but sturdy cookies, with minimal rise and flat tops. It's perfect for shortbread, which we like to dip in a raspberry glaze (see page 194). You start by combining all of the dry ingredients and then incorporating softened butter. Finally, you add any liquid ingredients. During this process, the butter coats the flour particles to minimize gluten development and yield a tender, crumbly cookie.

When we're working with melted butter, often for chewy cookies, we simply mix **by hand**. Vigorously mixing the ingredients together in a bowl with a silicone spatula facilitates gluten development without incorporating air in the way a stand mixer does. The result is chewy—not cakey—cookies.

Doneness Cues for Different Cookies

Recipes call to bake cookies to different degrees depending on the textural aim. Alongside baking times are, even more importantly, visual and tactile cues for when to pull cookies from the oven. Some cookies are harder to judge than others—like crunchy cookies you're trying to dry out fully or chocolaty cookies that are too dark to show browning. Here are some guidelines.

CHEWY COOKIES

It's important not to overbake; err on the side of underbaked.

- Edges should be set.
- Center should be soft and puffy.
- If the cookie has cracks, the cookie might look underbaked within them—that's OK.

CRISPY, CRUNCHY COOKIES

The goal is to dry these cookies out so they are crunchy even at the center.

- Look in any cracks to make sure cookies look dry.
- Check for adequate browning across the cookie.

BUTTER COOKIES

Buttery cookies such as shortbread and sablés should bake through but not overbrown.

- Cookies should be almost uniformly pale golden brown.
- Edges of cookies may be a bit more golden.

CUTOUT COOKIES

Thinly rolled cookies go from perfectly baked to overbaked quickly so keep a close eye.

- The cookies should just begin to brown around edges.
- They should show slight resistance when pressed.

CHOCOLATE BUTTER COOKIES

These cookies should finish like shortbread cookies, but you need to use different doneness cues since browning isn't visible.

- The edges of the cookies should be firm.
- When pressed with your finger, the cookie should reveal a slight indentation (see below).

BROWNIES

No one wants a dry brownie. Avoid overbaking them.

- A toothpick inserted in the center of the brownies should emerge with a few moist crumbs clinging to it (see below).

TEXTURE

One Cookie—Many Textures

We think textural variation—within the cookie itself or in what goes into it—is one of the most appealing qualities of a good cookie. Here are simple things you can do to achieve multiple compelling textures in a single elite cookie.

Bigger Cookies Can Be Better

A particularly easy way to get a cookie with a gradation of textures is to simply make the dough portions bigger. For chocolate chip cookies, for example, the classic Toll House recipe calls for dropping rounded tablespoons of dough onto the baking sheet. For us, that is unacceptably small. Below are cookies baked from 2 tablespoons of dough and ¼ cup of dough. The larger diameter increases the contrast between the crispy, more browned crust; the sturdy, chewy mantle; and the fudgy blond inner core. The smaller cookie has a more uniform texture and even bake and browning from edge to center.

How You Shape It

For chewy cookies in particular, the way you shape the dough portions before they bake impacts texture. Forming dough into balls or spheres causes cookies to spread more slowly in the center, where there is more dough, and faster along the edges, where the dough melts and thins out. The thinner edges brown and caramelize, while the centers bake less and maintain moisture and/or chewiness. For our Levain-Style Chocolate Chip Cookies (page 294), we roughly shape the dough portions. This creates mountainous cookies with a signature darkened crunchy shell around a soft interior.

Sometimes, however, we want a more even shape and texture, and we call for flattening dough after forming it into balls, as for our Chewy Sugar Cookies (page 62). This controls the cookies' spread so that it's even, with chewiness across the cookie and a uniformly light golden exterior, hallmarks of this nostalgic cookie.

Cold Cookies

Chilling cookie dough is another way to slow its spread and therefore bake a cookie with edges that are more cooked and caramelized than the center of the cookie (see page 12 for more information). You can see how this works with our Loaded White Chocolate–Macadamia Cookies on page 106. We also chill rolled-out dough for recipes like our Speculoos with Almonds (page 158) so that the cookies don't melt too fast and instead hold their pretty fluted shape through baking and emerge with a crispy texture.

Baking Time and Temperature

A shorter bake time in a hot-enough oven (see page 6 for more information) can give cookies textural contrast. This browns and cooks the cookies' exterior before the center has a chance to overbake. Some recipes suggest erring on the side of underbaking to capture this—cookies will continue to set on the hot baking sheet when they come out.

Something to Chew On: Mix-In Choices

No matter the texture of the crumb surrounding them, mix-ins can greatly impact the cookie eating experience, adding bits of interest throughout. They're a great way to create balance. Combining something creamy (melty chocolate chunks), something chewy (plump dried cherries), and something crunchy (toasty pecans) in our Chocolate Chunk Oatmeal Cookies with Pecans and Dried Cherries (page 125) makes this oatmeal cookie one of the most craveable cookies in the book. There are mix-ins in cookies throughout the book, but if you like lots of them, you should check out our Fully Loaded chapter (pages 104–147), which lives up to its name (some cookies are just as much mix-ins as dough!). Other texturally interesting incorporations include the chewy, stretchy (and pink!) mochi center in our Dragon Fruit Mochi-Stuffed Lime Cookies (page 70); the squidgy dried fruit filling in our Pumpkin Spice Hermits (page 84); the nutty granola baked into our Blueberry Jam Breakfast Cookies (page 133); and the almost-chewy fruit ribbon through our Passion Fruit Meringue Swirls (page 367).

The Cookie Baker's Cupboard

Cookies are often quicker and easier to make—and perhaps even more craveable—than other baked goods, so it's nice to have supplies to make them on hand at all times. Here's a guide to everything you need and nothing you don't to make The New Cookie. We think you'll welcome the new additions of items like black cocoa and glutinous rice flour to your collection.

Flour

Flour is arguably the most important ingredient for just about any cookies. It gives them structure, crumb, and texture, whether tough (bad), tender (good), or something in between (sometimes desired). While a majority of cookie recipes call for all-purpose flour, we also employ cake flour from time to time.

The main difference between types of flour is the amount of protein they contain. More protein leads to more gluten development, which translates to chewier cookies—or, depending on the proportion of other ingredients, tough, dense cookies. For that reason you won't see us using bread flour, the white flour with the highest protein content, in our cookies.

We develop our recipes with easy-to-find **Gold Medal Unbleached All-Purpose Flour**, which has a moderate protein content (10.5 percent protein) and is our preferred brand. (Pillsbury flour has a similar protein content.) If you're using King Arthur Unbleached All-Purpose Flour, which has a higher protein content (11.7 percent), in our recipes, the cookies may be a bit drier and denser. If you'd like to dabble in whole-grain flour baking, we love our Buckwheat Chocolate Chunk Cookies (page 54) made with the nutty pseudograin, but you can also try these cookies with spelt, rye, or whole-wheat flour.

Butter

Most recipes in this book use butter—rather than oil or shortening—for its satisfyingly rich flavor. But fat in cookies isn't just for flavor. The amount of fat in a recipe helps determine the texture of the cookie's crumb (see page 31); the more fat you add, the more tender your cookie.

We use only unsalted butter in our recipes so we can control the amount of salt that goes into the cookie. Another variable: Salted butter can also contain more water than unsalted butter does. We think you can save your money on premium European butters and cultured butters, as their extra richness doesn't come through in most cookies. Our favorite unsalted butter is **Challenge Unsalted Butter**. Butter can pick up off-flavors and turn rancid when kept in the refrigerator for longer than a month; freeze it if you need to store it longer.

Sugar

In addition to providing requisite sweetness, sugar contributes to the moisture level, chew, structure, and browning of cookies. **Granulated sugar** has a neutral flavor and an evenly ground, loose texture that incorporates well with other ingredients and dissolves relatively quickly.

Brown sugar is granulated sugar that's been combined with molasses. You can use light and dark brown sugar interchangeably in recipes that don't specify one or the other. Store brown sugar in an airtight container to prevent it from drying out; even better if you can pop in a Brown Sugar Bear, a clay bear that keeps the sugar extra soft. A slice of bread also works for a time. We've found that the molasses and moisture content of different brands of brown sugar can vary, so your cookies made with lots of brown sugar may bake up with slight variations in color, spread, and cracking (they'll all taste great!).

Confectioners' sugar is the most finely ground sugar. It's used for dusting cookies and for making glazes and icings, but it can also be incorporated into cookie dough when an ultrafine crumb is desired.

Some less standard sugars we like to keep? **Turbinado sugar**, referred to as raw sugar, is coarse and caramel-colored. Don't use it in dough unless you grind it (as we do in our Speculoos with Almonds [page 158]); it's too coarse to dissolve readily. But it's great for finishing cookies or rolling logs of cookie dough in. **Sanding sugar**, the semicoarse and often-colored sugar is also great for decorating cookies. And **maple sugar** is a bit of a splurge, but it makes a lovely maple cookie with the texture of a regular sugar cookie; something liquid syrup could not achieve.

Eggs

Eggs are magic: They bind, thicken, emulsify, and leaven. To standardize our baking, we use large eggs in all of our recipes. You want to use fresh eggs, as over time, the yolks and whites will become looser and lose their structure-lending properties. Check the sell-by date on the carton and store eggs in the back of the fridge (the coldest area) in the carton, which absorbs moisture.

Chemical Leaveners

A majority of cookies include some kind of chemical leavener to help them rise during baking. **Baking soda** is an alkali and therefore requires an acidic ingredient in the dough, such as sour cream, molasses, or brown sugar, in order to produce carbon dioxide. The leavening action happens right after mixing. In addition to leavening, baking soda also promotes spread (by disrupting gluten formation) and browning (by speeding up the Maillard reaction, which is the chemical process that happens when flavorful sugars and proteins caramelize).

Baking powder is a mixture of baking soda, a dry acid, and double-dried cornstarch, so it doesn't require acidic ingredients to act. The cornstarch absorbs moisture and prevents the premature production of gas. Baking powder works twice—when it first comes in contact with a liquid, and again in response to heat. Once a container is open it will lose effectiveness after six months.

Salt

Salt stimulates the palate, cuts through rich foods so they're not cloying, and brings out dimension, making sweet treats that much more appealing. You should use table salt in cookie dough or fillings, so it dissolves during baking, cooking, or with hydration. An adornment of a finishing salt adds surprising crunch that makes food pop. We keep Maldon Sea Salt on hand at all times for finishing foods because it's affordable and widely available. Its large, light, airy, thin flakes and pyramids have a delicate and shattering texture and soft crunch.

Oil

While it doesn't bring any flavor, vegetable oil can be a useful ingredient in cookies where we want a lot of chew (for more information, see page 31). We rarely use oil as the sole fat in a cookie; cookies made with only oil can be greasy and stodgy since oil doesn't aerate. They can also develop an almost fried exterior after baking.

Oats

Oatmeal cookies—chewy and raisined (see page 92), sandwich (see page 96), or crispy and caramelized (see page 160)—are a comforting favorite that are at their best when made with **old-fashioned rolled oats**. These are whole oats that are hulled, cleaned, steamed, and rolled, and their toasty flavor and hearty chew shine in cookies. They act like mix-ins in the cookie rather than like a starch. Quick-cooking oats can often be used in place of old-fashioned, but cookies made with them will be less chewy and more cakey. Avoid instant oats, which have a mushy texture when baked into cookies, and steel-cut oats, which won't soften in the dough.

Corn Flour

Not to be confused with cornmeal, corn flour is a flour ground from whole dried corn kernels. It gives baked goods a superlatively fresh-corn flavor with an undetectable texture. (Note that cornflour is the word used for cornstarch in the U.K.) In our Cranberry-Rosemary Corn Streusel Bars (page 256), the corn flour creates a streusel (and shortbread) with the texture of one made with standard wheat flour.

Glutinous Sweet White Rice Flour

Glutinous sweet rice flour may seem like a specialty flour, but we use it for two very fun cookies, our Dragon Fruit Mochi–Stuffed Lime Cookies (page 70) and our Strawberry Lemonade Coconut Mochi Bars (page 334). This flour is ground from short-grain sticky rice and therefore, when hydrated and cooked, takes on a stretchy, elastic texture. We developed our recipes with Koda brand Mochiko Flour.

Spices

It's time to open your mind (and spice cabinet) when it comes to spicing up cookies. We use garam masala in our molasses spice cookies (see page 83) for a touch of savor. We had fun spicing our snickerdoodles (see page 388) with the Iranian rose-scented spice blend advieh in place of the standard cinnamon. We encourage you to experiment with spices you love! Five-spice powder in Salted Caramel Apple Crumb Bars (page 259)? Why not? Don't like cardamom? Omit it from the Buckwheat Chocolate Chunk Cookies (page 54) and try allspice. Spices can also have a secondary role, like the cayenne pepper in our Double Gingersnaps (page 166), which makes the ginger taste extra spicy.

Black Cocoa Powder

We're kind of obsessed with black cocoa powder (see page 25). It has the most powerful chocolate flavor and incredible color for very dramatic cookies. We order black cocoa powder and prefer King Arthur Black Cocoa Powder, as it has the darkest color of cocoas we've tried. Other black cocoas work just fine but there is color variance across brands.

Milk Powders

Powdered milk is a milk product from which the water has been evaporated. **Nonfat dry milk powder** starts as pasteurized skim milk. We boost the browned butter in our Browned Butter Shortbread (page 201) with dry milk powder, as it really accentuates the butter's dairy notes for a cookie that lives up to every part of its name.

Malted milk powder is much more complex than dry milk powder: It's made from two powders. The first is malt powder. Malt powder is made by "malting" barley, a process that develops the barley's sugars. To that, milk solids (and salt) are added. Malted milk powder increases the toasty, nutty notes in desserts, so we love it in our updated take on a chocolate chip cookie, Salted Malted Milk Chocolate Chunk Cookies (page 56)—it ups the flavor of ordinary chocolate chip cookies exponentially.

Nuts

We love the richness and texture that nuts contribute to cookies, and you'll find nuts of all varieties ground into flour, chopped and mixed into doughs and batters, and sprinkled on top of baked cookies throughout this book. All nuts are high in oil and will become rancid rather quickly. In the test kitchen, we store nuts in the freezer in zipper-lock bags. Frozen nuts will keep for months, and there's no need to defrost before using. Often recipes call for toasting nuts, which enhances their flavor and gives them a satisfying, crunchy texture. We like to toast nuts when mixing them into doughs or batters, where they're prone to sogginess.

Sesame Seeds

Sesame seeds add flavor to recipes like Miso Magic Bars (page 272) and decoration and crunch to others. There are places where we want black sesame seeds specifically for their earthier, slightly more buttery flavor, like in our Yuzu and Black Sesame Thins (page 345). But in places where sesame seeds are decoration, like Salted Egg Yolk Shortbread Sandwiches (page 212), you can use either white or black.

Skinning Hazelnuts

Hazelnut skins can impart a bitter flavor and undesirable texture. To remove the skins, simply rub the hot toasted nuts inside a clean dish towel.

Nut Butters and Beyond

Many bakers have a jar of Skippy on hand, and that's great—it's our favorite peanut butter for baking. (We don't recommend natural peanut butter made only from peanuts; it can turn out greasy, tough cookies that spread too much.) But we used a number of different nut and seed products in the book that we think you'll love.

Pistachio cream is an ultracreamy product that's enriched with oils, sugar, and sometimes white chocolate; it fills our Chocolate-Pistachio Thumbprints (page 237). It's perfectly smooth and shouldn't be confused with pistachio butter, which is just ground pistachios and maybe some added oil, or highly concentrated pistachio paste.

Tahini has a strong nutty flavor in sweets such as our Browned Butter Halva Crunch Cookies (page 112). We also use another sesame product, roasted Chinese sesame paste. Roasting hulled seeds makes its flavor much stronger and it's texture much thicker than tahini, and it shines in a buttercream for our Salted Egg Yolk Shortbread Sandwiches (page 212).

Cookie Equipment

Cookies don't require too many pieces, but there is some equipment that's nice to have for the very best treats.

Digital Scale

We weigh ingredients to ensure consistent results. We prefer digital scales for their readability and precision. Look for one that has a large weight range and that can be "zeroed." The **OXO Good Grips 11 lb Food Scale with Pull Out Display** has clear buttons, and its display can be pulled out from the platform for easy viewing when weighing bulky items.

Liquid Measuring Cup

Cookies don't always include liquid ingredients such as milk, but when they do, we turn to the industry-standard durable, accurate **Pyrex 2-Cup Measuring Cup**.

Portion Scoops

We love having multiple sizes of portion scoops to easily and cleanly scoop drop cookie dough. Manufacturers identify scoops in different ways: by volume (listed in fluid ounces, tablespoons, or milliliters); by diameter; or, most commonly (and most confusingly), according to a numbered system unique to portion scoops. In this system, scoops are given numerical "sizes" based on the number of level scoops it would take to empty a quart. It would take 20 level scoops with a #20 size scoop, for example, and each scoop would hold about 3.2 tablespoons. You can use this to approximate 3-tablespoon portions—we are OK with a bit of deviation, up to a teaspoon—because it doesn't meaningfully change the yields or baking times of the recipes.

We recommend having the following portion scoop sizes:

¼ cup | #16 scoop
about 3 tablespoons | #20 scoop
about 2 tablespoons | #30 scoop
about 1 tablespoon | #60 scoop

Blade Grinder

You should have a grinder devoted solely to grinding whole spices and freeze-dried fruit to avoid unwanted coffee flavors and errant dark speckles. The **Krups Coffee and Spice Grinder** has been our longtime favorite for its clean, relatively even grinding and easy-to-use design.

Baking Sheets

If you're going to own only one kind of baking sheet (and you should buy at least two), get rimmed baking sheets. They're generally heavy-duty and easy to take in and out of the oven. You can fit a wire cooling rack inside for glazing and decorating cookies or for baking slices of biscotti (see pages 186–187). Of course, you can use them for savory cooking too. (Note: If you use your rimmed baking sheets for cooking a lot, they will darken over time and will impact the bake of your cookies, potentially causing quicker baking and browning of bottoms.) Our favorite is the **Nordic Ware Baker's Half Sheet**.

We do, however, recommend you own rimless baking sheets (also known as cookie sheets) in addition. We sometimes call for them for delicate cookies that we want to achieve even browning on all sides, such as our

Browned Butter Shortbread (page 201). Other times, we use a rimless baking sheet simply because there's room to fit more cookies on the sheet, with no real estate lost to the rim. A bonus: You can transfer all the cookies from the sheet to the wire rack with the parchment paper in one go. If you don't have rimless sheets, we'll let you know when you can flip over a rimmed sheet and use the bottom surface instead; however, this isn't an option for cookies with large yields. Our favorite rimless baking sheet is the **Vollrath Wear-Ever Aluminum Cookie Sheet with Natural Finish**.

Wire Cooling Rack

A wire rack allows air to circulate all around the cookies as they cool. Be sure to buy a sturdy one that will fit inside a standard 18 by 13-inch rimmed baking sheet. **The Checkered Chef Cooling Rack** is our favorite.

Baking Pans

For brownies and bars, we like pans that aren't too dark to prevent overbaking. Molded sides are easier to clean than folded metal, which traps crumbs. We like **Williams Sonoma Goldtouch Nonstick** (13 by 9 and 8-inch square), which have straight sides for tidy bars. We also like the helpful handles on the **All-Clad Pro-Release NonStick Bakeware 8 inch Square Cake Pan**.

Oven Thermometer

It's common for ovens to run hot or cold, which can lead to cookies that are either overbaked or underbaked. Know the exact temperature of your oven with a thermometer. We like **The CDN Pro Accurate Oven Thermometer**.

Instant-Read Thermometer

It is essential to take the temperature of some cookie fillings and confections, such as custard and caramel. A digital instant-read thermometer (rather than a slow-registering stick candy thermometer) will tell you the temperature of your food almost immediately. The **ThermoWorks Thermapen ONE** has every bell and whistle.

Stand Mixer

A stand mixer, with its hands-free operation, numerous attachments, and strong mixing arm, is a worthwhile investment if you plan on baking cookies regularly. A number of our recipes call for one. Heft matters, as does a strong motor that can mix stiff or chunky dough with ease. If beyond cookies you do a lot of heavy-duty, large-batch baking, especially breads, we suggest investing in the **Ankarsrum Original 6230 Creme and Stainless Steel 7 Liter Stand Mixer**. But we also like the **KitchenAid Classic Series 4.5 Quart Tilt-Head Stand Mixer** as a mid-priced option.

Food Processor

In addition to chopping nuts or grinding them to a fine flour, we use a food processor to make some cookie doughs. Look for a workbowl that has a capacity of at least 11 cups. With a powerful motor, responsive pulsing action, and sharp blades, the **Cuisinart Custom 14 Cup Food Processor** is a great choice.

Rolling Pin

There are many styles of rolling pins, but our preference is for French-style wood pins without handles. These pins come straight and tapered. We tend to reach for straight pins, which make achieving even dough thickness and rolling out large disks easy. Our favorite is the **J.K. Adams Plain Maple Rolling Dowel**.

Cookie Cutters

We hope you'll experiment with all kinds of cookie cutters. Seek out fun shapes that match the fun coating for Sparkling Blueberry-Lavender Shortbread Cookies (page 202). Make sandwich cookies other than rounds or squares. Mix and match shapes for cookies and their cutouts like we do on page 182 for our Blackberry-Thyme Linzer Cookies. Go fluted or straight-edge. Sharp metal cutters tend to work best (if you want just a basic set of different size round cutters, we like the **Ateco 5357 11-Piece Plain Round Cutter Set**). Just be sure to make cookies of all the same size (in inches), so they bake and brown at the same rate.

Measuring Cups

While we very much prefer to weigh our dry ingredients for cookie baking, we understand that some will still measure by volume. Look for heavy, well-constructed, evenly weighted stainless-steel models, with easy-to-read measurement markings. We recommend the very accurate **OXO Good Grips Stainless Steel Measuring Cups**.

Measuring Spoons

We prefer heavy steel spoons with long, sturdy, well-designed handles. Choose measuring spoons with deep bowls; shallow bowls allow more leavener or extract to spill with the shake of an unsteady hand. The **Cuisipro Stainless Steel 5-Piece Measuring Spoons** are our favorite set. Note: If you're making thumbprint cookies (see pages 230–239), you can use the bottom of this set's tablespoon measure to make an oval impression.

Piping Sets

Cookies such as Almond Joy Meringue Kisses (page 362) are piped onto baking sheets. Some cookies have frostings you can pipe artistically. Floppy cloth pastry bags can stain or hold smells. Canvas bags tend to be stiff. We prefer disposable plastic piping bags; they're easy to handle and effortless to clean. In addition you'll want a couple round and star tips, as well as four couplers, plastic nozzles that adhere the tip to the bag. We like **Wilton** supplies.

Bench Scraper

This basic tool is handy for transferring dough from one surface to another and for cutting dough into pieces. Our winner is the **Dexter-Russell Sani-Safe 6" x 3" Dough Cutter/Scraper**. It has a comfortable handle and the deeply beveled edge cuts through dough easily.

Bowl Scraper

The best way to remove sticky dough from the bowl is with a rigid curved scraper, which cleans the bowl and moves heavy dough easily. Our favorite models are made of contoured silicone covering a metal insert, like the **Fox Run Silicone Dough/Bowl Scraper**.

Silicone Baking Mat

Owning a silicone baking mat or two is valuable for sticky or paper-thin cookies such as Florentine Lace Cookies (page 168). You can use these instead of parchment for stick-proof results. Other benefits of baking mats are their heavy weight, which prevents them from moving or curling, and their surface, which ensures cookies with perfectly flat bottoms. Note: Because the mats are so slick, some cookies may spread out more on them, resulting in a slightly crispier final product. The gold-standard baking mat is **DeMarle Silpat Non-Stick Silicone Baking Mat**.

Keeping and Sharing Your Creations

How you treat your cookies after they bake is almost as important as what you do to make them. If you've built an incredible cookie, you want to experience and share an incredible cookie. This comes down to how you cool it and deliver it.

Cooling Cookies

As with many baked goods, a lot of cookies need to cool completely before you take a bite so that they set properly and exhibit the tender crumb, delicate snap, or appealing chew you worked for.

Many basic drop cookies require a short rest on the baking sheet—typically about 5 minutes—so they are firm enough to move; after that, they are transferred to a wire rack, where air can circulate around them, to finish cooling. Sometimes, for cookies we intentionally under-bake, we call for cooling the cookies completely on the warm sheet.

If you're filling a cookie with jam or chocolate, or topping it with frosting or glaze, it needs to cool completely—often 30 minutes—before you apply these ingredients. For layered and loaded bars and pans of brownies, you'll have to wait longer, often 2 hours or more.

We get it, though. The smell in the kitchen is intoxicating, and you want to experience some cookies when they're still fudgy or when their chocolate is still melty. If you have to sneak a bite of a warm-from-the-oven cookie, go ahead, we won't tell. We can live with your doing it with one of these. We suggest you add a glass of milk.

Chewy Chocolate Chip Cookies (50)

Buckwheat Chocolate Chunk Cookies (54)

Salted Malted Milk Chocolate Chunk Cookies (56)

Vegan Peanut Butter Chocolate Chip Cookies (59)

Loaded White Chocolate–Macadamia Cookies (106)

Peanut Butter Candy and Bacon Cookies (108)

Cookies and Cream Cookies (111)

S'mores Cookies (114)

Chewy, Gooey Biscoff Butter Cookies (120)

Chocolate Chunk Oatmeal Cookies with Pecans and Dried Cherries (125)

Triple Chocolate–Cherry Cookies (129)

Levain-Style Chocolate Chip Cookies (294)

Storing Baked Cookies

Cookie recipes usually yield a generous amount so, depending on your household size, you might want to keep them for a bit. There are ways to store cookies mid-process and after baking. You can also extend a cookie's life by applying glazes or frostings just before serving. Many cookies can be stored according to the methods below. These are general guidelines; see individual recipes for specific storage times. Our storage times reflect when the cookies are at top quality; use your discretion if you'd like to keep them longer.

Cookie Type	How to Store	How Long
Chewy Cookies	In an airtight container at room temperature	About 2 days
Shortbread Cookies	In an airtight container at room temperature	1 week
Crispy, Crunchy Cookies	In an airtight container at room temperature	3 days
Brownies and Blondies	In an airtight container in the refrigerator	3 days
Fruit-Based Bars	In an airtight container in the refrigerator	About 2 days
Cakey Cookies	In an airtight container at room temperature	About 3 days

Shop for Silica Packets

For crispy cookies that we want to keep that way, we love storing them with silica packets. The packets absorb moisture so you can keep the crunch for the shelf life of the cookie. We think silica packets are especially essential for storing meringue cookies. If you've made them before, you know that just a touch of humidity can turn them sticky, soft, and unappealing. You can order silica packets online.

Make-Ahead Possibilities

Cookies are perfect for any occasion—holidays, bake sales, school lunches, teatime, everyday desserts—and it's helpful to make them ahead.

REFRIGERATING DOUGH

If you're making cookies just for you or your family or roommates, you may want to refrigerate the dough and bake cookies a few at a time. Or, you may want to make your dough in advance and bake the day of an event. Is this OK? It depends on the type of leavener in the cookies. Dough made with baking soda alone holds well for two days but bakes up a little flatter on the third. Cookies made with both baking powder and soda begin to lose lift after a few days of dough storage (though we wouldn't recommend refrigerating a dough beyond three days because it could pick up off-flavors). Cookie dough made with only baking powder maintains good lift however long you store it. Unleavened cookies will hold just as long. Do not store batters or cookie dough with whipped eggs in the fridge. (Refrigerating has benefits beyond storage; see page 12 for more information.)

What kind of cookie dough is good to make and keep in the refrigerator?

- Drop cookie dough (cookie dough that you portion and place on the baking sheet) in a bowl; scoop and bake when you're ready.
- Slice-and-bake cookie dough logs wrapped in plastic; slice when you have the time.
- Cookie dough disks wrapped in plastic; roll and cut out shapes another day.

FREEZING DOUGH

By keeping unbaked cookie dough in the freezer, you can satisfy your craving for freshly baked cookies—just one or a whole batch—anytime. After making the dough, portion it out as you would for baking right away—either on parchment-lined baking sheets or on large plates—and place the dough portions in the freezer until they are frozen solid, at least 30 minutes. Remove the frozen unbaked cookies from the sheet, arrange them in a zipper-lock bag for dough balls or in layers in an airtight storage container for sliced or cutout cookies, and place them back in the freezer for up to two months. You may need to increase the recipe's baking time, but no defrosting is necessary. You can also freeze entire slice-and-bake dough logs and thaw them in the refrigerator until they're sliceable.

REVIVING STALE COOKIES

If you've had leftover cookies for too long, don't throw them out! To restore cookies to (almost) just-baked freshness, recrisp them in a 425-degree oven for 4 to 5 minutes. Let the cookies cool on the sheet for a couple of minutes and serve them warm.

Gifting, Swapping, and Shipping

Cookie swapping isn't just for the holidays. You can make anyone's day better with cookies, and they're among the best treats to give away, to the next-door neighbor or to a friend across the country—both deliveries are possible with the right selections and the right packing methods.

Cookies that have a generous shelf life are best for giving away, so the recipient tastes them at their best. Cookies that are baked until dried throughout, such as Double Gingersnaps (page 166) or Thin and Crispy Rosemary Toffee Cookies (page 152), remain intact, crunchy, and fresh-tasting. Shortbread and other butter cookies that are good for a week or more are ideal. Moist, dense brownies and blondies also fare well—but don't pack them with the others: The crunchy cookies will absorb moisture from the bar cookies and soften.

HOW TO PACK COOKIES

You can upcycle store-bought cookie tins, use a windowed bakery box, or look for secondhand cookie jars or tins to add a personal touch.

IN A ROUND TIN:

1. Line bottom and sides of cookie tin with parchment paper, waxed paper, crinkle-cut paper, or corrugated paper.

2. Cut lengths of corrugated cardboard or paper to fit snugly into interior of tin, creating sections for cookies. Make sure that cookies fit securely in each section and are not loose. Fold any overhanging parchment over top before closing tin.

Chewy cookies that started out moist, like Triple Citrus Gingerbread with White Chocolate (page 86), can end up stale during transit, and delicate lace cookies can break into shards. If a cookie has a glaze, consider it for a hand delivery rather than a shipped one so it's not ruined in travel. Sandwich cookies with fillings that don't drip are better for making the trip.

Cookies, especially those in this book, are fun, so beyond practicality, we recommend choosing a mix based on shapes, colors, textures and flavors. Another idea is to go monochrome with cookies of the same color (or flavor) family. And a gift doesn't have to be extravagant: Two to four very intentional cookies make an incredible box.

IN A LOAF PAN:

For square blondies, brownies, and bars or long cookies like biscotti, fit cookies snugly into disposable aluminum loaf pan with lid, lined with parchment paper.

IN A BAG:

Stack round cookies tall in a cellophane bag that holds them snugly and tie it closed.

IN A JAR:

For a cookie jar or other tall vessel, cut pieces of parchment or tissue paper to fit between layers of coated cookies like Millionaire's Shortbread (page 205).

Chapter 1

CHEWY AND GOOEY

ATK CLASSIC

Makes 16 cookies

Total Time 55 minutes, plus 30 minutes cooling

The chocolate chip cookie is the most iconic American treat, and when we set out to develop our recipe in the aughts, we wanted it to be the Platonic ideal—reliably moist and chewy with crisp edges and deep butterscotch notes. And we're happy that today, we still wouldn't change a thing. The key ingredient is browned butter. Melting the butter makes its water content readily available to interact with flour and create more gluten for a chewy texture; continuing to cook the butter until it browns contributes deep caramel notes, as does dissolving the sugar in the melted butter by whisking and briefly resting the mixture a few times. The dissolved sugar caramelizes more easily, creating a spectrum of toffee flavors, plus a crackly surface and crispy edges. Baking at a relatively high temperature—375 degrees—darkens the edges while the cookie centers stay soft. Studded with gooey chocolate and boasting a complex toffee flavor, these are chocolate chip cookies perfected.

CHEWY CHOCOLATE CHIP COOKIES

- 1¾ cups (249 grams) all-purpose flour
- ½ teaspoon baking soda
- 14 tablespoons (200 grams) unsalted butter, divided
- ¾ cup packed (149 grams) dark brown sugar
- ½ cup (99 grams) granulated sugar
- 2 teaspoons vanilla extract
- 1 teaspoon table salt
- 1 large egg plus 1 large yolk
- 1¼ cups (213 grams) semisweet or bittersweet chocolate chips
- ¾ cup (89 grams) pecans or walnuts, toasted and chopped (optional)

1 Adjust oven rack to middle position and heat oven to 375 degrees. Whisk flour and baking soda together in bowl.

2 Heat 10 tablespoons (143 grams) butter in 10-inch skillet over medium-high heat until melted, about 2 minutes. Continue to cook, swirling skillet and stirring constantly with silicone spatula, until butter is dark golden brown and has nutty aroma, 1 to 3 minutes. Transfer browned butter to large bowl and stir in remaining 4 tablespoons (57 grams) butter until melted. Whisk in brown sugar, granulated sugar, vanilla, and salt until incorporated. Whisk in egg and yolk until smooth and no lumps remain, about 30 seconds.

3 Let mixture stand for 3 minutes, then whisk for 30 seconds. Repeat process of resting and whisking 2 more times until mixture is thick, smooth, and shiny. Using silicone spatula, stir in flour mixture until just combined, about 1 minute. Stir in chocolate chips and pecans, if using.

4 Working with 3 tablespoons dough at a time, roll into balls and space them evenly on 2 parchment paper–lined baking sheets (8 dough balls per sheet). Bake cookies, 1 sheet at a time, until golden brown and edges have begun to set but centers are still soft and puffy, 10 to 14 minutes, rotating sheet halfway through baking. Transfer sheet to wire rack and let cookies cool completely on sheet before serving.

Storage: 2 days at room temperature

How We Get *Chewy* Chocolate Chip Cookies

- **Melt the butter** When butter melts, thewater in it separates from the fat and can then interact with the proteins in flour to create more structure-enhancing gluten for noticeably chewier results than creaming butter and sugar produces. We brown some of the butter for flavor (not all of it so we don't drive off too much moisture).

- **Increase the brown sugar** A 60:40 ratio of brown sugar to white sugar gives the cookies more moisture and chew without them falling apart.

- **Eliminate an egg white** Egg whites give cookies structure but they can also contribute to cakey, crumbly cookies; one whole egg and one egg yolk is just right.

- **Make bigger cookies** Using 3 tablespoons of dough instead of the 2 tablespoons in classic chocolate chip cookie recipes creates more textural contrast between a crispy edge and a chewy middle.

Crisp Edges
Relatively high baking temperature allows edges to crisp while center stays chewy.

Chewy Texture
Achieved by using melted butter, a high ratio of dark brown sugar to granulated, and generous dough portions.

Shiny, Craggy Top
Comes from caramelization of the granulated sugar.

Better Flavor through Sugar Science

Chocolate chips are in the name, but we think the element that makes these cookies so memorable and craveable is the deep, buttery toffee flavor that is unrivaled by other varieties of drop cookies. We wanted that flavor to shine in our chocolate chip cookies. Letting our butter-sugar mixture rest after whisking it together makes all the difference. Instead of cookies with a smooth, matte surface, our cookies emerge from the oven with a slightly glossy sheen and an alluring surface of cracks. One bite reveals a rush of deep, toffee-like flavor.

Sugar that is dissolved in liquid before baking caramelizes more readily than sugar that simply "melts" when exposed to the same amount of heat. Dissolved sugar breaks down more quickly from crystalline sucrose into glucose and fructose, which caramelize at a lower temperature to create new flavor compounds. As the dissolved, caramelized sugar cools, it takes on a brittle structure, which translates to a crispier texture. But that effect occurs mainly at the cookie's outer edges, where we want it. Just like an evaporating lake, as moisture on the perimeter disappears, the remaining moisture becomes concentrated in the center, where we want moist chewiness.

Is the dissolving/mixing/resting method an extra step? Yes, but it's worth it for chocolate chip cookies that are that much more delicious than the norm.

1

2

Mixing the Sugar

1 Whisk egg and yolk into browned butter-sugar mixture until smooth and no lumps remain, about 30 seconds.

2 Let mixture stand for 3 minutes, then whisk for 30 seconds.

3 Repeat process of resting and whisking 2 more times until mixture is thick, smooth, and shiny.

3

WHY THIS RECIPE WORKS We deepen the flavor of cookies with browned butter, brown sugar, and various baking techniques throughout the book, but using whole-grain flour is another delicious way to deep flavor—and it's incredible in these buttery chocolate chunk cookies. Whole-grain flours give rich, nutty flavor (and some nutrients) to baked goods. We tested a number in this variation on our Chewy Chocolate Chip Cookies (page 50), and we liked many of them. But buckwheat flour—a pseudograin actually ground from a seed—is distinctive in this cookie, especially when gently accented with ground cardamom. We add milk because the flour's high protein and fiber content causes it to absorb more liquid than all-purpose flour. The earthy flavors go well with rich chocolate, and this is a nice place to use dark. Roughly chopped chocolate gives a rustic, irregular distribution of chocolate streaks throughout; we reserve some extra-large shards for topping to ensure that each cookie features lustrous puddles of melted chocolate.

Makes 12 cookies

Total Time 1 hour, plus 30 minutes cooling

BUCKWHEAT CHOCOLATE CHUNK COOKIES

- 1 cup (142 grams) all-purpose flour
- ⅔ cup (104 grams) buckwheat flour
- 1 teaspoon table salt
- 1 teaspoon baking soda
- ½ teaspoon ground cardamom
- 14 tablespoons (200 grams) unsalted butter, divided
- ¾ cup packed (149 grams) dark brown sugar
- ½ cup (99 grams) granulated sugar
- 2 tablespoons whole milk
- 2 teaspoons vanilla extract
- 1 large egg plus 1 large yolk
- 8 ounces (227 grams) bittersweet chocolate (6 ounces/170 grams cut into rough ½-inch pieces, 2 ounces/57 grams cut into rough ¾-inch pieces)

Spelt, rye, or whole-wheat flour can be used in place of buckwheat flour if you prefer; measure the flour by weight.

1 Whisk all-purpose flour, buckwheat flour, salt, baking soda, and cardamom together in bowl.

2 Heat 10 tablespoons (143 grams) butter in 10-inch skillet over medium-high heat until melted, about 2 minutes. Continue to cook, swirling skillet and stirring constantly with silicone spatula, until butter is dark golden brown and has nutty aroma, 1 to 3 minutes. Transfer browned butter to large bowl and stir in remaining 4 tablespoons (57 grams) butter until me ted. Whisk in brown sugar, granulated sugar, milk, and vanilla until incorporated. Whisk in egg and yolk until smooth and no lumps remain, about 30 secconds.

3 Let mixture stand for 3 minutes, then whisk for 30 seconds. Repeat process of resting and whisking 2 more times until mixture is thick, smooth, and shiny. Using silicone spatula, stir in flour mixture until just combined, about 1 minute. Stir in ½-inch chocolate pieces, cover, and refrigerate for 30 minutes.

4 Adjust oven rack to middle position and heat oven to 350 degrees. Working with ¼ cup dough at a time, roll into balls and space them evenly on 2 parchment paper–lined baking sheets (6 balls per sheet). Press ¾-inch chocolate pieces evenly into tops of dough balls.

5 Bake cookies, 1 sheet at a time, until golden brown and edges have begun to set but centers are still soft and puffy, 10 to 14 minutes, rotating sheet halfway through baking. Transfer sheet to wire rack and let cookies cool completely on sheet before serving.

Storage: 2 days at room temperature

WHY THIS RECIPE WORKS For many, chocolate chip is The Cookie, so we challenged ourselves to create a deluxe, (better-than) bakery-style chocolate chip cookie—one so indulgent it would stop people in their tracks. We wanted to engineer crispy edges, a chewy-gooey center, big pools of chocolate, a dramatic sprinkling of flake salt, and flavor more caramelly-rich than in any cookie we've tasted. We add malted milk powder to make the cookie taste superlatively rich and robust. Interestingly, the flavor enhancer also substantially improves the cookie's texture, enhancing its chewiness, creating crispier caramelized edges, and contributing to a perfectly golden brown exterior. Milk chocolate enhances the cookie's maltiness (think: malted milk balls). We make this cookie big—bigger than any other in the book—to best achieve our dream contrast of texture—a crunchiness at the exterior and a middle that remains totally soft and chewy.

Makes 16 cookies

Total Time 1½ hours, plus 30 minutes chilling

SALTED MALTED MILK CHOCOLATE CHUNK COOKIES

- 16 tablespoons (228 grams) unsalted butter
- 2¼ cups (320 grams) all-purpose flour
- ¾ cup (106 grams) malted milk powder
- 1½ teaspoons baking soda
- 1 teaspoon table salt
- 1 cup packed (198 grams) dark brown sugar
- ½ cup (99 grams) granulated sugar
- 2 large eggs
- 1½ teaspoons vanilla extract
- 12 ounces (340 grams) thick bar milk chocolate, chopped into 1-inch pieces
- Flake sea salt

We chill the dough for a bit, finding that a range of time works. Just 30 minutes of chilling results in thinner, chewier cookies with the crispiest exterior, while 2 hours or more is best for thicker, fudgier centers. We prefer the way thick chocolate bars (like Tony's Chocolonely or vacuum-sealed blocks from the candy or baking aisle) melt in this cookie but you can use any brand in this recipe. We used Carnation brand malted milk powder to develop this recipe. Avoid sweetened or flavored malted milk powders. These cookies are very large and spread into giant 4½-inch-wide rounds while baking. If you don't haverimless baking sheets, use rimmed baking sheets and bake only four cookies on each sheet to accommodate their spread.

1 Heat butter in 10-inch skillet over medium-high heat until melted, about 2 minutes. Continue to cook, swirling skillet and stirring constantly with silicone spatula, until butter is dark golden brown and has nutty aroma, 1 to 3 minutes. Remove from heat and set aside to cool for 10 minutes. Whisk flour, malted milk powder, baking soda, and table salt together in bowl.

2 Scrape cooled butter and any milk solids at bottom of skillet into bowl of stand mixer. Fit mixer with paddle attachment and beat cooled butter, brown sugar, and granulated sugar on medium speed until well combined, about 1 minute, scraping down bowl as needed. Add eggs and vanilla and continue to beat until well incorporated, about 1 minute longer. Reduce speed to low, add flour mixture, and mix until most of flour has been incorporated, about 1 minute. Add chocolate and mix until just combined. Cover bowl with plastic wrap and chill dough for 30 minutes for a chewier cookie or up to 4 hours for a fudgier cookie.

3 Adjust oven rack to middle position and heat oven to 350 degrees. Working with heaping ¼ cup dough at a time, roll into balls and space them evenly on 3 parchment paper–lined rimless baking sheets (5 or 6 balls per sheet), orienting dough balls so any large chocolate chunks are facing up. (If you do not have 3 rimless baking sheets, reuse first sheet once it's cooled to room temperature.)

4 Bake cookies, 1 sheet at a time, until edges are golden but center is still puffy, 12 to 14 minutes, rotating sheet halfway through baking. Transfer sheet to wire rack and immediately sprinkle with flake sea salt. Let cookies cool on sheet for 10 minutes, then transfer to wire rack. Let cookies cool on wire rack for 10 minutes and serve warm or at room temperature.

Storage: 3 days at room temperature

WHY THIS RECIPE WORKS Peanut butter belongs with chocolate; therefore, it belongs in a chocolate chip cookie! This is one of our favorite chocolate chip cookie recipes and, as a bonus, the cookies are vegan. A modest amount of peanut butter in the dough satisfies our peanut craving while also providing richness and nuttiness to the cookie in the absence of butter. Coconut oil rounds out the rest of the fat that the usual amount of butter would provide in a chocolate chip cookie. We use all brown sugar to emphasize this cookie's depth of flavor and to make the center super soft and moist. Chopped peanuts give the cookies more nutty flavor and a great contrasting crunch.

Makes 18 cookies

Total Time 45 minutes, plus 30 minutes cooling

VEGAN PEANUT BUTTER CHOCOLATE CHIP COOKIES

- 2 cups (284 grams) all-purpose flour
- 1½ teaspoons baking powder
- ½ teaspoon baking soda
- ½ teaspoon table salt
- 1⅓ cups packed (264 grams) dark brown sugar
- ½ cup (105 grams) refined coconut oil, melted and cooled
- 6 tablespoons (89 grams) water
- ⅓ cup (87 grams) unsalted creamy peanut butter
- 2 teaspoons vanilla extract
- 1¼ cups (213 grams) semisweet chocolate chips or chunks
- ½ cup (71 grams) dry-roasted peanuts, chopped
- Flake sea salt

You can use natural peanut butter in this recipe, but the cookies will spread less. We prefer unsalted peanut butter in this recipe; if you only have salted peanut butter, reduce the salt in the recipe to ¼ teaspoon.

1 Adjust oven rack to middle position and heat oven to 350 degrees. Whisk flour, baking powder, baking soda, and table salt together in bowl.

2 Whisk sugar, melted oil, water, peanut butter, and vanilla in large bowl until well combined and smooth. Add flour mixture and stir until combined. Stir in chocolate chips and peanuts.

3 Working with 3 tablespoons dough at a time, roll into balls and space them evenly on 2 parchment paper–lined baking sheets (9 balls per sheet). Bake cookies, 1 sheet at a time, until light golden and edges have begun to set but centers are still soft, 12 to 14 minutes, rotating sheet halfway through baking. Transfer sheet to wire rack, sprinkle cookies with flake salt, and let cool completely on sheet before serving.

Storage: 3 days at room temperature

Makes 1 skillet cookie; serves 8

Total Time 55 minutes, plus 30 minutes cooling

WHY THIS RECIPE WORKS A big skillet cookie has a lot going for it: It's convenient (no scooping and baking multiple sheet pans), fun to serve (goes straight from the oven to the table), and full of contrasting textures (a cast-iron pan creates a great crust while the large-format bake ensures a soft middle). We wanted something a little different than regular chocolate chip. This milk chocolate and cinnamon skillet cookie has a big personality that matches its size, with sweet, aromatic cinnamon giving way to a finishing kick of cayenne and a crunchy topping of roasted, salted almonds. As with many of our cookies, we brown most of the butter to maximize nutty flavor; we're happy to do it since we bake the cookie in the same skillet anyway. You can serve the cookie warm from the skillet, with scoops of vanilla ice cream piled on top, if you like!

SPICED ALMOND CHIP SKILLET COOKIE

- 1¾ cups (249 grams) all-purpose flour
- 1 tablespoon ground cinnamon
- ½ teaspoon cayenne pepper
- ½ teaspoon baking soda
- 12 tablespoons (171 grams) unsalted butter, divided
- ¾ cup packed (149 grams) dark brown sugar
- ½ cup (99 grams) granulated sugar
- 2 teaspoons vanilla extract
- 1 teaspoon table salt
- 1 large egg plus 1 large yolk
- 1 cup (170 grams) milk chocolate chips
- ½ cup (79 grams) whole roasted salted almonds, chopped
- Flake sea salt

1 Adjust oven rack to upper-middle position and heat oven to 375 degrees. Whisk flour, cinnamon, cayenne, and baking soda together in bowl.

2 Heat 9 tablespoons (128 grams) butter in 12-inch cast-iron skillet over medium-high heat until melted, 2 to 4 minutes. Continue to cook, swirling skillet and stirring constantly with silicone spatula, until butter is dark golden brown and has nutty aroma, 1 to 3 minutes. Transfer browned butter to large bowl (set skillet aside to cool; do not clean) and stir in remaining 3 tablespoons butter until melted. Whisk in brown sugar, granulated sugar, vanilla, and table salt until incorporated. Whisk in egg and yolk until smooth and no lumps remain, about 30 seconds.

3 Let mixture stand for 3 minutes, then whisk for 30 seconds. Repeat process of resting and whisking 2 more times until mixture is thick, smooth, and shiny. Using silicone spatula, stir in flour mixture until just combined, about 1 minute. Stir in chocolate chips.

4 Transfer dough to now-empty cooled skillet and press with silicone spatula to fill skillet in even layer. Sprinkle almonds and flake sea salt over top and press lightly into dough. Transfer skillet to oven and bake until cookie is golden brown and edges are set, about 20 minutes, rotating skillet halfway through baking. Using pot holders, transfer skillet to wire rack and let cookie cool for 30 minutes. Slice cookie into wedges and serve warm.

Storage: 2 days at room temperature

ATK CLASSIC

Makes 24 cookies

Total Time 55 minutes, plus 20 minutes cooling

For a cookie with such a simple profile—butter and sugar—the sugar cookie remains a favorite thanks to the promise of a glimmering exterior crackle and comforting hallmark chew. Unlike many sugar cookies, we've engineered ours to actually live up to those promises. We whisk together a trio of liquid fats—vegetable oil, melted butter, and a bit of melted cream cheese (more on that later)—to make a soft dough by hand with the perfect amounts of saturated and unsaturated fat to build chew. The cookie isn't just sweet—generous vanilla extract perfumes the dough, and the cream cheese helps offset the white sugar with appealing tang. For a cookie that rises, spreads, and crackles to the trademark degree, we use both baking powder and soda; the soda reacts with the acidic cream cheese in the dough for the desired effect.

CHEWY SUGAR COOKIES

- 2¼ cups (320 grams) all-purpose flour
- 1 teaspoon baking powder
- ½ teaspoon baking soda
- ½ teaspoon table salt
- 1½ cups (297 grams) sugar, plus ⅓ cup (66 grams) for rolling
- 2 ounces (57 grams) cream cheese, cut into 8 pieces and softened
- 6 tablespoons (86 grams) unsalted butter, melted
- ⅓ cup (70 grams) vegetable oil
- 1 large egg
- 1 tablespoon whole milk
- 2 teaspoons vanilla extract

The final dough will be slightly softer than most cookie dough. For the best results, handle the dough as briefly and gently as possible when shaping the cookies; overworking the dough will result in flatter cookies.

1 Adjust oven rack to middle position and heat oven to 350 degrees. Whisk flour, baking powder, baking soda, and salt together in bowl.

2 Place 1½ cups (298 grams) sugar and cream cheese in large bowl. Whisk in melted butter (some lumps of cream cheese will remain). Whisk in oil until incorporated. Whisk in egg, milk, and vanilla until smooth. Using silicone spatula, fold in flour mixture until soft, homogeneous dough forms.

3 Spread remaining ⅓ cup (66 grams) sugar in shallow dish. Working with 2 tablespoons dough at a time, roll into balls, then roll in sugar to coat; space dough balls evenly on 2 parchment paper–lined baking sheets (12 dough balls per sheet). Using bottom of greased dry measuring cup, press each ball until 3 inches in diameter. Using sugar left in dish, sprinkle 2 teaspoons sugar over each sheet of cookies; discard extra sugar. (Raw cookies can be frozen for up to 1 month; bake frozen cookies in 350-degree oven for 17 to 22 minutes.)

4 Bake cookies, 1 sheet at a time, until edges are set and beginning to brown, 11 to 13 minutes, rotating sheet halfway through baking. Let cookies cool on sheet for 5 minutes, then transfer to wire rack. Let cookies cool completely before serving.

Storage: 3 days at room temperature

How We Get *Chewy* Sugar Cookies

- **Balance fats** Using both saturated and unsaturated fats—butter and oil—provides optimal chew.
- **Incorporate cream cheese** Including a bit of cream cheese as part of the saturated fat keeps the cookie chewy while adding some tang to cut the sweetness.
- **Double-up on leavener** Using baking soda, which interacts with the acidity in the cream cheese, in addition to powder creates a crackly top, which is an important contrast to the chewy interior.

Even Spread
Pressing the cookies to an even height before baking gives them the perfect uniform appearance.

Sparkly Coating
Rolling in sugar before baking creates the iconic look.

Chewy Cookie
Using both saturated (butter + cream cheese) and unsaturated (vegetable oil) fats creates a structure that bends just right.

Appealing Cracks
Using baking soda in addition to powder causes cookies to rise and collapse.

Creative *Sugar Cookie* Takes

- **Spice it up** Vanilla is nice, but spices add subtle perfume, as in our Olive Oil, Anise, and Orange Sugar Cookies (page 66), or lively appeal, as in our Garam Masala Molasses Cookies (page 83); you can even incorporate ground tea like matcha for color and flavor (see page 69).

- **Oil change** Vegetable oil is a good neutral choice, but you can also work with more flavorful oils like olive oil (see page 66).

- **Stuff it** We hide a mochi surprise in sugar cookie dough (see page 70).

- **Bake bars** We press lemon-scented sugar cookies into a pan to create sweet, chewy bars you can frost (see page 75).

Sugar Cookies' Chewy Secret

Getting the chew we want but usually miss from sugar cookies boils down to one thing: fat, specifically the ratio of saturated to unsaturated fat.

Fat can be divided into two broad types: saturated and unsaturated. Both types consist of carbon atoms strung together in long chains. In predominantly saturated fats such as butter, shortening, and lard, each of these carbon atoms has the maximum number of hydrogen atoms attached to it. The hydrogen acts as a buttress to keep the carbon chains rigid so that they pack together like a box of pencils, forming a fat that is solid even at room temperature.

Unsaturated fats, such as vegetable oils and olive oil, have fewer hydrogen atoms providing support, resulting in carbon chains that don't stick together tightly and fat that is liquid at room temperature.

A combination of rigid and flexible chains can give cookies a uniquely chewy texture. Here we hit close to a 1:2 ratio. We use butter for the saturated fat and vegetable oil for the unsaturated fat for a cookie that's rich but appropriately neutral in flavor. But other fats can work in different contexts. Our Olive Oil, Anise, and Orange Sugar Cookies (page 66) use olive oil for the unsaturated fat; our Classic Peanut Butter Cookies (page 98) put this combination of fats to work for chew and use peanut butter for the unsaturated fat.

Sugar Fix

Of course sugar cookies should be sweet, but we're not fans of one-note sweetness. Butter adds richness to our sugar cookies, but they still read a little bland in earlier bakes during recipe testing. We needed to take the edge off of the sugariness. Acidic lemon juice or zest had an assertive citrus flavor that took the cookies out of the "sugar" category and dropped them squarely into the lemon family. We often add buttermilk, sour cream, or yogurt to muffins and cakes to round out their flavors, but liquid made the dough much too soft.

We landed on a surprising addition, cream cheese, which enriches the dough's flavor without adding much liquid. This adds more saturated fat to our recipe's fat ratio (see Sugar Cookies' Chewy Secret), but it doesn't markedly affect the cookies' texture. It does, however, affect the flavor in a positive way, balancing the sweetness for a sugar cookie with more than one note.

Baking Powder and Baking Soda: Dynamic Duo

Our Chewy Sugar Cookies contain both baking soda and baking powder. Since each is a leavening agent, why do you need both? The two work in tandem to create cookies that not only rise but also spread to the right degree. Plus, in our recipe, baking soda has one more purely aesthetic effect: It creates cookies with an appealingly crackly top.

Baking powder is responsible for lift, since it is engineered to produce most of its gas after the cookies go into the oven, where the dough sets before these bubbles can burst.

But too much lift can mean cookies that turn out humped. A small amount of baking soda can even things out. Baking soda raises the pH of dough (baking powder does, too, but not as high), weakening gluten. Weaker gluten means less structure and cookies that spread. Goodbye, humped shapes.

As for crackly tops, baking soda reacts immediately in the wet dough to produce large bubbles of carbon dioxide that can't all be contained by the weakened dough. Before the cookies can set in the oven, the bubbles rise to the top and burst, leaving fissures in their wake.

Powder, No Soda
With only baking powder in the mix, cookies bake up humped, with less crackly tops.

Powder + Soda
Both leaveners in the dough lead to cookies that are perfectly mounded and nicely crackly.

Makes 24 cookies

Total Time 50 minutes, plus 30 minutes cooling

WHY THIS RECIPE WORKS If you like olive oil desserts, you'll love this olive oil sugar cookie, complemented by a very Sicilian combo of sweet and fragrant ground anise and orange zest. The sugar cookie's simple profile really lets the olive oil shine. Like the vegetable oil in our original Chewy Sugar Cookies (page 62), the olive oil in this cookie provides unsaturated fat in addition to the butter's saturated fat to give the cookie good chew.

OLIVE OIL, ANISE, AND ORANGE SUGAR COOKIES

- 2¼ cups (320 grams) all-purpose flour
- 1 teaspoon ground anise
- 1 teaspoon baking powder
- ½ teaspoon baking soda
- ½ teaspoon table salt
- ¼ teaspoon grated orange zest
- 1½ cups (297 grams) sugar, plus ⅓ cup (66 grams) for rolling
- 2 ounces (57 grams) cream cheese, cut into 8 pieces and softened
- 6 tablespoons (86 grams) unsalted butter, melted
- ⅓ cup (70 grams) extra-virgin olive oil
- 1 large egg
- 1 tablespoon whole milk
- 2 teaspoons vanilla extract

The final dough will be slightly softer than most cookie doughs. For the best results, handle the dough as briefly and gently as possible when shaping the cookies; overworking the dough will result in flatter cookies.

1 Adjust oven rack to middle position and heat oven to 350 degrees. Whisk flour, anise, baking powder, baking soda, and salt together in bowl.

2 Rub orange zest into 1½ cups (298 grams) sugar in large bowl until fragrant. Add cream cheese. Whisk in melted butter (some lumps of cream cheese will remain), then whisk in oil until incorporated. Whisk in egg, milk, and vanilla until smooth. Stir in flour mixture until soft, homogeneous dough forms.

3 Spread remaining ⅓ cup (66 grams) sugar in shallow dish. Working with 2 tablespoons dough at a time, roll into balls, then roll in sugar to coat; space dough balls evenly on 2 parchment paper–lined baking sheets (12 balls per sheet). Using bottom of greased dry measuring cup or drinking glass, press dough balls until 3 inches wide, then sprinkle 2 teaspoons remaining rolling sugar over each sheet of cookies.

4 Bake cookies, 1 sheet at a time, until edges are set and beginning to brown, 11 to 13 minutes, rotating sheet halfway through baking. Let cookies cool on sheet for 5 minutes, then transfer to wire rack. Let cookies cool completely before serving.

Storage: 2 days at room temperature

WHY THIS RECIPE WORKS Matcha, the powdered green tea originating in China and then produced in Japan, is a confection flavoring du jour all over the world. It's particularly right with our sugar cookies, where its savor is sweetened up and its earthiness is offset by the slight tang of cream cheese in the dough. Black sesame seeds, a common pairing for matcha in East Asian desserts, add nuttiness, little bits of texture, and visual appeal. Umami-boosted, tea-flavored treats have lots of interest, and this one goes down nicely with the spoonful of sugar.

Makes 24 cookies

Total Time 50 minutes, plus 30 minutes cooling

MATCHA AND BLACK SESAME SUGAR COOKIES

- 2¼ cups (320 grams) all-purpose flour
- 3 tablespoons black sesame seeds
- 1 tablespoon matcha powder
- 1 teaspoon baking powder
- ½ teaspoon baking soda
- ½ teaspoon table salt
- 1½ cups (297 grams) sugar, plus ⅓ cup (66 grams) for rolling
- 2 ounces (57 grams) cream cheese, cut into 8 pieces and softened
- 6 tablespoons (86 grams) unsalted butter, melted
- ⅓ cup (70 grams) vegetable oil
- 1 large egg
- 1 tablespoon milk

The final dough will be slightly softer than most cookie doughs. For the best results, handle the dough as briefly and gently as possible when shaping the cookies; overworking the dough will result in flatter cookies.

1 Adjust oven rack to middle position and heat oven to 350 degrees. Whisk flour, sesame seeds, matcha powder, baking powder, baking soda, and salt together in bowl.

2 Place 1½ cups (298 grams) sugar and cream cheese in large bowl. Whisk in melted butter (some lumps of cream cheese will remain), then whisk in oil until incorporated. Whisk in egg and milk until smooth. Stir in flour mixture until soft, homogeneous dough forms.

3 Spread remaining ⅓ cup (66 grams) sugar in shallow dish. Working with 2 tablespoons dough at a time, roll into balls, then roll in sugar to coat; space dough balls evenly on 2 parchment paper–lined baking sheets (12 balls per sheet). Using bottom of greased dry measuring cup or drinking glass, press dough balls until 2 inches wide, then sprinkle 2 teaspoons remaining rolling sugar over each sheet of cookies.

4 Bake cookies, 1 sheet at a time, until edges are set and beginning to brown, 11 to 13 minutes, rotating sheet halfway through baking. Let cookies cool on sheet for 5 minutes, then transfer to wire rack. Let cookies cool completely before serving.

Storage: 2 days at room temperature

DRAGON FRUIT MOCHI-STUFFED LIME COOKIES

Makes 16 cookies

Total Time 1¼ hours, plus 35 minutes cooling

WHY THIS RECIPE WORKS Mochi-stuffed cookies have become a popular dessert for their surprising collision of textures and flavors: From the outside, they look like regular cookies, but biting into one reveals a gooey, stretchy mochi center. We think that contrast is even more striking with vibrant color, so we make a bright pink filling using thawed and pureed frozen dragon fruit for the liquid (in place of water or some kind of milk) that brings the mochi together. The tropical fruit lends mellow sweetness and a bold magenta hue, while its natural sugars and pectin make the mochi softer and more tender than traditional versions. That's especially important in this cookie, where we want a filling that stays pliable even after baking. Wrapped in a lime-scented sugar cookie dough and rolled in chopped toasted cashews for crunch, these cookies deliver a dynamic blend of crisp edges, chewy cookie crumb, and a stretchy, fruity center.

MOCHI

- ⅔ cup (104 grams) sweet rice flour
- 3 tablespoons sugar
- ¼ teaspoon table salt
- 6½ ounces (184 grams/1½ cups) frozen dragon fruit chunks, thawed
- ¼ cup (59 grams) lime juice (2 limes)

COOKIES

- 2¼ cups (320 grams) all-purpose flour
- 1 teaspoon baking powder
- ½ teaspoon baking soda
- ½ teaspoon table salt
- 1½ cups (297 grams) sugar
- 2 ounces (57 grams) cream cheese, cut into 8 pieces and softened
- 6 tablespoons (86 grams) unsalted butter, melted
- ⅓ cup (70 grams) vegetable oil
- 1 large egg
- 1 tablespoon whole milk
- 1 tablespoon grated lime zest
- ⅓ cup (47 grams) roasted cashews, chopped fine

You can substitute frozen mango or frozen tropical fruit mix for the frozen dragon fruit and macadamia nuts, pistachios, almonds, sweetened dried coconut, or crystallized ginger for the cashews. Be sure to use sweet white (or glutinous) rice flour for this recipe, such as Mochiko flour. Plain white rice flour will not create the chewy texture that is essential to this recipe. These cookies are best served warm.

1 For the mochi: Whisk rice flour, sugar, and salt together in bowl. Process dragon fruit chunks and lime juice in blender until smooth, about 30 seconds. Add to flour mixture and whisk until no lumps remain. Microwave, covered, until mixture is cohesive, thick, and sticky (has texture of wet Play-Doh), 3 to 4 minutes, stirring halfway through microwaving. Scrape mochi from sides of bowl and stir mixture well until homogeneous. Set aside to cool, covered, for 15 minutes.

2 For the cookies: Adjust oven rack to middle position and heat oven to 350 degrees. Whisk flour, baking powder, baking soda, and salt together in bowl.

3 Place sugar and cream cheese in large bowl. Whisk in melted butter (some lumps of cream cheese will remain), then whisk in oil until incorporated. Whisk in egg, milk, and zest until smooth. Stir in flour mixture until soft, homogeneous dough forms.

••• CONTINUED •••

4 Working with 3 tablespoons dough at a time, roll into balls and space them evenly on 2 parchment paper–lined baking sheets (8 balls per sheet). Using your fingers, press dough balls until 3½ inches wide.

5 Using silicone spatula, stir mochi filling to incorporate any condensation. Working with your dampened hands, place 1 tablespoon cooled mochi in center of each cookie dough disk. Wrap edges of dough up and around filling and seal dough at top. Reshape into smooth ball, pinching and smoothing any cracks if needed. Return to sheets and sprinkle with cashews.

6 Bake cookies, 1 sheet at a time, until edges are set and just beginning to brown, 13 to 15 minutes, rotating sheet halfway through baking. Let cookies cool on sheet for 5 minutes, then transfer to wire rack. Let cookies cool for 20 minutes before serving.

Storage: 2 days at room temperature

FORMING THE COOKIES

1. Using your fingers, press each dough ball until 3½ inches wide.

2. Working with your dampened hands, place 1 tablespoon cooled mochi in center of each cookie dough disk, and wrap edges of dough up and around filling and seal dough at top.

3. Reshape dough into smooth ball, pinching and smoothing any cracks if needed.

4. Return dough balls to sheets and sprinkle with finely chopped cashews.

1
2
3
4

WHY THIS RECIPE WORKS These chewy, zingy bars are like a cross between our sugar cookies (see page 62) and a traditional layered lemon bar (see page 260). We incorporate lemon zest and juice into our dough, which provides floral citrus pucker. Instead of forming cookie balls with the sugar cookie dough, we pat it into a pan, and we spread the baked cookie with a thin layer of a potent lemony glaze that further enunciates the sweet-tart balance. We like adding a smattering of yellow sprinkles so these easy bars look as sunny as they taste.

Makes 24 cookies

Total Time 1 hour, plus 3 hours cooling and setting

LEMON COOKIE BARS

BARS

- 2¼ cups (320 grams) all-purpose flour
- ½ teaspoon baking soda
- ½ teaspoon table salt
- 2 cups (396 grams) granulated sugar
- 6 tablespoons (86 grams) unsalted butter, melted
- ⅓ cup (70 grams) vegetable oil
- 2 ounces (57 grams) cream cheese, cut into 8 pieces and softened
- 1 large egg plus 1 large yolk
- 5 teaspoons grated lemon zest plus 3 tablespoons juice (2 lemons)
- 2 teaspoons vanilla extract

GLAZE

- 1½ tablespoons lemon juice
- 1 tablespoon cream cheese, softened
- 1 cup (113 grams) confectioners' sugar
- 3 tablespoons yellow sprinkles (optional)

To ensure that the glaze has the proper consistency, it's best to weigh the confectioners' sugar. The glaze will feel thick—and that's OK. It should sit atop the bars and not soak in.

1 For the bars: Adjust oven rack to middle position and heat oven to 325 degrees. Make foil sling for 13 by 9-inch baking pan by folding 2 long sheets of aluminum foil; first sheet should be 13 inches wide and second sheet should be 9 inches wide. Lay sheets of foil in pan perpendicular to each other, with extra foil hanging over edges of pan. Push foil into corners and up sides of pan, smoothing foil flush to pan. Grease foil.

2 Whisk flour, baking soda, and salt together in bowl. Whisk sugar, melted butter, oil, and cream cheese together in second bowl (some lumps of cream cheese will remain). Add egg and yolk, lemon zest and juice, and vanilla and whisk until smooth. Stir in flour mixture until just combined.

3 Transfer batter to prepared pan, smoothing top with silicone spatula. Bake until light golden brown and toothpick inserted in center comes out clean, 33 to 38 minutes, rotating pan halfway through baking. Let bars cool completely in pan on wire rack, about 2 hours.

4 For the glaze: Once bars are cooled, whisk lemon juice and cream cheese together in bowl. Whisk in sugar until smooth. Spread evenly over bars. Scatter sprinkles, if using, over top. Let sit until glaze is set, about 1 hour.

5 Using foil overhang, lift bars out of pan and transfer to cutting board. Cut into 24 pieces before serving.

Storage: 3 days at room temperature

Makes 24 cookies

Total Time 50 minutes, plus 30 minutes cooling

WHY THIS RECIPE WORKS These ultrachewy cookies turn up the volume on the classic by swapping out mild granulated sugar for robust, caramelly dark brown sugar. Browning the butter, unsurprisingly, works particularly beautifully here, and its butterscotch and toffee notes help the brown sugar really shine. The toasty, nutty butter combined with the brown sugar make this a very homey cookie. For the signature crystalline sugar-cookie coating, we stick with brown sugar so the pure flavor hits the palate right away, but we add a little granulated sugar to the mix to prevent clumping.

BROWN SUGAR COOKIES

- 2 cups plus 2 tablespoons (302 grams) all-purpose flour
- ½ teaspoon baking soda
- ¼ teaspoon baking powder
- 14 tablespoons (200 grams) unsalted butter, divided
- 1¾ cups packed (347 grams) dark brown sugar, plus ¼ cup (50 grams) for rolling
- 1 tablespoon vanilla extract
- ½ teaspoon table salt
- 1 large egg plus 1 large yolk
- ¼ cup (50 grams) granulated sugar for rolling

1 Adjust oven rack to middle position and heat oven to 350 degrees. Whisk flour, baking soda, and baking powder together in bowl.

2 Heat 10 tablespoons (143 grams) butter in 10-inch skillet over medium-high heat, about 2 minutes. Continue to cook, swirling skillet and stirring constantly with silicone spatula, until butter is dark golden brown and has nutty aroma, 1 to 3 minutes. Transfer browned butter to large bowl and stir in remaining 4 tablespoons (57 grams) butter until melted. Whisk in 1¾ cups (347 grams) brown sugar, vanilla, and salt until incorporated. Whisk in egg and yolk until smooth and no lumps remain, about 30 seconds. Stir in flour mixture until just combined, about 1 minute.

3 Combine remaining ¼ cup (50 grams) brown sugar and granulated sugar in shallow dish. Working with 2 tablespoons dough at a time, roll into balls, then roll in sugar to coat; space dough balls evenly on 2 parchment paper–lined baking sheets (12 balls per sheet).

4 Bake cookies, 1 sheet at a time, until edges have begun to set but centers are still soft, puffy, and cracked (cookies will look raw between cracks and seem underdone), 12 to 14 minutes, rotating sheet halfway through baking. Let cookies cool on sheet for 5 minutes, then transfer to wire rack. Let cookies cool completely before serving.

Storage: 2 days at room temperature

WHY THIS RECIPE WORKS This chewy, rich, black tea–scented cookie takes inspiration from the incredible flavor of brown sugar milk tea, a boba shop favorite. In this popular drink, a deep-brown sugar syrup made from Taiwanese sugar is drizzled on the insides of the glass (earning its moniker "tiger milk tea") before chewy tapioca pearls (boba), bathed in the same syrup, are added to the bottom. Then, a mix of creamy milk and fragrant black tea is poured in. Although we couldn't incorporate boba into the cookies (the pearls harden), we were able to approximate the super deep, dark Taiwanese sugar, by adding molasses to a dark brown sugar cookie base for lots of extra depth and chew. Infusing the butter with tea leaves gives the most pronounced tea aroma and flavor to counterbalance the sugar. A final milky glaze brings the concept together for a surprising treat that milk tea enthusiasts and newcomers alike will savor.

Makes 18 cookies

Total Time 1½ hours, plus 1 hour sitting and cooling

BROWN SUGAR MILK TEA COOKIES

COOKIES

- 16 tablespoons (228 grams) unsalted butter
- 2 tablespoons English breakfast tea leaves
- 2 cups (284 grams) all-purpose flour
- ½ teaspoon table salt
- ½ teaspoon baking soda
- ¼ teaspoon baking powder
- 1½ cups packed (297 grams) dark brown sugar
- 2 large eggs
- 1 tablespoon molasses

GLAZE

- 3 tablespoons milk, plus extra as needed
- 1 tablespoon English breakfast tea leaves
- 1 ounce (28 grams) cream cheese, softened
- 1 cup (113 grams) confectioners' sugar

For the best tea flavor, use a high quality, loose leaf English breakfast tea, or equal parts Assam and Ceylon loose leaf teas. Do not use bagged tea as the cut of the tea leaves is too fine.

1 **For the cookies:** Heat butter in medium saucepan over medium-low heat until melted. Stir in tea leaves and bring to simmer. Reduce heat to low to maintain bare simmer for 5 minutes. Remove from heat, cover, and let sit for 30 minutes to extract flavor from tea leaves.

2 Adjust oven rack to middle position and heat oven to 350 degrees. Strain butter-tea mixture through fine mesh strainer into large bowl, pressing on tea leaves to extract as much butter as possible (you should have about ¾ cup melted butter). Discard tea leaves. Whisk flour, salt, baking soda, and baking powder together in second bowl.

3 Add sugar, eggs, and molasses to cooled butter, whisking until smooth. Stir in flour mixture until just combined.

4 Working with 2 heaping tablespoons of dough at a time, roll into balls and space evenly on 2 parchment paper–lined baking sheets (9 balls per sheet). Bake cookies, 1 sheet at a time, until edges are set but center is still puffy, 12 to 14 minutes, rotating sheet halfway through baking (cookies will look raw between cracks and seem underdone). Let cookies cool on sheet for 5 minutes, then transfer to wire rack. Let cookies cool completely before glazing.

5 **For the glaze:** Microwave milk until steaming, 30 to 45 seconds. Add tea leaves and let steep for 5 minutes, then strain milk mixture through fine mesh strainer, pressing on tea leaves to extract as much milk as possible; discard tea leaves. (You should have about 2 tablespoons milk tea).

6 Whisk cream cheese and 2 tablespoons milk tea in medium bowl until smooth, then whisk in sugar. (Glaze should be thick and pourable. Add extra milk, drop by drop, if needed, to achieve desired consistency.)

7 Drizzle glaze attractively over cooled cookies. Let sit until glaze is set, about 15 minutes, before serving.

Storage: 3 days at room temperature

Makes 24 cookies

Total Time 55 minutes, plus 30 minutes cooling

WHY THIS RECIPE WORKS There are sugar cookies, and brown sugar cookies, and molasses cookies, so why doesn't maple syrup star in a cookie? We think maple syrup is one of the most appealing sweeteners, its incredible toasty caramel notes conjuring coziness. To create a chewy sugar cookie with rich maple flavor, we couldn't just pour in maple syrup for the sugar, as the liquid sweetener softens the cookies much too much. We turn to maple sugar, which is pure crystallized maple syrup, for just the right amount of moisture. It's pricier than regular sugar (a delicious splurge), but we were able to cut it with some brown sugar without diminishing maple flavor. We love how some flake salt mixed with the final sprinkle of maple sugar really highlights its multidimensional flavor.

MAPLE SUGAR COOKIES

- 2 cups plus 2 tablespoons (302 grams) all-purpose flour
- ½ teaspoon table salt
- ½ teaspoon baking soda
- ¼ teaspoon baking powder
- 14 tablespoons (200 grams) unsalted butter, divided
- 1 cup (198 grams) maple sugar plus 1 tablespoon for sprinkling
- ¾ cup packed (149 grams) light brown sugar, plus ¼ cup (50 grams) for rolling
- 1 tablespoon vanilla extract
- 1 large egg plus 1 large yolk
- ¼ cup (50 grams) granulated sugar for rolling
- ½ teaspoon flake sea salt

Maple sugar is available at high-end grocery stores and online.

1 Adjust oven rack to middle position and heat oven to 350 degrees. Whisk flour, table salt, baking soda, and baking powder together in bowl.

2 Heat 10 tablespoons (143 grams) butter in 10-inch skillet over medium-high heat until melted, about 2 minutes. Continue to cook, swirling skillet and stirring constantly with silicone spatula until butter is dark golden brown and has nutty aroma, 1 to 3 minutes. Transfer browned butter to large bowl and stir in remaining 4 tablespoons (57 grams) butter until melted. Whisk in 1 cup maple sugar, ¾ cup brown sugar, and vanilla until incorporated. Whisk in egg and yolk until smooth and no lumps remain, about 30 seconds. Stir in flour mixture until just combined, about 1 minute.

3 Combine granulated sugar and remaining ¼ cup brown sugar in shallow dish. Working with 2 tablespoons dough at a time, roll into balls, then roll in sugar to coat; space dough balls evenly on 2 parchment paper–lined baking sheets (12 balls per sheet).

4 Combine remaining 1 tablespoon maple sugar and flake sea salt in bowl. Bake cookies, 1 sheet at a time, until edges have begun to set but centers are still soft, puffy, and cracked (cookies will look raw between cracks and seem underdone), 12 to 14 minutes, rotating sheet halfway through baking. Transfer sheet to wire rack and immediately sprinkle with maple sugar mixture. Let cookies cool on sheet for 5 minutes, then transfer to wire rack. Let cool completely before serving.

Storage: 2 days at room temperature

WHY THIS RECIPE WORKS Our molasses spice cookies are charmingly crackled and crinkled, with an uncommonly moist, chewy interior; undertones of dark, bittersweet molasses; and a spicy flavor provided by a blend we had a hunch would invigorate the cookie: garam masala. This warming blend, an essential component of Indian savory cooking (the term means "warm spice" in Hindi), typically features cinnamon, pepper, cardamom, and coriander with other spices such as cumin, fennel, mace, or nutmeg playing supporting roles. The earthy, floral depth of garam masala, used in place of traditional cookie spices (cinnamon, ginger, cloves, and allspice), lends a certain je ne sais quoi to our cookies. Making the blend ourselves (instead of buying it) gives us the ability to control the quantity of each spice. We particularly like the unexpected savory notes that cumin and coriander add to the mix, so we add whole cumin and coriander seeds to the rolling sugar for more fragrance and crunch. These flavors are so intriguing in a cookie that they keep us coming back for more.

Makes 22 cookies

Total Time 55 minutes, plus 30 minutes cooling

GARAM MASALA MOLASSES COOKIES

- 2 teaspoons ground cinnamon
- 1½ teaspoons pepper
- 1 teaspoon ground cardamom
- 1 teaspoon ground coriander
- 1 teaspoon ground cumin
- 2¼ cups (319 grams) all-purpose flour
- 1 teaspoon baking soda
- ½ teaspoon table salt
- 12 tablespoons (171 grams) unsalted butter, softened
- ⅓ cup packed (66 grams) dark brown sugar
- ⅓ cup (66 grams) granulated sugar, plus ½ cup (99 grams) for rolling
- ½ cup (156 grams) molasses
- 1 large egg yolk
- 1 teaspoon vanilla extract
- 1 teaspoon cumin seeds
- 1 teaspoon coriander seeds

The final dough will be slightly softer than most cookie doughs.

1 Adjust oven rack to middle position and heat oven to 375 degrees. Whisk cinnamon, pepper, cardamom, coriander, and cumin together in large bowl; measure out and reserve 1 teaspoon spice mixture for rolling. Whisk flour, baking soda, and salt into remaining spice mixture in bowl.

2 Using stand mixer fitted with paddle, beat butter, brown sugar, and ⅓ cup (66 grams) granulated sugar at medium-high speed until pale and fluffy, 3 to 5 minutes, scraping down sides of bowl as needed. Add molasses, egg yolk, and vanilla and continue to beat until well incorporated, about 1 minute longer. Reduce speed to low; add flour mixture; and mix until dough is uniform, about 1 minute.

3 Whisk remaining ½ cup (99 grams) granulated sugar, reserved 1 teaspoon spice mixture, cumin seeds, and coriander seeds together in shallow dish. Working with 2 tablespoons dough at a time, roll into balls, then roll in sugar mixture to coat, pressing gently to adhere seeds; space dough balls evenly on 2 parchment paper–lined baking sheets (11 balls per sheet).

4 Bake cookies, 1 sheet at a time, until browned and puffy and edges have begun to set but centers are still soft (cookies will look raw between cracks and seem underdone), about 11 minutes, rotating sheet halfway through baking. Let cookies cool on sheet for 5 minutes, then transfer to wire rack. Let cookies cool completely before serving.

Storage: 5 days at room temperature

WHY THIS RECIPE WORKS What on earth is a hermit, you ask? Unless you're from New England, you might not be familiar with this old-fashioned cookie that's cut into chewy bars. The classic version is studded with raisins, spiced with cinnamon and allspice, and has deep molasses flavor. It's a fine tradition, but we thought it was time for an update. Enter the pumpkin spice hermit—just as toothsome as the original, but with sweet, jammy dates instead of raisins. A mix of brown sugar and granulated sugar produces cookies with nice structure and chew, and is neutral enough in flavor to allow the pumpkin pie spice blend to come through. Baking the hermits one sheet at a time ensures proper development of the characteristic cracks on top. A simple icing and sprinkle of pepitas offer a finishing touch, and one more opportunity to infuse spices and a little crunch into every bite.

Makes 20 cookies

Total Time 55 minutes, plus 1 hour cooling and setting

PUMPKIN SPICE HERMITS

HERMITS

- 2 cups (284 grams) all-purpose flour
- ½ teaspoon baking soda
- ½ teaspoon table salt
- ¾ cup (114 grams) pitted dates, chopped coarse
- 8 tablespoons (114 grams) unsalted butter
- 1 tablespoon pumpkin pie spice
- ¾ cup packed (149 grams) dark brown sugar
- ½ cup (99 grams) granulated sugar
- 2 large eggs

ICING

- ¾ cup (85 grams) confectioners' sugar
- 1½ tablespoons milk
- ½ teaspoon pumpkin pie spice
- ¼ cup (37 grams) roasted salted pepitas (optional)

1 For the hermits: Adjust oven rack to middle position and heat oven to 350 degrees. Whisk flour, baking soda, and salt together in bowl.

2 Place chopped dates in large bowl. Heat butter in 10-inch skillet over medium-high heat until melted, about 2 minutes. Continue to cook, swirling skillet and stirring constantly with silicone spatula, until butter is dark golden brown and has nutty aroma, 1 to 3 minutes. Stir in pumpkin pie spice and cook until fragrant, about 15 seconds. Add butter mixture to bowl with dates, stirring to coat. Whisk brown sugar and granulated sugar into date mixture until well combined, then whisk in eggs. Stir in flour mixture until just combined (dough will be sticky).

3 Transfer one-quarter of dough to parchment paper–lined rimmed baking sheet and shape into 9 by 2-inch rectangle using your lightly moistened hands. Repeat with second quarter of dough, spacing rectangles about 4 inches apart on sheet. Repeat on second parchment-lined sheet.

4 Bake cookies, 1 sheet at a time, until edges are lightly browned and have begun to set but centers are still soft (cookies will look raw between cracks and seem underdone), 10 to 12 minutes, rotating sheet halfway through baking. Let cookies cool on sheet for 5 minutes, then transfer to wire rack. Let cool completely before icing.

5 For the icing: Whisk confectioners' sugar, milk, and pumpkin pie spice together in small bowl. Drizzle evenly over cooled bars and sprinkle with pepitas, if using. Let stand until glaze is set, about 30 minutes. Before serving, transfer bars to cutting board and slice into 2-inch-wide cookies.

Storage: 5 days at room temperature

WHY THIS RECIPE WORKS We love gingerbread but if we're going to bake it every year, we think it needs an exciting update. These cookies are perfectly soft and chewy—like we enjoy our annual gingerbread—but enlivened with bright, surprising flavor from lemon, lime, and orange zests. Plenty of butter, brown sugar, and molasses give the cookies chew; we roll them to an even ¼ inch so that the cookies are soft across the batch. Finally, we watch the cookies carefully as they bake and remove them from the oven as soon as the edges are set (but the centers remain puffy) to ensure they stay soft after cooling. These updated gingerbreads deserve something different than piped icing. Dipping them in two tones of white chocolate gives them a striking, modern look; plus, the white chocolate tempers some of the punch and pucker.

Makes about 30 cookies

Total Time 1½ hours, plus 1½ hours chilling and cooling

TRIPLE CITRUS GINGERBREAD WITH WHITE CHOCOLATE

- 3¼ cups (462 grams) all-purpose flour
- ¾ cup packed (149 grams) dark brown sugar
- 2 tablespoons ground ginger
- 1 teaspoon ground cinnamon
- ¾ teaspoon baking soda
- ½ teaspoon table salt
- 12 tablespoons (171 grams) unsalted butter, melted and cooled
- ¾ cup (233 grams) molasses
- 2 tablespoons milk
- 1 tablespoon grated fresh ginger
- 1 tablespoon grated orange zest
- 1 tablespoon grated lemon zest
- 1 tablespoon grated lime zest
- 1½ cups (255 grams) white chocolate chips
- 3 tablespoons refined coconut oil
- Gel food coloring

Let the melted butter cool before adding it in step 1, or the dough will be too sticky to work with. Because we roll the dough between sheets of parchment paper (no additional flour is added), the scraps can be rerolled and cut as many times as necessary. Be sure to use oil-based gel food coloring, not water-based food coloring, or the chocolate will seize. You can use any color you'd like in any amount you prefer.

1 Process flour, sugar, ground ginger, cinnamon, baking soda, and salt in food processor until combined, about 10 seconds. Add melted butter, molasses, milk, fresh ginger, orange zest, lemon zest, and lime zest and process until soft dough forms and no streaks of flour remain, about 20 seconds, scraping down sides of bowl as needed.

2 Transfer dough to lightly floured counter and knead until dough forms cohesive ball, about 20 seconds. Divide dough in half. Form each half into 5-inch disk, wrap disks tightly in plastic wrap, and refrigerate for at least 1 hour or up to 24 hours.

3 Adjust oven racks to upper-middle and lower-middle positions and heat oven to 350 degrees. Working with 1 disk of dough at a time, roll dough between 2 large sheets of parchment to ¼-inch thickness. (Keep second disk of dough refrigerated while rolling out first.) Peel off top parchment sheet and use 3-inch round cookie cutter to cut out cookies. Peel away scraps from around rounds and space rounds ¾ inch apart on 2 parchment paper–lined baking sheets. Knead dough scraps to bring back together, then repeat rolling and cutting. (If you need more than 2 sheets to fit all the cookies, reuse sheets once they have cooled to room temperature.)

4 Bake until cookies are puffy and just set around edges, 9 to 11 minutes, switching and rotating sheets halfway through baking. Let cookies cool on sheets for 10 minutes, then transfer to wire rack and let cool completely.

5 Microwave white chocolate chips and coconut oil in bowl at 50 percent power until melted, about 2 minutes, stirring once halfway through microwaving. Remove from microwave and stir until completely smooth. Transfer half of melted chocolate to second bowl and stir in food coloring until desired shade is reached.

6 Working with 1 cookie at a time, dip partially into colored chocolate, then transfer to wire rack set in rimmed baking sheet. Refrigerate cookies on sheet until coating is set, about 5 minutes. Working with 1 cookie at a time, dip partially into bowl of white chocolate, overlapping first coating by about half. Return dipped cookie to wire rack and let sit until coating sets, about 15 minutes, before serving.

Storage: 3 days at room temperature

WHY THIS RECIPE WORKS These date-based cookies, inspired by the comforting English dessert sticky toffee pudding, are soft, slightly gooey, and loaded with rich toffee flavor. For a chewy, deeply flavored cookie, we use dark brown sugar and molasses, which impart moisture and rich molasses notes to the dough. We fold in a generous amount of chopped dates to form the requisite sticky interior with pops of caramel flavor. An ample amount of butter and an extra egg yolk boost the richness of the base. Finally, for a cookie-appropriate glaze (rather than the sticky, drippy caramel in the original dessert), we cook butter and brown sugar into a luxurious toffee topping and mix in confectioners' sugar so it sets up beautifully.

Makes 16 cookies

Total Time 1¼ hours, plus 30 minutes cooling

STICKY TOFFEE DATE COOKIES

COOKIES

- 1⅔ cups (237 grams) all-purpose flour
- 1 teaspoon table salt
- ¾ teaspoon baking soda
- 12 tablespoons (171 grams) unsalted butter, softened
- 1 cup packed (198 grams) dark brown sugar
- 1 large egg plus 1 large yolk
- 2 tablespoons vanilla extract
- 2 tablespoons molasses
- 2 cups (304 grams) pitted dates, chopped

GLAZE

- 4 tablespoons (57 grams) unsalted butter
- 5 teaspoons water
- ¼ cup packed (50 grams) dark brown sugar
- ⅛ teaspoon table salt
- ½ cup (57 grams) confectioners' sugar

We developed this recipe using Medjool and Deglet Noor pitted dates. Do not substitute prechopped dates.

1 **For the cookies:** Adjust oven rack to middle position and heat oven to 375 degrees. Whisk flour, salt, and baking soda together in bowl.

2 Using stand mixer fitted with paddle, beat butter and brown sugar on medium speed until pale and fluffy, 3 to 5 minutes, scraping down bowl as needed. Add egg and yolk, vanilla, and molasses and continue to beat until incorporated, about 1 minute. Reduce speed to low; add flour mixture; and mix until dough is just combined and no dry flour remains, about 1 minute. Add dates and mix until evenly incorporated, about 15 seconds.

3 Working with 3 tablespoons dough at a time, roll into balls and space them evenly over 2 parchment paper–lined baking sheets (8 balls per sheet). Bake cookies, 1 sheet at a time, until edges are browned and centers are puffed and lightly browned, 10 to 12 minutes, rotating sheet halfway through baking. Let cookies cool on sheet for 5 minutes, then transfer to wire rack. Let cookies cool completely before glazing.

4 **For the glaze:** Melt butter with water in small saucepan over medium-low heat. Whisk in brown sugar and salt and continue to cook, whisking often, until mixture is gently bubbling all over and lightened in color, about 2 minutes. Transfer butter mixture to bowl and whisk in confectioners' sugar until smooth.

5 Top each cookie with about 1 teaspoon glaze, using back of spoon to spread glaze evenly over cookie. Let glaze set for at least 15 minutes before serving.

Storage: 4 days at room temperature

WHY THIS RECIPE WORKS Matcha is a dessert darling, but this tender-chewy cookie gives hojicha the dessert platform it deserves. The roasty-toasty ruddy Japanese green tea shines in a sweet setting, with butter and brown sugar enriching its earthy notes. We call for light brown sugar so the caramel notes complement rather than overpower the hojicha. White chocolate chips add pops of sweetness that balance the tea's savory flavor, and a coating of finely chopped pistachios brings out the green color and aptly accessorizes the cookie with a sweet crunch. Hojicha enthusiasts will adore this cookie, while those new to the tea will be inspired to change their latte order.

Makes 16 cookies

Total Time 50 minutes, plus 30 minutes cooling

HOJICHA PISTACHIO COOKIES

- 1⅔ cups (237 grams) all-purpose flour
- 2 tablespoons hojicha powder
- 1 teaspoon baking soda
- ½ teaspoon table salt
- 12 tablespoons (171 grams) unsalted butter, softened
- ¾ cup packed (149 grams) light brown sugar
- ½ cup (99 grams) granulated sugar
- 2 large eggs
- 2 teaspoons vanilla extract
- ½ cup (85 grams) white chocolate chips
- 1 cup (145 grams) shelled pistachios, chopped fine

1 Adjust oven rack to lower-middle position and heat oven to 350 degrees. Whisk flour, hojicha powder, baking soda, and salt together in bowl.

2 Using stand mixer fitted with paddle, beat butter, brown sugar, and granulated sugar on medium speed until pale and fluffy, 3 to 5 minutes, scraping down bowl as needed. Add eggs and vanilla and continue to beat until well incorporated, about 1 minute. Reduce speed to low; add flour mixture; and mix until dough is uniform, about 1 minute. Add chocolate chips and mix until just combined.

3 Place pistachios in bowl. Working with 3 tablespoons dough at a time, roll into balls and drop into pistachios. Working with a few dough balls at a time, coat 1 side of dough balls; space dough balls evenly on 2 parchment paper–lined baking sheets (8 balls per sheet). Bake cookies, 1 sheet at a time, until edges are set and just beginning to brown, about 12 minutes, rotating sheet halfway through baking. Transfer sheet to wire rack and let cookies cool completely on sheet before serving.

Storage: 3 days at room temperature

WHY THIS RECIPE WORKS Almost every chewy oatmeal cookie is the same (underwhelming, overly spiced, kind of crumbly, and a replica of the one on the Quaker can), so we're delighted to present this old-fashioned cookie for modern sensibilities: It has crispy edges; a dense, chewy middle; plump raisins; and true oaty flavor. We think you'll crave it just as much as chocolate chip cookies (as long as you have a good relationship with raisins). We employ some of our go-to chewy cookie tricks: Use more brown sugar; melt and brown the butter; use some oil; and add an extra egg yolk. But the biggest improvement to our oatmeal raisin cookies may be adding more salt than other recipes call for. It tempers the sweetness and complements the oats in a really beautiful way.

Makes 20 cookies

Total Time 50 minutes, plus 30 minutes cooling

CHEWY OATMEAL COOKIES

- 1 cup (142 grams) all-purpose flour
- ¾ teaspoon table salt
- ½ teaspoon baking soda
- 4 tablespoons (57 grams) unsalted butter
- ¼ teaspoon ground cinnamon
- ¾ cup packed (149 grams) dark brown sugar
- ½ cup (99 grams) granulated sugar
- ½ cup (105 grams) vegetable oil
- 1 teaspoon vanilla extract
- 1 large egg plus 1 large yolk
- 3 cups (255 grams) old-fashioned rolled oats
- ½ cup (71 grams) raisins (optional)

Regular old-fashioned rolled oats work best in this recipe. Do not use extra-thick rolled oats. If you omit the raisins, the recipe will yield 18 cookies.

1 Adjust oven rack to middle position and heat oven to 375 degrees. Whisk flour, salt, and baking soda together in bowl.

2 Heat butter in 8-inch skillet over medium-high heat until melted, about 2 minutes. Continue to cook, swirling skillet and stirring constantly, until butter is dark golden brown and has nutty aroma, 1 to 3 minutes. Transfer browned butter to large bowl and whisk in cinnamon. Whisk in brown sugar, granulated sugar, oil, and vanilla until incorporated. Add egg and yolk and whisk until smooth and no lumps remain. Stir in flour mixture until combined, about 1 minute. Stir in oats and raisins, if using (mixture will be stiff).

3 Working with 3 tablespoons dough at a time, roll into balls and space them evenly on 2 parchment paper–lined baking sheets (10 balls per sheet). Using your dampened hand, press dough balls until 2½ inches wide.

4 Bake cookies, 1 sheet at a time, until edges are set and lightly browned and centers are still soft but not wet, 8 to 10 minutes, rotating sheet halfway through baking. Let cookies cool on sheet for 5 minutes, then transfer to wire rack. Let cookies cool completely before serving.

Storage: 2 days at room temperature

Makes 24 cookies

Total Time 1¼ hours

WHY THIS RECIPE WORKS Daniella Senior, owner of Colada Shop, a Washington, D.C.–based restaurant group serving Cuban food, coffee, and cocktails, shared her fruity new way with oatmeal cookies with us. Merging the flavors she grew up with and an old-fashioned American cookie results in a sweet-salty delight that guests can't get enough of—neither can we. Daniella says, "I've basically been in the United States for the same amount of time that I've been out of it, so it feels like this cookie represents a crossroads of where I am in my life." This cookie well depicts baking in the United States today.

OAT GUAVA COOKIES

- 3⅓ cups (283 grams) old-fashioned rolled oats
- 1½ cups (213 grams) all-purpose flour
- 1 teaspoon ground cinnamon
- ½ teaspoon table salt
- ½ teaspoon baking powder
- ½ teaspoon baking soda
- 16 tablespoons (228 grams) unsalted butter, softened
- 1 cup packed (198 grams) light brown sugar
- ¾ cup (149 grams) granulated sugar, divided
- 2 large eggs
- 1½ teaspoons vanilla extract
- ½ cup (41 grams) shredded sweetened coconut, toasted
- 8 ounces (227 grams) guava paste, chilled and cut into ½-inch pieces (1 cup)

These cookies are big and benefit from the extra space provided by rimless baking sheets.

1 Adjust oven rack to middle position and heat oven to 350 degrees. Whisk oats, flour, cinnamon, salt, baking powder, and baking soda together in large bowl.

2 Using stand mixer fitted with paddle, beat butter, brown sugar, and ½ cup granulated sugar on medium-high speed until pale and fluffy, 3 to 5 minutes, scraping down bowl as needed. Add eggs and vanilla and continue to beat until well incorporated, about 1 minute longer. Reduce speed to low, add flour mixture, and mix until just combined. Add coconut and mix until just combined.

3 Toss chilled guava paste with remaining ¼ cup granulated sugar in bowl until well coated. Stir guava mixture into cookie dough with silicone spatula until just incorporated. Working with heaping ¼ cup dough at a time, roll into balls and space them evenly on 3 parchment paper–lined rimless baking sheets (8 balls per sheet). Using dry measuring cup or drinking glass, press to ¾-inch thickness. (If you do not have 3 rimless baking sheets, reuse first sheet once it's cooled to room temperature.)

4 Bake cookies, 1 sheet at a time, until edges are browned and set and centers are puffed with some pale, raw spots, 15 to 18 minutes, rotating sheet halfway through baking. Let cookies cool on sheet for 5 minutes, then transfer to wire rack. Serve warm or at room temperature.

Storage: 2 days at room temperature

Makes 12 sandwich cookies

Total Time 1½ hours, plus 30 minutes cooling

WHY THIS RECIPE WORKS These iconic soft, chewy oatmeal cookies sandwiching a creamy, snow-white marshmallow filling are instantly recognizable for their signature look, but they have a freshly baked flavor Little Debbie can't beat. Unlike standard oatmeal raisin cookies (see page 92), these packaged pies have a uniform texture and appearance, so we grind the oats and raisins in the food processor before baking the dough. We use extra baking soda and bake the cookies at a high temperature (400 degrees) so the cookies spring up in the oven and then deflate as they cool, re-creating the distinct dark cracks of the Little Debbie cookies. Nailing the filling is as easy as combining marshmallow crème, softened butter, and confectioners' sugar (with just a touch of vanilla extract and salt) in the food processor.

OATMEAL CREME PIES

COOKIES

- 1 cup (142 grams) all-purpose flour
- 1 teaspoon table salt
- ¾ teaspoon baking soda
- 3 cups (255 grams) old-fashioned rolled oats
- ½ cup (71 grams) raisins
- ¾ cup packed (149 grams) dark brown sugar
- ½ cup (99 grams) granulated sugar
- ½ cup (105 grams) vegetable oil
- 4 tablespoons (57 grams) unsalted butter, melted
- 2 teaspoons molasses
- ¼ teaspoon ground cinnamon
- 1 large egg plus 1 large yolk
- 1 teaspoon vanilla extract

FILLING

- 1¼ cups (141 grams) Fluff brand marshmallow crème
- ¾ cup (85 grams) confectioners' sugar
- 6 tablespoons (85 grams) unsalted butter, softened
- ½ teaspoon vanilla extract
- ¼ teaspoon table salt

Regular old-fashioned rolled oats work best in this recipe. Do not use extra-thick rolled oats. For cookies with just the right amount of spread and chew, we strongly recommend that you weigh your ingredients. The cookies will seem underdone when you pull them from the oven. This is OK; they will continue to bake as they cool on the baking sheet for 5 minutes. This method ensures that the cookies remain chewy once they have cooled.

1 **For the cookies:** Adjust oven rack to middle position and heat oven to 400 degrees. Whisk flour, salt, and baking soda together in bowl. Process oats and raisins in food processor until very finely ground, about 1 minute.

2 Whisk brown sugar, granulated sugar, oil, melted butter, molasses, and cinnamon in large bowl until smooth. Whisk in egg and yolk and vanilla until well combined. Stir in flour mixture until no dry flour remains. Stir in oat-raisin mixture until evenly distributed. (Mixture will be stiff; once dough begins to stiffen, you may want to mix with your hands.)

3 Working with 1½ tablespoons dough at a time, roll into balls and space them evenly on 2 parchment paper–lined baking sheets (12 balls per sheet). Using dry measuring cup or drinking glass, press balls to ½-inch thickness.

4 Bake cookies, 1 sheet at a time, until tops begin to crack at edges, 5 to 7 minutes, rotating sheet halfway through baking. Let cookies cool on sheet for 5 minutes, then transfer to wire rack. Let cookies cool completely before filling.

5 **For the filling:** Process all ingredients in now-empty processor until smooth and fluffy, about 30 seconds, scraping down sides of bowl as needed. Transfer to bowl and stir to incorporate any dry sugar.

6 Before serving, spread 1 scant tablespoon filling on bottoms (flat sides) of each of 12 cookies. Top with remaining cookies to form sandwiches.

Storage: 3 days at room temperature

Makes 24 cookies

Total Time 50 minutes, plus 30 minutes cooling

WHY THIS RECIPE WORKS These are the lunchbox classic—soft, satisfying, very peanut butter-y cookies with crunchy peanuts throughout and a charming crosshatched top. Lots of peanutty flavor, however, means lots of peanut butter, which, because of its starch content, can interrupt the cookie's chewy texture, producing drier, more stunted cookies. We needed to add some saturated fat for maximal chew. We melt the small amount of butter in the recipe so we can mix it by hand. Dark brown sugar deepens the color of the dough, and honey aids in browning as the cookies bake.

CLASSIC PEANUT BUTTER COOKIES

- 1½ cups (213 grams) all-purpose flour
- 1 teaspoon baking soda
- ½ teaspoon table salt
- 1½ cups packed (297 grams) dark brown sugar
- 1 cup (261 grams) creamy peanut butter
- 2 large eggs
- 4 tablespoons (57 grams) unsalted butter, melted and cooled
- 2 tablespoons honey
- 1 teaspoon vanilla extract
- ½ cup (71 grams) dry-roasted peanuts, chopped fine

To ensure that the cookies have the proper texture, use a traditional creamy peanut butter in this recipe; do not substitute chunky or natural peanut butter. You can substitute light brown sugar for the dark, but your cookies will be lighter in color.

1 Adjust oven rack to middle position and heat oven to 350 degrees. Whisk flour, baking soda, and salt together in bowl.

2 Whisk sugar, peanut butter, eggs, melted butter, honey, and vanilla in large bowl until smooth. Add flour mixture and stir until soft, homogeneous dough forms. Stir in peanuts until evenly distributed.

3 Working with 2 tablespoons dough at a time, roll into balls and space them evenly on 2 parchment paper–lined baking sheets (12 balls per sheet). Using fork, make crosshatch design on cookies, pressing until dough ball spreads to about 2 inches wide.

4 Bake cookies, 1 sheet at a time, until edges are just set and just beginning to brown, 10 to 12 minutes, rotating sheet halfway through baking. Let cookies cool on sheet for 5 minutes, then transfer to wire rack. Let cookies cool completely before serving.

Storage: 3 days at room temperature

WHY THIS RECIPE WORKS These cookies, incredibly, achieve the crisp-chewy texture of a good sugar cookie and the toffee-like flavor of a chocolate chip cookie, with notes of deeply toasted coconut—and without butter. Or eggs. Or even vanilla. After discovering that store-bought coconut butter could be slowly browned to produce a caramelly, intensely flavored paste, we knew we had to use it in a cookie. Because this vegan cookie contains only six ingredients, the browned coconut butter flavor is front and center. Brown sugar accentuates the coconut butter's flavor, and, in the absence of eggs or butter, water plays an important role in hydrating this cookie dough.

Makes 16 cookies

Total Time 1¼ hours, plus 50 minutes cooling

BROWNED COCONUT BUTTER COOKIES

- 1 (15-ounce) jar coconut butter
- 1½ cups (213 grams) all-purpose flour
- ¾ teaspoon baking powder
- ½ teaspoon baking soda
- ½ teaspoon table salt
- 1⅓ cups packed (264 grams) brown sugar
- 6 tablespoons plus 2 teaspoons (99 grams) water
- ½ cup (41 grams) sweetened shredded coconut
- Flake sea salt

1 Place jar of coconut butter in pot of just-simmering water until coconut butter is softened enough to be easily scooped from jar. (Avoid using microwave for this step as coconut butter may heat unevenly and burn in spots.)

2 Transfer coconut butter to large saucepan and cook over medium-low heat, stirring frequently, until medium brown, 6 to 8 minutes. Remove from heat and let cool slightly, about 20 minutes. Transfer ¾ cup (174 grams) browned coconut butter to large bowl. (Remaining browned coconut butter can be refrigerated in airtight container for up to 1 month.)

3 Adjust oven rack to middle position and heat oven to 350 degrees. Whisk flour, baking powder, baking soda, and salt together in bowl. Add sugar and water to reserved browned butter in bowl and whisk until well combined and smooth. Stir in flour mixture until just combined.

4 Working with 2 tablespoons dough at a time, roll into balls and space evenly on 2 parchment paper–lined baking sheets (8 balls per sheet). Using greased dry measuring cup or drinking glass, press each dough ball to 3-inch-wide disk. Sprinkle with coconut and flake sea salt and gently press to adhere.

5 Bake cookies, 1 sheet at a time, until edges are set and just beginning to brown, 15 to 17 minutes, rotating sheet halfway through baking. Let cookies cool on sheet for 5 minutes, then transfer to wire rack. Let cookies cool completely before serving.

Storage: 5 days at room temperature

Makes about 30 cookies

Total Time 25 minutes, plus 1 hour chilling

WHY THIS RECIPE WORKS These chewy, boozy, fruity cookies are inspired by the simple decadence of rum balls, the wafer-based confection often given at holidays. For this version, we opt for the complementary flavors of dried cherries and amaretto. A mixture of crushed vanilla wafer cookies and coconut flakes creates a chewy dough, which we roll in toasted coconut for extra flavor and crunch. Chilling yields a soft cookie with a satisfying bite, studded with bursts of fruitiness and scented with sophisticated boozy flavor.

NO-BAKE CHERRY-AMARETTO BALLS

- 2½ cups (205 grams) sweetened shredded coconut, divided
- 5 cups (312 grams) vanilla wafer cookies
- ½ cup (57 grams) dried sweetened cherries, chopped
- ½ cup (130 grams) amaretto
- 1 cup (113 grams) confectioners' sugar
- ⅛ teaspoon table salt
- ¼ cup (82 grams) light corn syrup

You can use sweetened or unsweetened dried cherries in this recipe, but we prefer sweetened.

1 Toast 1 cup (82 grams) coconut in 10-inch skillet over medium-low heat, stirring often, until golden, 3 to 5 minutes. Transfer to shallow dish and set aside.

2 Process wafer cookies and remaining 1½ cups (123 grams) coconut in food processor until finely ground, about 20 seconds; transfer to large bowl. Stir in cherries, amaretto, sugar, salt, and corn syrup until evenly combined.

3 Working with 1 tablespoon dough at a time, roll into balls with your moistened hands, then roll in toasted coconut to coat, pressing to adhere. Transfer coated balls to plate and refrigerate until firm, at least 1 hour. Serve.

Storage: 1 week in refrigerator

Chapter 2

FULLY LOADED

ATK CLASSIC

Makes 16 cookies

Total Time 1 hour

We define a loaded cookie as a big one, where the dough is really just a binder for an outrageous amount of mix-ins. They're hyperflavorful cookies with all kinds of textures (and often melted chocolate moments) in every bite. This basic, exemplary version is a classic (but never tired!) combo of creamy white chocolate and salty, crunchy macadamia nuts. To make a loadable dough, we use both brown sugar and granulated sugar, with a higher proportion of brown sugar, to give the dough the right amount of depth without it overshadowing all *the stuff*. We make the dough in the mixer rather than by hand to give it lift and enough structure to handle everything we throw at it. Baking at a hot 425 degrees for a short time browns and sets the exterior while keeping the interior chewy and fudgy. We serve these cookies warm so they're a bit gooey, heightening the texture contrast of the mix-ins.

LOADED WHITE CHOCOLATE–MACADAMIA COOKIES

- 2¼ cups (319 grams) all-purpose flour
- 1 teaspoon table salt
- ¾ teaspoon baking soda
- 1 cup packed (198 grams) light brown sugar
- 12 tablespoons (170 grams) unsalted butter, melted
- ½ cup (99 grams) granulated sugar
- 2 large eggs
- 1½ teaspoons vanilla extract
- 1¼ cups (154 grams) chopped salted dry-roasted macadamia nuts
- 6 ounces (170 grams) white chocolate, chopped

Underbaking the cookies ensures that they remain chewy even once they've cooled.

1 Adjust oven rack to middle position and heat oven to 425 degrees. Whisk flour, salt, and baking soda together in bowl.

2 Using stand mixer fitted with paddle, beat brown sugar, melted butter, and granulated sugar on medium speed until well combined, about 1 minute, scraping down bowl as needed. Add eggs and vanilla and beat until fully incorporated, about 30 seconds. Reduce speed to low; add flour mixture; and mix until mostly incorporated but some streaks of flour remain, about 30 seconds. Add macadamia nuts and chocolate and mix until evenly distributed, about 30 seconds.

3 Working with ¼ cup dough at a time, roll into balls between your dampened hands and space them evenly on 2 parchment paper–lined baking sheets (8 balls per sheet). Using your hand, flatten dough balls to ¾-inch thickness.

4 Bake cookies, 1 sheet at a time, until centers of cookies are puffed and lightly golden, 8 to 10 minutes, rotating sheet halfway through baking. (Cookies will seem underdone but will continue to bake as they cool.) Let cookies cool on sheet for 5 minutes, then transfer to wire rack and let cool for 10 minutes. Serve warm or at room temperature.

Storage: 2 days at room temperature

Creative *Loaded Cookie* Takes

- **Chocolate-chip it** If you can never get enough chocolate, skip the white chocolate and nuts and fill this durable base dough with milk, semisweet, and/or bittersweet chocolate to your heart's content.

- **Get snacky** Use small candies like M&M's, or chop up candy bars to stir in. Prefer salty snacks? Mix in chopped pretzels or trail mix.

- **Double the cookie** You can add cookies to cookies by chopping up Oreos (see page 111), gingersnaps, or other packaged cookies and stuffing this dough with them.

Chewy Cookie
Underbaking ensures chewy-fudgy centers.

Tons of Mix-Ins
Dough holds together carefully chosen add-ins with lots of contrasting flavors and textures.

Melty Chocolate
Serving the cookies warm is the ultimate indulgence.

Makes 16 cookies
Total Time 1¼ hours

WHY THIS RECIPE WORKS Peanut butter and bacon occasionally find each other in sandwiches—some find it silly, some find it brilliant. If you're in the latter camp, this cookie is for you. Rather than make a peanut butter cookie dough, we use a classic brown sugar–y cookie base so that the smoky flavor of the crispy bacon mix-in comes through and a bite isn't overwhelmingly rich. The peanut butter comes in the form of Reese's Pieces that are mixed in with the bacon and add crunch, color, and peanutty flavor.

PEANUT BUTTER CANDY AND BACON COOKIES

- 9 ounces (255 grams) bacon, cut into ½-inch pieces
- 2¼ cups (320 grams) all-purpose flour
- 1 teaspoon table salt
- ¾ teaspoon baking soda
- 1 cup packed (198 grams) light brown sugar
- 12 tablespoons (171 grams) unsalted butter, melted
- ½ cup (99 grams) granulated sugar
- 2 large eggs
- 1½ teaspoons vanilla extract
- 1½ cups (306 grams) Reese's Pieces

Underbaking the cookies ensures that they remain chewy once cool.

1 Adjust oven rack to middle position and heat oven to 425 degrees. Cook bacon in 12-inch nonstick skillet over medium heat until crispy, 7 to 9 minutes. Using slotted spoon, transfer bacon to paper towel–lined plate and let cool completely. Whisk flour, salt, and baking soda together in bowl.

2 Using stand mixer fitted with paddle, beat brown sugar, melted butter, and granulated sugar on medium speed until well combined, about 1 minute, scraping down bowl as needed. Add eggs and vanilla and beat until fully incorporated, about 30 seconds. Reduce speed to low; add flour mixture; and mix until mostly incorporated but some streaks of flour remain, about 30 seconds. Add Reese's Pieces and bacon and mix until evenly distributed, about 30 seconds.

3 Working with ¼ cup dough at a time, roll into balls between your dampened hands and space them evenly on 2 parchment paper–lined baking sheets (8 balls per sheet). Using your hand, flatten dough balls to ¾-inch thickness.

4 Bake cookies, 1 sheet at a time, until centers of cookies are puffed and lightly golden, 8 to 10 minutes, rotating sheet halfway through baking. (Cookies will seem underdone but will continue to bake as they cool.) Let cookies cool on sheet for 5 minutes, then transfer to wire rack and let cool for 10 minutes. Serve warm or at room temperature.

Storage: 2 days at room temperature

Makes 16 cookies

Total Time 1 hour

WHY THIS RECIPE WORKS These cookies are for the Oreo lovers, the ones who always order cookies 'n' cream ice cream, and the ones who just can't get enough cookies! We add chopped Oreo cookies, along with chopped creamy white chocolate, to brown sugar–y cookie dough for a cookie-in-cookie treat. Milk just might have a new favorite cookie.

COOKIES AND CREAM COOKIES

- 2¼ cups (320 grams) all-purpose flour
- 1 teaspoon table salt
- ¾ teaspoon baking soda
- 1 cup packed (198 grams) light brown sugar
- 12 tablespoons (171 grams) unsalted butter, melted
- ½ cup (99 grams) granulated sugar
- 2 large eggs
- 1½ teaspoons vanilla extract
- 15 Oreo cookies, chopped
- 4 ounces (113 grams) white chocolate, chopped

Underbaking the cookies ensures that they remain chewy once cool.

1 Adjust oven rack to middle position and heat oven to 425 degrees. Whisk flour, salt, and baking soda together in bowl.

2 Using stand mixer fitted with paddle, beat brown sugar, melted butter, and granulated sugar on medium speed until well combined, about 1 minute, scraping down bowl as needed. Add eggs and vanilla and beat until fully incorporated, about 30 seconds. Reduce speed to low; add flour mixture; and mix until mostly incorporated but some streaks of flour remain, about 30 seconds. Add cookies and chocolate and mix until evenly distributed throughout dough, about 30 seconds.

3 Working with ¼ cup dough at a time, roll into balls between your dampened hands and space them evenly on 2 parchment paper–lined baking sheets (8 balls per sheet). Using your hand, flatten dough balls to ¾-inch thickness.

4 Bake cookies, 1 sheet at a time, until centers of cookies are puffed and lightly golden, 8 to 10 minutes, rotating sheet halfway through baking. (Cookies will seem underdone but will continue to bake as they cool.) Let cookies cool on sheet for 5 minutes, then transfer to wire rack and let cool for 10 minutes. Serve warm or at room temperature.

Storage: 2 days at room temperature

Makes 16 cookies

Total Time 1¼ hours

WHY THIS RECIPE WORKS Halva—a dense tahini and sugar confection—is excellent on its own, but as an add-in, it makes one of the best cookies we've ever had. Derived from the Arabic word for "sweet," halva in different forms is popular across Asia, the Mediterranean, and North Africa. When eaten alone, halva crumbles into delicate shards before dissolving on your tongue; baked into the dough, its unique texture provides contrast to a thick, chewy browned butter cookie. We use a generous piece of halva in each cookie and, for more texture and crunch, we also incorporate pistachios and sesame seeds. The goodies don't end there: White chocolate provides pockets of sweetness that tame the bold cookie. Finally, we add orange blossom water and orange zest, which impart floral notes and further sophistication to this incredible treat.

BROWNED BUTTER HALVA CRUNCH COOKIES

- 2¼ cups (320 grams) all-purpose flour
- 1 teaspoon table salt
- ¾ teaspoon baking soda
- 12 tablespoons (171 grams) unsalted butter
- 1 cup packed (198 grams) light brown sugar
- ½ cup (99 grams) granulated sugar
- 1 teaspoon grated orange zest
- 2 large eggs
- 2 teaspoons orange blossom water
- 6 ounces (170 grams) white chocolate, chopped
- 1 cup (145 grams) shelled pistachios, toasted and chopped
- ½ cup (71 grams) sesame seeds
- 8 ounces (227 grams) halva, cut into 16 rough 1-inch squares

Storage: 2 days at room temperature

Halva sometimes includes nuts or other flavorings (vanilla, rose water, cocoa); you can use any type of sesame-based halva. We love the floral aroma orange blossom water provides this cookie, but you can omit it if you prefer.

1 Adjust oven rack to middle position and heat oven to 375 degrees. Whisk flour, salt, and baking soda together in bowl. Heat butter in 10-inch skillet over medium-high heat until melted, about 2 minutes. Continue to cook, swirling skillet and stirring constantly with silicone spatula, until butter is dark golden brown and has nutty aroma, 1 to 3 minutes longer. Transfer browned butter to second bowl and let cool slightly, about 10 minutes.

2 Using stand mixer fitted with paddle, beat brown sugar, granulated sugar, orange zest, and cooled browned butter on medium speed until well combined, about 1 minute, scraping down bowl as needed. Add eggs and orange blossom water and beat until fully incorporated, about 30 seconds. Reduce speed to low; add flour mixture; and mix until mostly incorporated but some streaks of flour remain, about 30 seconds. Add white chocolate and pistachios and mix until evenly distributed, about 30 seconds.

3 Place sesame seeds in shallow dish. Working with ¼ cup dough at a time, roll into balls between your dampened hands, then roll in sesame seeds to coat; space dough balls 2 inches apart on 2 parchment paper–lined baking sheets (8 balls per sheet). Press 1 piece halva into center of each ball, flattening dough ball so cookie is about 2½ inches wide.

4 Bake cookies, 1 sheet at a time, until firm around edges and lightly golden, 12 to 14 minutes, rotating sheet halfway through baking. Let cookies cool on sheet for 5 minutes, then transfer to wire rack and let cool for 10 minutes. Serve warm or at room temperature.

Makes 16 cookies

Total Time 1 hour

WHY THIS RECIPE WORKS S'mores on their own are really meant for the outdoors, where simple foods are important and where sweets are more snack than indulgence. Take s'mores indoors and you can turn these graham cracker sandwiches from just a little austere to over the top. We pack cookie dough with chopped bittersweet chocolate, graham crackers (only lightly crushed so that every munch has a crunch), and mini marshmallows, which melt and peek out of the cookies playfully.

S'MORES COOKIES

- 2¼ cups (320 grams) all-purpose flour
- 1 teaspoon table salt
- ¾ teaspoon baking soda
- 1 cup packed (198 grams) light brown sugar
- 12 tablespoons (171 grams) unsalted butter, melted
- ½ cup (99 grams) granulated sugar
- 2 large eggs
- 1½ teaspoons vanilla extract
- ¾ cup (36 grams) mini marshmallows
- 3 whole graham crackers, lightly crushed (¾ cup)
- 4 ounces (113 grams) bittersweet chocolate, chopped

Underbaking the cookies ensures that they remain chewy once cool.

1 Adjust oven rack to middle position and heat oven to 425 degrees. Whisk flour, salt, and baking soda together in bowl.

2 Using stand mixer fitted with paddle, beat brown sugar, melted butter, and granulated sugar on medium speed until well combined, about 1 minute, scraping down bowl as needed. Add eggs and vanilla and beat until fully incorporated, about 30 seconds. Reduce speed to low; add flour mixture; and mix until mostly incorporated but some streaks of flour remain, about 30 seconds. Add marshmallows, graham crackers, and chocolate and mix until evenly distributed, about 30 seconds.

3 Working with ¼ cup dough at a time, roll into balls between your dampened hands and space them evenly on 2 parchment paper–lined baking sheets (8 balls per sheet). Using your hand, flatten dough balls to ¾-inch thickness.

4 Bake cookies, 1 sheet at a time, until centers of cookies are puffed and lightly golden, 8 to 10 minutes, rotating sheet halfway through baking. (Cookies will seem underdone but will continue to bake as they cool.) Let cookies cool on sheet for 5 minutes, then transfer to wire rack and let cool for 10 minutes. Serve warm or at room temperature.

Storage: 2 days at room temperature

WHY THIS RECIPE WORKS With its elegant swirling of dark chocolate and bittersweet orange doughs, this cookie reminds us of Terry's Chocolate Orange, the British candy you whack into segments and unwrap. Although common in confections, the pairing of chocolate and orange isn't so often found in a cookie. We make sugar cookie dough, divide it in half, and load one half with melted chocolate and chocolate chunks and the other half with fresh orange zest and candied orange peel. To mix it all up, we roll portions of each dough into marbled balls. These beautiful cookies deliver both chocolate and orange flavor in a creative package—no whacking required!

Makes 16 cookies

Total Time 50 minutes, plus 30 minutes cooling

CHOCOLATE-ORANGE TWIST COOKIES

- 2¼ cups (320 grams) all-purpose flour
- 1 teaspoon baking powder
- ½ teaspoon baking soda
- ½ teaspoon table salt
- 1½ cups (297 grams) sugar
- 2 ounces (57 grams) cream cheese, softened and cut into 8 pieces
- 6 tablespoons (85 grams) unsalted butter, melted
- ⅓ cup (70 grams) vegetable oil
- 1 large egg
- 1 tablespoon milk
- 2 teaspoons vanilla extract
- 4 ounces (113 grams) bittersweet chocolate, chopped, divided
- 2 tablespoons chopped candied orange peel
- 1 tablespoon grated orange zest

1 Adjust oven rack to middle position and heat oven to 350 degrees. Line 2 baking sheets with parchment paper. Whisk flour, baking powder, baking soda, and salt together in bowl.

2 Whisk sugar, cream cheese, melted butter, and oil in large bowl until no lumps of cream cheese remain. Add egg, milk, and vanilla and whisk until smooth. Stir in flour mixture until soft, homogeneous dough forms. Transfer half of dough to second bowl.

3 Microwave 2 ounces chopped chocolate in bowl at 50 percent power, stirring occasionally, until melted, 1 to 3 minutes. Add to 1 bowl of dough along with remaining chopped chocolate, stirring until fully combined. Stir candied orange peel and orange zest into other bowl of dough. (You should have 1 chocolate dough and 1 blond dough.)

4 Measure out about 1 tablespoon of each dough flavor, rounding each into individual balls. Pull each ball into 2 pieces, then compress into 1 large ball, alternating dough flavors. Roll into smooth ball and place on prepared baking sheet. Repeat with remaining dough, spacing dough balls about 3 inches apart on 2 sheets. (You should have 16 cookies; if you have extra dough, distribute it among dough balls and reroll into smooth balls.) Using bottom of dry measuring cup or drinking glass, press each ball to ½-inch thickness.

5 Bake cookies, 1 sheet at a time, until edges are set and just beginning to brown, 12 to 14 minutes, rotating sheet halfway through baking. Let cookies cool on sheet for 5 minutes, then transfer to wire rack. Let cookies cool completely before serving.

Storage: 2 days at room temperature

SHAPING THE COOKIES

1. Pull each flavor dough ball into 2 pieces.

2. Compress dough pieces into 1 large ball, alternating dough flavors. Roll into balls.

3. Press dough balls to ½-inch thickness.

1

2

3

WHY THIS RECIPE WORKS This delightfully over-the-top spiced cookie recipe is pretty meta; it not only calls for stuffing a cookie with a cookie, but also incorporates the popular condiment cookie butter. An ode to an icon—speculoos-inspired crispy Biscoff cookies (see page 158)—our chewy cookie dough includes cinnamon, ginger, and cloves. We also add a bit of espresso powder for depth and a touch of bitterness. We wrap the flavorful dough around frozen portions of creamy, spreadable Biscoff cookie butter, leaving a slight amount of the filling exposed. The cookie butter bakes into molten pools, perfect for capturing a sprinkling of flaky sea salt. For contrasting texture, we stir chopped hazelnuts into the dough and stick half of a packaged Biscoff cookie into the filling after baking. The biscuit is an obvious hint at what's within, but you'll have to take a bite to discover all of the layers of richness in this mammoth cookie.

Makes 16 cookies

Total Time 1¼ hours, plus 1 hour chilling and cooling

CHEWY, GOOEY BISCOFF BUTTER COOKIES

- 1 cup (283 grams) Biscoff cookie butter, chilled
- 2¼ cups (320 grams) all-purpose flour
- 2 teaspoons ground cinnamon
- 1 teaspoon ground ginger
- 1 teaspoon table salt
- ¾ teaspoon baking soda
- ¼ teaspoon ground cloves
- 12 tablespoons (171 grams) unsalted butter
- 1 cup packed (198 grams) light brown sugar
- ½ cup (99 grams) granulated sugar
- 2 large eggs
- 2 teaspoons instant espresso powder
- 1 teaspoon vanilla extract
- 1 cup (143 grams) hazelnuts, toasted, skinned, and chopped
- Flake sea salt
- 8 Biscoff cookies, broken in half (optional)

Chilling the Biscoff cookie butter and using a 1-tablespoon cookie scoop makes it easier to portion before freezing it. You can use creamy or crunchy cookie butter.

1 Using greased 1-tablespoon scoop, scoop Biscoff butter into sixteen portions on large plate; freeze until firm, about 30 minutes.

2 Adjust oven rack to middle position and heat oven to 375 degrees. Line 2 baking sheets with parchment paper. Whisk flour, cinnamon, ginger, table salt, baking soda, and cloves together in bowl. Heat butter in 10-inch skillet over medium-high heat until melted, about 2 minutes. Continue to cook, swirling skillet and stirring constantly with silicone spatula, until butter is dark golden brown and has nutty aroma, 1 to 3 minutes longer. Transfer browned butter to second bowl and let cool slightly, about 10 minutes.

3 Using stand mixer fitted with paddle, beat brown sugar, granulated sugar, and cooled browned butter on medium speed until well combined, about 1 minute, scraping down bowl as needed. Add eggs, espresso powder, and vanilla and beat until fully incorporated, about 30 seconds. Reduce speed to low; add flour mixture; and mix until mostly incorporated but some streaks of flour remain, about 30 seconds. Add hazelnuts and mix until evenly distributed, about 30 seconds.

4 Working with ¼ cup dough at a time, roll into balls between your hands. Use your fingers to flatten 1 dough ball into 2½-inch-wide disk. Place 1 frozen ball of filling in center of disk, then wrap edges of dough up and around filling, leaving top of filling uncovered (opening should be roughly ½ inch wide). Smooth any cracks on underside of dough ball with your fingers. Repeat with remaining dough balls and filling, spacing filled dough balls, open side up, 2 inches apart on prepared sheets (8 balls per sheet). (Return filling balls to freezer if any become too soft to work with.)

5 Bake cookies, 1 sheet at a time, until firm around edges and light golden, 12 to 14 minutes, rotating sheet halfway through baking. Transfer sheet to wire rack; immediately sprinkle with flake sea salt and press Biscoff cookie half, if using, into filling. Let cookies cool on sheet for 5 minutes, then transfer to wire rack. Let cookies cool completely before serving.

Storage: 2 days at room temperature

1

STUFFING AND SHAPING THE COOKIES

1. Place 1 frozen ball of filling in center of 1 dough disk, then wrap edges of dough up and around filling.

2. Leave top of filling uncovered (opening should be roughly ½ inch wide). Smooth any cracks on underside of dough ball with your fingers.

2

Why This Recipe Works These chewy-gooey cookies are baked with a marshmallow in the center, which puffs up in the oven like a hot air balloon and collapses into a golden sweet blanket over the cookie's center. The marshmallow caramelizes while the cookie bakes and adds toasty notes in addition to pleasant sweetness to the rich peanut butter base. Chopped peanuts add a welcome crunchy texture. Once you meet this cookie, you'll skip the fluffernutter sandwiches and move right to dessert.

Makes 24 cookies

Total Time 55 minutes, plus 30 minutes cooling

MOLTEN TOASTED MARSHMALLOW PEANUT BUTTER COOKIES

- 1½ cups (213 grams) all-purpose flour
- 1 teaspoon baking soda
- ½ teaspoon table salt
- 1½ cups packed (298 grams) dark brown sugar
- 1 cup (261 grams) creamy peanut butter
- 2 large eggs
- 4 tablespoons (57 grams) unsalted butter, melted and cooled
- 2 tablespoons honey
- 1 teaspoon vanilla extract
- ¾ cup (107 grams) dry-roasted peanuts, chopped fine, divided
- 24 large marshmallows
- Flake sea salt

1 Adjust oven rack to middle position and heat oven to 350 degrees. Whisk flour, baking soda, and table salt together in medium bowl.

2 Whisk sugar, peanut butter, eggs, melted butter, honey, and vanilla together in large bowl until smooth. Add flour mixture and stir with rubber spatula until soft, homogeneous dough forms. Stir in ½ cup (71 grams) peanuts.

3 Working with 2½ tablespoons dough at a time, roll dough into balls, then space evenly on 2 parchment paper–lined baking sheets (12 dough balls per sheet). Using bottom of dry measuring cup or drinking glass, press each dough ball until about 2 inches wide. Firmly press 1 marshmallow, rounded side down, into center of each cookie, pressing until cookie spreads to about 2½ inches wide. Using lightly moistened fingertips, smooth any cracked edges.

4 Bake cookies, 1 sheet at a time, until marshmallows are puffed and lightly browned on top and edges of cookies are just set, 10 to 12 minutes, rotating sheet halfway through baking. Remove sheet from oven, sprinkle with remaining ¼ cup (36 grams) peanuts and sea salt to taste, and let cookies cool on sheet for 5 minutes. Transfer cookies to wire rack and let cool completely before serving.

Storage: 3 days at room temperature

WHY THIS RECIPE WORKS These superlative oatmeal cookies showcase generous pieces of bittersweet chocolate; crunchy, buttery toasted pecans; and chewy, tart dried cherries, wrapped in a deeply chewy, molasses-y dough. The cookie is jam-packed, but the lineup of mix-ins is carefully curated, with a sophisticated balance of flavor and texture. Dark brown sugar in the cookie dough provides both molasses flavor and chewiness; making big cookies and baking them just until set yet slightly underdone further ensures good chew. Since the thick oatmeal dough is so chock-full, we flatten the dough balls to encourage spread.

Makes 16 cookies

Total Time 55 minutes, plus 30 minutes cooling

CHOCOLATE CHUNK OATMEAL COOKIES WITH PECANS AND DRIED CHERRIES

- 1¼ cups (178 grams) all-purpose flour
- ¾ teaspoon baking powder
- ½ teaspoon baking soda
- ½ teaspoon table salt
- 1¼ cups (106 grams) old-fashioned rolled oats
- 1 cup (119 grams) pecans, toasted and chopped
- 1 cup (113 grams) dried sour cherries, chopped coarse
- 4 ounces (113 grams) bittersweet chocolate, chopped into ½-inch pieces
- 12 tablespoons (171 grams) unsalted butter, softened
- 1½ cups packed (298 grams) dark brown sugar
- 1 large egg
- 1 teaspoon vanilla extract

You can substitute walnuts or skinned hazelnuts for the pecans and dried cranberries for the cherries. Quick oats can be used in place of the old-fashioned oats, but they will yield a cookie with slightly less chew.

1 Adjust oven racks to upper-middle and lower-middle positions and heat oven to 350 degrees. Whisk flour, baking powder, baking soda, and salt together in bowl. Stir oats, pecans, cherries, and chocolate together in second bowl.

2 Using stand mixer fitted with paddle, beat butter and sugar on medium speed until no lumps of sugar remain, about 1 minute, scraping down bowl as needed. Add egg and vanilla and beat until fully incorporated, about 30 seconds. Reduce speed to low; add flour mixture; and mix until just combined, about 30 seconds. Add oat mixture and mix until just incorporated. Give dough final stir by hand.

3 Working with ¼ cup dough at a time, roll into balls and space them 2½ inches apart on 2 parchment paper–lined baking sheets (8 balls per sheet). Using bottom of greased dry measuring cup or drinking glass, press each ball to 1-inch thickness.

4 Bake cookies until golden and edges have begun to set but centers are still soft (cookies will look raw between cracks and seem underdone), 20 to 22 minutes, switching and rotating sheets halfway through baking. Let cookies cool on sheets for 5 minutes, then transfer to wire rack. Let cookies cool completely before serving.

Storage: 2 days at room temperature

Makes 16 cookies

Total Time 1 hour, plus 30 minutes cooling

WHY THIS RECIPE WORKS Some say the combination of mix-ins in this hearty yet indulgent cookie—rolled oats, chocolate chips, toasted nuts, and flakes of coconut—originally sustained American cattle workers. Others celebrate their common use in Texan desserts. No matter, these nostalgic Texas-size cookies are sure to steal a Texas-size piece of your heart. Since all the dry oats and coconut absorb moisture in the dough, we add an egg plus an extra yolk and melt the butter to keep the dough moist and to give the cookies appealing chew. The baked cookies are big, rustic, and full of flavor.

TEXAS TRAIL COOKIES

- 1¼ cups (177 grams) all-purpose flour
- ¾ teaspoon baking powder
- ½ teaspoon baking soda
- ½ teaspoon table salt
- 1½ cups packed (298 grams) light brown sugar
- 12 tablespoons (170 grams) unsalted butter, melted and cooled
- 1 large egg plus 1 large yolk
- 1 teaspoon vanilla extract
- 1¼ cups (106 grams) old-fashioned rolled oats
- 1 cup (119 grams) pecans, toasted and chopped coarse
- 1 cup (82 grams) sweetened shredded coconut
- ⅔ cup (113 grams) semisweet chocolate chips

We prefer old-fashioned rolled oats in this recipe, but you can use quick or instant oats in a pinch. Do not use thick-cut oats here; the cookies will spread too much. These cookies are big and spread wide, and they benefit from the extra space provided by a rimless baking sheet when baking. You can use a rimmed baking sheet, but you will need to divide the cookies among three sheets and bake them in three batches to avoid overcrowding.

1 Adjust oven rack to middle position and heat oven to 350 degrees. Whisk flour, baking powder, baking soda, and salt together in bowl.

2 Whisk sugar, melted butter, egg and yolk, and vanilla together in large bowl. Stir in flour mixture until no dry streaks remain. Stir in oats, pecans, coconut, and chocolate chips (mixture will be sticky).

3 Using greased ¼-cup measure, scoop dough and space 2½ inches apart on 2 parchment paper–lined rimless baking sheets (8 portions per sheet). Divide any remaining dough among portions.

4 Bake cookies, 1 sheet at a time, until edges are browned and set and centers are puffed with pale, raw spots, 15 to 17 minutes, rotating sheet halfway through baking. Let cookies cool on sheet for 5 minutes, then transfer to wire rack. Let cookies cool completely before serving.

Storage: 2 days at room temperature

WHY THIS RECIPE WORKS The sweet-tart, earthy taste of cherries complements rich chocolate in this classic pairing (see: cherry cordials, Black Forest cake, and a certain beloved ice cream pint). Although chocolate can so easily overpower its fruit counterpart in desserts, in this rich fudgy-chewy chocolate-cherry cookie, the two are true equals. Plumping dried cherries in cherry liqueur intensifies their flavor and keeps them jammy, so there are bright, tangy bursts in every bite. Dutch-processed cocoa gives the cookies a rich, deep chocolate flavor, so we add white and semisweet chocolate chips for creamy contrast. A subtle but important enhancement: almond extract, which amplifies cherry notes and ties all the flavors together.

Makes 24 cookies

Total Time 1 hour, plus 30 minutes cooling

TRIPLE CHOCOLATE–CHERRY COOKIES

- 1½ cups (170 grams) dried cherries
- ⅓ cup (87 grams) cherry liqueur
- 2 tablespoons water
- 1 cup (85 grams) Dutch-processed cocoa powder
- ¾ cup (107 grams) all-purpose flour
- ½ teaspoon table salt
- ¼ teaspoon baking soda
- 1 cup packed (198 grams) dark brown sugar
- 8 tablespoons (114 grams) unsalted butter, melted
- 2 large eggs
- 2 teaspoons vanilla extract
- ¼ teaspoon almond extract
- 6 ounces (170 grams) white chocolate, chopped
- 3 ounces (85 grams) semisweet chocolate, chopped

You can substitute a cherry brandy, such as kirsch, for the liqueur, but the flavor will be more boozy. To skip the alcohol, substitute ½ cup tart cherry juice for the cherry liqueur and water. Do not use natural cocoa powder; the cookies will be too dry. The cookies will seem underdone but will continue to set as they cool.

1 Adjust oven rack to middle position and heat oven to 375 degrees. Microwave cherries, liqueur, and water in bowl until bubbling around edges, about 90 seconds. Let sit at room temperature for 15 minutes. Drain cherries in fine-mesh strainer set over bowl, pressing on cherries to extract as much liquid as possible; discard liquid or save for another use.

2 Whisk cocoa, flour, salt, and baking soda together in bowl. Whisk sugar and melted butter together in large bowl. Whisk eggs, vanilla, and almond extract into sugar mixture until creamy and smooth, about 30 seconds. Stir in cocoa mixture until no dry flour remains. Fold in white and semisweet chocolates and soaked cherries.

3 Working with 2 tablespoons dough at a time, roll into balls and space them evenly on 2 parchment paper–lined baking sheets (12 balls per sheet).

4 Bake cookies, 1 sheet at a time, until edges are just set and centers are puffed but still soft, 7 to 8 minutes, rotating sheet halfway through baking. Let cookies cool completely on sheet before serving.

Storage: 4 days at room temperature

Makes 24 cookies

Total Time 1 hour, plus 30 minutes resting

WHY THIS RECIPE WORKS Snackers: Think outside the bag with this salty-sweet cookie! It pairs the best two salty snacks, pretzels and potato chips, in a crispy cookie. The crushed chips and pretzels add a savory edge to the cookie dough, which we roll into balls and coat with sugar before baking. We flatten each dough ball so that when the cookies cool, they have a surface for spreading with a sweet butterscotch frosting that's the perfect foil for the salty, snacky cookie. A sprinkling of chopped pecans on top adds lasting crunch. Like most of our favorite snacks, this one beckons us to keep eating it.

CRUNCHY SALTY SNACK COOKIES WITH CARAMEL FROSTING

COOKIES

- 12 tablespoons (171 grams) unsalted butter, softened
- ½ cup (99 grams) granulated sugar, plus ¼ cup (50 grams) for rolling
- 1 teaspoon vanilla extract
- ⅛ teaspoon table salt
- 1½ cups (213 grams) all-purpose flour
- 2 ounces (57 grams) potato chips, crushed (⅔ cup)
- ¾ ounce (21 grams) mini pretzels, crushed (¼ cup)

FROSTING

- ½ cup packed (99 grams) light brown sugar
- ¼ cup (58 grams) heavy cream
- 3 tablespoons unsalted butter
- Pinch table salt
- ½ teaspoon vanilla extract
- 1 cup (113 grams) confectioners' sugar
- ¼ cup (30 grams) pecans, toasted and chopped fine

1 **For the cookies:** Adjust oven rack to middle position and heat oven to 350 degrees. Using stand mixer fitted with paddle, beat butter, ½ cup sugar, vanilla, and salt on medium-high speed until pale and fluffy, about 3 minutes. Reduce speed to low, add flour, and mix until incorporated. Stir in potato chips and pretzels.

2 Spread remaining ¼ cup sugar in shallow dish. Working with heaping 1 tablespoon dough at a time, roll into 24 balls. Roll balls in sugar to coat and space them 2 inches apart on 2 parchment paper–lined baking sheets (12 balls per sheet). Using bottom of greased measuring cup or drinking glass, press dough to ¼-inch thickness.

3 Bake cookies, 1 sheet at a time, until set and edges are golden, about 15 minutes, rotating sheet halfway through baking. Let cookies cool on sheets for 5 minutes, then transfer to wire rack. Let cookies cool completely.

4 **For the frosting:** Meanwhile, bring brown sugar, cream, butter, and salt to boil in medium saucepan over medium heat. Remove from heat and stir in vanilla. Transfer to bowl and let cool completely, about 20 minutes. Whisk in confectioners' sugar.

5 Stir frosting, then spread 1 teaspoon over top of each cookie. Sprinkle cookies with pecans; let sit until frosting is set, about 30 minutes, before serving.

Storage: 3 days at room temperature

Makes 12 cookies

Total Time 1¼ hours, plus 1¼ hours cooling

WHY THIS RECIPE WORKS If other baked goods are acceptable at breakfast, why not cookies? These cookies, with a fruity jam layer and loads of granola, satisfy on busy mornings when you need breakfast—but you also want a treat. We make a pat-in-the-pan brown sugar cookie dough and spread it with bright blueberry jam. Then we stir together spiced, maple-sweetened granola ingredients and bake them right into the dough for a tight marriage of chewy cookie and crunchy, satisfying granola. Piped (or dolloped) with a tangy homemade blueberry yogurt topping, this cookie makes perfect sense as breakfast. On the go? You can omit the topping.

BLUEBERRY JAM BREAKFAST COOKIES

YOGURT TOPPING

- ½ cup (119 grams) plain Greek yogurt
- 1 teaspoon lemon juice
- 2 tablespoons blueberry jam

COOKIES

- ¾ cup plus 2 tablespoons (135 grams) all-purpose flour
- ¾ teaspoon table salt, divided
- ¼ teaspoon baking soda
- 6 tablespoons (85 grams) unsalted butter
- ½ cup plus 2 tablespoons packed (125 grams) dark brown sugar
- 5 tablespoons (66 grams) vegetable oil, divided
- 1 large egg
- ⅓ cup (94 grams) blueberry jam
- 3 tablespoons maple syrup
- 1 teaspoon ground ginger
- 1¼ cups (106 grams) old-fashioned rolled oats
- ¼ cup (39 grams) whole raw almonds, chopped
- ¼ cup (36 grams) raw cashews, chopped

1 **For the yogurt topping:** Whisk yogurt and lemon juice together in bowl. Using spoon, gently swirl jam into yogurt mixture. Refrigerate until ready to use. (Topping can be refrigerated for up to 2 days.)

2 **For the cookies:** Adjust oven rack to middle position and heat oven to 350 degrees. Make foil sling for 8-inch square baking pan by folding 2 long sheets of aluminum foil so each is 8 inches wide. Lay sheets of foil in pan perpendicular to each other, with extra foil hanging over edges of pan. Push foil into corners and up sides of pan, smoothing foil flush to pan. Grease foil.

3 Whisk flour, ½ teaspoon salt, and baking soda together in bowl. Heat butter in 10-inch skillet over medium-high heat until melted, about 2 minutes. Continue to cook, swirling skillet and stirring constantly with silicone spatula, until butter is dark golden brown and has nutty aroma, 1 to 3 minutes longer; transfer to medium bowl. Whisk sugar and 2 tablespoons vegetable oil into hot butter until combined. Whisk in egg until smooth. Stir in flour mixture. Transfer dough to prepared pan and press into even layer. Dollop with jam, then spread into even layer over top.

4 Whisk maple syrup, ginger, and remaining ¼ teaspoon salt together in large bowl, then whisk in remaining 3 tablespoons oil until combined. Fold in oats, almonds, and cashews until well coated. Spread oat mixture into even layer over top of jam; then, using stiff metal spatula, compress oat mixture until very compact. Bake until evenly golden brown, 40 to 45 minutes, rotating pan halfway through baking.

5 Let cookies cool in pan on wire rack for 45 minutes. Using foil sling, lift cookies out of pan, discard foil, and let cool completely on rack. Transfer cookies to cutting board. Cut in half, then cut each half crosswise into 6 rectangles (you should have twelve 1⅓-inch-wide rectangles). Just before serving, dollop or pipe yogurt topping decoratively onto bars.

Storage: untopped, 3 days at room temperature

Makes 15 bars

Total Time 1¼ hours, plus 1 hour cooling

WHY THIS RECIPE WORKS This oatmeal cookie bar boldly leans into contrasting flavors, using a generously piped whipped topping instead of sugary frosting to counter (rather than augment) the sweetness of a date- and brown sugar–packed base. Labneh, the thick and tangy strained yogurt common in Middle Eastern cuisine, combines with tahini (and just 2 tablespoons of sugar) for a creamy, tangy topping with nutty complexity and intriguing savor. To take the cookie's flavor and texture a step further, we sprinkle it with an orange zest–enhanced dukkah garnish. The zest in the Egyptian nut-and-spice mix really brightens up the cookie and brings all the flavors together for an exciting and surprising treat that's also chewy, rich, and comforting.

OATMEAL-DATE BARS WITH WHIPPED LABNEH

BARS

- 1 cup (142 grams) all-purpose flour
- ¾ teaspoon table salt
- ½ teaspoon baking powder
- 2 cups (304 grams) pitted dates, cut into ½-inch pieces
- 4 tablespoons (57 grams) unsalted butter
- ¾ cup packed (149 grams) brown sugar
- ½ cup (99 grams) granulated sugar
- ½ cup (105 grams) vegetable oil
- 1 large egg plus 1 large yolk
- 1 teaspoon vanilla extract
- 2 cups (170 grams) old-fashioned rolled oats

TOPPING

- 2 tablespoons chopped toasted pistachios
- 1 teaspoon toasted sesame seeds
- 1 teaspoon coriander seeds, toasted and ground coarse
- ½ teaspoon fennel seeds, toasted and ground coarse
- ½ teaspoon flake sea salt
- ½ teaspoon grated orange zest
- 2 cups (476 grams) labneh
- ¾ cup (185 grams) tahini
- 2 tablespoons granulated sugar

1 **For the bars:** Adjust oven rack to middle position and heat oven to 375 degrees. Make foil sling for 13 by 9-inch baking pan by folding 2 long sheets of aluminum foil; first sheet should be 13 inches wide and second sheet should be 9 inches wide. Lay sheets of foil in pan perpendicular to each other, with extra foil hanging over edges of pan. Push foil into corners and up sides of pan, smoothing foil flush to pan. Grease foil.

2 Whisk flour, salt, and baking powder together in bowl. Add dates and toss to coat in flour mixture, breaking any pieces that stick together.

3 Heat butter in 8-inch skillet over medium-high heat until melted, about 2 minutes. Continue to cook, swirling skillet and stirring constantly with silicone spatula, until butter is dark golden brown and has nutty aroma, 1 to 3 minutes. Transfer to large bowl, scraping out browned milk solids with spatula.

4 Whisk brown sugar, granulated sugar, and oil into browned butter until no lumps of sugar remain. Add egg and yolk and vanilla and whisk until smooth. Stir in flour-date mixture until soft, homogeneous dough forms. Stir in oats (mixture will be stiff).

5 Transfer dough to prepared pan and press into even layer. Bake until golden brown, 16 to 18 minutes, rotating pan halfway through baking. Let bars cool in pan on wire rack for 1 hour.

6 **For the topping:** Combine pistachios, sesame seeds, coriander seeds, fennel seeds, salt, and orange zest in small bowl; set aside. Whisk labneh, tahini, and sugar together in separate bowl. (Pistachio mixture and labneh mixture can be refrigerated separately for up to 24 hours; let labneh mixture sit at room temperature for 30 minutes before using.)

7 Using foil overhang, lift bars out of pan and transfer to cutting board; discard foil. Using chef's knife, cut bars lengthwise into thirds (you should have 3 roughly 13 by 3-inch rectangles), then cut each rectangle into 5 pieces (you should have 15 roughly 3 by 2½-inch pieces). Just before serving, dollop or pipe labneh mixture decoratively onto each cookie, then sprinkle with pistachio mixture.

Storage: untopped, 2 days at room temperature

WHY THIS RECIPE WORKS Hiding a surprise peanut butter filling in a double-chocolate cookie is a great party trick. Anyone who loves peanut butter cups would love to find a creamy, salty, peanutty center in a fudgy, crackly, slightly chewy, intensely chocolaty cookie. Adding bittersweet chocolate as well as Dutch-processed cocoa powder to the dough gives it potent chocolate flavor. Increasing the standard ratio of flour to sugar, fat, and egg keeps the dough from becoming sticky, making it easy to wrap it around chilled balls of thick peanut butter filling.

Makes 16 cookies

Total Time 1¼ hours, plus 1 hour freezing and cooling

PEANUT BUTTER–STUFFED CHOCOLATE COOKIES

FILLING

- ½ cup (131 grams) creamy peanut butter
- ½ cup (57 grams) confectioners' sugar
- ¼ teaspoon table salt

DOUGH

- 1½ cups (213 grams) all-purpose flour
- ¼ cup (21 grams) Dutch-processed cocoa powder
- 1 teaspoon baking powder
- ¼ teaspoon baking soda
- ¾ teaspoon table salt
- 10 ounces (284 grams) bittersweet chocolate, chopped fine, divided
- 3 tablespoons vegetable oil
- 1 tablespoon unsalted butter
- 1 tablespoon vanilla extract
- 1 cup (198 grams) granulated sugar, plus ⅓ cup (66 grams) for rolling
- 2 large eggs
- ½ cup (57 grams) confectioners' sugar for rolling

Once baked and cooled, these cookies are best stored in the refrigerator.

1 For the filling: Combine peanut butter, sugar, and salt in bowl. Using fork or your hands, stir and mash mixture until thoroughly combined and no dry pockets of sugar remain. Divide filling into 16 equal portions (about 2 teaspoons each). Roll each portion into ball and place on large plate. Freeze until firm, about 30 minutes.

2 For the dough: Meanwhile, adjust oven racks to upper-middle and lower-middle positions and heat oven to 300 degrees. Line 2 baking sheets with parchment paper. Whisk flour, cocoa, baking powder, baking soda, and salt together in bowl. Microwave 6 ounces (170 grams) chocolate, oil, and butter in bowl at 50 percent power, stirring occasionally, until melted, about 3 minutes. Whisk vanilla into melted chocolate mixture.

3 Whisk 1 cup granulated sugar and eggs in large bowl until thoroughly combined. Add melted chocolate mixture and whisk until uniform. Add flour mixture and stir until combined. Fold in remaining 4 ounces (114 grams) chopped chocolate.

4 Divide dough into 16 equal portions, about scant 3 tablespoons each; divide any remaining dough evenly among portions. Working with 1 dough ball at a time, use your fingers to flatten into 3-inch-wide disk. Place 1 frozen ball of filling in center of disk, then wrap edges of dough up and around filling. Seal dough and shape into smooth ball.

●●● CONTINUED ●●●

5 Spread confectioners' sugar and remaining ⅓ cup granulated sugar in 2 separate shallow dishes. Roll dough balls first in granulated sugar, then in confectioners' sugar to coat. Evenly space dough balls on prepared baking sheets (8 balls per sheet).

6 Using bottom of dry measuring cup or drinking glass, flatten dough balls into 2-inch-wide disks. (Dough balls will crack at edges; this is OK. If filling shows through any large cracks, pinch dough together to seal cracks.) Bake until cookies are puffed, edges are just set, and cookies no longer look raw between cracks, about 22 minutes, switching and rotating sheets halfway through baking. Transfer sheets to wire racks and let cookies cool completely on sheets before serving.

Storage: 2 days at room temperature

STUFFING AND SHAPING THE COOKIES

1. Using your fingers, flatten 1 dough portion into disk with roughly 3-inch diameter. Place 1 ball of chilled filling in center of disk.

2. Wrap edges of dough up and around filling.

3. Seal dough, shape into smooth ball, and roll in sugar.

4. Flatten dough balls into 2-inch-wide disks using bottom of dry measuring cup. Seal any cracks where filling shows through.

1

2

3

4

Makes 12 cookies

Total Time 1 hour, plus 2½ hours chilling and cooling

WHY THIS RECIPE WORKS Baker and chef Adrian Lipscombe is the mastermind behind turning a beloved layer cake into a unique, fun, and especially eye-catching colossal cookie. We adapted Adrian's bakery-shop recipe for the home cook. A sturdy cream cheese filling is hidden by bright-red cookie dough that's enlivened with vibrant lemon zest and studded with finely chopped pecans and creamy, sweet white chocolate chips. A bit of whole-wheat flour added to the dough not only lends it a pleasant nutty, earthy flavor but also contributes good structure needed for this stuffed cookie.

STUFFED RED VELVET COOKIES

FILLING

- ½ cup (57 grams) confectioners' sugar
- 4 ounces (113 grams) cream cheese, softened
- 2 tablespoons unsalted butter, softened
- ⅛ teaspoon vanilla extract
- Pinch table salt

COOKIES

- 2⅔ cups (379 grams) all-purpose flour
- ⅔ cup (104 grams) whole-wheat flour
- 1 tablespoon unsweetened cocoa powder
- 1¼ teaspoons table salt
- 1 teaspoon baking soda
- 16 tablespoons (228 grams) unsalted butter, melted
- 1 cup packed (198 grams) light brown sugar
- ½ cup (99 grams) granulated sugar
- 2 large eggs
- 1½ teaspoons grated lemon zest
- 2 teaspoons vanilla extract
- 1 tablespoon red food coloring
- 1 cup (170 grams) white chocolate chips
- ½ cup (60 grams) finely chopped pecans

You can use either liquid or gel food coloring in this recipe. You can substitute an additional ½ cup of white chocolate chips for the pecans if you prefer.

1 For the filling: Using stand mixer fitted with paddle, beat all ingredients on low speed until sugar is mostly moistened, about 1 minute. Increase speed to medium-high and beat until fluffy and smooth, 2 to 3 minutes, scraping down bowl as needed.

2 Line large, flat plate with parchment paper. Scoop filling into twelve 1-tablespoon portions on prepared plate. Use back of spoon to lightly flatten each portion into rough disk shape (no greater than 1½ inches in diameter). Freeze until solid, at least 2 hours. (Filling can be frozen for up to 1 week.)

3 For the cookies: Adjust oven rack to middle position and heat oven to 425 degrees. Line 2 baking sheets with parchment paper. Whisk all-purpose flour, whole-wheat flour, cocoa, salt, and baking soda together in bowl.

4 Whisk melted butter, brown sugar, and granulated sugar together in large bowl. Whisk in eggs, lemon zest, vanilla, and food coloring. Stir in half of flour mixture, then stir in chocolate chips, pecans, and remaining flour mixture until evenly combined. (Mixture will be stiff; once dough begins to stiffen, you may want to mix it with your hands.)

5 Working with ⅓ cup dough at a time, roll into balls, then flatten into disk shape, about 3 inches in diameter. Working quickly, place 1 disk of frozen filling in center of each dough disk. Wrap edges of dough up and around filling, seal dough, and shape into smooth disk shape (about 3½ inches in diameter and ½ inch thick), taking care to ensure filling remains in center of each disk. Space disks evenly on prepared baking sheets (6 disks per sheet).

6 Bake cookies, 1 sheet at a time, until edges of cookies are beginning to puff and crack, 7 to 8 minutes, rotating sheet halfway through baking. Let cookies cool completely on sheet before serving.

Storage: 2 days at room temperature

Makes 24 brownies

Total Time 1¾ hours, plus 2 hours cooling

WHY THIS RECIPE WORKS A twofer treat for the indecisive, a brookie, as the name suggests, is a playful combination of brownie and cookie, and we know a thing or two about the best of both. To create a texturally and flavorfully dynamic dessert that has two distinct sections, we really lean into emphasizing the brownie's fudginess and the cookie's chewiness. We forgo leaveners to give the brownie a gooey, barely set texture, and use unsweetened chocolate and cocoa powder, bolstered with espresso powder, to make it deeply and darkly chocolaty. And for the cookie, browning the butter enhances the dough's butterscotch notes. Generous scoops of cookie stand tall in the squidgy squares of brownie.

ULTIMATE BROOKIES

COOKIE

- 1¾ cups (249 grams) all-purpose flour
- ½ teaspoon baking soda
- 14 tablespoons (200 grams) unsalted butter, divided
- ¾ cup packed (149 grams) dark brown sugar
- ½ cup (99 grams) granulated sugar
- 2 teaspoons vanilla extract
- 1 teaspoon table salt
- 1 large egg plus 1 large yolk
- 1¼ cups (213 grams) bittersweet chocolate chips

BROWNIE

- 4 tablespoons (57 grams) unsalted butter, cut into 4 pieces
- 2 ounces (57 grams) unsweetened chocolate, chopped
- ⅓ cup (28 grams) Dutch-processed cocoa powder
- 1 tablespoon instant espresso powder
- 1 teaspoon table salt
- ½ cup plus 2 tablespoons (148 grams) boiling water
- 2½ cups (495 grams) granulated sugar
- ½ cup plus 2 tablespoons (131 grams) vegetable oil
- 2 large eggs plus 2 large yolks
- 2 teaspoons vanilla extract
- 1¾ cups (249 grams) all-purpose flour
- ½ teaspoon flake sea salt (optional)

For an accurate measurement of boiling water, bring a full kettle to a boil, then measure out the desired amount.

1 Adjust oven rack to middle position and heat oven to 350 degrees. Make foil sling for 13 by 9-inch baking pan by folding 2 long sheets of aluminum foil; first sheet should be 13 inches wide and second sheet should be 9 inches wide. Lay sheets of foil in pan perpendicular to each other, with extra foil hanging over edges of pan. Push foil into corners and up sides of pan, smoothing foil flush to pan. Grease foil.

2 **For the cookie:** Whisk flour and baking soda together in large bowl; set aside. Heat 10 tablespoons (143 grams) butter in 10-inch skillet over medium-high heat until melted, about 2 minutes. Continue to cook, swirling skillet and stirring constantly with silicone spatula, until butter is dark golden brown and has nutty aroma, 1 to 3 minutes longer. Remove skillet from heat and transfer browned butter to second large bowl. Stir remaining 4 tablespoons (57 grams) butter into hot butter until completely melted.

3 Add brown sugar, granulated sugar, vanilla, and salt to bowl with butter and whisk until no lumps of sugar remain. Add egg and yolk and whisk until smooth. Let mixture stand for 3 minutes, then whisk until mixture is thick and shiny, about 1 minute. Stir in flour mixture until just combined. Fold in chocolate chips until evenly distributed and no dry flour remains.

4 **For the brownie:** Combine butter, chocolate, cocoa powder, espresso powder, and salt in now-empty large bowl. Add boiling water and whisk until butter and chocolate are completely melted, about 1 minute. Add sugar, oil, eggs and yolks, and vanilla and whisk until smooth. Gently whisk in flour until just incorporated. Transfer batter to prepared pan.

5 Dollop heaping tablespoon mounds of cookie dough evenly over brownie batter (cookie dough can touch edges of pan), about 24 portions. Bake until toothpick inserted into cookie layer comes out clean, 40 to 45 minutes, rotating pan halfway through baking. Transfer pan to wire rack and let cool for 1 hour.

6 Using foil overhang, lift brookies out of pan; let cool completely on wire rack,about 1 hour. Cut into 24 pieces and sprinkle with flake sea salt, if using, before serving.

Storage: 4 days at room temperature

Makes 20 sandwiches

Total Time 1½ hours, plus 8½ hours cooling and freezing

WHY THIS RECIPE WORKS One of the best ways to load cookies is to pack two with a generous scoop of cold, creamy ice cream. This is an M&M's sundae in handheld form—sugar cookies filled with crispy, chocolaty M&M's Minis and vanilla ice cream with a fudgy swirl. To make this happen, the cookies need to be soft straight from the freezer, and the sandwich should be easy to eat. We've nailed cookies that are chewy at room temperature, but here they need retooling. Leaving out an egg white, adding some corn syrup, and baking the cookies quickly in a hot oven all ensure the cookies are soft from the freezer. Cold temperatures dull your palate, so we pump up the flavor, increasing the salt and vanilla. This is ice cream with all the fixins—no spoon needed.

M&M'S FUDGE RIPPLE ICE CREAM SANDWICHES

- 2⅓ cups (331 grams) all-purpose flour
- 1½ teaspoons table salt
- ¾ teaspoon baking soda
- 12 tablespoons (171 grams) unsalted butter, melted
- 1 cup packed (198 grams) light brown sugar
- ½ cup (99 grams) granulated sugar
- 2 tablespoons light corn syrup
- 1 large egg plus 1 large yolk
- 1 tablespoon vanilla extract
- 1¼ cups (255 grams) M&M's Minis
- 3 pints fudge ripple ice cream

These cookies benefit from the extra space provided by a rimless baking sheet. You can use a rimmed baking sheet, but you will need to divide the cookies among three sheets and bake them in three batches to avoid overcrowding. If your ice cream is very hard when fully frozen, let it soften slightly in the refrigerator before scooping. If you have it, a portion scoop that holds ¼ cup (a #16 scoop) works well for portioning the ice cream.

1 Adjust oven rack to middle position and heat oven to 400 degrees. Line 2 rimless baking sheets with parchment paper. Whisk flour, salt, and baking soda together in bowl.

2 Whisk melted butter, brown sugar, granulated sugar, and corn syrup together in large bowl until well combined, about 30 seconds. Whisk in egg and yolk and vanilla until fully combined and mixture is smooth and creamy, about 30 seconds. Stir in half of flour mixture. Stir in candies and remaining flour mixture until no dry flour remains.

3 Working with heaping 1 tablespoon dough at a time, roll into balls between your hands and space them evenly on prepared sheets (20 balls per sheet). Using your hand, flatten balls to ¾-inch thickness.

4 Bake cookies, 1 sheet at a time, until centers of cookies are puffed and lightly golden, about 8 minutes, rotating sheet halfway through baking. (Cookies will seem underdone.) Let cookies cool on sheet for 5 minutes, then transfer to wire rack and let cool completely. Place 1 empty sheet, still lined with parchment, in freezer.

5 Place 4 cookies upside down on counter. Working quickly, deposit large scoop (about ¼ cup) of ice cream in center of each cookie. Place 1 cookie right side up on top of each scoop. Gently press and twist each sandwich between your hands until ice cream spreads to edges of cookies (edges may be uneven; ice cream can be neatened after freezing). Transfer sandwiches to prepared sheet in freezer. Repeat with remaining cookies and remaining ice cream. Cover sandwiches with plastic wrap and freeze for at least 8 hours before serving. (Once frozen, sandwiches can be individually wrapped tightly in plastic wrap, transferred to zipper-lock bag, and frozen for up to 2 months.)

Storage: 2 months in freezer

Makes 20 sandwiches

Total Time 1½ hours, plus 8½ hours cooling and freezing

WHY THIS RECIPE WORKS Gourmet cookies and artisanal ice creams are increasingly the norm, squashing any notion that treats like ice cream sandwiches are just for kids. This sandwich is a bit refined but full of flavor. Butterscotch cookies bring out the caramel notes in coffee ice cream, while the coffee leaves the sweet treat with a hint of balancing bitterness. Our cookie dough uses a lot of brown sugar and so is already full of butterscotch notes, but we bolster that here by stirring in butterscotch chips.

BUTTERSCOTCH COFFEE ICE CREAM SANDWICHES

- 2⅓ cups (331 grams) all-purpose flour
- 1½ teaspoons table salt
- ¾ teaspoon baking soda
- 12 tablespoons (171 grams) unsalted butter, melted
- 1 cup packed (198 grams) light brown sugar
- ½ cup (99 grams) granulated sugar
- 2 tablespoons light corn syrup
- 1 large egg plus 1 large yolk
- 1 tablespoon vanilla extract
- 1¼ cups (213 grams) butterscotch chips
- 3 pints coffee ice cream

These cookies benefit from the extra space provided by a rimless baking sheet. You can use a rimmed baking sheet, but you will need to divide the cookies among three sheets and bake them in three batches to avoid overcrowding. If your ice cream is very hard when fully frozen, let it soften slightly in the refrigerator before scooping. If you have it, a portion scoop that holds ¼ cup (a #16 scoop) works well for portioning the ice cream.

1 Adjust oven rack to middle position and heat oven to 400 degrees. Line 2 rimless baking sheets with parchment paper. Whisk flour, salt, and baking soda together in bowl.

2 Whisk melted butter, brown sugar, granulated sugar, and corn syrup together in large bowl. Whisk in egg and yolk and vanilla until mixture is smooth and creamy, about 30 seconds. Stir in half of flour mixture. Stir in butterscotch chips and remaining flour mixture until no dry flour remains.

3 Working with 1 heaping tablespoon dough at a time, roll into balls between your hands and space them evenly on prepared sheets (20 balls per sheet). Using your hand, flatten dough balls to ¾-inch thickness.

4 Bake cookies, 1 sheet at a time, until centers of cookies are puffed and lightly golden, about 8 minutes, rotating sheet halfway through baking. (Cookies will seem underdone.) Let cookies cool on sheet for 5 minutes, then transfer to wire rack and let cool completely. Place 1 empty sheet, still lined with parchment, in freezer.

5 Place 4 cookies upside down on counter. Working quickly, deposit large scoop (about ¼ cup) of ice cream in center of each cookie. Place 1 cookie right side up on top of each scoop. Gently press and twist each sandwich between your hands until ice cream spreads to edges of cookies (edges may be uneven; ice cream can be neatened after freezing). Transfer sandwiches to prepared sheet in freezer. Repeat with remaining cookies and remaining ice cream. Cover sandwiches with plastic wrap and freeze for at least 8 hours before serving. (Once frozen, sandwiches can be individually wrapped tightly in plastic wrap, transferred to zipper-lock bag, and frozen for up to 2 months.)

Storage: 2 months in freezer

Chapter 3

CRISPY AND CRUNCHY

ATK CLASSIC

Makes 16 cookies

Total Time 30 minutes, plus 30 minutes cooling

While our Chewy Chocolate Chip Cookies (page 50) are rich with a chewy center, sometimes we get a hankering for another style: a thin, crisp cookie—one that's perfectly flat, almost like praline in appearance, and packs a big crunch. Melted butter and a little milk help the dough spread thin. Whole eggs encourage rise, so we use only egg yolks in this dough so the thin cookies will spread flat. Using mini chocolate chips instead of regulation size helps keep the cookies flat. While brown sugar gives cookies nice flavor, it also contributes moisture that lasts through baking, which foils crunch; using equal parts brown and granulated gives these cookies just the right balance of butterscotch flavor and good crunch. To banish any last bit of chew, we swap the all-purpose flour we typically use for cookies with cake flour; its lower protein content encourages less gluten development for a cookie that's light and crisp.

THIN AND CRISPY CHOCOLATE CHIP COOKIES

- 1¼ cups (142 grams) cake flour
- ¾ teaspoon table salt
- ¼ teaspoon baking soda
- 8 tablespoons (114 grams) unsalted butter, melted and cooled
- ⅓ cup (66 grams) granulated sugar
- ⅓ cup packed (66 grams) dark brown sugar
- 2 large egg yolks
- 1½ tablespoons whole milk
- 2 teaspoons vanilla extract
- ¾ cup (128 grams) mini semisweet chocolate chips

1 Adjust oven rack to middle position and heat oven to 350 degrees. Whisk flour, salt, and baking soda together in bowl.

2 Using stand mixer fitted with paddle, beat melted butter, granulated sugar, and brown sugar on medium speed until well combined, about 1 minute, scraping down bowl as needed. Increase speed to medium-high and beat until mixture is lightened in color, about 1 minute. Add egg yolks, milk, and vanilla and beat until fully incorporated. Reduce speed to low; add flour mixture; and mix until just combined, scraping down bowl as needed. Add chocolate chips and mix until evenly distributed throughout dough, about 30 seconds.

3 Divide dough into 16 equal portions (about scant 2 tablespoons each), spaced evenly on 2 parchment paper–lined baking sheets (8 portions per sheet). Using your moistened fingers, press dough portions to ½-inch thickness. Bake cookies, 1 sheet at a time, until deep golden brown, 16 to 18 minutes, rotating sheet halfway through baking. Transfer sheets to wire rack and let cookies cool completely on sheets before serving.

Storage: 3 days at room temperature

For the *Crispiest* Chocolate Chip Cookies

- **Choose cake flour** The low-protein flour develops less gluten than all-purpose flour and creates a more delicate cookie.
- **Combine brown and white sugar** The mix provides butterscotch flavor without too much of the moisture that keeps cookies soft after baking and cooling outside of the oven.
- **Use only yolks** Egg yolks provide structure without creating lift.
- **Dial in leavener** A little baking soda is needed to aerate the crumb for a delicate crunch but not so much that it lifts the cookies significantly.
- **Bake longer** The cookies need more time in the oven than many to get crispy.
- **Add liquid** A little milk helps the cookies spread adequately.
- **Flatten** Pressing dough portions to uniform thickness promotes spread.

Crisp, with Caramel Flavor
The cookies have a generous baking time.

Significant Spread
Melted butter and milk loosen up the dough.

Light Texture
We use cake flour for delicacy and just enough baking soda to open the crumb.

Small Mix-Ins
Mini chocolate chips maintain a low profile.

WHY THIS RECIPE WORKS Caramel and rosemary are not a common flavor combination like chocolate and vanilla, but the pairing can find its way into high-end confections thanks to an irresistible interplay of sweet and savory. In this cookie, we use toffee as our cooked-sugar component because we love its deep flavor, buttery richness, and crunchy texture, and when baked, it softens into chewy little golden pools. Introduce the rosemary (minced for seamless integration) and toffee to a thin, crispy cookie, and you achieve even more textural interest. The resulting treat feels both familiar and unexpected—buttery and sweet, yet elevated with an herbaceous perfume that keeps the cookie from becoming cloying.

Makes 16 cookies

Total Time 55 minutes, plus 30 minutes cooling

THIN AND CRISPY ROSEMARY TOFFEE COOKIES

- 1¼ cups (142 grams) cake flour
- ¾ teaspoon table salt
- ¼ teaspoon baking soda
- 8 tablespoons (114 grams) unsalted butter, melted and cooled
- ⅓ cup (66 grams) granulated sugar
- ⅓ cup packed (66 grams) dark brown sugar
- 2 large egg yolks
- 1½ tablespoons whole milk
- 1 tablespoon minced fresh rosemary
- 2 teaspoons vanilla extract
- ¾ cup (106 grams) plain toffee bits

We like Heath Bar Bits of Brickle in this recipe but you can substitute chopped-up Heath Bars or any toffee.

1 Adjust oven rack to middle position and heat oven to 350 degrees. Whisk flour, salt, and baking soda together in bowl.

2 Using stand mixer fitted with paddle, beat melted butter, granulated sugar, and brown sugar on medium speed until well combined, about 1 minute, scraping down bowl as needed. Increase speed to medium-high and beat until mixture is lightened in color, about 1 minute. Add egg yolks, milk, rosemary, and vanilla and beat until fully incorporated. Reduce speed to low; add flour mixture and mix until just combined, scraping down bowl as needed. Add toffee bits and mix until evenly distributed throughout dough, about 30 seconds.

3 Divide dough into 16 equal portions (about scant 2 tablespoons each) and space evenly on 2 parchment paper–lined baking sheets (8 portions per sheet). Using your moistened fingers, press dough portions to ½-inch thickness. Bake cookies, 1 sheet at a time, until deep golden brown, 16 to 18 minutes, rotating sheet halfway through baking. Transfer sheets to wire rack and let cookies cool completely on sheet before serving.

Storage: 3 days at room temperature

Makes 16 cookies

Total Time 1½ hours, plus 30 minutes cooling

WHY THIS RECIPE WORKS This pretty cookie has balanced sweetness and really tastes of Thai tea. Joe Gitter, the recipe developer behind this thin cookie with broad flavor, says of his inspiration, "As an Englishman who appreciates a properly strong cup of tea, I've always admired Thai iced tea's unapologetic boldness, that intense, amber-orange brew balanced by the sweet richness of condensed milk." Translating that distinctive tea flavor into cookies presents a challenge: Tea can easily get lost among butter, sugar, and flour. Our solution is to make a hot milk infusion, steeping finely pulverized tea leaves in warm milk to extract maximum flavor before incorporating it into the dough. The result is a crispy, delicate cookie (perfect with tea?) that carries the tea's earthy intensity without being overwhelmed. The colored glaze adds the appropriate extra sweetness and is swirled to mimic those beautiful skeins of evaporated milk created from pouring it over the bright-orange Thai tea.

THAI TEA CRISPS

COOKIES

- 2 tablespoons Thai tea leaves (6 bags)
- 3 tablespoons whole milk, warm (140 degrees)
- 1¼ cups (142 grams) cake flour
- ¾ teaspoon table salt
- ¼ teaspoon baking soda
- 8 tablespoons (114 grams) unsalted butter, melted and cooled
- ⅓ cup (66 grams) granulated sugar
- ⅓ cup packed (66 grams) dark brown sugar
- 2 large egg yolks
- ½ teaspoon vanilla extract

GLAZE

- 2 tablespoons cream cheese, at room temperature
- ¼ cup (61 grams) whole milk, plus extra as needed
- 3 cups (339 grams) confectioners' sugar
- Yellow gel food coloring
- Red gel food coloring

We developed this recipe using ChaTraMue Thai tea; avoid Thai tea blends that contain whole spices. A spice grinder makes quick work of grinding the tea; a mortar and pestle will also work. It's important to cool the butter before adding it to the sugar in the mixer. If you've got them, wear food-handling gloves when pressing the cookies in step 3, as the Thai tea can stain your hands. Do not use liquid food coloring, as it will add too much water to the glaze. You can omit the food coloring if desired.

1 **For the cookies:** Adjust oven rack to middle position and heat oven to 325 degrees. Process tea in spice grinder until finely ground, about 15 seconds, then sift through fine-mesh strainer into small bowl; discard any tea left in strainer. Stir warm milk into sifted tea and let sit for 5 minutes. Whisk flour, salt, and baking soda together in medium bowl.

2 Using stand mixer fitted with paddle, mix melted butter, granulated sugar, and brown sugar on low speed until fully combined, about 1 minute. Increase speed to medium-high and beat until mixture is lightened in color, about 1 minute. Reduce speed to low; add milk-tea mixture, egg yolks, and vanilla; and mix until combined, about 1 minute. Slowly add flour mixture and mix until just combined, about 1 minute, scraping down bowl as needed. Let dough sit for 15 minutes.

••• CONTINUED •••

3 Divide dough into 16 equal portions (about scant 2 tablespoons each) and space evenly on 2 parchment paper–lined baking sheets (8 portions per sheet). Using your moistened fingers, press dough portions to ½-inch thickness. Bake cookies, 1 sheet at a time, until deep golden brown, 23 to 25 minutes, rotating sheet halfway through baking. Let cookies cool on sheet for 5 minutes, then transfer to wire rack and let cool completely.

4 For the glaze: Whisk cream cheese and milk in medium bowl until combined and no lumps remain. Whisk in confectioners' sugar until smooth. Add extra milk, drop by drop, as needed until glaze is thin enough to spread easily. Transfer 3 tablespoons glaze to separate small bowl. Stir yellow food coloring and red food coloring into remaining glaze until uniform in color and desired shade has been reached.

5 Spread 2 teaspoons colored glaze over each cookie, leaving ½-inch border. Drizzle ½ teaspoon white glaze over orange glaze on each cookie. Using toothpick or wooden skewer, swirl white glaze into orange glaze to create attractive design on each cookie. Let glaze dry completely, about 30 minutes, before serving.

Storage: unglazed, 3 days at room temperature; 24 hours glazed

GLAZING THE COOKIES

1. Spread 2 teaspoons colored glaze over each cookie, leaving ½-inch border.

2. Drizzle ½ teaspoon white glaze over orange glaze.

3. Swirl white glaze into orange glaze.

WHY THIS RECIPE WORKS Known by many Americans as Biscoff, these much-loved Belgian cookies—with a familiar presence on countless flights—have a crisp, light, open-crumbed texture and a blend of caramelized sugar and warm spice flavors. Our homemade speculoos, encrusted with sliced almonds, reach even higher heights. To achieve the appropriate texture, we roll the dough thin so it bakes up dry and crisp, and we use only enough sugar to lightly sweeten the dough. In the OG speculoos, that sugar is hard-to-find Belgian brown sugar; we use turbinado (which we grind in a food processor that's then used to make the dough) in our homage to its subtle caramel taste. Adding baking powder along with the usual baking soda produces an open, airy crumb. Biscoff cookies are spiced only with cinnamon, but we craved more dimension; some cardamom and cloves bring more interest without calling attention to themselves.

Makes 32 cookies

Total Time 1 hour, plus 2 hours chilling and cooling

SPECULOOS WITH ALMONDS

- 1½ cups (213 grams) all-purpose flour
- 5 teaspoons ground cinnamon
- 1 teaspoon ground cardamom
- ¼ teaspoon ground cloves
- ¼ teaspoon baking powder
- ¼ teaspoon baking soda
- ¼ teaspoon table salt
- ¾ cup (170 grams) turbinado sugar
- 8 tablespoons (114 grams) unsalted butter, cut into ½-inch pieces and chilled
- 1 large egg
- ½ cup (50 grams) sliced almonds

For the proper flavor, we strongly recommend using turbinado sugar (commonly sold as Sugar in the Raw); if you can't find it, you can use ¾ cup plus 2 tablespoons packed (170 grams) light brown sugar and skip the grinding in step 2. Do not use cookie molds or an embossed rolling pin for the speculoos; the cookies will not hold decorations. We call for rimless baking sheets for baking the cookies so you can fit the optimal number of cookies on each sheet.

1 Whisk flour, cinnamon, cardamom, cloves, baking powder, baking soda, and salt together in bowl. Using pencil and ruler, draw 12 by 10-inch rectangle in center of each of 2 large sheets of parchment paper, crisscrossing lines at corners. (Use crisscrosses to help line up top and bottom sheets as dough is rolled.)

2 Process sugar in food processor for 30 seconds (some grains will be smaller than granulated sugar; others will be larger). Add butter and process until uniform mass forms and no large pieces of butter are visible, about 30 seconds, scraping down sides of bowl as needed. Add egg and process until smooth and paste-like, about 10 seconds, scraping down sides of bowl as needed. Add flour mixture and process until no dry flour remains but mixture is still crumbly, about 30 seconds, scraping down sides of bowl as needed.

3 Transfer dough to bowl and knead gently with silicone spatula until uniform and smooth, about 10 seconds. Place 1 piece of parchment on counter with pencil side facing down (you should be able to see rectangle through paper). Place dough in center of marked rectangle and press into 9 by 6-inch rectangle. Place second sheet of parchment over dough with pencil side facing up, so dough is in center of marked rectangle. Using pencil marks as guide, press and roll dough into 12 by 10-inch rectangle of even ⅜-inch thickness with rolling pin, squaring sides with bench scraper as you go. Gently peel off top layer of parchment. Sprinkle sliced almonds evenly over dough. Using rolling pin, gently press almonds into dough. Return parchment to dough, flip dough over, and transfer with parchment to baking sheet. Refrigerate until dough is firm, at least 1½ hours (or freeze for 30 minutes). (Rolled dough can be wrapped in plastic wrap and refrigerated for up to 5 days.)

4 Adjust oven racks to upper-middle and lower-middle positions and heat oven to 300 degrees. Line 2 rimless baking sheets with parchment. Transfer chilled dough to counter. Gently peel off top layer of parchment. Using fluted pastry wheel (or chef's knife or pizza cutter) and ruler, trim off rounded edges of dough that extend over marked edges of 12 by 10-inch rectangle. Cut dough lengthwise into 8 equal strips about 1¼ inches wide. Cut each strip crosswise into 4 equal pieces about 3 inches long. Transfer cookies to prepared sheets, spacing them at least ½ inch apart. Bake until cookies are lightly and evenly browned, 30 to 32 minutes, switching and rotating sheets halfway through baking. Transfer sheets to wire rack and let cookies cool completely on sheets before serving.

Storage: 3 weeks at room temperature

WHY THIS RECIPE WORKS This is a refined oatmeal cookie: It's thin, crisp, and delicate, and the flavor of buttery oats, partnered with sweet, nutty coconut, really stands out. Creaming the butter and sugar introduces air that helps the cookies dry out and develop irresistible crispness in the oven. Our Chewy Oatmeal Cookies (page 92) use a majority brown sugar; here we use a majority granulated to reduce moisture so that even the center of the cookies is dry enough to develop a pleasant crunch. The more neutral sugar also helps the oat and coconut flavors shine. Using a generous amount of both baking soda and powder causes the cookies to puff, collapse, and spread thin. We press the dough portions flat and bake them one sheet at a time until the cookies are fully set and evenly browned from edge to center. The result is caramelized oat flavor and a cookie that's made for a cup of tea.

Makes 24 cookies

Total Time 1 hour, plus 30 minutes cooling

COCONUT OATMEAL COOKIES

- 1 cup (142 grams) all-purpose flour
- ¾ teaspoon baking powder
- ½ teaspoon baking soda
- ½ teaspoon table salt
- 14 tablespoons (200 grams) unsalted butter, softened
- 1 cup (198 grams) granulated sugar
- ¼ cup packed (50 grams) light brown sugar
- 1 large egg
- 1 teaspoon vanilla extract
- 2 cups (170 grams) old-fashioned rolled oats
- 1½ cups (86 grams) sweetened flaked coconut

Do not use quick or instant oats. Place the cookies on the baking sheet in three rows, with three cookies in the outer rows and two cookies in the center row.

1 Adjust oven rack to middle position and heat oven to 350 degrees. Whisk flour, baking powder, baking soda, and salt together in bowl.

2 Using stand mixer fitted with paddle, beat butter, granulated sugar, and brown sugar on medium speed until pale and fluffy, 3 to 5 minutes, scraping down bowl as needed. Add egg and vanilla and continue to beat until well incorporated, about 1 minute longer. Reduce speed to low; add flour mixture; and mix until just combined, scraping down bowl as needed. With mixer running, gradually add oats and coconut and mix until evenly distributed throughout dough, about 30 seconds.

3 Working with 2 tablespoons dough at a time, roll into balls and space them 2½ inches apart on 3 parchment paper–lined baking sheets (8 balls per sheet). Using your fingertips, gently press each ball to ¾-inch thickness. (If you do not have 3 baking sheets, reuse first sheet once it's cooled to room temperature.)

4 Bake, 1 sheet at a time, until cookies are deep golden brown, edges are crisp, and centers yield to slight pressure when pressed, 13 to 16 minutes, rotating sheet halfway through baking. Transfer sheet to wire rack and let cookies cool completely on sheet before serving.

Storage: 3 days at room temperature

Makes about 40 cookies

Total Time 1 hour, plus 2 hours chilling and cooling

WHY THIS RECIPE WORKS Supercrunchy grocery store oatmeal cookies, with a crackled surface and an appealing landscape of glaze, are a nostalgic treat with a demure size and really big crunch. We love that you can eat more than one in a sitting, and they're just as good a week later. Baking the cookies for a generous amount of time (relative to their small size) ensures that they dry out and get crunchy. Taking inspiration from coffee breaks, we add espresso powder to the dough and icing to introduce a homemade twist to the warm, toasty flavor profile. The icing is thick so it doesn't run into the cookies' cracks.

ICED ESPRESSO OATMEAL CRUNCHIES

COOKIES

- 1⅔ cups (142 grams) old-fashioned rolled oats
- ¾ cup packed (149 grams) dark brown sugar
- ½ cup (71 grams) all-purpose flour
- ½ teaspoon table salt
- ½ teaspoon baking soda
- 8 tablespoons (114 grams) unsalted butter, cut into ½-inch pieces and chilled
- 1 large egg yolk
- 2 teaspoons instant espresso powder
- 1 teaspoon vanilla extract

ICING

- 1 large egg white
- ½ teaspoon instant espresso powder
- 1⅓ cups (151 grams) confectioners' sugar

ICING THE COOKIES

1. Dip just top of 1 cookie into icing.

2. Lift cookie from icing and let excess drip back into bowl.

With so much sugar, the icing is safe at room temperature for up to 1 week but if you're concerned about raw egg white, you can substitute pasteurized.

1 For the cookies: Process oats in food processor until coarse flour forms, 15 to 20 seconds. Add sugar, flour, salt, and baking soda and process until fully incorporated, 10 to 15 seconds. Add butter pieces and process until butter is incorporated and mixture resembles wet sand, about 45 seconds. Whisk egg yolk, 2 teaspoons espresso powder, and vanilla together in bowl, then add to food processor and process until cohesive dough forms, 15 to 20 seconds.

2 Transfer mixture to clean counter and press and knead until no dry oat pockets remain. Divide dough in half, then press and roll each piece into 1-inch wide log, about 10 inches long. Wrap logs tightly in plastic wrap and twist ends tightly to seal; refrigerate until firm, at least 1 hour or up to 24 hours.

3 Adjust oven racks to upper-middle and lower-middle positions and heat oven to 350 degrees. Working with 1 dough log at a time, trim ends, then slice chilled dough into ½-inch-thick rounds, rotating dough as you slice to prevent any flat edges from forming; space dough rounds evenly on 2 parchment paper–lined baking sheets (about 20 rounds per sheet). Bake until uniformly golden and firm to touch, 14 to 16 minutes, switching and rotating sheets halfway through baking. Let cookies cool on sheets for 5 minutes, then transfer to wire rack. Let cookies cool completely before icing.

4 For the icing: Whisk egg white and espresso powder together until espresso powder is dissolved. Whisk in sugar until smooth (icing will be quite thick; if too thick to adhere to cookies, whisk in ½ to 1 teaspoon water). Working with 1 cookie at a time, dip top into icing without fully submerging (only craggy peaks of each cookie should be coated). Lift cookie from icing, letting excess icing drip back into bowl, then invert cookie and return to rack. Let cookies sit until icing is set, about 30 minutes, before serving.

Storage: 1 week at room temperature

Makes 24 cookies

Total Time 1¼ hours, plus 30 minutes cooling

WHY THIS RECIPE WORKS If you like almonds, these might be their greatest expression in a cookie: The chocolate-covered treats feature almond flavor in three ways. Roasted, crushed almonds are studded throughout the dough as well as sprinkled on top for added crunch. Almond butter adds richness and a subtle toasty warmth to the dough. And almond extract adds sweet, fruity complexity and an immediately recognizable almond flavor. We use equal parts granulated and confectioners' sugar for a pleasing balance of crunch and crumbliness in texture. A quick dip in melted chocolate (tempered for lasting shine and snap) makes these cookies extra special.

CHOCOLATE-DIPPED ALMOND COOKIES

- ¾ cup (107 grams) all-purpose flour
- ¾ cup (118 grams) roasted salted almonds, crushed, divided
- ¼ teaspoon table salt
- 8 tablespoons (114 grams) unsalted butter, softened
- ¼ cup (65 grams) creamy almond butter
- ¼ cup (50 grams) granulated sugar
- ¼ cup (28 grams) confectioners' sugar
- 1 large egg yolk
- ¼ teaspoon vanilla extract
- ¼ teaspoon almond extract
- 8 ounces (227 grams) bittersweet chocolate (170 grams chopped fine, 57 grams grated), divided

Storage: 4 days at room temperature

To crush the almonds, place them in a zipper-lock bag and use a rolling pin.

1 Adjust oven rack to middle position and heat oven to 350 degrees. Whisk flour, ½ cup (79 grams) crushed almonds, and salt together in bowl.

2 Using stand mixer fitted with paddle, beat butter, almond butter, granulated sugar, and confectioners' sugar on medium speed until pale and fluffy, 3 to 5 minutes, scraping down bowl as needed. Add egg yolk, vanilla, and almond extract and continue to beat until well incorporated. Reduce speed to low; add flour mixture; and mix until just combined and no dry flour remains, about 1 minute.

3 Working with 1 tablespoon dough at a time, roll into balls and space them evenly on 2 parchment paper–lined baking sheets (12 balls per sheet). Refrigerate until just firm, about 10 minutes. Using lightly floured bottom of dry measuring cup, flatten dough balls to ¼-inch thickness.

4 Bake cookies, 1 sheet at a time, until edges are set and bottoms are lightly browned, 10 to 12 minutes, rotating sheet halfway through baking. Transfer sheet to wire rack and let cookies cool completely on sheet.

5 While cookies are cooling, microwave chopped chocolate in bowl at 50 percent power, stirring often, until about two-thirds melted, 1 to 2 minutes. Add grated chocolate and stir until smooth, returning to microwave for no more than 5 seconds at a time to complete melting as needed.

6 Carefully dip half of each cooled cookie in melted chocolate, scraping off excess with offset spatula; return cookies to cooled parchment-lined sheets. Sprinkle remaining ¼ cup (39 grams) crushed almonds over warm chocolate (about ½ teaspoon per cookie) and refrigerate cookies until chocolate is set, about 15 minutes, before serving.

ATK CLASSIC

Makes 80 cookies

Total Time 2 hours, plus 1½ hours chilling and cooling

Most gingersnap recipes don't live up to their name on either account. For homemade gingersnaps that rival the snap and spice of store-bought cookies, the first step is to dry out the cookies (in a good way) and make them crunchy. We approach this from several angles: We cut back on the amount of moist brown sugar, and we brown the butter, which evaporates some of the water in it. Using plenty of baking soda results in attractive fissures on the tops of our cookies, which also serve as channels for moisture to escape. Finally, a lower oven temperature and longer baking time dry them out enough to yield our desired snappy texture. To spice up the snap, we double the amount of dried ginger called for in most recipes and give it lots of help in the form of fresh ginger, as well as black pepper and a secret heat weapon: cayenne pepper.

DOUBLE GINGERSNAPS

- 2½ cups (355 grams) all-purpose flour
- 2 teaspoons baking soda
- ½ teaspoon table salt
- 12 tablespoons (171 grams) unsalted butter
- 2 tablespoons ground ginger
- 1 teaspoon ground cinnamon
- ¼ teaspoon ground cloves
- ¼ teaspoon pepper
- Pinch cayenne pepper
- 1¼ cups packed (248 grams) dark brown sugar
- ¼ cup (78 grams) molasses
- 2 tablespoons finely grated fresh ginger
- 1 large egg plus 1 large yolk
- ½ cup (99 grams) granulated sugar for rolling

Storage: 2 weeks at room temperature

For efficiency, form the second batch of cookies while the first batch bakes.

1 Whisk flour, baking soda, and salt together in bowl; set aside. Heat butter in 10-inch skillet over medium-high heat until melted, about 2 minutes. Continue to cook, swirling skillet and stirring constantly with silicone spatula, until butter is just beginning to brown, 1 to 3 minutes longer. Transfer browned butter to large bowl and whisk in ground ginger, cinnamon, cloves, pepper, and cayenne. Let cool slightly, about 2 minutes.

2 Whisk brown sugar, molasses, and fresh ginger into butter mixture until combined. Whisk in egg and yolk until combined. Stir in flour mixture until just combined. Cover bowl tightly with plastic wrap and refrigerate until dough is firm, about 1 hour.

3 Adjust oven racks to upper-middle and lower-middle positions and heat oven to 300 degrees. Spread granulated sugar in shallow dish. Divide dough into heaping teaspoon portions; roll dough portions into 1-inch balls. Working in batches of 10, roll balls in sugar to coat; space dough balls evenly on 2 parchment paper–lined baking sheets (20 balls per sheet).

4 Place 1 sheet on upper rack and bake cookies for 15 minutes. Transfer partially baked top sheet to lower rack, rotating sheet, and place second sheet of dough balls on upper rack. Continue to bake until cookies on lower sheet just begin to darken around edges, 10 to 12 minutes longer. Remove lower sheet of cookies and transfer upper sheet to lower rack, rotating sheet; continue to bake until cookies begin to darken around edges, 15 to 17 minutes longer.

5 Slide baked cookies, still on parchment, onto wire rack and let cool completely before serving. (Set aside sheets to cool completely before reusing.)Repeat with remaining dough balls.

For the *Crunchiest* Gingersnaps

- **Load up on leavener** Lots of baking soda creates fissures that help moisture escape the cookie.
- **Reduce the sugar** Gingersnaps need dark brown sugar for flavor—but not too much because it holds on to moisture.
- **Brown the butter** In addition to adding deep flavor, browning the butter evaporates some of its moisture.
- **Bake low and slow** A longer baking time at a lower temperature dries out the small cookies without burning them.
- **Switch oven racks** Baking each tray on the top rack before moving it to the cooler bottom rack also assists in creating fissures.

Baking Soda Bonanza

We use a dramatic amount of baking soda—a full 2 teaspoons—and no baking powder to create a gingersnap with extra snap and large fissures. The weaker gluten structure created in this environment means a more porous structure from which air bubbles and moisture can escape. It also means that the dough will collapse after its initial rise in the oven, leading to the cracks that also allow more moisture to evaporate.

Makes 24 cookies

Total Time 1½ hours, plus 30 minutes chilling

WHY THIS RECIPE WORKS These wafer-thin disks are sophisticated but still utterly craveable, with ground almonds bound by buttery cooked caramel and slicked with bittersweet chocolate. And, despite their placement at fancy pastry shops, they're utterly attainable at home too. To achieve thin, delicate, filigreed Florentines, we use coarsely ground almonds, very little flour, and enough cream to make the batter spread flat and become lacy. We bake the cookies until they're dark golden brown from edge to edge for toasty notes and the deepest caramelized flavor. The traditional orange flavor comes from marmalade and orange zest in the batter, and the zigzag of snappy chocolate is achieved through microwave tempering.

FLORENTINE LACE COOKIES

- 2 cups (256 grams) slivered almonds
- ¾ cup (173 grams) heavy cream
- ½ cup (99 grams) sugar
- 4 tablespoons (57 grams) unsalted butter, cut into 4 pieces
- ¼ cup (74 grams) orange marmalade
- 3 tablespoons all-purpose flour
- 1 teaspoon vanilla extract
- ¼ teaspoon grated orange zest
- ¼ teaspoon table salt
- 4 ounces (113 grams) bittersweet chocolate (85 grams chopped fine, 28 grams grated), divided

It's important to cook the cream mixture until it's thick and starting to brown at the edges; undercooked dough will be too runny to portion. Don't be concerned if some butter separates from the dough. For the most uniform cookies, make sure that your parchment paper lies flat, or use a silicone baking mat.

1 Adjust oven racks to upper-middle and lower-middle positions and heat oven to 350 degrees. Process almonds in food processor until they resemble coarse sand, about 30 seconds.

2 Bring cream, sugar, and butter to boil in medium saucepan over medium-high heat. Cook, stirring frequently, until mixture begins to thicken, 5 to 6 minutes. Continue to cook, stirring constantly, until mixture begins to brown at edges and is thick enough to leave trail that doesn't immediately fill in when silicone spatula is scraped along pan bottom, 1 to 2 minutes longer (it's OK if some darker speckles appear in mixture). Remove pan from heat and stir in ground almonds, marmalade, flour, vanilla, orange zest, and salt until combined.

3 Drop twelve 1-tablespoon portions dough onto 2 parchment paper–lined baking sheets (6 portions per sheet), spaced at least 3½ inches apart. When dough is cool enough to handle, use your dampened fingers to press each portion into 2½-inch circle.

4 Bake cookies until deep brown from edge to edge, 15 to 17 minutes, switching and rotating sheets halfway through baking. Transfer cookies, still on parchment, to wire racks. Let sheets cool for 10 minutes before placing clean parchment on sheets and repeating with remaining dough. Let cookies cool completely.

5 Microwave chopped chocolate in bowl at 50 percent power, stirring often, until about two-thirds melted, 1 to 2 minutes. Add grated chocolate and stir until smooth, returning to microwave for no more than 5 seconds at a time to complete melting if necessary. Transfer chocolate to small zipper-lock bag or piping bag and snip off corner, making hole no larger than ¹⁄₁₆ inch.

6 Pipe zigzag of chocolate over each cookie on wire racks, distributing chocolate evenly among all cookies. Refrigerate until chocolate is set, about 30 minutes, before serving.

Storage: 4 days at room temperature

Makes 40 sandwich cookies

Total Time 1 hour, plus 1½ hours chilling and cooling

WHY THIS RECIPE WORKS Whether you're a dunker or you prefer to twist and lick, you'll find these homemade Oreos have so much more flavor than the reference. For the midnight-black color of an Oreo, we turn to black cocoa powder (for more information, see page 24). Black cocoa has almost no fat in it, so we cut it with some Dutch-processed cocoa to prevent our cookies from crumbling. A little espresso powder, in combination with the cocoas, gives our cookies a deep chocolaty punch that you can't find in the packaged version. Blending butter and shortening together for the filling results in a rich, round flavor as well as the essential meltaway texture of a classic Oreo.

CHOCOLATE-VANILLA CRÈME SANDWICH COOKIES

COOKIES

- 3 tablespoons (43 grams) unsalted butter, melted and cooled, plus 5 tablespoons (71 grams) softened
- ¼ cup (21 grams) black cocoa powder
- 2 tablespoons Dutch-processed cocoa powder
- ½ teaspoon instant espresso powder
- ½ cup (99 grams) granulated sugar
- ¼ teaspoon table salt
- 1 large egg yolk
- 1½ teaspoons vanilla extract
- 1 cup (142 grams) all-purpose flour

FILLING

- 2 tablespoons unsalted butter, softened
- 2 tablespoons vegetable shortening
- 1 cup (113 grams) confectioners' sugar
- ½ teaspoon vanilla extract
- Pinch table salt

It is important to slice these cookies exactly to size so they bake evenly and are thin enough to have the classic Oreo snap.

1 **For the cookies:** Stir melted butter, black cocoa, Dutch-processed cocoa, and espresso powder in bowl until combined and smooth.

2 Using stand mixer fitted with paddle, beat remaining 5 tablespoons (71 grams) butter, sugar, salt, and cocoa mixture on medium-high speed until fluffy, about 2 minutes, scraping down bowl as needed. Add egg yolk and vanilla and continue to beat until well incorporated, about 1 minute longer. Reduce speed to low, add flour, and mix until dough is uniform, about 1 minute.

3 Transfer dough to counter and divide in half. Roll each piece of dough into 6-inch log. Wrap logs tightly in plastic wrap and twist ends tightly to seal; refrigerate until firm, at least 1 hour or up to 3 days.

4 Adjust oven racks to upper-middle and lower-middle positions and heat oven to 325 degrees. Trim ends of chilled dough logs, then slice into ⅛-inch-thick rounds, rotating dough as you slice to prevent any flat edges from forming; space dough rounds ½ inch apart on 2 parchment paper–lined baking sheets. Poke each round with tines of fork.

5 Bake until cookies are firm and reveal slight indentation when pressed with your finger, 14 to 16 minutes, switching and rotating sheets halfway through baking. Let cookies cool on sheets for 5 minutes, then transfer to wire rack and let cool completely.

6 **For the filling:** Using clean, dry mixer bowl and paddle, mix butter, shortening, sugar, vanilla, and salt on medium-low speed until combined, about 1 minute. Increase speed to medium-high and beat until light and fluffy, about 2 minutes.

7 Before serving, working with 1 cookie at a time, place rounded ½ teaspoon filling in center of upturned cookie. Place second cookie on top of filling, pressing gently until filling spreads to edges.

Storage: 1 week at room temperature

Makes 24 sandwich cookies

Total Time 1¼ hours, plus 1½ hours cooling and setting

WHY THIS RECIPE WORKS Jam is a timeless pairing with peanut butter because it adds brightness to the super-rich spread, which is especially welcome in this crunchy, extra-peanutty sandwich cookie. We reach the pinnacle of peanut flavor in the cookies by replacing a portion of flour with finely chopped peanuts, in addition to the obvious inclusion of peanut butter in the dough. Adding a full teaspoon of baking soda encourages air bubbles within the dough to inflate so rapidly that they burst before the cookies set, leaving the cookies flat for sandwiching with creamy filling. We warm the peanut butter and butter for the filling in the microwave so the filling is easy to pipe in a ring on a cookie bottom. A generous dollop of jam goes in the center, and the peanut butter seal prevents it from oozing out when the cookies are sandwiched.

PB&J SANDWICH COOKIES

COOKIES

- 1¼ cups (178 grams) dry-roasted peanuts
- ¾ cup (107 grams) all-purpose flour
- 1 teaspoon baking soda
- ½ teaspoon table salt
- ½ cup (131 grams) creamy peanut butter
- ½ cup (99 grams) granulated sugar
- ½ cup packed (99 grams) light brown sugar
- 3 tablespoons unsalted butter, melted
- 3 tablespoons whole milk
- 1 large egg

FILLING

- ¾ cup (196 grams) creamy peanut butter
- 3 tablespoons unsalted butter
- 1 cup (113 grams) confectioners' sugar
- 1 cup (281 grams) seedless strawberry jam

Do not use unsalted peanut butter. We like strawberry jam here, but feel free to use the jam of your choice. Take care when processing the peanuts—you want to chop them, not turn them into a paste.

1 **For the cookies:** Adjust oven racks to upper-middle and lower-middle positions and heat oven to 350 degrees. Pulse peanuts in food processor until finely chopped, about 8 pulses. Whisk flour, baking soda, and salt together in bowl. Whisk peanut butter, granulated sugar, brown sugar, melted butter, milk, and egg together in second bowl. Using silicone spatula, stir flour mixture into peanut butter mixture until combined. Stir in chopped peanuts until evenly distributed.

2 Drop 1 tablespoon dough mounds evenly onto 2 parchment paper–lined baking sheets (12 mounds per sheet). Using your dampened hand, press each mound until 2 inches in diameter.

3 Bake cookies until deep golden brown and firm to touch, 15 to 18 minutes, switching and rotating sheets halfway through baking. Let cookies cool on sheets for 5 minutes, then transfer to wire rack and let cool completely. (Set aside sheets to cool completely before reusing.) Repeat with remaining dough.

4 **For the filling:** Microwave peanut butter and butter until melted and warm, about 40 seconds. Using silicone spatula, stir in confectioners' sugar. Transfer to pastry bag fitted with ½-inch round or star tip.

5 Holding 1 upturned cookie in your hand, pipe ring of peanut butter cream on top, leaving ⅛-inch border. Spoon 2 teaspoons jam inside peanut butter ring. Place second cookie on top of filling, pressing gently until filling spreads to edges. Repeat with remaining cookies, filling, and jam. Let filling set for 1 hour before serving.

Storage: 3 days at room temperature

Makes 20 sandwiches

Total Time 1¼ hours, plus 1 hour 10 minutes chilling and cooling

COOKIES

- 1¾ cups plus 2 tablespoons (267 grams) all-purpose flour
- 2 tablespoons unsweetened cocoa powder
- ½ teaspoon table salt
- ¼ teaspoon baking powder
- ¼ teaspoon baking soda
- ¾ cup (149 grams) granulated sugar
- ½ cup (105 grams) refined coconut oil
- 2 tablespoons whole milk
- 1 large egg
- 1 teaspoon vanilla extract

FILLING

- 4 tablespoons (57 grams) unsalted butter, softened
- 2 tablespoons plus 2 teaspoons refined coconut oil
- 1⅓ cups (151 grams) confectioners' sugar
- 4 teaspoons unsweetened cocoa powder
- 4 teaspoons malted milk powder
- ½ teaspoon vanilla extract
- ⅛ teaspoon table salt

CHOCOLATE COATING

- 12 ounces (340 grams) milk chocolate (255 grams chopped fine, 85 grams grated)
- 1 tablespoon refined coconut oil

WHY THIS RECIPE WORKS Imagine two tender cocoa-kissed biscuits that bake up firm yet yielding, sandwiching a light malted chocolate filling and totally enrobed in chocolate. There's no need to stop at imagining Tim Tams, Australia's beloved cookie (often called the country's Oreo), when you can make them at home. The trick to making Tim Tams as perfectly pretty as those from an assembly line is mixing coconut oil with the melted chocolate for dipping; this loosens the chocolate for easy dipping, achieves the signature glossy shell and irresistible snap, and seals in the creamy center. We also make use of coconut oil in the cookie for the right texture. Our filling boasts buttery richness and the subtle toastiness of real malt powder. These are the kind of cookie that invites you to pause for tea—or to try the "Tim Tam slam" (biting the ends off a cookie and drinking a hot beverage through it, which melts the filling).

DOUBLE CHOCOLATE TIM TAMS

1 **For the cookies:** Whisk flour, cocoa, salt, baking powder, and baking soda together in bowl. Using pencil and ruler, draw 10 by 6-inch rectangle in center of each of 2 large sheets of parchment paper, crisscrossing lines at corners. (Use crisscrosses to help line up top and bottom sheets as dough is rolled.)

2 Using stand mixer fitted with paddle, beat sugar and oil on medium-high speed until fluffy, about 2 minutes. Reduce speed to low; add milk, egg, and vanilla; and beat until combined, about 30 seconds. Slowly add flour mixture and beat until just combined, about 1 minute, scraping down bowl as needed. Divide dough in half. Place each piece of dough on sheet of plastic wrap and flatten each into 4-inch disk. Wrap each disk tightly in plastic and refrigerate until firm but still malleable, about 20 minutes.

3 Adjust oven racks to upper-middle and lower-middle positions and heat oven to 325 degrees. Line 2 baking sheets with parchment.

4 Place 1 piece of parchment on counter with pencil side facing down (you should be able to see rectangle through paper) and lightly dust with flour. Place 1 piece of dough in center of marked rectangle (keep second piece of dough in refrigerator until ready to roll). Lightly flour top of dough, then place second sheet of parchment over dough with pencil side facing up, so dough is in center of marked rectangle. Using pencil marks as guide, press and roll dough into 10 by 6-inch rectangle of even thickness with rolling pin, squaring sides with bench scraper as you go.

••• CONTINUED •••

5 Gently peel off top layer of parchment. Using sharp knife (or pizza cutter) and ruler, trim off rounded edges of dough that extend over marked edges of 10 by 6-inch rectangle. Cut dough into 4 equal strips about 2½ inches wide. Cut each strip crosswise into 5 equal pieces about 1¼ inches long. Transfer cookies to 2 parchment-lined baking sheets, spacing them at least ¼ inch apart. Repeat with remaining piece of dough, reusing marked sheets of parchment. (You should have 40 rectangles; gently reroll scraps ⅛ inch thick, cut into rectangles, and transfer to prepared sheets if desired.)

6 Bake until cookies are firm and reveal slight indentation when pressed with your finger, 22 to 24 minutes, switching and rotating sheets halfway through baking. Let cookies cool on sheets for 5 minutes, then transfer to wire rack and let cool completely.

7 **For the filling:** Meanwhile, using clean, dry mixer bowl and paddle, mix butter, oil, sugar, cocoa powder, malt powder, vanilla, and salt on medium-low speed until combined, about 1 minute. Increase speed to medium-high and beat until light and fluffy, about 2 minutes. Place half of cookies upside down on counter. Place 1½ teaspoons filling in center of each cookie, then spread filling to edges. Place second cookie on top of filling, right side up, pressing gently to adhere.

8 **For the chocolate coating:** Microwave chopped chocolate in medium bowl at 50 percent power, stirring often, until about two-thirds melted, 2 to 4 minutes. (Melted chocolate should not be much warmer than body temperature; check by holding bowl in palm of your hand.) Add grated chocolate and coconut oil and stir until smooth, returning to microwave for no more than 5 seconds at a time to finish melting if necessary.

9 Place 1 sandwich cookie in chocolate and, using 2 forks, gently flip to fully coat all sides. Lift cookie out of chocolate with fork. Using offset spatula, spread chocolate on top of cookie into thin, even layer, allowing excess to run off sides. Tap fork against edge of bowl, then wipe underside of fork on edge of bowl to remove excess chocolate from bottom of cookie. Using second fork, slide sandwich cookie onto parchment-lined sheet. Run fork in wavy pattern through chocolate. Repeat with remaining sandwich cookies, returning chocolate to microwave for no more than 5 seconds at a time if it becomes too firm. Refrigerate sandwich cookies until chocolate is set, about 20 minutes, before serving.

Storage: 1 week at room temperature

COATING THE COOKIES

1. Place 1 sandwich cookie in chocolate and, using 2 forks, gently flip to fully coat all sides.

2. Lift cookie out of chocolate with fork. Using offset spatula, spread chocolate on top of cookie into thin, even layer.

3. Tap fork against edge of bowl, then wipe underside of fork on edge of bowl to remove excess chocolate from bottom of cookie.

4. Using second fork, slide sandwich cookie onto parchment-lined sheet. Run fork in wavy pattern through chocolate.

1

2

3

4

Makes about 70 cookies

Total Time 1½ hours, plus 1¼ hours chilling and cooling

WHY THIS RECIPE WORKS No longer wanting to count the days until the cookie season arrives, we decided to re-create Thin Mints, the best-selling Girl Scout cookies with a crisp chocolate coating and cool mint flavor. To keep the mint flavor in check, we use peppermint oil in the chocolate coating only and omit it from the chocolate cookie itself. Thin Mints get their ultracrisp, short texture from palm kernel oil, but we found that coconut oil, a saturated fat that the home cook is more likely to have in their pantry, does the trick. Our tempered chocolate-mint coating is just as attractive and crisp as the one from the manufacturer, and—like the Girl Scout variety—these cookies are extra-cool eaten from the freezer.

THIN CHOCOLATE-MINT COOKIES

COOKIES

- 1½ cups (213 grams) all-purpose flour
- ½ cup (43 grams) unsweetened cocoa powder
- ½ teaspoon table salt
- ¼ teaspoon baking powder
- ¼ teaspoon baking soda
- ½ cup (105 grams) refined coconut oil, chilled
- ¾ cup (149 grams) sugar
- 2 tablespoons whole milk
- 1 large egg
- 1 teaspoon vanilla extract

CHOCOLATE COATING

- 1 pound (454 grams) semisweet chocolate (340 grams chopped fine, 114 grams grated)
- ⅛ teaspoon peppermint oil

1 **For the cookies:** Whisk flour, cocoa, salt, baking powder, and baking soda together in bowl. Using stand mixer fitted with paddle, beat oil and sugar on medium-high speed until fluffy, about 2 minutes, scraping down bowl as needed. Reduce speed to low; add milk, egg, and vanilla; and beat until combined, about 30 seconds. Add flour mixture and beat until just combined, about 1 minute. Divide dough in half. Place each piece of dough on sheet of plastic wrap and flatten each into 4-inch disk. Wrap each disk tightly in plastic wrap and refrigerate for at least 45 minutes or up to 3 days.

2 Adjust oven racks to upper-middle and lower-middle positions and heat oven to 350 degrees. Working with 1 disk of dough at a time, roll into ⅛-inch-thick circle, 11 inches wide, between 2 large sheets of lightly floured parchment paper. Remove top piece of parchment. Using 1¾-inch round cookie cutter, cut dough into rounds. Gently reroll scraps up to 2 times and cut into rounds. Space rounds ½ inch apart on 2 parchment-lined baking sheets. Bake until cookies are very firm, 16 to 18 minutes, switching and rotating sheets halfway through baking. Let cookies cool on sheets for 5 minutes, then transfer to wire rack and let cool completely.

3 **For the chocolate coating:** Line baking sheet with parchment. Microwave finely chopped chocolate and oil in bowl at 50 percent power, stirring often, until about two-thirds melted, 2 to 4 minutes. Add grated chocolate and stir until smooth, returning to microwave for no more than 5 seconds at a time to complete melting if necessary.

4 Place 1 cookie on fork and dip bottom of cookie in chocolate. Using offset spatula, spread chocolate over top of cookie, creating thin coating. Transfer cookie to prepared sheet and repeat with remaining cookies. Let cookies sit until chocolate sets, about 15 minutes, before serving.

Storage: 2 weeks at room temperature

Makes 24 sandwich cookies

Total Time 1½ hours, plus 1½ hours chilling and cooling

WHY THIS RECIPE WORKS We have a hard time keeping chocolate out of recipes, and we found a way to sneak it into a souped-up Linzer cookie with deeply flavored black cherry preserves. To accommodate the extra richness from the chocolate, we omit the nuts from the cookie dough and make a more basic butter cookie. To maintain a subtle nutty aroma, we add almond extract (in addition to cinnamon) to perfume the dough. Once the bottom cookies cool, we spread them with melted bittersweet chocolate, which provides deep,dark contrast to the buttery cookie. After it's set we top it with the requisite jam. We like the choice of black cherry preserves, which have a unique, almost wine-y flavor that's a sophisticated match for the dark chocolate and a complementary pairing for the almond-scented dough. With a snow shower of confectioners' sugar, these small sandwich cookies are a hit at the holidays.

BLACK CHERRY AND CHOCOLATE LINZER COOKIES

- 2⅓ cups (331 grams) all-purpose flour
- 1 teaspoon baking powder
- ½ teaspoon table salt
- ½ teaspoon ground cinnamon
- 1 cup (198 grams) superfine sugar
- 12 tablespoons (171 grams) unsalted butter, softened
- 2 large eggs
- ½ teaspoon almond extract
- 1 cup (170 grams) bittersweet chocolate chips
- 1 cup (281 grams) black cherry preserves
- Confectioners' sugar

If you can't find superfine sugar, you can process regular granulated sugar to superfine consistency in about 30 seconds in a food processor. We used a 2½-inch fluted round cutter for the cookies; you can use any shape cookie cutter, though you may get a different number of cookies. Reuse the baking sheets for the cutout cookies once they're cooled to room temperature. You can dust the cookie tops with confectioners' sugar before sandwiching the cookies if desired.

1 Whisk flour, baking powder, salt, and cinnamon together in bowl. Using stand mixer fitted with paddle, beat superfine sugar and butter on medium speed until pale and fluffy, 3 to 5 minutes, scraping down bowl as needed. Add eggs and almond extract and continue to beat until well incorporated, about 1 minute longer. Reduce speed to low; add flour mixture; and mix until dough is uniform, about 1 minute. Divide dough in half. Place each piece of dough on sheet of plastic wrap and flatten each into 5-inch disk. Wrap each disk tightly in plastic and refrigerate for at least 1 hour or up to 3 days.

2 Adjust oven racks to upper-middle and lower-middle positions and heat oven to 375 degrees. Roll 1 disk of dough into ⅛-inch-thick circle, about 13 inches wide, on lightly floured counter. Using 2½-inch cutter, cut dough into 24 cookies, gently gathering scraps and rerolling once; space cookies ½ inch apart on 2 parchment paper–lined baking sheets. Bake until edges are lightly browned, about 7 minutes, switching and rotating sheets halfway through baking. Let cookies cool on sheets for 5 minutes, then transfer to wire rack. (Set aside sheets to cool completely before reusing.)

3 Roll out second disk of dough into ⅛-inch-thick circle, about 13 inches wide. Using 2½-inch cutter, cut dough into 24 cookies, gathering scraps and rerolling once. Using smaller cutter, cut out centers of cookies. Space cookies ½ inch apart on now-empty prepared sheets. Bake until edges are lightly browned, about 7 minutes, switching and rotating sheets halfway through baking. Let cookies cool on sheets for 5 minutes, then transfer to wire rack and let cool completely.

4 Before serving, microwave chocolate chips in bowl at 50 percent power, stirring occasionally, until melted, 2 to 4 minutes. Spread bottom of each solid cookie with chocolate; let sit for 5 minutes until chocolate is set. Spread 2 teaspoons preserves over chocolate on each cookie. Dust tops of cutout cookies with confectioners' sugar. Carefully top bottom cookies with cutout cookies, pressing lightly to adhere.

Storage: 3 days at room temperature

Makes 18 cookies

Total Time 50 minutes, plus 1½ hours chilling, cooling, and setting

WHY THIS RECIPE WORKS Changing the jam filling and adding herbs to the dough are simple but pleasantly surprising ways to put a twist on classic linzer cookies, without detracting from their festive elegance. Here, woodsy thyme gives our crisp cookie a slightly savory edge, while seedless blackberry jam—amped up with lemon zest and infused with a sprig of thyme—provides an eye-catching inky color and subtle earthy undertone. We simmer the jam for just a few minutes and employ a cornstarch–lemon juice slurry to create a thick filling that won't squish out the sides of the cookie.

BLACKBERRY-THYME LINZER COOKIES

- 2 teaspoons cornstarch
- 1 teaspoon grated lemon zest plus 1 teaspoon juice
- ¾ cup (211 grams) seedless blackberry jam
- 1 sprig fresh thyme, plus 2 teaspoons chopped thyme
- ⅔ cup (75 grams) confectioners' sugar
- ½ cup (79 grams) whole blanched almonds, toasted
- 1 cup (142 grams) all-purpose flour
- ½ teaspoon table salt
- 6 tablespoons (86 grams) unsalted butter, cut into ½-inch pieces and chilled
- 1 large egg yolk
- 1 tablespoon heavy cream
- ½ teaspoon vanilla extract
- Confectioners' sugar (optional)

Storage: 3 days at room temperature

Watch the cookies with cutouts because they bake a bit faster. We mixed and matched cutout shapes for a modern look; you can use any shape cookie cutter, though you may get a different number of cookies. You can dust the cookie tops with confectioners' sugar before sandwiching the cookies if desired.

1 Whisk cornstarch and lemon juice together in small bowl; set aside. Bring jam and thyme sprig to simmer in small saucepan over medium heat and cook, stirring frequently, for 3 minutes. Whisk cornstarch mixture into jam and simmer until thickened and glossy, about 2 minutes (jam will continue to thicken as it cools); remove from heat, discard thyme, and let cool completely.

2 While jam cools, process sugar, almonds, chopped thyme, and lemon zest in food processor until almonds are finely ground, about 20 seconds. Add flour, salt, and butter and pulse until mixture resembles coarse meal, 15 to 20 pulses. Add egg yolk, cream, and vanilla, and process until dough forms ball, about 20 seconds. Transfer dough to counter and flatten into 4-inch disk. Wrap disk tightly in plastic wrap and refrigerate for at least 30 minutes or up to 3 days.

3 Adjust oven racks to upper-middle and lower-middle positions and heat oven to 375 degrees. Transfer dough to counter and roll into ⅛-inch-thick circle, about 11 inches wide, on lightly floured counter. Using 2-inch cutter, cut out 18 cookies. Using smaller cutter, cut out centers of cookies. Space cookies ¾ inch apart on parchment paper–lined baking sheet. Gather and reroll scraps, then use 2-inch cutter to cut out 18 more cookies (do not cut out centers); space them ¾ inch apart on second parchment paper–lined baking sheet. (You should have 18 solid and 18 cutout cookies.) Bake until edges are lightly browned, about 8 minutes, switching and rotating sheets halfway through baking. Let cookies cool on sheets for 5 minutes, then transfer to wire rack and let cool completely.

4 Spread bottom of each solid cookie with 1 teaspoon jam. Dust tops of cutout cookies with confectioners' sugar, if desired. Carefully top bottom cookies with cutout cookies, pressing lightly to adhere. Let cookies set for 30 minutes before serving.

ATK CLASSIC

Makes about 32 cookies

Total Time 1¾ hours, plus 30 minutes cooling

Biscotti literally means "twice baked"; they're baked once as a single oblong loaf and then sliced into thin planks, which are returned to the oven to fully dry. Italians typically like their biscotti dry and hard, whereas Americans tend to favor a buttery, tender version. We wanted a cookie that falls in between, one that has plenty of crunch but isn't tooth-breaking. Biscotti made with little (or no) fat are rocks, while doughs enriched with a full stick of butter bake up too soft. We found 4 tablespoons to be just the right balance, making a cookie that's both crunchy and tender. Whipping the eggs provides lift, and swapping in ground almonds for some of the flour makes the cookies more tender by breaking up the crumb and interrupting gluten development. The fragrant slices are perfect alongside a cup of coffee—or, as in Italy, a glass of sweet vin santo.

ALMOND BISCOTTI

- 1¼ cups (196 grams) whole almonds, lightly toasted, divided
- 1¾ cups (249 grams) all-purpose flour
- 2 teaspoons baking powder
- ¼ teaspoon table salt
- 2 large eggs, plus 1 large white beaten with pinch table salt
- 1 cup (198 grams) sugar
- 4 tablespoons (57 grams) unsalted butter, melted and cooled
- 1½ teaspoons almond extract
- ½ teaspoon vanilla extract

Storage: 1 month at room temperature

The almonds will continue to toast during baking, so toast them just until they're fragrant.

1 Adjust oven rack to middle position and heat oven to 325 degrees. Using ruler and pencil, draw two 8 by 3-inch rectangles, spaced 4 inches apart, on sheet of parchment paper. Grease rimmed baking sheet and place parchment on it, pencil side down.

2 Pulse 1 cup almonds in food processor until coarsely chopped, 8 to 10 pulses; transfer to bowl and set aside. Process remaining ¼ cup almonds in now-empty food processor until finely ground, about 45 seconds. Add flour, baking powder, and salt; process to combine, about 15 seconds; transfer to large bowl. Process 2 eggs in now-empty food processor until lightened in color and almost doubled in volume, about 3 minutes. With processor running, slowly add sugar until thoroughly combined, about 15 seconds. Add melted butter, almond extract, and vanilla and process until combined, about 10 seconds. Transfer egg mixture to bowl with flour mixture along with chopped almonds and fold until just combined.

3 Divide dough in half. Using your lightly oiled hands, form each half into 8 by 3-inch rectangle, using lines on parchment as guide and smoothing tops and sides of loaves. Gently brush tops of rectangles with egg white mixture.

4 Bake until loaves are golden and just beginning to crack on top, 25 to 30 minutes, rotating sheet halfway through baking. Let loaves cool on sheet for 30 minutes, then transfer to cutting board. Set wire rack in rimmed baking sheet. Using serrated knife and gentle sawing motion, slice each loaf on slight bias into ½-inch-thick slices. Arrange slices, cut side down, about ¼ inch apart on prepared rack. Bake until crisp and golden brown on both sides, 25 to 30 minutes, flipping slices and rotating sheet halfway through baking. Let biscotti cool completely on wire rack before serving.

For Perfectly *Crunchy-Tender* Biscotti

- **Use moderate butter** Four tablespoons of butter—more than in Italian versions but less than in American—makes dough that's neither too hard nor too rich.
- **Whip the whole eggs** Whipping the eggs gives the dough lift so it's not dense.
- **Grind some of the almonds** Cutting the flour with an almond meal interrupts the gluten matrix and creates microscopic fault lines in the crumb that make it easy to bite through.

Biscotti *Swaps*

- **Go nuts** Make biscotti with pistachios (see page 188) or hazelnuts (see page 190), which have a similar amount of fat as almonds.

- **Flavor liberally** Don't be shy when changing the extract to vanilla or trying a spirit or floral water; or adding spices or citrus zest.

- **Mix in other flavors** Bring chocolate or fruit into the equation by replacing some of the chopped nuts with chopped bar chocolate or dried fruit.

For Double-Baked Cookies, Double– or Triple–the Spice

While turning out batch after batch of biscotti, we noticed that many of the flavors we added to the dough, such as almond extract and aromatic orange zest, started off strong and fragrant but faded once the cookies had baked twice, since the successive exposure to heat kills off many of their volatile flavor compounds. To compensate, we loaded up on them, in some cases tripling the amount we started with.

Shaping Biscotti

1 Form each half into 8 by 3-inch rectangle, using lines on parchment as guide, and smooth tops and sides of loaves, and gently brush tops with egg white beaten with salt.

2 Bake until loaves are golden and just beginning to crack on top. Let loaves cool on sheet for 30 minutes, then, using serrated knife and gentle sawing motion, slice each loaf on slight bias into ½-inch-thick slices.

3 Arrange slices, cut side down, about ¼ inch apart on prepared rack.

4 Bake until crisp and golden brown on both sides, 25 to 30 minutes, flipping slices and rotating sheet halfway through baking.

1

2

3

4

WHY THIS RECIPE WORKS Without being overtly spicy, pink peppercorns lend bright, zingy flavor to anything they touch, with desserts like these crisp biscotti being a great place for them. A bit of a misnomer, the little red spheres aren't actually peppercorns, but the ripe berries of the Peruvian (*Schinus molle*) and Brazilian (*Schinus terebinthifolius*) pepper trees. We experimented with different quantities of the spice, both in the dough and sprinkled on top, and arrived at what we think is the perfect amount to uplift our cookies without being overpowering. We bring out the citrusy notes of pink peppercorns with more citrus in the form of orange zest. Pistachios add contrasting color and texture, and a finishing drizzle of melted white chocolate tempers the kick of the peppercorns and elevates the biscotti to special-occasion status.

Makes about 32 cookies

Total Time 1¾ hours, plus 1 hour cooling and setting

PINK PEPPERCORN–PISTACHIO BISCOTTI WITH WHITE CHOCOLATE

- 1¼ cups (181 grams) shelled pistachios, divided
- 1¾ cups (249 grams) all-purpose flour
- 2 teaspoons baking powder
- ½ teaspoon table salt
- 2 large eggs
- 1 cup (198 grams) sugar
- 4 tablespoons (57 grams) unsalted butter, melted and cooled
- 1 tablespoon grated orange zest
- 2 teaspoons vanilla extract
- 2 tablespoons pink peppercorns, divided
- ¾ cup (128 grams) white chocolate chips

1 Adjust oven rack to middle position and heat oven to 325 degrees. Using ruler and pencil, draw two 8 by 3-inch rectangles, spaced 4 inches apart, on sheet of parchment paper. Grease rimmed baking sheet and place parchment on it, pencil side down.

2 Process ¼ cup pistachios in food processor until finely ground, about 45 seconds. Add flour, baking powder, and salt and process until combined, about 15 seconds; transfer to large bowl. Process eggs in now-empty processor until lightened in color and almost doubled in volume, about 3 minutes. With processor running, slowly add sugar until thoroughly combined, about 15 seconds. Add melted butter, orange zest, and vanilla and process until combined, about 10 seconds. Transfer egg mixture to bowl with flour mixture along with 1 tablespoon peppercorns and remaining pistachios and fold until just combined.

3 Divide dough in half. Using your lightly oiled hands, form each half into 8 by 3-inch rectangle, using lines on parchment as guide and smoothing tops and sides of loaves. Bake until loaves are golden and just beginning to crack on top, 25 to 30 minutes, rotating sheet halfway through baking.

4 Let loaves cool on sheet for 30 minutes, then transfer to cutting board. Using serrated knife and gentle sawing motion, slice each loaf on slight bias into ½-inch-thick slices. Lay slices cut side down, about ¼ inch apart, on wire rack set in rimmed baking sheet. Bake until crisp and golden brown on both sides, 25 to 30 minutes, flipping slices and rotating sheet halfway through baking. Let biscotti cool completely on wire rack.

5 Lightly crush remaining 1 tablespoon peppercorns using bottom of dry measuring cup. Microwave white chocolate in bowl at 50 percent power, stirring occasionally, until melted, 2 to 4 minutes. Drizzle biscotti decoratively with chocolate and sprinkle with crushed peppercorns. Let biscotti sit until chocolate is firm, about 30 minutes, before serving.

Storage: 1 month at room temperature

WHY THIS RECIPE WORKS Twice-baked cookies are twice as nice if chocolate-flavored. But chocolate biscotti can fall short on chocolate flavor due to the extra time drying in the oven, which can dull the delicate flavor compounds. For intensely chocolaty biscotti, we start with cocoa powder (plus some espresso powder) because it carries intense chocolate flavor and is easy to incorporate. For the requisite nutty element, we love hazelnuts, a favorite partner to chocolate. Lightly toasting the nuts gives them roasty flavor to balance the chocolate. These cookies are so rich in taste that the typical chocolate dip is unnecessary.

Makes about 32 cookies

Total Time 1¾ hours, plus 30 minutes cooling

CHOCOLATE-HAZELNUT BISCOTTI

- 1¼ cups (179 grams) hazelnuts, toasted and skinned, divided
- 1¼ cups (178 grams) all-purpose flour
- ½ cup (43 grams) unsweetened cocoa powder
- 2 teaspoons baking powder
- 1 teaspoon instant espresso powder
- ¼ teaspoon table salt
- 2 large eggs, plus 1 large white beaten with pinch salt
- 1 cup (198 grams) sugar
- 4 tablespoons (57 grams) unsalted butter, melted and cooled
- ½ teaspoon vanilla extract

Storage: 1 month at room temperature

1 Adjust oven rack to middle position and heat oven to 325 degrees. Using ruler and pencil, draw two 8 by 3-inch rectangles, spaced 4 inches apart, on piece of parchment paper. Grease rimmed baking sheet and place parchment on it, pencil side down.

2 Pulse 1 cup hazelnuts in food processor until coarsely chopped, 8 to 10 pulses; transfer to bowl and set aside. Process remaining ¼ cup hazelnuts in now-empty processor until finely ground, about 45 seconds. Add flour, cocoa, baking powder, espresso powder, and salt and process until combined, about 15 seconds; transfer flour mixture to large bowl.

3 Process 2 eggs in now-empty processor until lightened in color and almost doubled in volume, about 3 minutes. With processor running, slowly add sugar until thoroughly combined, about 15 seconds. Add melted butter and vanilla and process until combined, about 10 seconds. Transfer egg mixture to bowl. Sprinkle half of flour mixture over egg mixture and, using silicone spatula, gently fold until just combined. Add remaining flour mixture and chopped hazelnuts and gently fold until just combined.

4 Divide dough in half. Using your lightly oiled hands, form each half into 8 by 3-inch rectangle, using lines on parchment as guide and smoothing tops and sides of loaves. Gently brush tops of rectangles with egg white mixture. Bake until loaves are set and beginning to crack on top, 25 to 30 minutes, rotating sheet halfway through baking.

5 Let loaves cool on baking sheet for 30 minutes. Transfer loaves to cutting board. Using serrated knife and gentle sawing motion, slice each loaf on slight bias into ½-inch-thick slices. Lay slices cut side down, about ¼ inch apart, on wire rack set in rimmed baking sheet. Bake until crisp on both sides, about 35 minutes, flipping slices and rotating sheet halfway through baking. Let biscotti cool completely on wire rack, about 1 hour, before serving.

Chapter 4

BUTTER MAKES IT BETTER

ATK CLASSIC

Makes 28 cookies

Total Time 45 minutes, plus 2 hours chilling, cooling, and resting

Shortbread looks humble, but there's a reason it's one of the British Isles' most famous tea cakes—and might just be your favorite cookie. Good shortbread has a tawny brown color, and its crumb should be, as the name suggests, "short," meaning that it's very tender from limited gluten formation and crumbles with pure, buttery richness. For this exemplary version, we use confectioners' sugar for the sweetener to avoid granularity in the crumb, and we employ the reverse creaming mixing method (see page 32) to curb gluten development and create less aeration. To limit gluten formation further, we look to shortbread's past and replace some of the flour with ground oats and a modest amount of cornstarch. (Scottish shortbread was first a way to turn leftover oat bread into something special.) Not every recipe with the shortbread moniker follows these rules, but when you want something classic that nods to the original Scottish shortbread, they're the best way to get there. And while these buttery cookies are delicious as they are, we like to elevate and brighten them with a raspberry glaze. (You can omit the glaze or dip the shortbread in melted chocolate, if you like.)

RASPBERRY-DIPPED SHORTBREAD

SHORTBREAD

- ½ cup (43 grams) old-fashioned rolled oats
- 1½ cups (213 grams) all-purpose flour
- ⅔ cup (76 grams) confectioners' sugar
- ¼ cup (28 grams) cornstarch
- ½ teaspoon table salt
- 14 tablespoons (200 grams) unsalted butter, cut into ⅛-inch-thick slices and chilled

RASPBERRY GLAZE

- ½ cup freeze-dried raspberries
- ½ cup (105 grams) refined coconut oil
- ¾ cup (85 grams) confectioners' sugar

Storage: 1 week at room temperature

1 For the shortbread: Pulse oats in spice grinder until reduced to fine powder, about ten 5-second pulses (you should have ⅓ cup oat flour; discard any extra). Using stand mixer fitted with paddle, mix oat flour, all-purpose flour, sugar, cornstarch, and salt on low speed until combined. Add butter and mix until dough just forms and pulls away from sides of bowl, 5 to 10 minutes.

2 Transfer dough to center of sheet of plastic wrap. Draw edges of plastic over dough and press firmly on sides and top to form rough 8 by 6-inch rectangle. Wrap in plastic wrap and use bench scraper to press sides and top into smooth, compact 7 by 5-inch rectangle, adjusting plastic as needed. Refrigerate dough until firm, at least 30 minutes or up to 3 days.

3 Adjust oven rack to middle position and heat oven to 425 degrees. Using chef's knife, cut dough in half lengthwise (you should have two 7-inch-long by 2½-inch-wide rectangles). Cut rectangles crosswise into ½-inch-thick slices (you should have 28 slices) and space them about ½ inch apart on parchment paper–lined baking sheet.

4 If desired, use wooden skewer or fork to poke 8 to 10 holes in center of each slice. Place sheet in oven and immediately reduce oven temperature to 300 degrees. Bake until pale golden, 20 to 30 minutes, rotating sheet halfway through baking. Transfer sheet to wire rack and let cool completely.

5 **For the raspberry glaze:** Set wire rack in parchment paper–lined rimmed baking sheet. Pulse freeze-dried raspberries in spice grinder until reduced to fine powder, about 5 pulses (you should have ⅓ cup fruit powder). Sift powder through fine-mesh strainer to remove any seeds; discard seeds. Microwave oil in bowl at 50 percent power, stirring occasionally, until melted, 1 to 2 minutes. Stir in fruit powder and sugar until completely smooth. Working quickly with 1 shortbread cookie at a time, dip half of cookie into glaze. Lift up from glaze (do not turn upright) and gently shake side to side to allow excess coating to drip off evenly. Transfer (upright) to prepared rack and let sit until firm, about 1 hour. (If glaze begins to solidify during dipping, microwave until fluid, about 10 seconds. Stir to recombine before continuing.)

How We Achieve *Tender* Raspberry-Dipped Shortbread

- **Reverse cream** Adding butter to the dry ingredients when mixing coats them with fat to prevent excess gluten development.
- **Use confectioners' sugar** The fine sugar goes texturally undetected in the cookie.
- **Reduce gluten** Replacing some of the flour with oats and cornstarch reduces the gluten content while ensuring deep flavor.

Shortest in Class
Reverse creaming ground oats, cornstarch, and confectioners' sugar with lots of butter prevents aeration for a fine texture and minimizes gluten development to keep the crumb charmingly short.

Slicing Shortbread

1 Using bench scraper to press sides and top into smooth, compact 7 by 5-inch rectangle; refrigerate until firm.

2 Using chef's knife, cut dough in half lengthwise (you should have two 7-inch-long by 2½-inch-wide rectangles).

3 Cut rectangles crosswise into ½-inch-thick slices (you should have 28 slices).

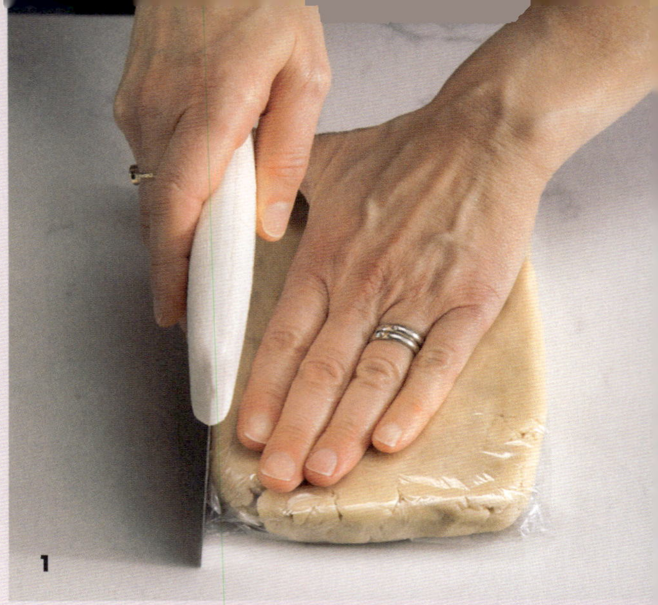

Coating Cookies

1 Working quickly with 1 cookie at a time, dip half of cookie into mixture.

2 Lift up from mixture (do not turn upright) and gently shake side to side to allow excess coating to drip off evenly.

3 Transfer (upright) to wire rack and let sit until firm, about 1 hour.

Creative *Shortbread* Takes

- **Shape it** Instead of slicing and baking, roll and cut out dough into desired shapes (see page 202) or create wedges, a traditional technique (see page 198).

- **Flavor it** Shortbread is a blank canvas for adding extracts or mix-ins or dipping in chocolate instead of coating.

- **Color it** Coating warm shortbread in a mixture of ground freeze-dried fruit and confectioners' sugar (see page 202) colors the cookie and gives it a fruity finish.

Makes 16 wedges

Total Time 1¼ hours, plus 50 minutes chilling and cooling

WHY THIS RECIPE WORKS Baked in traditional wedges but (clearly) boasting a chocolate update, this shortbread is flavored singularly by unsweetened cocoa powder. Melted chocolate, with its high fat content, would make the already butter-filled dough too soft. We like the clear chocolate flavor of the cocoa and we reduce some of the flour to accommodate it (just ¼ cup cocoa delivers big chocolate flavor). Rolling the dough on parchment paper prevents it from sticking, and baking the shortbread on a double layer of parchment helps absorb some of the rich cookie's butter. An optional sprinkling of granulated sugar gives the chocolate-brown shortbread some sparkling dimension.

CHOCOLATE SHORTBREAD

- 2 cups (284 grams) all-purpose flour
- ¼ cup (21 grams) Dutch-processed cocoa powder
- ½ teaspoon table salt
- 16 tablespoons (228 grams) unsalted butter, softened
- ½ cup (57 grams) confectioners' sugar
- 1 tablespoon granulated sugar (optional)

1 Whisk flour, cocoa, and salt together in bowl. Using stand mixer fitted with paddle, beat butter and confectioners' sugar on medium speed until pale and fluffy, 3 to 5 minutes. Reduce speed to low; add flour mixture; and mix until dough is uniform, about 1 minute.

2 Using your hands, press dough into cohesive ball in bowl. Transfer dough to lightly floured counter and knead until very smooth, about 3 minutes. Press dough into disk. Roll dough into 9-inch round (about ½ inch thick) on sheet of parchment paper.

3 Transfer dough and parchment to parchment-lined baking sheet. Using your fingers, flute dough edge, then poke dough all over with fork and score into 16 wedges. Cover with plastic wrap and refrigerate dough for at least 20 minutes or up to 24 hours.

4 Adjust oven rack to middle position and heat oven to 300 degrees. Sprinkle granulated sugar, if using, evenly over dough. Bake shortbread until edges are firm and indentation partially fills back in when pressed, 40 to 45 minutes, rotating sheet halfway through baking.

5 Transfer sheet to wire rack and, using chef's knife, cut through scored marks into separate wedges. Let shortbread cool on sheet for 10 minutes, then transfer wedges to wire rack. Let shortbread cool completely before serving.

Storage: 1 week at room temperature

Makes 54 cookies

Total Time 1¼ hours, plus 2½ hours cooling

WHY THIS RECIPE WORKS Browned butter makes just about anything better, and this shortbread is salty-sweet, with toasty notes and really rich, nutty depth. Melted butter makes tough, greasy shortbread, so after we brown the butter—20 tablespoons of it—we cool it back to solid form before creaming it with sugar and a little milk powder. The granulated sugar caramelizes and the milk powder emphasizes the sweet dairy notes in the butter. This shortbread is great for gifts that will surprise recipients with remarkable butterscotch flavor.

BROWNED BUTTER SHORTBREAD

- 20 tablespoons (285 grams/ 2½ sticks) unsalted butter
- 2 cups (284 grams) all-purpose flour
- 1 teaspoon table salt
- ½ teaspoon baking powder
- ½ teaspoon baking soda
- 1⅓ cups (264 grams) sugar
- ¼ cup (21 grams) nonfat dry milk powder
- 2 teaspoons vanilla extract
- 2 teaspoons water

Storage: 1 week at room temperature

If preferred, in step 1, you can cool the browned butter in the refrigerator until opaque, about 30 minutes. A rimless cookie sheet helps achieve evenly baked cookies; if you do not have one, use an overturned rimmed baking sheet.

1 Adjust oven rack to middle position and heat oven to 325 degrees. Heat butter in 12-inch skillet over medium-high heat until melted, about 2 minutes. Continue to cook, swirling skillet and stirring constantly with silicone spatula, until butter is dark golden brown and has nutty aroma, 1 to 3 minutes. Scrape browned butter and any milk solids at bottom of skillet into bowl of stand mixer; let cool until opaque in color and completely cool, about 2 hours.

2 Whisk flour, salt, baking powder, and baking soda together in bowl. Using stand mixer fitted with paddle, beat cooled butter, sugar, and milk powder on medium speed until pale and fluffy, 3 to 5 minutes, scraping down bowl as needed. Add vanilla and water and continue to beat until well incorporated, about 1 minute longer. Reduce speed to low; add flour mixture; and mix until dough is uniform, about 1 minute.

3 Transfer dough to counter and divide in half. Working with 1 piece of dough at a time (keep remaining piece covered with plastic wrap), place in center of large sheet of parchment paper and press into 4-inch square. Top with second large sheet parchment then roll dough, between parchment, into 10-inch square (about ¼ inch thick). Remove top piece of parchment.

4 Using pizza cutter or chef's knife, trim away outer ½ inch of dough to make clean square shape with neat edges. Cut dough lengthwise into three 3-inch-wide strips, then cut crosswise into nine 1-inch-wide strips (you should have 27 rectangles). Slide sheet of parchment onto rimless baking sheet (leaving cookies touching). Repeat with remaining dough.

5 Bake cookies, 1 sheet at a time, until edges are just golden, 17 to 19 minutes, rotating sheet halfway through baking. Let cookies cool on sheet for 10 minutes. Using chef's knife, recut shortbread to separate, then let cool completely on sheet before serving.

Makes 16 cookies

Total Time 1¼ hours, plus 1¼ hours chilling and cooling

WHY THIS RECIPE WORKS This pretty purple cookie is inspired by a memorable lavender shortbread that recipe developer Stephanie Winter enjoyed on a trip to the San Juan Islands of Washington state, where the herb grows abundantly. The flavor lent itself to additions in her own cookie: lemon and vibrant blueberry, which she adds in two impactful ways. Dried blueberries distribute bits of chew throughout the cookie, which she makes satisfyingly thick. Deviating from our Raspberry-Dipped Shortbread (page 194), she creams the butter and sugar so she can use the mixer to distribute the berries and give the surrounding crumb a bit of lift. After baking, she coats the cookies in a mixture of ground freeze-dried blueberries and confectioners' sugar, made whimsical with the (optional) addition of edible glitter. The blueberry flavor hits the palate right away, punctuated by dried berries and perfumed delicately by lavender and lemon.

SPARKLING BLUEBERRY-LAVENDER SHORTBREAD COOKIES

COOKIES

- 14 tablespoons (200 grams) unsalted butter, cut into ½-inch pieces and chilled
- ⅔ cup (75 grams) confectioners' sugar
- ½ cup (83 grams) dried blueberries
- 1 tablespoon grated lemon zest
- 1½ teaspoons dried lavender
- ½ teaspoon table salt
- 2 cups (284 grams) all-purpose flour

BLUEBERRY SUGAR

- 1 cup freeze dried blueberries, divided
- ¼ cup (28 grams) confectioners' sugar, divided
- ¼ teaspoon edible glitter (optional)

We used a 2¼-inch flower cutter; you can use any shape cookie cutter, though you may get a different number of cookies. Be sure to coat the cookies while they're still warm or the blueberry sugar won't adhere uniformly. (Rewarm the cookies if necessary; see page 9.)

1 **For the cookies:** Using stand mixer fitted with paddle, beat butter, sugar, dried blueberries, lemon zest, lavender, and salt on medium speed until pale and fluffy, 3 to 5 minutes, scraping down bowl as needed. Add flour and mix on low speed until no dry flour remains, about 30 seconds. Scrape down bowl, then beat on medium-low speed until dough forms, about 1 minute.

2 Using your hands, press dough into cohesive ball in bowl. Transfer to lightly floured counter and roll dough into ½-inch-thick circle (about 9 inches wide). Using 2¼-inch cutter, cut dough into 16 cookies, gathering scraps and rerolling once; space cookies ½ inch apart on parchment paper–lined baking sheet. Cover sheet with plastic wrap and refrigerate for at least 45 minutes or up to 24 hours.

3 Adjust oven rack to middle position and heat oven to 300 degrees. Bake shortbread until edges are just starting to turn golden brown and indentation partially fills in when pressed, 35 to 40 minutes, rotating sheet halfway through baking. Transfer sheet to wire rack and let cool for 5 minutes.

4 **For the blueberry sugar:** While cookies bake, pulse half of freeze-dried blueberries with 2 tablespoons sugar in spice grinder until reduced to fine powder, about 5 pulses. Sift blueberry sugar through fine mesh strainer into shallow dish. Repeat with remaining freeze-dried blueberries and remaining 2 tablespoons sugar. Whisk in edible glitter, if using.

5 Working quickly with 1 cookie at a time, toss in blueberry sugar to coat and gently tap to remove excess. Transfer to wire rack and let cool completely before serving.

Storage: 1 week at room temperature

Makes 40 cookies

Total Time 1¼ hours, plus 1 hour 50 minutes cooling

WHY THIS RECIPE WORKS Millionaire's shortbread is a fitting name for this rich British cookie/confectionery hybrid that features a crunchy shortbread base; a chewy, caramel-like filling; and a shiny, snappy chocolate top. (Incidentally, its doppelgänger, the Twix bar, was also invented in the UK, but these rich, substantial cookies are even better.) The pat-in-the pan base comes together easily with melted butter—no mixer or food processor required. Sweetened condensed milk in the caramel portion gives it a luxurious creaminess. The snappy top layer breaks to reveal luscious caramel and buttery cookie.

MILLIONAIRE'S SHORTBREAD

CRUST

- 2½ cups (355 grams) all-purpose flour
- ½ cup (99 grams) granulated sugar
- ¾ teaspoon table salt
- 16 tablespoons (228 grams) unsalted butter, melted

FILLING

- 1 (14-ounce) can sweetened condensed milk
- 1 cup packed (198 grams) brown sugar
- ½ cup (116 grams) heavy cream
- ½ cup (164 grams) corn syrup
- 8 tablespoons (114 grams) unsalted butter
- ½ teaspoon table salt

CHOCOLATE

- 8 ounces (227 grams) bittersweet chocolate (170 grams chopped fine, 57 grams grated)

Storage: 1 week at room temperature

1 For the crust: Adjust oven rack to lower-middle position and heat oven to 350 degrees. Make foil sling for 13 by 9-inch baking pan by folding 2 long sheets of aluminum foil; first sheet should be 13 inches wide and second sheet should be 9 inches wide. Lay sheets of foil in pan perpendicular to each other, with extra foil hanging over edges of pan. Push foil into corners and up sides of pan, smoothing foil flush to pan. Grease foil.

2 Combine flour, sugar, and salt in medium bowl. Add melted butter and stir with silicone spatula until flour is evenly moistened. Crumble dough evenly over bottom of prepared pan and press firmly into even layer. Using fork, pierce dough at 1-inch intervals. Bake until light golden brown and firm to touch, 25 to 30 minutes. Transfer pan to wire rack. Using sturdy metal spatula, press on entire surface of warm crust to compress (this will make finished bars easier to cut). Let crust cool until it is just warm, at least 20 minutes.

3 For the filling: Stir all ingredients together in large, heavy-bottomed saucepan. Cook over medium heat, stirring frequently, until mixture registers between 236 and 239 degrees (temperature will fluctuate), 16 to 20 minutes. Pour over crust and spread to even thickness (mixture will be very hot). Let cool completely, about 1½ hours.

4 For the chocolate: Microwave chopped chocolate in bowl at 50 percent power, stirring every 15 seconds, until melted but not much warmer than body temperature (check by holding bowl in palm of your hand), 1 to 2 minutes. Add grated chocolate and stir until smooth, returning to microwave for no more than 5 seconds at a time to finish melting if necessary. Spread chocolate evenly over surface of filling. Refrigerate shortbread until chocolate is just set, about 10 minutes.

5 Before serving, use foil overhang to lift shortbread out of pan and transfer to cutting board; discard foil. Using serrated knife and gentle sawing motion, cut shortbread in half crosswise to create two 9 by 6½-inch rectangles. Cut each rectangle in half to make four 9 by 3¼-inch strips. Cut each strip crosswise into 10 pieces.

Sablé means "sandy" in French, and that texture defines these butter cookies—if you can capture it. We took every measure to achieve a sweet, buttery cookie with the lightness and inviting granular texture that separates sablés from shortbread. We learned that removing moisture from the cookie made it so that the granulated sugar couldn't completely dissolve in the baked cookie, creating a crumbly texture. So we removed moisture to the max. First we cut back on butter (which is 20 percent water), then we removed the egg white and used just the yolk. This made a dryer dough but we wanted to do even better. We found recipes that hard-boil the egg yolk (which is 50 percent water) before creaming it with the butter, and this made a supremely sandy cookie.

Makes about 40 cookies

Total Time 55 minutes, plus 2½ hours chilling and cooling

SABLÉS

- 1 large egg, plus 1 large egg white, lightly beaten with 1 teaspoon water
- 10 tablespoons (143 grams) unsalted butter, softened
- ⅓ cup plus 1 tablespoon (78 grams) granulated sugar
- ¼ teaspoon table salt
- 1 teaspoon vanilla extract
- 1½ cups (213 grams) all-purpose flour
- 4 teaspoons turbinado sugar

1 Place egg in small saucepan, cover with water by 1 inch, and bring to boil over high heat. Remove pan from heat, cover, and let sit for 10 minutes. Meanwhile, fill small bowl with ice water. Using slotted spoon, transfer egg to ice water and let stand for 5 minutes. Crack egg and peel shell. Separate yolk from white; discard white. Press yolk through fine-mesh strainer into bowl of stand mixer.

2 Add butter, granulated sugar, and salt to cooked egg yolk in bowl of stand mixer, then beat with paddle on medium speed until pale and fluffy, 3 to 5 minutes, scraping down bowl as needed. Add vanilla and continue to beat until well incorporated. Reduce speed to low; add flour; and mix until just combined, about 30 seconds. Using silicone spatula, press dough into cohesive mass.

3 Transfer dough to counter and divide in half. Roll each piece of dough into 6-inch log. Wrap logs tightly in plastic wrap and twist ends tightly to seal; chill until firm, at least 2 hours in refrigerator or 45 minutes in freezer. (Wrapped dough can be refrigerated for up to 3 days or frozen for up to 2 weeks. Thaw in refrigerator before slicing and baking.)

4 Adjust oven racks to upper-middle and lower-middle positions and heat oven to 350 degrees. Working with 1 dough log at a time, slice chilled dough into ¼-inch-thick rounds, rotating dough as you slice to prevent any flat edges from forming; space dough rounds 1 inch apart on 2 parchment paper–lined baking sheets. Using pastry brush, gently brush cookies with egg white mixture and sprinkle evenly with turbinado sugar.

5 Bake cookies until centers are pale golden brown and edges are slightly darker than centers, about 15 minutes, switching and rotating sheets halfway through baking. Let cookies cool on sheets for 5 minutes, then transfer to wire rack. Let cookies cool completely before serving.

Storage: 1 week at room temperature

Chocolate Sablés

Reduce flour to 1⅓ cups (189 grams) and add ¼ cup (21 grams) Dutch-processed cocoa powder with flour in step 2.

ATK CLASSIC

How We Achieve *Sandy* Sablés

- **Dry it out** Limiting the moisture in cookie dough reduces how much sugar is dissolved, leaving behind intact granules that deliver a sandy consistency.
- **Scale back** the butter This is meant to be a rich cookie, but keep the butter in check, as it's 20 percent water.
- **Lose the egg white** This short cookie doesn't need the watery egg white.
- **Hard-boil the yolk** This is the last step for reducing any bit of excess moisture.

Seeing the Sand

Sablés get a compact, sandy texture from visible granulated sugar that's undissolved in the cookie.

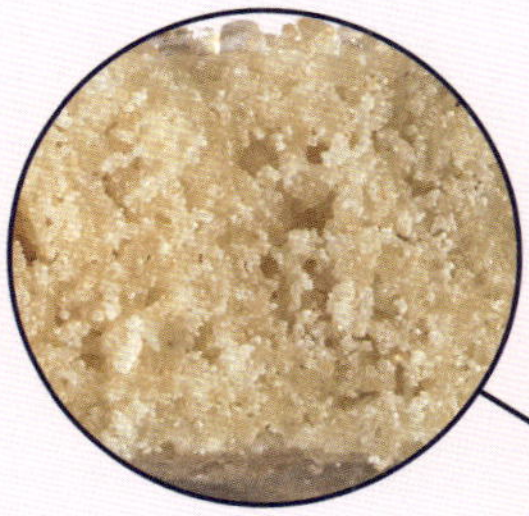

Standard Shortbread has a fine crumb from reverse creaming, cornstarch, and plenty of butter; confectioners' sugar goes undetected.

Hard Boiled and Baked

In our quest to reduce the moisture in our sablé dough, we used just the egg yolk (which is about 50 percent water, compared to the white's 90 percent) instead of a whole egg. The perfectionist's (that's us!) upgrade, however, is to use hard-cooked egg yolks. We press a hard-cooked egg yolk through a fine-mesh strainer before adding it with the other ingredients. Once cooked, the yolk's water becomes unavailable to dissolve sugar, which means the sugar's crystalline texture remains in the baked and cooled cookie. And don't worry; there are no bits of egg in the final cookie.

Making Spirals

At their simplest, sablés are shaped like icebox cookies (see page 214); the dough is rolled into a log, chilled, and then sliced into rounds. But this style of cookie lends itself to shapes. We love how graphic these Black and White Spirals are. They use the classic dough and the chocolate variation. Follow these steps and photos to try them yourself.

Creative *Sablé* Takes

- **Flavor it** You can add your favorite extract to the dough in place of the vanilla, or follow our steps to flavoring the dough with saffron (see page 200) or chocolate (see page 206).

- **Add contrast** Create new textures by breaking up the sandy cookie with chopped mix-ins like nuts or chocolate chunks.

1

2

Black and White Spiral Sablés

1 Make 1 batch each of plain and chocolate dough. Divide each batch in half and roll each dough portion into 8 by 6-inch rectangle on parchment paper.

2 Stack 1 rectangle of chilled plain dough on top of 1 rectangle of chilled chocolate dough and square edges.

3 Roll dough stack into 9 by 6-inch rectangle. Starting at long end, roll dough into tight pinwheel log. Repeat with remaining dough.

3

WHY THIS RECIPE WORKS Earthy pistachio and aromatic saffron pair in many cultures throughout West Asia, South Asia, and Europe, and this elegant, modestly rich butter cookie gives the nut and spice duo a place to shine—in taste and brilliant color too! To infuse flavor, we had to work around the core discovery in our sablés: We get the sandiest texture from eliminating as much moisture as possible; meanwhile, saffron's flavor compounds are mostly water soluble. Since we didn't need the aroma of vanilla extract here, we removed it and steeped the saffron in just 1 teaspoon of hot water so we didn't add more liquid. Adding half the pistachios (ground) to the dough and reserving the rest (chopped) for coating the slice-and-bake logs distributes the taste and provides a pretty finish without compromising the cookie's crisp texture.

Makes about 40 cookies

Total Time 1 hour, plus 2½ hours chilling and cooling

SAFFRON SABLÉS WITH PISTACHIOS

- 1 large egg, plus 1 large egg white, lightly beaten with 1 teaspoon water
- ¼ teaspoon saffron threads, crumbled
- ½ cup (73 grams) shelled pistachios
- 1¼ cups (178 grams) all-purpose flour
- ½ teaspoon table salt
- 10 tablespoons (143 grams) unsalted butter, softened
- ⅓ cup plus 1 tablespoon (78 grams) sugar

1 Place egg in small saucepan, cover with 1 inch water, and bring to boil over high heat. Remove pan from heat, cover, and let sit 10 minutes. Meanwhile, fill small bowl with ice water. Using slotted spoon, transfer egg to ice water and let stand for 5 minutes. Crack egg and peel shell. Separate yolk from white; discard white. Press yolk through fine-mesh strainer into bowl of stand mixer; set aside. Combine 1 teaspoon hot water and saffron in small bowl and let steep for 5 minutes.

2 Pulse pistachios in food processor until finely chopped, 15 to 20 pulses; measure out and reserve ¼ cup finely chopped pistachios in shallow dish. Continue processing remaining pistachios in processor until finely ground, about 45 seconds. Add flour and salt; process to combine, about 15 seconds.

3 Add butter and sugar to cooked egg yolk in bowl of stand mixer, then beat with paddle on medium speed until pale and fluffy, 3 to 5 minutes, scraping down bowl as needed. Add saffron liquid and continue to beat until well incorporated, about 1 minute. Reduce speed to low; add flour mixture; and mix until just combined, about 30 seconds. Using silicone spatula, press dough into cohesive mass.

4 Transfer dough to counter and divide in half. Roll each piece of dough into 6-inch log. Wrap logs tightly in plastic wrap and twist ends tightly to seal; chill until firm, at least 2 hours in refrigerator or 45 minutes in freezer. (Wrapped dough can be refrigerated for up to 3 days or frozen for up to 2 weeks. Thaw in refrigerator before slicing and baking.)

5 Adjust oven racks to upper-middle and lower-middle positions and heat oven to 350 degrees. Using pastry brush, gently brush logs with egg white mixture, then roll in reserved chopped pistachios, pressing to adhere. Working with 1 dough log at a time, using chef's knife, slice chilled dough into ¼-inch-thick rounds, rotating dough as you slice to prevent any flat edges from forming; space dough rounds 1 inch apart on 2 parchment paper–lined baking sheets.

6 Bake until centers of cookies are pale golden brown (edges slightly darker), about 15 minutes, switching and rotating sheets halfway through baking. Let cookies cool on sheets for 5 minutes, then transfer to wire rack. Let cookies cool completely before serving.

Storage: 1 week at room temperature

Makes 20 sandwich cookies

Total Time 1 hour, plus 40 minutes chilling and cooling

WHY THIS RECIPE WORKS These sandwiches feature cookies more deeply rich and uniquely savory than any we've had. We use hard-cooked egg yolk to create the sandiest Sablés (page 206), and we realized this opened an intriguing possibility. Salted duck egg yolks are enjoyed in China, where the tradition likely originated, as well as in other Asian countries that adopted the practice to extend the shelf life of eggs and also to intensify flavor. Compared to chicken egg yolks, duck egg yolks have a higher fat content; when cured, the golden orbs turn savory and luscious. Used for the hard-cooked yolk in this stand-out sablé, they add buttery richness and a pleasant hint of salt to each bite. We sandwich Chinese roasted sesame seed paste between two cookies, which elevates them with toasty flavor and umami.

SALTED EGG YOLK SHORTBREAD SANDWICHES

COOKIES

- 12 tablespoons (171 grams) unsalted butter, softened
- ¾ cup (85 grams) confectioners' sugar
- 3 frozen salted duck egg yolks, thawed
- ½ teaspoon table salt
- 1½ cups (213 grams) all-purpose flour
- 1 large egg yolk, lightly beaten with 1 tablespoon water
- 2 teaspoons sesame seeds

FILLING

- 3 tablespoons unsalted butter, softened
- ⅓ cup (82 grams) Chinese roasted sesame seed paste
- ¾ cup (85 grams) confectioners' sugar
- Pinch table salt

You can substitute tahini for the roasted sesame seed paste but the cookie filling will be looser and less deeply flavored. The salted egg yolk is the primary flavor in the cookies; don't omit it. We used a 1¾-inch fluted square cutter; you can use any shape cookie cutter, though you may get a different number of cookies.

1 **For the cookies:** Using stand mixer fitted with paddle, beat butter, sugar, thawed salted egg yolks, and salt on medium speed until pale and fluffy, 3 to 5 minutes, scraping down bowl as needed. Stop mixer; add flour and mix on low speed until no dry flour remains, about 30 seconds. Scrape down bowl, then increase speed to medium-low and beat until dough just forms, about 30 seconds.

2 Transfer dough to center of large lightly floured sheet of parchment paper and press into 8 by 6-inch oval. Sprinkle dough lightly with flour, then place second large sheet of parchment over top. Roll dough into 13 by 12-inch oval of even ⅛-inch thickness. Using 1¾-inch cutter, cut dough into cookies, gathering scraps and rerolling once; space cookies ½ inch apart on 2 parchment-lined baking sheets. Cover sheets with plastic wrap and refrigerate for 20 minutes.

3 Adjust oven racks to upper-middle and lower-middle positions and heat oven to 325 degrees. Brush tops of dough with egg wash and sprinkle half of cookies with sesame seeds. Bake until edges of cookies are golden brown, 12 to 15 minutes, switching and rotating sheets halfway through baking. Let cookies cool on sheets for 5 minutes, then transfer to wire rack and let cool completely.

4 **For the filling:** Using stand mixer fitted with whisk attachment, mix butter and sesame paste at medium-high speed until smooth, about 1 minute, scraping down bowl halfway through mixing. Add confectioners' sugar and salt and mix at medium-low speed until most of sugar is moistened, about 45 seconds. Scrape down bowl and mix at medium speed until fully combined, about 15 seconds. Scrape down bowl, increase speed to medium-high, and whip until fluffy and lightened in color, 1 to 2 minutes.

5 Before serving, working with cookies without sesame seeds, place 1 teaspoon filling on flat side of each cookie. Top with remaining cookies, sesame seed side out, pressing gently until filling spreads to edges.

Storage: unfilled, 1 week at room temperature; 1 day filled

Makes about 50 cookies

Total Time 1½ hours, plus 1 hour 20 minutes chilling and cooling

WHY THIS RECIPE WORKS We appreciate holiday cookie cutters and colorful, iced delights, but festive, flavorful cookies don't need to be so elaborate. These stir-together slice-and-bake cookies have buttery taste (check), colorful (and flavorful!) decoration (check), and gifting capabilities (check). Cinnamon gives the cookies holiday spice (cardamom works too), while a pretty magenta raspberry coating offers bracing contrast. We place a wire rack on the cookies and dust them with freeze-dried raspberry powder to create a checkered pattern. The cookies start with melted butter, rather than softened or chilled, so we can skip creaming or processing and instead mix the dough by hand—a little baking powder opens up air pockets in the dough to keep it from being dense. An egg yolk contributes to a firm and crumbly texture; it also extends the cookies' shelf life to 10 days, so these are great for gifting and swapping.

SIMPLEST RASPBERRY-CINNAMON SLICE-AND-BAKES

- 1¾ cups (249 grams) all-purpose flour
- ¾ teaspoon ground cinnamon
- ½ teaspoon table salt
- ½ teaspoon baking powder
- 16 tablespoons (228 grams) unsalted butter, melted and cooled
- ¾ cup (149 grams) sugar
- 1 large egg yolk
- 2 teaspoons vanilla extract
- 1 cup freeze-dried raspberries

1 Whisk flour, cinnamon, salt, and baking powder together in bowl. Whisk melted butter, sugar, egg yolk, and vanilla in second bowl until very smooth. Add flour mixture and stir with silicone spatula or wooden spoon until well combined (dough will be loose). Let dough rest until firm, about 5 minutes.

2 Transfer dough to counter and divide in half. Roll each piece of dough into 1¼-inch-wide log, about 10 inches long. Wrap logs tightly in plastic wrap and twist ends tightly to seal; refrigerate until firm, at least 1 hour or up to 3 days.

3 Adjust oven rack to middle position and heat oven to 350 degrees. Let chilled dough sit on counter to soften slightly, about 15 minutes. Pulse freeze-dried raspberries in spice grinder until reduced to fine powder, about ten 5-second pulses. Transfer to fine-mesh strainer and set aside.

4 Working with 1 dough log at a time, slice chilled dough into ¼-inch-thick rounds, rotating dough as you slice to prevent any flat edges from forming; space dough rounds 1 inch apart on 2 parchment paper–lined baking sheets. Let rest at room temperature for 10 minutes. Bake cookies, 1 sheet at a time, until edges are just golden, 10 to 12 minutes, rotating sheet halfway through baking. Let cookies cool for 2 minutes, then gently invert wire rack on top of cookies, being careful not to press them. Dust cookies with raspberry powder until evenly coated, then carefully remove rack. Let cookies cool on sheet for 10 minutes, then transfer to wire rack and let cool completely before serving.

Storage: 10 days at room temperature

Makes about 56 checkerboard cookies, plus about 20 scrap marbled cookies

Total Time 1¼ hours, plus 3½ hours chilling and cooling

WHY THIS RECIPE WORKS This holiday cookie is not only striking and deliciously pepperminty, but also a part of a rich historical tradition of cookie assembly. The checkerboard cookie, or Schackrutor, became a staple cookie in Sweden during the 19th-century rise of the kaffehus (coffee shop), where assortments of small cookies were often served. It wasn't long until these patterned treats made their way into American kitchens, and they were especially popular during the Christmas season. They look intricate, but they're universally achievable thanks to our streamlined process. We make one dough and then divide it in half to color. We roll each dough into a square that we stack (with an egg white "glue"); cut into strips; and stack again, alternating color blocks and ensuring clean angles. This process does yield scraps but we're crafty about it; we use them to make additional round cookies with a cool marbled design.

PEPPERMINT CHECKERBOARDS

- 2¼ cups (320 grams) all-purpose flour
- ½ teaspoon table salt
- 16 tablespoons (228 grams) unsalted butter, softened
- ¾ cup (149 grams) granulated sugar
- ½ cup (57 grams) confectioners' sugar
- 2 large egg yolks, plus 1 large egg white, lightly beaten with 1 teaspoon water
- ¾ teaspoon peppermint extract
- Red gel food coloring

We like gel food coloring, as we can use very little and achieve great color: Start with 8 drops to achieve the look you see in the photo, but you may need to use more depending on the type of food coloring you use (see page 21 for more information).

1 For the checkerboards: Whisk flour and salt together in bowl. Using stand mixer fitted with paddle, beat butter, granulated sugar, and confectioners' sugar on medium speed until pale and fluffy, 3 to 5 minutes, scraping down bowl as needed. Add egg yolks and peppermint extract and continue to beat until well incorporated, about 1 minute longer. Reduce speed to low; slowly add flour mixture; and mix until cohesive dough forms, 1 to 2 minutes. Remove half of dough from mixer and set aside.

2 Add food coloring to remaining dough in mixer and mix on low speed until fully combined and no streaks remain, about 1 minute, scraping down paddle and bowl halfway through.

3 Transfer colored dough to large sheet of lightly floured parchment paper. Press and roll into 9-inch square, about ¼ inch thick. Transfer parchment and dough to rimmed baking sheet; wrap tightly with plastic wrap; and refrigerate until firm, about 1 hour or up to 3 days. Repeat with reserved blond dough.

4 Brush chilled blond dough square with thin layer of egg wash, then place red dough square on top, lining up edges as best as possible. Using very light pressure, roll top of red dough square with rolling pin to help adhere doughs.

••• CONTINUED •••

Storage: 10 days at room temperature

5 Use a ruler and chef's knife to mark center of dough along top and bottom edges then, using marks as guide, cut vertically through both layers of dough to create two 4½-inch-wide dough rectangles. Brush top of 1 piece lightly with egg wash, then stack second piece on top, rotating so cut sides are on the same side and aligning edges as best as possible. Use rolling pin to adhere dough pieces, then trim unsliced long edge to form 4-inch-wide rectangle, reserving scraps in bowl. (If dough begins to feel soft, transfer to parchment-lined rimmed baking sheet and refrigerate until firm.)

6 With short side of dough rectangle parallel to counter edge, cut dough lengthwise into eight ½-inch-wide strips. Place 1 dough strip flat on counter with red stripe along leftmost edge; brush lightly with egg wash. Top with second dough strip, with blond stripe on leftmost edge, lining up edges as best as possible. Brush top lightly with egg wash. Repeat with 2 more dough strips, alternating orientation of blond and red stripes to create checkerboard pattern, brushing lightly with egg wash between each layer, and lining up edges as best as possible as you go. Gently roll top layer to adhere doughs. (If dough begins to feel soft, refrigerate remaining 4 dough strips while you work.)

7 Trim 1 inch from each short end of rectangle to reveal checkerboard pattern; add trimming to bowl with dough scraps. Wrap rectangle with plastic and chill until firm, at least 1 hour or up to 3 days. Repeat stacking, egg washing, adhering, trimming, and chilling remaining 4 strips of dough. (Dough rectangles can be frozen for up to 1 month. Thaw overnight in refrigerator before slicing and baking.)

8 Press reserved dough scraps together into rough log, then roll into 1½-inch-wide log. Wrap with plastic and refrigerate until firm, at least 1 hour or up to 24 hours.

9 Adjust oven racks to upper-middle and lower-middle positions and heat oven to 325 degrees. Working with 1 chilled dough rectangle at a time, slice crosswise into ¼-inch-thick rectangles and space evenly on 2 parchment paper–lined rimmed baking sheets (28 per sheet). Bake until edges are light golden brown, 12 to 15 minutes, switching and rotating sheets halfway through baking. Let cookies cool on sheets for 5 minutes, then transfer to wire rack and let cool completely.

10 **For the marbled cookies:** While checkerboard cookies cool, trim ends of scrap dough log, then slice crosswise into ¼-inch-thick rounds, rolling dough log as you slice. Arrange evenly over one-third of parchment-lined sheet (or wait until checkerboard cookies and sheets have cooled completely and reuse parchment and sheet). Adjust oven rack to middle position. Bake marbled cookies until edges are light golden brown, 12 to 15 minutes, rotating sheet halfway through baking. Let cookies cool on sheets for 5 minutes, then transfer to wire rack. Let cookies cool completely before serving.

Makes about 65 cookies

Total Time 50 minutes, plus 1½ hours chilling and cooling

WHY THIS RECIPE WORKS Honestly, we're quite enamored with these cookies: The marbling is hyper-realistic, the black and white scheme is sophisticated, and the chocolate-vanilla flavor is as great as the cookie's good looks. But most of all, we're in love with these cookies because we discovered a method that—unlike every other complicated marble cookie recipe out there—is dead simple. Using the mixer to marble the chocolate and vanilla doughs makes a complicated-looking cookie supersimple to execute—we give the two just a quick mix. The "black" part of the marble is achieved through a combination of black cocoa powder and melted chocolate, so that the dough has great cocoa taste without being dry. The baked cookies are incredibly tender yet crunchy, with a long shelf life for gifting.

EASIEST-EVER MARBLED BUTTER COOKIES

3 Microwave milk and salt for dough in bowl until just warm (about 110 degrees), 30 to 45 seconds. Sprinkle yeast over warm milk and stir to combine. Add milk mixture to dough and mix with your hands until combined, about 30 seconds. Transfer dough to counter (don't wash bowl) and knead until smooth, about 2 minutes. Return dough to bowl, cover tightly, and let stand at room temperature for 30 minutes.

4 While dough rests, line 2 rimmed baking sheets with parchment paper. Divide filling into 30 equal portions, weighing about ½ ounce each, and roll into balls. Place balls on 1 half of 1 prepared sheet. Cover with damp dish towel.

5 Transfer dough to counter and divide in half (dough will be slightly tacky, soft, and somewhat elastic). Roll each piece of dough into 15-inch log and cut into 15 equal pieces. Roll each portion into ball and place on sheet with filling. Cover with damp dish towel.

6 Adjust oven rack to middle position and heat oven to 350 degrees. Place 1 dough ball in palm of your hand and gently press into 3-inch round of even thickness. Place 1 filling ball in center of dough. Bring sides of dough up around filling and pinch top to seal. Roll ball until smooth, place on second prepared baking sheet, and cover with damp dish towel. Repeat with remaining dough and filling.

7 Place 1 filled ball in ma'amoul mold and gently press until cookie fills crevices and top is flat. Turn mold over and tap edge on edge of counter so cookie releases onto palm of your hand. (If cookie sticks, line mold with plastic wrap.) Return cookie, pattern side up, to baking sheet. Repeat, placing 15 cookies, evenly spaced, on each sheet.

8 Bake cookies, 1 sheet at a time, until bottoms are light golden, 15 to 20 minutes, rotating sheet halfway through baking. Transfer baking sheet to wire rack and let cool on sheet for 20 minutes. Dust liberally with confectioners' sugar before serving.

Storage: 2 weeks at room temperature

1

2

3

SHAPING MA'AMOUL

1. Place 1 dough ball in palm of your hand and gently press into 3-inch round. Place 1 filling ball in center of dough.

2. Bring sides of dough up and around filling and pinch top to seal; roll ball until smooth.

3. Place filled ball in mold and gently press until cookie fills crevices and top is flat. Turn mold over and tap edge on edge of counter to release cookie.

Makes about 40 cookies

Total Time 1¼ hours, plus 50 minutes chilling and cooling

WHY THIS RECIPE WORKS These crisp, meltingly tender shortbread cookies, scented with anise and coated in cinnamon sugar, are the state cookie of New Mexico, where they're served at any special celebration or holiday. While their texture is traditionally produced by lard, we create it with a combination of equal parts shortening and butter for balance of tenderness and buttery-rich flavor (and for those who might not keep lard on hand). The cookies come in many shapes and sizes, but we're partial to the diamond shape that's commonly used for weddings. To finish the cookies, we coat them in cinnamon sugar using the traditional method: gently toss the still-warm cookies in the sugary coating so it adheres.

NEW MEXICAN BISCOCHITOS

- 1 cup (198 grams) sugar
- 1 teaspoon ground cinnamon
- 1 tablespoon anise seeds
- 8 tablespoons (114 grams) unsalted butter, softened
- 8 tablespoons (88 grams) vegetable shortening, cut into 1-inch pieces
- ½ teaspoon salt
- 1 large egg yolk
- 1 teaspoon vanilla extract
- 2 cups (284 grams) all-purpose flour

For a traditional take, use lard in place of vegetable shortening. Don't let the cookies cool on the baking sheets for longer than 5 minutes before coating or the cinnamon sugar won't adhere.

1 Combine sugar and cinnamon in small bowl; spread ½ cup cinnamon sugar in shallow dish. Grind anise seeds in spice grinder until finely ground, about 10 seconds.

2 Using stand mixer fitted with paddle, beat butter, shortening, salt, remaining ½ cup cinnamon sugar, and ground anise on medium speed until pale and fluffy, 3 to 5 minutes, scraping down bowl as needed. Add egg yolk and vanilla and continue to beat until well incorporated, about 1 minute longer. Reduce speed to low, add flour, and mix until dough is uniform, about 10 seconds.

3 Roll dough into 9-inch circle on large sheet of parchment paper. Transfer dough, still on parchment, to large plate; cover with plastic wrap and refrigerate until firm, about 30 minutes.

4 Adjust oven racks to upper-middle and lower-middle positions and heat oven to 350 degrees. Line 2 baking sheets with parchment paper. Transfer dough, still on parchment, to cutting board. Using chef's knife or pizza cutter, cut dough lengthwise into 1-inch-wide strips, then cut diagonally into 1-inch-wide strips to form diamonds; space diamonds evenly on prepared sheets, about 20 per sheet.

5 Bake cookies until set and just starting to brown, about 15 minutes, switching and rotating sheets halfway through baking. Let cookies cool on sheets for 5 minutes. Gently toss warm cookies, a few at a time, in reserved cinnamon sugar; transfer cookies to wire rack. Let cookies cool completely before serving.

Storage: 3 days at room temperature

WHY THIS RECIPE WORKS One of the best ways on earth to enjoy the butterscotch-y goodness of dulce de leche is between a pair of buttery, citrus-scented cookies in the Latin American confection called alfajores de maicena. Named for the cornstarch (maicena) in the dough, the cookies are so delicate that they crumble as you eat them, their buttery flavor melding with the rich toffee notes of the dulce de leche. We found that adding some flour to the cornstarch in the dough creates powdery-soft cookies with enough structure to hold together when sandwiched. For the filling, we keep things simple and turn to commercial dulce de leche and doctor it with some flavor-boosting vanilla extract and salt. We love these cookies bristling with flecks of coconut, a customary addition.

Makes 26 sandwich cookies

Total Time 2¼ hours

COCONUT ALFAJORES

FILLING

- 2 (13.4-ounce) cans Nestlé La Lechera Dulce de Leche
- 1 teaspoon vanilla extract
- ¼ teaspoon table salt

COOKIES

- 1½ cups (170 grams) cornstarch
- 1⅓ cups (189 grams) all-purpose flour
- 1 teaspoon baking powder
- ¼ teaspoon table salt
- 16 tablespoons (228 grams) unsalted butter, softened
- ½ cup (99 grams) sugar
- 3 large egg yolks
- 1 tablespoon brandy (optional)
- 1 teaspoon grated lemon zest
- 1 teaspoon vanilla extract
- 1 cup (82 grams) unsweetened shredded coconut

Alfajores are fragile, so we've designed this recipe to make a few extra cookies in case some break. It's essential to buy the Nestlé La Lechera brand of canned dulce de leche, or the filling won't have the right consistency.

1 **For the filling:** Transfer dulce de leche to medium bowl. Stir in vanilla and salt until thoroughly incorporated. Cover and refrigerate until mixture is completely chilled, at least 2 hours.

2 **For the cookies:** While filling chills, whisk cornstarch, flour, baking powder, and salt together in medium bowl. Using stand mixer fitted with paddle, beat butter and sugar on medium-high speed until pale and fluffy, 3 to 5 minutes, scraping down bowl as needed. Add egg yolks; brandy, if using; lemon zest; and vanilla and continue to beat until well incorporated, about 1 minute longer. Reduce speed to low; add cornstarch mixture; and mix until dough is uniform, about 1 minute.

3 Transfer dough to counter and divide in half. Place 1 piece of dough in center of large sheet of parchment paper and press with your hand to ½-inch thickness. Place second large sheet of parchment over dough and roll dough ¼ inch thick. Using your flat hand on parchment, smooth out wrinkles on both sides. Transfer dough with parchment to rimmed baking sheet. Repeat pressing, rolling, and smoothing second piece of dough, then stack on top of first piece on sheet. Freeze until dough is firm, about 30 minutes.

4 Adjust oven racks to upper-middle and lower-middle positions and heat oven to 350 degrees. Transfer 1 piece of dough to counter. Peel off top layer of parchment and replace loosely. Flip dough and parchment. Peel away second piece of parchment and place on baking sheet. Using 2-inch round cutter, cut dough into rounds; space rounds ½ inch apart on prepared sheet. Repeat with second piece of dough, then roll, chill, and cut scraps until you have 26 rounds on each sheet.

5 Bake until tops are set but still pale and bottoms are light golden, 10 to 12 minutes, switching and rotating sheets halfway through baking. Let cookies cool on sheets for 5 minutes, then transfer to wire rack and let cool completely.

6 To assemble, place half of cookies upside down on counter. Place about 2 teaspoons filling on each upside-down cookie. Hold 1 topped cookie on your fingers. Place second, untopped cookie on top of filling, right side up, and press gently with your other fingers until filling spreads to edges. Repeat with remaining cookies.

7 Place coconut in small bowl. Working with 1 cookie at a time, roll sides of cookies in coconut, pressing gently to help coconut adhere to exposed filling. If not serving immediately, refrigerate; allow refrigerated cookies to sit out at room temperature for 10 minutes before serving.

Storage: 5 days in refrigerator

Makes 36 cookies

Total Time 1¼ hours, plus 30 minutes cooling

WHY THIS RECIPE WORKS Not every print has to be a thumb, and we really *love* filling hearts with creamy lemon curd in these darling sweet-and-tangy raspberry cookies. Making a heart-shaped indentation is simple, and there are two options: pressing an oval shaped measuring spoon or an inverted greased handle of a spoon into a V shape. We do this as soon as the baked cookies come out of the oven, when they're still soft, so they hold the heart shape. Then we coat them in ground freeze-dried raspberries, which adhere to the warm cookie before we fill the hearts with curd. The coating for these colorful cookies is inspired by Jesse Szewczyk's Tutti-Frutti Thumbprint Cookies.

RASPBERRY-LEMON SWEETHEART THUMBPRINTS

COOKIES

- 2¼ cups (320 grams) all-purpose flour
- ¾ teaspoon table salt
- ½ teaspoon baking soda
- ¼ teaspoon baking powder
- 12 tablespoons (171 grams) unsalted butter, softened
- ⅔ cup (132 grams) sugar
- 3 ounces (85 grams) cream cheese, softened
- 1 large egg
- 1½ teaspoons vanilla extract
- 6 tablespoons (113 grams) lemon curd

RASPBERRY SUGAR

- 1 cup freeze-dried raspberries, divided
- ½ cup (99 grams) sugar

You can use your favorite seedless jam or jelly in place of the lemon curd if you prefer; if using jam, microwave until loose and bubbling around edges, about 30 seconds before filling cookies. Be sure to coat the cookies while they're still warm or the raspberry sugar won't adhere uniformly. (Rewarm the cookies if necessary; see page 9.) See page 10 for more flavor inspiration.

1 For the cookies: Adjust oven rack to middle position and heat oven to 350 degrees. Whisk flour, salt, baking soda, and baking powder together in bowl; set aside.

2 Using stand mixer fitted with paddle, beat butter and sugar on medium speed until pale and fluffy, 3 to 5 minutes, scraping down sides of bowl as needed. Add cream cheese, egg, and vanilla and beat until well incorporated, about 1 minute. Reduce speed to low; add flour mixture; and beat until dough is uniform, about 1 minute.

3 Working with 1 tablespoon dough at a time, roll into balls and space evenly on 2 parchment paper–lined baking sheets (18 balls per sheet). Using bottom of greased dry measuring cup or drinking glass, press each dough ball to ¾-inch thickness (pinch together any large cracks that form). Bake 1 sheet of cookies until beginning to turn golden around edges, about 14 minutes, rotating sheet halfway through baking.

4 **For the raspberry sugar:** While cookies bake, working in 2 batches, pulse freeze-dried raspberries with sugar in spice grinder until reduced to fine powder, about five 1-second pulses. Sift sugar mixture through fine-mesh strainer into shallow dish; set aside.

5 Transfer cookies on sheet to wire rack and immediately make ¼-inch-deep heart-shaped indentation in center of each cookie by pressing oval shaped ¼-teaspoon measuring spoon or inverted greased handle of spoon into each cookie in V shape. While cookies are still hot, toss each cookie in sugar mixture in dish to coat. Tap cookie gently to remove excess sugar, then transfer to wire rack to fill and cool. Repeat baking, indenting, and coating remaining sheet of cookies.

6 Carefully fill each indentation with ½ teaspoon curd, pouring and spreading curd in heart shape to fill indentation. Let cookies cool completely before serving.

Storage: unfilled, 2 days at room temperature; 1 day filled

FORMING THE HEARTS

1. When baked cookies are hot from oven, make ¼-inch-deep heart-shaped indentation in centers with oval-shaped ¼-teaspoon measuring spoon.

2. Finish heart by making second indentation in V shape.

1

2

Makes 48 cookies

Total Time 1½ hours, plus 30 minutes cooling

WHY THIS RECIPE WORKS Inspired by chewy tamarind candies of different varieties found in Mexico, the Caribbean, and Southeast Asia, we make a bright and tangy tamarind caramel to fill a buttery, coconut-encrusted thumbprint vessel. The caramel texture is just right for cookies: It's thin enough for appealing stretch but set just enough so that it doesn't pour out between nibbles. It's optional, but for Tajín heads, we think a dusting of the salty, tart Mexican chili seasoning over the caramel really heightens the tamarind flavor and adds a touch more dimension to this fun treat.

COCONUT THUMBPRINTS WITH TAMARIND CARAMEL

TAMARIND CARAMEL

- 1 cup (198 grams) sugar
- ¼ cup (59 grams) water
- 2 tablespoons light corn syrup
- 3 tablespoons tamarind juice concentrate
- 2 tablespoons unsalted butter
- 1 teaspoon vanilla extract
- ½ teaspoon table salt

THUMBPRINTS

- 2¼ cups (320 grams) all-purpose flour
- ½ teaspoon table salt
- ½ teaspoon baking soda
- ¼ teaspoon baking powder
- 12 tablespoons (170 grams) unsalted butter, softened
- ⅔ cup (132 grams) sugar
- 4½ ounces (128 grams) cream cheese, softened
- 1 large egg
- 1½ teaspoons vanilla extract
- 1½ cups (123 grams) shredded sweetened coconut

Tajín Clásico Seasoning (optional)

Don't confuse tamarind juice concentrate with tamarind paste, which may contain seeds and fibers of fruit pulp. If you can't find tamarind concentrate substitute with equal parts lime juice.

1 **For the tamarind caramel:** Bring sugar, water, and corn syrup to boil in large saucepan over medium-high heat. Cook, without stirring, until mixture is straw-colored, 6 to 8 minutes. Reduce heat to low and continue to cook, swirling saucepan occasionally, until mixture is amber-colored and registers between 360 and 370 degrees, 2 to 5 minutes.

2 Off heat, carefully stir in tamarind juice concentrate, butter, vanilla, and salt (mixture will bubble and steam) until smooth. Return to medium heat and cook until caramel is bubbling and registers 240 degrees, about 1 minute. Carefully transfer caramel to heatproof bowl and let cool while baking cookies. (Caramel can be cooled completely, covered, and stored at room temperature for up to 24 hours. If caramel becomes too thick to spoon into cookies, microwave at 50 percent power in 5-second intervals.)

3 **For the thumbprints:** Adjust oven rack to middle position and heat oven to 350 degrees. Whisk flour, salt, baking soda, and baking powder together in bowl. Using stand mixer fitted with paddle, beat butter and sugar on medium speed until pale and fluffy, 3 to 5 minutes, scraping down sides of bowl as needed. Add cream cheese, egg, and vanilla and beat until well incorporated, about 1 minute longer. Reduce speed to low; add flour mixture; and mix until dough is uniform, about 1 minute.

4 Spread coconut in shallow dish. Working with 1 tablespoon dough at a time, roll into balls between your dampened hands, then roll in coconut, pressing to adhere. Space evenly on 2 parchment paper–lined baking sheets (24 balls per sheet). Using bottom of greased dry measuring cup or drinking glass, press each dough ball to ¾-inch thickness (pinch together any large cracks that form).

5 Bake cookies, 1 sheet at a time, until just beginning to set, about 10 minutes. Transfer sheet to wire rack and immediately make ¼-inch-deep indentation in center of each cookie with greased rounded 1-tablespoon measure.

6 Rotate sheet and continue to bake cookies until light golden around edges, about 10 minutes. Transfer sheet to wire rack, then spoon 1 teaspoon caramel into indent of each cookie and sprinkle with Tajín, if using. Let cookies cool completely on sheet before serving.

Storage: 1 week at room temperature

WHY THIS RECIPE WORKS Rich chocolate and sweet, earthy pistachio are a time-honored pairing, but the Dubai chocolate bar trend really put the spotlight on the duo. The world doesn't need another Dubai chocolate dessert, and we instead wanted to put the chocolate and the pistachio in sharp focus in a cookie. We think smooth pistachio cream is one of the best expressions of pistachio flavor. We pair the luxurious spread with dark chocolate thumbprint cookies. Crusted in chopped pistachios, the cookies sport a striking contrast of midnight brown and vibrant green. Pressing each cookie with the back of a tablespoon measure before and after baking gives us a consistent hollow in which to add a scoop of filling.

Makes 18 cookies

Total Time 55 minutes, plus 30 minutes cooling

CHOCOLATE-PISTACHIO THUMBPRINTS

- 1½ cups (213 grams) all-purpose flour
- ½ cup (43 grams) Dutch-processed cocoa powder
- ½ teaspoon table salt
- ¼ teaspoon baking powder
- ¼ teaspoon baking soda
- 8 tablespoons (114 grams) unsalted butter, softened
- 1 cup (198 grams) sugar
- 1 large egg
- 2 teaspoons vanilla extract
- ⅓ cup (48 grams) shelled pistachios, finely chopped
- 6 tablespoons (104 grams) pistachio cream

Dutch-processed cocoa has deeper flavor than natural cocoa. We used Peppertux's Vegan Pistachio Cream when developing this recipe, other brands may have different colors and consistencies. Finely chopping the pistachios ensures they adhere well to the dough.

1 Adjust oven rack to middle position and heat oven to 350 degrees. Whisk flour, cocoa powder, salt, baking powder, and baking soda together in bowl. Using stand mixer fitted with paddle, beat butter and sugar on medium-high speed until light and fluffy, 3 to 5 minutes. Add egg and vanilla and continue to beat until well incorporated, about 1 minute longer, scraping down bowl as needed. Reduce speed to low; add flour mixture; and mix until dough is uniform, about 1 minute.

2 Place pistachios in shallow dish. Working with 1½ tablespoons dough at a time, roll into balls, then roll in pistachios, pressing to adhere. Space evenly on 2 parchment paper–lined baking sheets (9 balls per sheet). Using bottom of greased dry measuring cup or drinking glass, press each dough ball to ¾-inch thickness (pinch together any large cracks that form). Bake cookies, 1 sheet at a time, until edges are set, 10 to 12 minutes, rotating sheet halfway through baking.

3 Transfer sheet to wire rack and immediately use back of rounded tablespoon measure to make ¼-inch-deep indentation in center of each cookie. Spoon 1 teaspoon pistachio cream into indent. Let cookies cool on sheet for 5 minutes, then, if necessary, use back of spoon to gently spread pistachio cream to fill depression. Transfer cookies to wire rack and let cool completely before serving.

Storage: 3 days at room temperature

Makes 24 cookies

Total Time 55 minutes, plus 30 minutes cooling

WHY THIS RECIPE WORKS This might be the most-holiday holiday cookie ever, with spiced gingerbread cookie dough holding a creamy filling inspired by the season's best sipper. With a hint of custardy richness from a binding egg yolk and tang from cream cheese, the eggnog center is an excellent foil to the deep molasses flavor of the gingerbread. Some black pepper reinforces the spicy flavor of the cookie, while cinnamon and nutmeg warm the filling with their classic flavor.

GINGERBREAD EGGNOG THUMBPRINTS

EGGNOG FILLING

- 6 ounces (170 grams) cream cheese, softened
- 1 large egg yolk
- ⅓ cup (66 grams) granulated sugar
- 1 tablespoon bourbon or rum
- ¼ teaspoon ground cinnamon
- ¼ teaspoon ground nutmeg, plus extra for serving

COOKIES

- 2¾ cups (391 grams) all-purpose flour
- 1 teaspoon ground cinnamon
- 1 teaspoon ground ginger
- ½ teaspoon ground cloves
- ½ teaspoon baking powder
- ½ teaspoon baking soda
- ½ teaspoon table salt
- ¼ teaspoon pepper
- 12 tablespoons (171 grams) unsalted butter, softened
- ½ cup (99 grams) granulated sugar
- ½ cup (156 grams) molasses
- 1 large egg
- ⅓ cup (76 grams) sparkling sugar or turbinado, for rolling

Make sure your cream cheese is softened to prevent lumps in the filling. For extra eggnog flavor, grate fresh nutmeg directly over each cookie.

1 For the eggnog filling: Combine all ingredients in bowl, stirring vigorously with silicone spatula until well combined and smooth; set aside.

2 For the cookies: Adjust oven rack to middle position and heat oven to 350 degrees. Whisk flour, cinnamon, ginger, cloves, baking powder, baking soda, salt, and pepper together in bowl.

3 Using stand mixer fitted with paddle, beat butter and granulated sugar on medium speed until pale and fluffy, 3 to 5 minutes, scraping down bowl as needed. Add molasses and egg and continue to beat until well incorporated, about 1 minute longer. Reduce speed to low, add flour mixture, and mix until dough is uniform, about 1 minute.

4 Spread sparkling sugar in shallow dish. Working with 1½ tablespoons dough at a time, roll into balls, then roll in sparkling sugar, pressing to adhere. Space dough balls evenly on 2 parchment paper–lined baking sheets (12 dough balls per sheet). Using rounded 1-tablespoon measure, make indentation in center of each dough ball. Pinch together any large cracks, then divide filling evenly among indentations in dough balls, about 1½ teaspoons per cookie.

5 Bake cookies, 1 sheet at a time, until edges are just set, 10 to 12 minutes, rotating sheet halfway through baking. Transfer sheet to wire rack and let cookies cool completely on sheet. Sprinkle with extra nutmeg before serving.

Storage: 3 days at room temperature

Makes 32 cookies

Total Time 1 hour, plus55 minutes cooling and setting

WHY THIS RECIPE WORKS These exquisite parallelograms of buttery cookie encasing vibrant jam are like a thumbprint but even easier and quicker. That's why this cookie's inspiration, the winning cookie entry in 1954's Pillsbury Bake-Off, were called Split Seconds. We tweaked the blue-ribbon version, making the sugar cookie–like dough more the texture of shortbread (and flavoring it with cardamom) and diluting the jam (we like apricot) with a bit of water before filling the cookies so it doesn't bake up candy-like. With a drizzle of icing, these diagonals will stand out on your holiday spread—in a split second.

APRICOT-CARDAMOM DIAGONALS

- 16 tablespoons (228 grams) unsalted butter, softened
- ½ cup (99 grams) granulated sugar
- ½ teaspoon ground cardamom
- ½ teaspoon table salt
- 2½ cups (355 grams) all-purpose flour
- ¾ cup (211 grams) apricot preserves
- 1 teaspoon lemon juice
- ¾ cup (85 grams) confectioners' sugar
- 1 tablespoon hot water

You can use an overturned rimmed baking sheet instead of a rimless baking sheet. Smucker's apricot preserves work well here. A pastry bag makes it easy to fill the troughs with jam, but if you don't have one you can use a small spoon.

1 Adjust oven rack to middle position and heat oven to 350 degrees. Using stand mixer fitted with paddle, beat butter, granulated sugar, cardamom, and salt onmedium-high speed until pale and fluffy, 3 to 5 minutes. Stop mixer. Add flour and mix on low speed until mixture comes together into crumbly dough, about 2 minutes, scraping down bowl halfway through mixing. Transfer to work surface and knead gently until dough forms smooth ball.

2 Divide dough into 4 equal pieces. Gently roll and pinch each piece into 14-inch log (if dough cracks, pinch it back together). Arrange logs lengthwise on parchment paper–lined rimless baking sheet. Press your index finger along length of 1 log to create trough that is ¾ inch wide and ¼ to ⅓ inch deep, using fingers of your other hand to mold sides of trough. Repeat with remaining logs.

3 Whisk preserves and lemon juice in bowl until smooth. Transfer mixture to piping bag fitted with ¼-inch round tip and pipe evenly among troughs. Bake until logs are lightly browned and firm to touch, about 30 minutes, rotating sheet halfway through baking. Let cool on sheet until just warm to touch.

4 Gently slide logs into center of sheet until touching. Whisk confectioners' sugar and water in small bowl until smooth. (If mixture is too thick to drizzle, whisk in more water, ½ teaspoon at a time.) Using spoon, drizzle icing over cookies. Let sit until icing is set, 25 to 30 minutes.

5 Run thin metal spatula under 1 log to release from parchment. Carefully transfer log to cutting board. Using sharp chef's knife at 45-degree angle, trim ½ inch from each end of log and discard trim. Slice remaining length on diagonal into 8 pieces. Repeat with remaining logs. Serve.

Storage: 3 days at room temperature

MAKING THE LOGS

1. Press your index finger along length of logs to create trough ¾ inch wide and ¼ inch to ⅓ inch deep, using fingers of your other hand to mold sides.

2. Pipe preserve mixture evenly among dough logs.

1

2

Makes about 30 cookies

Total Time 2 hours, plus 2 hours chilling

WHY THIS RECIPE WORKS Hamantaschen, the iconic triangular butter cookies shaped around a lush filling, are as lively as the Jewish holiday they're eaten on, Purim. A poppyseed filling is one of the most traditional but still one of our favorites, thick and rich from the poppy seeds but also from the heavy cream and the butter that finishes it, and fragrant from honey and brightening lemon zest. For a cookie dough that keeps its shape in the oven and doesn't open or leak, we use a small amount of cream cheese in place of some butter to increase pliability. Rolling the dough to a thin ⅛ inch makes the cookie pleasingly crispy, not dense or tough. While the cookie is a symbol of Purim, we think you should try these packages of poppyseed goodness any time of year.

HAMANTASCHEN WITH POPPY SEED FILLING

FILLING

- 1 cup (136 grams) poppy seeds
- ½ cup (116 grams) heavy cream
- ¼ cup (84 grams) honey
- ⅛ teaspoon table salt
- 1 tablespoon unsalted butter
- 1 teaspoon grated lemon zest plus 1 teaspoon juice
- ½ teaspoon vanilla extract

DOUGH

- 10 tablespoons (143 grams) unsalted butter, softened
- ¾ cup (149 grams) sugar
- 1 ounce cream cheese
- ¾ teaspoon table salt
- 1 large egg
- 2 teaspoons vanilla extract
- 2½ cups (355 grams) all-purpose flour

Poppy seeds have a high oil content and can turn rancid quickly; we recommend buying a fresh package for this recipe since their flavor plays a prominent role. Store any unused poppy seeds in the freezer.

1 For the filling: Working in 3 batches, grind poppy seeds in spice grinder until fine and powdery (but stop before paste forms), 15 to 30 seconds per batch (scrape bottom of spice grinder clean between batches). Bring cream, honey, and salt to simmer in small saucepan over medium heat. Stir in ground poppy seeds and cook, stirring occasionally, until mixture is thickened, liquid is absorbed, and seeds begin to clump together, 2 to 3 minutes. Off heat, stir in butter, lemon zest and juice, and vanilla. Transfer filling to bowl and let cool completely, about 1 hour. (Cooled filling can be refrigerated for up to 3 days.)

2 For the dough: Using stand mixer fitted with paddle, beat butter, sugar, cream cheese, and salt on medium speed until pale and fluffy, 3 to 5 minutes, scraping down bowl as needed. Add egg and vanilla and continue to beat until well incorporated, about 1 minute longer. Reduce speed to low; add flour; and mix until dough is uniform, about 1 minute. Divide dough in half. Transfer each half to sheet of plastic wrap; form into 6-inch disk; wrap tightly; and refrigerate until firm, at least 2 hours or up to 3 days.

••• CONTINUED •••

3 Adjust oven rack to middle position and heat oven to 350 degrees. Line rimmed baking sheet with parchment paper. Unwrap 1 dough disk, place in center of large piece of parchment, and cover with second large piece of parchment. Roll dough into 12-inch round of uniform ⅛-inch thickness, occasionally flipping dough and gently peeling off and replacing parchment to avoid creases. Refrigerate rolled dough sheet between parchment while repeating rolling (between parchment) with remaining dough disk.

4 Working with first dough sheet, peel off top piece of parchment, then use 3-inch round cutter to cut out 11 or 12 rounds; space evenly on prepared baking sheet. Dollop 1 heaping teaspoon filling in center of each round. Working with 1 round at a time, fold 3 sides of dough over filling to create triangle shape, overlapping dough at corners and leaving small window of filling exposed. Gently press corners to seal and press any cracked edges back together. (If dough becomes too fragile to work with, return briefly to refrigerator.) Bake cookies until evenly golden brown around edges, 16 to 20 minutes. Let cookies cool on sheet for 5 minutes, then transfer to wire rack.

5 Repeat cutting, filling, and baking with second dough sheet. Gather dough scraps from both dough rounds into rough disk shape and reroll to ⅛-inch thickness, then repeat cutting. Rerolled dough should yield 4 to 8 additional rounds. (Do not reroll scraps a second time and chill dough if it becomes too soft at any point during rolling.) Repeat filling, shaping, and baking. Let cookies cool completely before serving.

Storage: 3 days at room temperature

SHAPING HAMANTASCHEN

1. Fold in 1 edge of dough about ¾ inch, partially covering filling to establish shape.

2. Fold in second edge of dough, overlapping first flap at corner.

3. Fold in last edge of dough, overlapping second flap at corner and tucking underneath first flap at opposite corner.

4. Pinch all corners lightly to seal. Press any cracked edges back together.

1

2

3

4

Makes 20 oatcakes

Total Time 1¼ hours, plus 30 minutes cooling

WHY THIS RECIPE WORKS Classic Cape Breton oatcakes are decidedly cookies—richer and sweeter than their spartan Scottish counterparts, like a crunchy oaten shortbread. A mix of brown and white sugar lends the oatcakes a toffee-like complexity while allowing the nutty oats to shine. Mixing the ingredients in a food processor chops up the oats, making the dough easier to cut into neat cakes. Kosher salt provides pops of salinity to contrast with the cakes' sweetness, and a low-and-slow bake ensures that the finished oatcakes are evenly crisp and brown—and leaves plenty of time to decide what tea to brew on the side.

CAPE BRETON OATCAKES

- 1¼ cups (178 grams) all-purpose flour
- ⅓ cup (66 grams) brown sugar
- ¼ cup (50 grams) granulated sugar
- 1¼ teaspoons kosher salt
- ¾ teaspoon baking powder
- 1¼ cups (106 grams) old-fashioned rolled oats
- 8 tablespoons (114 grams) unsalted butter, melted and hot
- 2 tablespoons hot water

We developed this recipe with Domino brown sugar, which has a fine texture similar to granulated sugar; avoid using a coarser sugar (many organic brands are coarse) as it may make your dough unworkably crumbly. We developed this recipe with Diamond Crystal kosher salt; if using Morton kosher salt, decrease the amount to 1 teaspoon. Do not substitute quick or instant oats in this recipe.

1 Using pencil and ruler, draw 12 by 10-inch rectangle in center of each of 2 large sheets of parchment paper, crisscrossing lines at corners.

2 Process flour, brown sugar, granulated sugar, salt, and baking powder in food processor until fully blended, about 10 seconds. Add oats and pulse until oats are coarsely chopped, about 4 pulses. Add butter and water and pulse until most ingredients are evenly moistened, about 6 pulses. Transfer mixture to work surface and press and knead until all ingredients are evenly moistened. Gather into 1-inch-thick disk (mixture will be crumbly).

3 Place 1 piece of parchment on counter with pencil side facing down (you should be able to see rectangle through paper). Place dough in center of marked rectangle and press to ½-inch thickness. Place second sheet of parchment over dough, with pencil side facing up, so dough is in center of marked rectangle. Using pencil marks as guide, use rolling pin to roll dough into 12 by 10-inch rectangle of even thickness (roll firmly from center outward to create even thickness). If dough extends beyond rectangle in some spots and falls short in other places, trim excess and use to patch bare spots; after patching, replace parchment and roll firmly to create smooth top. Peel off top layer of parchment and reserve.

4 Using chef's knife or pizza cutter and ruler, trim edges of dough that extend over marked edges of rectangle. Discard scraps. Transfer dough, still on parchment, to rimmed baking sheet. Freeze until dough is firm, at least 15 minutes (alternatively you may refrigerate dough for at least 30 minutes). While dough is chilling, adjust oven rack to middle position and heat oven to 300 degrees.

5 Transfer dough, still on parchment, to counter. Place reserved parchment, pencil side down, on baking sheet. Cut dough lengthwise into 5 equal strips about 2 inches wide. Cut each strip crosswise into 4 equal pieces to create 20 rectangles. Transfer rectangles to prepared sheet, spacing them evenly and placing any thinner pieces toward center of sheet.

6 Bake until oatcakes are firm to touch and uniformly golden, 32 to 36 minutes, rotating sheet halfway through baking. Transfer sheet to wire rack and let oatcakes cool completely on sheet before serving.

Storage: 3 weeks at room temperature

Chapter 5

SINK YOUR TEETH IN

Makes 24 bars

Total Time 1 hour, plus 2 hours cooling

Cherry streusel bars are a study in contrasts: light, crisp oat topping strewn atop a filling of vibrant fruit, all supported by a shortbread base that's tender but sturdy enough so you can enjoy this mini feast for the senses anywhere. To streamline these three-layer bars, we make one dough and use it for both the base and the streusel topping (for which we stir in a couple of crunchy additions). The best cherry flavor comes from a mixture of frozen cherries and jarred cherry preserves, a winning combination that requires no stovetop cooking time.

CHERRY STREUSEL BARS

CRUST

- 2½ cups (355 grams) all-purpose flour
- ⅔ cup (132 grams) granulated sugar
- ½ teaspoon table salt
- 16 tablespoons (228 grams) unsalted butter, cut into ½-inch pieces and chilled

CHERRY FILLING

- 9 ounces (255 grams/2 cups) frozen sweet cherries, thawed
- 1 cup (281 grams) cherry preserves
- 2 teaspoons lemon juice
- ¼ teaspoon almond extract
- Pinch table salt

STREUSEL

- ½ cup (43 grams) old-fashioned rolled oats
- ½ cup (64 grams) slivered almonds, chopped
- ¼ cup packed (50 grams) brown sugar
- 2 tablespoons unsalted butter, cut into ½-inch pieces and softened

Storage: 3 days at room temperature

Measure the cherries while they are still frozen and then transfer them to a paper towel–lined baking sheet to thaw. One 12-ounce jar of cherry preserves is more than enough preserves for this recipe.

1 For the crust: Adjust oven rack to middle position and heat oven to 375 degrees. Make foil sling for 13 by 9-inch baking pan by folding 2 long sheets of aluminum foil; first sheet should be 13 inches wide and second sheet should be 9 inches wide. Lay sheets of foil in pan perpendicular to each other, with extra foil hanging over edges of pan. Push foil into corners and up sides of pan, smoothing foil flush to pan. Grease foil.

2 Process flour, sugar, and salt in food processor until combined, about 5 seconds. Add butter and pulse until mixture resembles wet sand, about 15 pulses.

3 Transfer 1¼ cups dough to medium bowl and set aside. Transfer remaining dough to prepared pan and press firmly into even layer (dough will be slightly dry). Bake until light golden brown, 16 to 18 minutes, rotating pan halfway through baking.

4 For the cherry filling: Meanwhile, wipe processor bowl clean with paper towels. Pulse all ingredients in food processor until finely chopped, about 7 pulses; set aside.

5 For the streusel: Add oats, almonds, and sugar to reserved dough and toss to combine. Add butter and rub mixture between your fingers until butter is fully incorporated and mixture forms small clumps. Set aside streusel.

6 Transfer filling to pan and spread evenly over crust (crust needn't be cool). Sprinkle streusel evenly over filling (do not press streusel into filling). Bake until filling is bubbling and streusel is deep golden brown, 24 to 28 minutes, rotating pan halfway through baking. Transfer pan to wire rack and let bars cool completely, about 2 hours. Using foil overhang, lift bars out of pan. Cut into 24 pieces before serving.

ATK CLASSIC

How We Achieve *Structurally Sound* Cherry Streusel Bars

- **Make a double-duty shortbread** You can use the same simple mixture of sugar, flour, and plenty of butter for both the sturdy bottom layer and the base for the top layer.

- **Open a jar of preserves** Adding preserves to thawed frozen fruit makes the filling cohesive without the need for cooking.

- **Enhance the dough** Oats, sugar, and a bit more butter transform the reserved base dough into a light, crumbly streusel topping that adheres nicely to the fruit filling.

Robust Cherry Layer
Punchy jam and frozen sweet cherries combine.

Crumbly Streusel
Oats and nuts give the topping textural interest.

Sturdy Shortbread Base
Pressing the dough into the pan creates a firm (yet tender) foundation.

Making a Foil Sling

For bar cookies, simply greasing a baking pan isn't enough: Sticky fillings can glue bars to the pan. We line the pans with aluminum foil (or parchment paper) in a way that makes them simple to remove.

Fold 2 long sheets of aluminum foil to match width of pan. For rectangular pan, sheets will be 2 different widths. Place sheets of foil perpendicular to each other, with extra foil hanging over edges of pan. Push foil into corners, smoothing foil flush with pan.

Making a Crust

A great streusel bar has a solid, level crust. Sprinkle flour mixture evenly over pan bottom and press down firmly (you can use flat bottom of dry measuring cup, metal spatula, or your hands) to make sure crust is level from edge to edge.

Cutting Even, Precise Bars

1 Using foil sling, lift bars from pan before cutting.

2 Use ruler to measure and mark even intervals.

3 Using sharp chef's knife, slice desired number of bars.

1

2

3

Makes 16 bars

Total Time 1 hour, plus 2 hours cooling

WHY THIS RECIPE WORKS A deep, dark chocolate crust and a luscious raspberry filling combine to deliver a streusel bar far more audaciously flavored than your average bar. We use lots of cocoa for the crust and incorporate chopped bittersweet chocolate and walnuts into the streusel for even more flavor and appealing texture. The raspberry filling, a classic pairing with chocolate, delivers a tart and fruity counterpoint to the rich cocoa.

CHOCOLATE RASPBERRY STREUSEL BARS

CRUST AND STREUSEL

- 1¼ cups (178 grams) all-purpose flour
- ½ cup (43 grams) unsweetened cocoa powder
- ⅓ cup (66 grams) sugar
- ½ teaspoon table salt
- 10 tablespoons (143 grams) unsalted butter, melted
- 2 ounces (57 grams) bittersweet chocolate, chopped
- ⅓ cup (35 grams) walnuts, chopped

RASPBERRY FILLING

- ¾ cup (211 grams) seedless raspberry jam
- 3¾ ounces (106 grams/¾ cup) frozen raspberries, thawed
- 1 tablespoon lemon juice

We like the consistent quality and availability of frozen berries for this recipe; simply microwave them for about 1 minute to thaw.

1 **For the crust and streusel:** Adjust oven rack to lower-middle position and heat oven to 350 degrees. Make foil sling for 8-inch square baking pan by folding 2 long sheets of aluminum foil so each is 8 inches wide. Lay sheets of foil in pan perpendicular to each other, with extra foil hanging over edges of pan. Push foil into corners and up sides of pan, smoothing foil flush to pan. Grease foil.

2 Whisk flour, cocoa, sugar, and salt together in bowl. Add melted butter and stir until flour is evenly moistened. Crumble two-thirds of dough evenly over bottom of prepared pan and press firmly into even layer. Bake crust until firm to touch, 20 to 22 minutes, rotating pan halfway through baking. Transfer pan to wire rack.

3 Stir chocolate and walnuts into remaining dough and mix until mixture is texture of coarse meal with pea-size clumps; set aside streusel.

4 **For the raspberry filling:** Using fork, mash jam, raspberries, and lemon juice together in bowl until few berry pieces remain. Spread berry mixture evenly over crust (crust needn't be cool). Sprinkle streusel evenly over filling. Bake until filling is bubbling around edges, 22 to 25 minutes, rotating pan halfway through baking. Transfer pan to wire rack and let bars cool completely, about 2 hours. Using foil overhang, lift bars out of pan. Cut into 16 pieces before serving.

Storage: 3 days at room temperature

Makes 24 bars

Total Time 1¼ hours, plus 2 hours cooling

WHY THIS RECIPE WORKS The buttery sweetness of corn meets cranberries' tart, vivid bite in these striking layered bars. The base combines all-purpose and corn flours for a sandy, tender crust with a subtle earthiness and noticeable corn flavor—without the grit that cornmeal would contribute. Rosemary threads through the cookie and filling to add a piney savor. The jewel-toned cranberry filling, simmered until the berries just burst, is jammy and lush. On top, the crust mixture reappears as a streusel, baking into golden crumbles that are crisp-edged and buttery. A drizzle of orange glaze seeps into the crumbles and fruit and ties the layers together with tangy sweetness.

CRANBERRY-ROSEMARY CORN STREUSEL BARS

CRANBERRY FILLING

- 18 ounces (510 grams/4½ cups) frozen cranberries
- 2 cups (396 grams) granulated sugar
- 2 teaspoons grated orange zest plus ½ cup (118 grams) juice
- ½ teaspoon table salt
- 1 sprig fresh rosemary

CRUST AND STREUSEL

- 2 cups (284 grams) all-purpose flour
- 1¾ cups (227 grams) corn flour
- ½ cup plus 2 tablespoons (124 grams) granulated sugar
- 1½ teaspoons minced fresh rosemary
- ¾ teaspoon table salt
- 20 tablespoons (285 grams/2½ sticks) unsalted butter, melted

GLAZE

- ½ cup (57 grams) confectioners' sugar
- 1 tablespoon orange juice

We like the fine consistency of corn flour here; you can use fine cornmeal but the crust and streusel will be slightly gritty. Do not use masa harina, which has a very pronounced corn flavor. You'll need to juice two to three oranges to yield ½ cup plus 1 tablespoon orange juice. Once baked, the cranberry filling is quite sticky; use parchment paper, not aluminum foil, to line the pan and make sure there are no gaps in the corners of your parchment sling to ensure easy removal.

1 For the cranberry filling: Bring cranberries, sugar, orange zest and juice, salt, and rosemary sprig to boil in medium saucepan over high heat, stirring occasionally. Reduce to medium-high and cook until about one-quarter of cranberries have burst, about 10 minutes. Transfer to bowl, discard rosemary sprig, and set aside to cool while making crust.

2 For the crust and streusel: Adjust oven rack to lower-middle position and heat oven to 350 degrees. Grease 13 by 9-inch baking pan. Make parchment sling for pan by folding 2 long sheets of parchment; first sheet should be 13 inches wide and second sheet should be 9 inches wide. Lay sheets of parchment in pan perpendicular to each other, with extra parchment hanging over edges of pan. Push parchment into corners and up sides of pan, smoothing parchment flush to pan, making sure there are no gaps in parchment on corners. Grease parchment.

3 Whisk flour, corn flour, sugar, rosemary, and salt together in medium bowl. Add melted butter and stir until flour is evenly moistened. Transfer one-third of flour mixture to separate bowl and set aside.

4 Crumble remaining flour mixture into prepared pan and press firmly into even layer. Bake until firm to touch and edges are light golden, 20 to 22 minutes, rotating pan halfway through baking.

5 Transfer cooled filling evenly to baked crust (crust needn't be cool) and spread into even layer. Crumble reserved flour mixture evenly over top and bake until fruit is bubbling around edges and topping is light golden, 25 to 30 minutes, rotating pan halfway through baking. Let bars cool completely in pan on wire rack, about 2 hours. Using parchment overhang, remove bars from pan.

6 For the glaze: Whisk sugar and orange juice together in bowl; drizzle over bars. Cut into 24 pieces before serving.

Storage: 3 days at room temperature

Makes 24 bars

Total Time 2 hours, plus 4 hours cooling

WHY THIS RECIPE WORKS These crumb bars pack all the autumnal appeal of an apple pie in a convenient, portable, and easy-to-make bar cookie format, doused with the irresistible flavor of salty-gooey caramel. A simple stir-together dough serves as both the sturdy base crust and the crumbled topping. We mix tart, lively Granny Smith apples with a glug of store-bought caramel sauce for a rich, gooey filling, and add brown sugar for depth, lemon juice for brightness, and a sprinkle of cinnamon for spicy warmth. Before serving, we drizzle the bars with extra caramel sauce and a final sprinkle of flaky, crunchy salt.

SALTED CARAMEL APPLE CRUMB BARS

CRUST AND STREUSEL

- 3¾ cups (533 grams) all-purpose flour
- 2 cups packed (396 grams) dark brown sugar
- 24 tablespoons (342 grams/ 3 sticks) unsalted butter, melted
- 1½ teaspoons table salt
- 1½ teaspoons baking powder
- ¾ teaspoon baking soda

APPLE FILLING

- 3 pounds Granny Smith apples, peeled, cored, and sliced ¼ inch thick
- ¾ cup (241 grams) jarred caramel sauce, divided
- ⅓ cup packed (66 grams) dark brown sugar
- 1 tablespoon grated lemon zest plus 2 tablespoons juice
- 1 teaspoon ground cinnamon
- ¼ teaspoon table salt

- 2 teaspoons flake sea salt

We developed these bars using Stonewall Kitchen jarred caramel sauce; other brands of jarred caramel sauce, such as Smucker's, can be used, but do not use looser caramel sauces that are packaged in squeeze bottles.

1 For the crust and streusel: Adjust oven rack to middle position and heat oven to 350 degrees. Make foil sling for 13 by 9-inch baking pan by folding 2 long sheets of aluminum foil; first sheet should be 13 inches wide and second sheet should be 9 inches wide. Lay sheets of foil in pan perpendicular to each other, with extra foil hanging over edges of pan. Push foil into corners and up sides of pan, smoothing foil flush to pan. Grease foil.

2 Stir all ingredients in bowl until no dry spots remain and mixture forms clumps. Reserve one-third of flour mixture and refrigerate until ready to use (mixture will firm as it chills).

3 Crumble remaining flour mixture into prepared pan and press firmly into even layer. Bake until pale golden, 15 to 20 minutes, rotating pan halfway through baking. Transfer pan to wire rack and let crust cool for 20 minutes.

4 For the apple filling: Combine apples, ½ cup (160 grams) caramel sauce, sugar, lemon zest and juice, cinnamon, and table salt in large bowl, then spread into even layer over crust. Crumble reserved chilled flour mixture evenly over top. Bake until top is golden and crisp, 55 minutes to 1 hour 5 minutes.

5 Transfer pan to wire rack and let bars cool completely, about 4 hours. Using foil overhang, remove bars from pan. Cut into 24 pieces, drizzle with remaining ¼ cup caramel sauce, and sprinkle with flake sea salt before serving.

Storage: 2 days in refrigerator

The sweet-tart taste of a good lemon bar is pure sunshine in edible form and its textural contrast—silky custard atop a crisp shortbread base—is sublime. Our crust uses granulated sugar for a delicate crunch and melted butter for ease; just stir and pat in the pan, then bake until golden brown to ensure lasting crispness. For a brightly flavored filling, we include lemon zest as well as juice, and we add a couple teaspoons of cream of tartar to reinforce the tang. Cooking the filling on the stove before baking it on the crust both shortens the oven time and protects against overcooked edges.

Makes 12 bars

Total Time 55 minutes, plus 2 hours cooling

LEMON BARS

CRUST

- 1 cup (142 grams) all-purpose flour
- ¼ cup (50 grams) granulated sugar
- ½ teaspoon table salt
- 8 tablespoons (114 grams) unsalted butter, melted

LEMON FILLING

- 1 cup (198 grams) granulated sugar
- 2 tablespoons all-purpose flour
- 2 teaspoons cream of tartar
- ¼ teaspoon table salt
- 3 large eggs plus 3 large yolks
- 2 teaspoons grated lemon zest plus ⅔ cup (158 grams) juice (4 lemons)
- 4 tablespoons (57 grams) unsalted butter, cut into 8 pieces

Confectioners' sugar for dusting (optional)

Do not substitute bottled lemon juice for fresh here.

1 For the crust: Adjust oven rack to middle position and heat oven to 350 degrees. Make foil sling for 8-inch square baking pan by folding 2 long sheets of aluminum foil so each is 8 inches wide. Lay sheets of foil in pan perpendicular to each other, with extra foil hanging over edges of pan. Push foil into corners and up sides of pan, smoothing foil flush to pan. Grease foil.

2 Whisk flour, sugar, and salt together in bowl. Add melted butter and stir until combined. Crumble mixture into prepared pan and press firmly into even layer (do not wash bowl). Bake until dark golden, 19 to 24 minutes, rotating pan halfway through baking.

3 For the lemon filling: While crust bakes, whisk sugar, flour, cream of tartar, and salt together in now-empty bowl. Whisk in eggs and yolks until no streaks of egg remain. Whisk in lemon zest and juice. Transfer mixture to saucepan and cook over medium-low heat, stirring constantly, until mixture thickens and registers 160 degrees, 5 to 8 minutes. Off heat, stir in butter. Strain filling through fine-mesh strainer set over bowl.

4 Pour filling over hot crust and tilt pan to spread evenly. Bake until filling is set and barely jiggles when pan is shaken, 8 to 12 minutes. (Filling around perimeter may be slightly raised.) Let bars cool completely in pan on wire rack, about 2 hours. Using foil overhang, remove bars from pan. Cut into 12 pieces, wiping knife clean between cuts as necessary. Dust bars with confectioners' sugar, if using, before serving.

Storage: 2 days at room temperature

ATK CLASSIC

How We Achieve *Luscious* Lemon Bars

- **Use granulated sugar in the base** Many lemon bar crusts are made with confectioners' sugar, but we like how the crystalline texture of granulated gives the crust crispness.

- **Bake the base until golden brown** Sufficient baking protects the crust from getting soggy once the filling is baked on.

- **Precook the filling** Essentially making a lemon curd on the stovetop means less time in the oven and a consistent texture from edge to center.

- **Strain the filling** Straining removes zest and bits of cooked egg, ensuring a silky-smooth filling.

Smooth Filling
We strain out the zest once it's given up its flavor.

Lightly Crunchy Crust
Granulated sugar gives it a crisp bite.

Makes 16 bars

Total Time 1¼ hours, plus 2 hours cooling

WHY THIS RECIPE WORKS In these colorful two-tone bars, a slightly floral Meyer lemon filling and a fruity, flavor-packed wild blueberry filling meld harmoniously into a delightful jammy texture perched atop a crisp, buttery foundation (the same pat-in-the-pan crust as in our Lemon Bars). The simple flour-thickened lemon filling goes straight from the mixing bowl to the oven, which frees up time to make the blueberry topping: a strained puree of wild blueberries and sugar that's thickened with pectin. The pectin also gives these bars their gorgeous glossy, almost mirror-like surface.

MEYER LEMON–BLUEBERRY REFLECTION BARS

CRUST

- 1 cup (142 grams) all-purpose flour
- ¼ cup (50 grams) granulated sugar
- ½ teaspoon table salt
- 8 tablespoons (114 grams) unsalted butter, melted

MEYER LEMON FILLING

- 1½ cups (297 grams) granulated sugar
- 1 tablespoon grated Meyer lemon zest plus ½ cup (118 grams) juice (5 Meyer lemons)
- 2 large eggs plus 2 large egg yolks
- ¼ cup (35 grams) all-purpose flour

WILD BLUEBERRY FILLING

- 12 ounces (340 grams/2¼ cups) frozen wild blueberries, thawed
- ⅓ cup (66 grams) sugar
- 1 tablespoon low- or no-sugar-needed fruit pectin (such as Sure-Jell)

If Meyer lemons aren't available, you can replicate the flavor by using 6 tablespoons regular lemon juice and 2 tablespoons orange juice. Wild blueberries are available in the freezer section of most grocery stores. We recommend Sure-Jell Premium Fruit Pectin for Less or No Sugar Needed Recipes; other brands such as Ball set up grainier. If making these bars ahead, refrigerate them uncut and blot surface condensation with a paper towel before cutting.

1 Adjust oven rack to middle position and heat oven to 350 degrees. Grease 8-inch square pan. Make foil sling by folding 2 long sheets of aluminum foil so each is 8 inches wide. Lay sheets of foil in pan perpendicular to each other, with extra foil hanging over edges of pan. Push foil into corners and up sides of pan, smoothing foil flush to pan. Grease foil.

2 **For the crust:** Whisk flour, sugar, and salt together in medium bowl. Add melted butter and stir until combined. Crumble mixture into prepared pan and press firmly into even layer (do not wash bowl). Bake until golden, 20 to 22 minutes, rotating pan halfway through baking.

3 **For the Meyer lemon filling:** Whisk sugar, lemon zest and juice, eggs and yolks, and flour together in now-empty bowl. Pour over warm crust and bake until filling has set around edges but jiggles slightly in center when shaken, 20 to 22 minutes, rotating pan halfway through baking. Transfer pan to wire rack.

4 **For the wild blueberry filling:** Process thawed blueberries and any juices with sugar in food processor until smooth, about 1 minute. Strain puree through fine-mesh strainer into medium saucepan, pressing on solids to extract as much puree as possible (you should have about ¾ cup); discard solids. Whisk in pectin and bring to simmer over medium heat; cook, stirring constantly, for 2 minutes. (Blueberry mixture will not be thickened.) Slowly and gradually pour blueberry mixture over warm lemon filling, then let sit until bars are cooled completely, about 2 hours. Using foil overhang, remove bars from pan. Cut into 16 pieces before serving.

Storage: 24 hours in refrigerator

WHY THIS RECIPE WORKS With a full pound of toasted pecans piled high on a buttery crust and held in place by a lightly sweet glaze, these bars really let their star ingredient shine. The generous amount of nuts forms a thick layer, allowing for a combination of textures in every bite—some nuts are slicked with glaze and chewy, while those sitting on top are crisp. Brown sugar, butter, and vanilla add depth to the easy corn syrup glaze, and, because the topping isn't wet, there's no need to prebake the crust. We simply pat it into the pan, spread the pecans on top, and bake.

Makes 24 bars

Total Time 1 hour, plus 2 hours cooling

ULTRANUTTY PECAN BARS

CRUST

- 1¾ cups (249 grams) all-purpose flour
- 6 tablespoons (74 grams) granulated sugar
- ½ teaspoon table salt
- 8 tablespoons (114 grams) unsalted butter, melted

TOPPING

- ¾ cup packed (149 grams) light brown sugar
- ½ cup (164 grams) light corn syrup
- 7 tablespoons (100 grams) unsalted butter, melted and hot
- 1 teaspoon vanilla extract
- ½ teaspoon table salt
- 4 cups (476 grams) pecans, toasted

- ½ teaspoon flake sea salt (optional)

The edges will be slightly firmer than the center. If desired, trim ¼ inch from the edges before cutting into bars.

1 Adjust oven rack to lowest position and heat oven to 350 degrees. Grease 13 by 9-inch baking pan. Make parchment sling by folding 2 long sheets of parchment paper; first sheet should be 13 inches wide and second sheet should be 9 inches wide. Lay sheets of parchment in pan perpendicular to each other, with extra parchment hanging over edges of pan. Push parchment into corners and up sides of pan, smoothing parchment flush to pan. Grease parchment.

2 **For the crust:** Whisk flour, sugar, and salt together in medium bowl. Add melted butter and stir with wooden spoon until dough begins to form. Using your hands, continue to combine until no dry flour remains and small portion of dough holds together when squeezed in palm of your hand. Crumble mixture into prepared pan and press firmly into even layer.

3 **For the topping:** Whisk sugar, corn syrup, melted butter, vanilla, and table salt in medium bowl until smooth (mixture will look separated at first but will become homogeneous), about 20 seconds. Fold pecans into sugar mixture until evenly coated.

4 Pour topping over crust, then spread into even layer, pushing to edges and into corners (there will be bare patches). Bake until topping is evenly distributed and rapidly bubbling across entire surface, 23 to 25 minutes, rotating pan halfway through baking.

5 Transfer pan to wire rack and sprinkle with flake sea salt, if using. Let bars cool completely in pan on rack, about 2 hours. Using foil overhang, remove bars from pan. Cut into 24 pieces before serving.

Storage: 5 days at room temperature

WHY THIS RECIPE WORKS These satisfyingly chewy bars marry luscious, buttery-soft caramel with crisp toasted pistachios. Cacao nibs punctuate the filling with extra crunch, and their roasted cocoa flavor provides an earthy counterpoint to the sweetness of the caramel and shortbread base. To make sure the caramel is just the right texture—holding its shape around the nuts without hurting our teeth—we cook it to 245 degrees, for a soft caramel. A quick bake atop the crust makes everything cohesive and increases chewiness. A final sprinkling of flake sea salt pulls all the flavors into focus.

Makes 16 bars

Total Time 1½ hours, plus 2 hours cooling and chilling

CARAMEL PISTACHIO BARS WITH CACAO NIBS

CRUST

- 1¼ cups (178 grams) all-purpose flour
- ¼ cup packed (50 grams) dark brown sugar
- ¼ teaspoon table salt
- 8 tablespoons (114 grams) unsalted butter, melted

FILLING

- 1¼ cups (248 grams) granulated sugar
- ¼ cup (82 grams) light corn syrup
- ¼ cup (59 grams) water
- ½ cup (116 grams) heavy cream
- 8 tablespoons (114 grams) unsalted butter, cut into 8 pieces
- 1 teaspoon vanilla extract
- 1 teaspoon table salt
- 1½ cups (218 grams) shelled pistachios
- 2 tablespoons cacao nibs

- ¼ teaspoon flake sea salt

The caramel will appear loose after baking but sets as it cools. You can substitute any chopped toasted nut for pistachios or use a combination.

1 Adjust oven rack to lower-middle position and heat oven to 325 degrees. Grease 8-inch square baking pan. Make parchment sling by folding 2 long sheets of parchment paper so each is 8 inches wide. Lay sheets of parchment in pan perpendicular to each other, with extra parchment hanging over edges of pan. Push parchment into corners and up sides of pan, smoothing parchment flush to pan. Grease parchment.

2 **For the crust:** Whisk flour, sugar, and salt together in bowl. Add melted butter and stir until flour is evenly moistened. Crumble mixture into prepared pan and press firmly into even layer. Bake until light golden and firm to touch, 25 to 28 minutes, rotating pan halfway through baking. Transfer pan to wire rack then, using sturdy metal spatula, press on entire surface of warm crust to compress. Let crust cool while preparing filling.

3 **For the filling:** Combine sugar, corn syrup, and water in medium saucepan. Bring to boil over medium-high heat and cook, without stirring, until mixture is light amber in color, 8 to 10 minutes. Reduce heat to medium-low and continue to cook, swirling saucepan occasionally, until mixture is just beginning to brown, is bubbling vigorously, and registers between 320 and 330 degrees in several places, 2 to 5 minutes.

4 Off heat, carefully stir in cream, butter, vanilla, and table salt (mixture will bubble and steam). Return saucepan to medium heat and cook, stirring frequently, until smooth and registers 240 to 245 degrees in several places, about 2 minutes. Off heat, stir in pistachios and cacao nibs.

5 Pour filling over crust in pan (crust needn't be completely cooled) and spread into even layer. Bake until filling is dark amber, about 25 minutes, rotating pan halfway through baking.

6 Transfer pan to wire rack and let cool for 1 hour. Transfer pan to refrigerator and chill until completely set, at least 1 hour. Using foil overhang, remove bars from pan. Cut bars in half, then slice each half crosswise into 8 equal pieces. Sprinkle bars with flake salt before serving.

Storage: 1 week in refrigerator

Makes 16 wedges

Total Time 1½ hours, plus 2 hours 10 minutes cooling

WHY THIS RECIPE WORKS Our giant riff on classic Girl Scout Samoa cookies (also called Caramel deLites) is a simple bar cookie built in a round springform pan that captures the charm—and varying textures—of the original version. To give this large-format cookie the signature "O" shape of the small Girl Scout cookie, we cut a circle out of the middle of the crust with a round cutter and leave the cutter in place while baking and topping the cookie. Each bite of short vanilla cookie, chewy caramel, crispy bits of toasted coconut, and snappy tempered chocolate drizzle brings back memories for those familiar and creates a new (and maybe even better) sensation for those tasting the "deLite" for the first time.

GIANT COCONUT-CARAMEL SHORTBREAD COOKIE

CRUST

- 1⅔ cups (237 grams) all-purpose flour
- ⅓ cup (66 grams) granulated sugar
- 1 teaspoon table salt
- 10 tablespoons (143 grams) unsalted butter, melted
- 1 tablespoon vanilla extract

FILLING

- ½ cup packed (99 grams) brown sugar
- ⅔ cup (210 grams) sweetened condensed milk
- ¼ cup (58 grams) heavy cream
- ¼ cup (82 grams) corn syrup
- 4 tablespoons (57 grams) unsalted butter
- ¾ teaspoon table salt
- 1 tablespoon vanilla extract
- 1½ cups (123 grams) toasted unsweetened shredded coconut, divided

CHOCOLATE

- 10 ounces (284 grams) bittersweet chocolate (8 ounces/227 grams chopped fine, 2 ounces/57 grams grated)

We developed this recipe with Bob's Red Mill Unsweetened Shredded Coconut. To toast the coconut, spread it evenly on a rimmed baking sheet and bake it at 325 degrees for 10 to 15 minutes, stirring halfway through baking.

1 Adjust oven rack to upper-middle position and heat oven to 350 degrees. Grease 9-inch springform pan and ovensafe 2-inch round cutter.

2 For the crust: Combine flour, sugar, and salt in bowl. Add melted butter and vanilla; stir with silicone spatula until evenly moistened. Crumble dough over bottom of prepared pan and press firmly into even layer. Using fork, poke dough all over.

3 Press 2-inch round cutter into center of dough. Keeping cutter in place and using small spoon or offset spatula, gently remove center round of dough; discard or bake separately. Bake crust (with cutter in place) until edges are light golden brown, about 20 minutes, rotating pan halfway through baking. Using bottom of dry measuring cup, gently press on entire surface of warm crust to compress. Let crust cool for at least 20 minutes.

4 For the filling: Meanwhile, combine sugar, condensed milk, cream, corn syrup, butter, and salt in small heavy-bottomed saucepan. Cook over medium-low heat, stirring frequently with silicone spatula, until mixture registers between 236 and 239 degrees in several places (temperature will fluctuate), 16 to 20 minutes. Off heat, stir in vanilla and 1 cup (82 grams) coconut. Pour caramel mixture over crust (with cutter in place) and, using spatula, spread to even thickness (mixture will be very hot). Sprinkle evenly with remaining ½ cup (41 grams) coconut. Let cool completely, at least 1½ hours. (Cookie can be loosely wrapped in plastic wrap and stored at room temperature for up to 24 hours.)

5 For the chocolate: Microwave chopped chocolate in liquid measuring cup at 50 percent power, stirring every 15 seconds, until melted but not much warmer than body temperature (check by holding in palm of your hand), 1 to 2 minutes. Add grated chocolate and stir until smooth, returning to microwave for no more than 5 seconds at a time to finish melting if necessary.

••• CONTINUED •••

6 Remove side of pan and cutter in center of dough; invert cookie onto inverted rimmed baking sheet. Pour ¼ cup melted chocolate onto cookie in even band around hole in center, about ½ inch from hole. Using small offset spatula, gently spread chocolate to completely cover cookie. Repeat with additional ¼ cup chocolate. Refrigerate until chocolate is set, 20 to 25 minutes.

7 If remaining ½ cup chocolate has hardened, microwave, stirring every 10 seconds, until just remelted. Transfer chocolate to pastry bag or small zipper-lock bag and snip off corner, making about ⅛-inch hole. Invert cookie, chocolate side down, onto wire rack. Carefully place rack in now-empty rimmed baking sheet. Pipe remaining chocolate in zigzags across caramel layer. Refrigerate until set, about 10 minutes. Using large offset spatula, transfer cookie to cutting board. Using chef's knife, cut cookie into 2-inch wedges. Serve.

Storage: 4 days at room temperature

CRAFTING THE COOKIE

1. Press 2-inch round cutter into center of dough. Using small spoon, remove dough round in cutter. Bake crust until light golden brown, about 20 minutes

2. Using bottom of dry measuring cup, gently press on entire surface of warm crust to compress.

3. Pour caramel mixture over cooled crust and spread to even thickness. Sprinkle evenly with coconut and let cool completely.

4. Invert cookie onto inverted rimmed baking sheet and pour ¼ cup melted chocolate onto cookie in even band around hole in center, about ½ inch from hole. Spread chocolate to completely cover cookie and repeat with additional ¼ cup chocolate.

1

2

3

4

MISO MAGIC BARS

Makes 16 bars

Total Time 1 hour, plus 2 hours cooling

WHY THIS RECIPE WORKS While the magic bars we had in childhood have all the nostalgia and sweetness of a bunk bed at sleepaway camp, adults deserve a little magic, too, and these roasty-toasty, toffee-flavored, nut- and seed–packed bars make for an enchanting cookie break. Balancing (and reducing) the sweetness was the most important step to transforming our bars, so we brought in miso. This umami-packed ingredient, mixed into the condensed milk that traditionally holds these bars together, enhances all the nutty flavors, while adding its own depth and bit of salty savor. Sesame seeds and toasted sesame oil give the base layer incredible nuttiness. We replace the very-sweet butterscotch chips with toffee bits. Peanuts and chocolate (here, bittersweet) never miss and, unlike other nuts we tried, the peanuts stand out against the other big, bold flavors in this bar. The final sweetened shredded coconut layer is a must, but instead of adding it and then fully saturating the bars with the milk mixture, we apply some coconut before pouring on the miso-milk mixture and more halfway through baking so there's a crunchy top.

- 5 whole graham crackers, broken into 1-inch pieces
- 3 tablespoons sugar
- ¼ teaspoon table salt
- ¼ cup (36 grams) sesame seeds
- 4 tablespoons (57 grams) unsalted butter, melted
- ½ teaspoon toasted sesame oil
- 1 (14-ounce) can sweetened condensed milk
- 2 tablespoons white miso
- ½ cup (85 grams) bittersweet chocolate chips
- 1 cup (142 grams) Heath Bar Bits of Brickle
- ½ cup (71 grams) dry-roasted peanuts
- 1 cup (82 grams) sweetened shredded coconut, divided

We like Heath Bar Bits of Brickle in this recipe but you can substitute Heath Bars chopped into ¼-inch pieces or any toffee bits; alternatively, you can substitute an equal amount of Butterfinger Bits. We developed this recipe with white miso but red miso would also work. The sweetened condensed milk can make getting these bars out of the pan a little tricky; use parchment paper, not aluminum foil, to line the pan, make sure there are no gaps in the corners of the sling, and grease the pan and the parchment.

1 Adjust oven rack to upper-middle position and heat oven to 350 degrees. Grease 8-inch square baking pan. Make parchment sling for baking pan by folding 2 long sheets of parchment paper so each is 8 inches wide. Lay sheets of parchment in pan perpendicular to each other, with extra parchment hanging over edges of pan. Push parchment into corners and up sides of pan, smoothing parchment flush to pan. Grease parchment.

2 Pulse crackers, sugar, and salt in food processor until finely ground, about 15 pulses. Transfer crumbs to bowl, then stir in sesame seeds, melted butter, and sesame oil and mix until evenly moistened. Spread crumb mixture in prepared pan and press firmly into even layer. Bake until golden brown and firm, about 12 minutes, rotating pan halfway through baking.

3 Whisk sweetened condensed milk and miso together in bowl. Sprinkle chocolate chips, toffee bits, peanuts, and ½ cup (41 grams) coconut, in that order, over warm crust. Drizzle sweetened condensed milk mixture over top and bake for 18 minutes.

4 Sprinkle remaining ½ cup (41 grams) coconut over top and bake until coconut is lightly toasted, 10 to 13 minutes. Transfer pan to wire rack and let bars cool completely in pan, about 2 hours. Using parchment overhang, remove bars from pan. Cut into 16 pieces before serving.

Storage: 2 weeks at room temperature

WHY THIS RECIPE WORKS Chocolate turtle candies hit every texture (crunchy, chewy, creamy) and three popular tastes (nutty, rich, sweet)—we love these qualities in cookies too. To reimagine this classic candy as a bar cookie, we start with a chocolate shortbread base. For a caramel layer with sliceable chew, we cook dulce de leche, butter, sugar, cream, and corn syrup, and then stir in pecans. We finish the bars by swirling chocolate chips into the still-warm caramel and add another handful of pecans and a sprinkle of flake sea salt to heighten all the flavors.

Makes 24 bars

Total Time 1 hour, plus 3 hours setting

TURTLE BARS

CRUST

- 1⅔ cups (237 grams) all-purpose flour
- ½ cup (99 grams) granulated sugar
- ⅓ cup (28 grams) unsweetened cocoa powder
- ¾ teaspoon table salt
- 12 tablespoons (171 grams) unsalted butter, melted

TOPPING

- 1 (13.4-ounce) can dulce de leche
- 1 cup packed (198 grams) light brown sugar
- ½ cup (116 grams) heavy cream
- ½ cup (164 grams) light corn syrup
- 8 tablespoons (114 grams) unsalted butter
- ½ teaspoon table salt
- 2 cups (238 grams) coarsely chopped pecans, toasted, divided
- 1 cup (170 grams) semisweet chocolate chips
- ½ teaspoon flake sea salt

1 Adjust oven rack to middle position and heat oven to 350 degrees. Grease 13 by 9-inch baking pan. Make parchment sling by folding 2 long sheets of parchment paper; first sheet should be 13 inches wide and second sheet should be 9 inches wide. Lay sheets of parchment in pan perpendicular to each other, with extra parchment hanging over edges of pan. Push parchment into corners and up sides of pan, smoothing parchment flush to pan. Grease parchment.

2 **For the crust:** Combine flour, sugar, cocoa, and salt in bowl. Add melted butter and stir with silicone spatula until evenly moistened. Crumble mixture into prepared pan and press firmly into even layer. Bake until crust is fragrant and looks dry, 18 to 20 minutes, rotating pan halfway through baking. Transfer pan to wire rack to cool while making topping.

3 **For the topping:** Combine dulce de leche, sugar, cream, corn syrup, butter, and table salt in large saucepan. Bring to boil over medium heat, stirring frequently with silicone spatula. Once boiling, continue to cook, stirring frequently to prevent scorching, until mixture registers between 235 and 240 degrees in several places, 9 to 11 minutes longer. (Mixture will be thick and bubbling vigorously.) Off heat, stir in 1½ cups (179 grams) pecans. Pour caramel mixture over crust (crust needn't be completely cooled) and spread to even thickness. Sprinkle with chocolate chips and let sit until chocolate chips have softened, about 5 minutes.

4 Using butter knife, swirl softened chocolate chips through caramel mixture. Sprinkle with remaining ½ cup (60 grams) pecans and flake sea salt. Let bars sit at room temperature until chocolate is set, at least 3 hours. Using parchment overhang, remove bars from pan. Cut into 24 pieces before serving.

Storage: 5 days at room temperature

Makes 24 bars

Total Time 1¾ hours, plus 6 hours cooling and chilling

WHY THIS RECIPE WORKS Lush cheesecake topped with glistening strawberries is an iconic pairing; the juicy, slightly acidic berries balance the cheesecake's richness. For our bars, we wanted the strawberry component to be neater and incorporated in every bite. We bake a cream cheese filling atop a crisp graham cracker crust; then we puree fresh strawberries and stir them into a sour cream topping. We garnish each square with a strawberry slice.

STRAWBERRY CHEESECAKE BARS

CRUST

- 9 whole graham crackers, broken into pieces
- ½ cup (99 grams) sugar
- ¾ cup (107 grams) all-purpose flour
- ¼ teaspoon table salt
- 8 tablespoons (114 grams) unsalted butter, melted

FILLING

- 1½ pounds (680 grams) cream cheese
- 1 cup (198 grams) sugar
- 3 large eggs
- 2 teaspoons vanilla extract

TOPPING

- 6 ounces (170 grams) strawberries, hulled (1 heaping cup), plus 5 hulled strawberries
- ½ cup (99 grams) plus 1 teaspoon sugar, divided
- 2 cups (475 grams) sour cream

1 Adjust oven rack to middle position and heat oven to 300 degrees. Make foil sling for 13 by 9-inch baking pan by folding 2 long sheets of aluminum foil; first sheet should be 13 inches wide and second sheet should be 9 inches wide. Lay sheets of foil in pan perpendicular to each other, with extra foil hanging over edges of pan. Push foil into corners and up sides of pan, smoothing foil flush to pan. Grease foil.

2 **For the crust:** Process cracker pieces and sugar in food processor until finely ground, about 30 seconds. Add flour and salt and pulse to combine, about 2 pulses. Add melted butter and pulse until crumbs are evenly moistened, about 10 pulses.

3 Spread crumb mixture in prepared pan and, using bottom of dry measuring cup, firmly pack crust into even layer. Bake until fragrant and beginning to brown around edges, about 20 minutes, rotating pan halfway through baking. Transfer pan to wire rack and let cool completely.

4 **For the filling:** In clean, dry processor bowl, process cream cheese and sugar until smooth, about 3 minutes, scraping down sides of bowl as needed. With processor running, add eggs, one at a time, until just incorporated, about 30 seconds. Scrape down sides of bowl. Add vanilla and process to combine, about 10 seconds. Pour cream cheese mixture over cooled crust then bake until center is almost set but still jiggles slightly when pan is shaken, about 45 minutes, rotating pan halfway through baking.

5 **For the topping:** While bars bake, in clean, dry processor bowl, process 6 ounces strawberries and ½ cup (99 grams) sugar until smooth, about 30 seconds. Combine strawberry puree and sour cream in bowl until homogeneous.

6 Remove pan from oven, then pour strawberry mixture over cheesecake (cheesecake layer should be completely covered). Return pan to oven and bake until topping is just set, about 15 minutes. Let cheesecake cool completely in pan on wire rack, about 2 hours. Refrigerate until cold and set, at least 4 hours or up to 24 hours.

7 Slice hulled strawberries thin and gently toss with remaining 1 teaspoon sugar in bowl. Using foil overhang, remove cheesecake from pan. Cut into 24 pieces, dipping knife in very hot water and wiping knife clean and dry between cuts as necessary. Garnish each piece with 1 strawberry slice before serving.

Storage: 2 days in refrigerator

WHY THIS RECIPE WORKS Cooling, sweet, tangy, and full of mango flavor, our mango lassi bars capture everything we love about the refreshing Indian drink. While the traditional beverage generally uses fresh or frozen mangos blended with yogurt, we rely on freeze-dried fruit to intensely flavor a mix of sweetened yogurt and heavy cream—with just a touch of cardamom—that whips up creamy and airy. A crisp coconut and lime crust is a sturdy base and a complementary pairing. And for a dramatic, colorful finish, we swirl a simple bright-orange mango puree into the lassi layer.

Makes 16 bars

Total Time 1¼ hours, plus 2½ hours cooling and chilling

MANGO LASSI BARS

CRUST

- ½ cup (71 grams) all-purpose flour
- 6 tablespoons (21 grams) unsweetened flaked coconut
- 3 tablespoons sugar
- 1½ teaspoons grated lime zest
- ¼ teaspoon table salt
- 5 tablespoons (71 grams) unsalted butter, melted

MANGO PUREE

- ½ cup (127 grams) unsweetened mango puree
- 2 tablespoons sugar
- 1 tablespoon lime juice

MANGO FILLING

- 2 teaspoons unflavored gelatin
- 3 tablespoons water
- 1¼ cups freeze-dried mangos
- 1½ cups (357 grams) plain Greek yogurt
- ⅔ cup (132 grams) sugar
- ¼ teaspoon ground cardamom
- ⅛ teaspoon table salt
- 1 cup (231 grams) heavy cream

Unsweetened mango puree can be found in the freezer section of well-stocked grocery stores. If you do not have a spice grinder, you can grind the freeze-dried mangos in a blender. The mango filling will start to set after the gelatin is added, so do not delay in pouring it into the crust and swirling in the mango puree.

1 Adjust oven rack to middle position and heat oven to 350 degrees. Make foil sling for 8-inch square baking pan by folding 2 long sheets of aluminum foil so each is 8 inches wide. Lay sheets of foil in pan perpendicular to each other, with extra foil hanging over edges of pan. Push foil into corners and up sides of pan, smoothing foil flush to pan. Grease foil.

2 **For the crust:** Whisk flour, coconut, sugar, lime zest, and salt together in bowl. Add melted butter and stir until flour is evenly moistened. Crumble mixture into prepared pan and press firmly into even layer. Bake crust until golden brown and firm to touch, about 16 minutes, rotating pan halfway through baking. Transfer pan to wire rack and let cool completely, about 30 minutes.

3 **For the mango puree:** Bring all ingredients to simmer in small saucepan over medium heat. Reduce heat to low and simmer until reduced by half, about 10 minutes (you should have scant ⅓ cup puree). Transfer to bowl and refrigerate, stirring puree occasionally while making filling.

4 **For the mango filling:** Sprinkle gelatin over water in small bowl and let sit until gelatin softens, about 5 minutes. Microwave until mixture is bubbling around edges and gelatin dissolves, about 30 seconds. Meanwhile, pulse freeze-dried mangos in spice grinder until reduced to fine powder, about 5 pulses (you should have ¼ cup fruit powder).

5 Using stand mixer fitted with whisk attachment, whip freeze-dried mango powder, yogurt, sugar, cardamom, and salt on medium speed until well combined, about 1 minute. Scrape down sides of bowl, then add heavy cream and whip on medium-high speed until whisk leaves trail in mixture, about 30 seconds. Add dissolved gelatin mixture and whip until mixture holds soft peaks, 30 to 45 seconds.

6 Transfer filling to cooled crust, then use offset spatula to smooth top. Whisk cooled mango puree to recombine, then dollop in 9 places over filling. Using chopstick or skewer, swirl mango puree into filling, making marbled pattern. Refrigerate until set, about 2 hours.

7 Using foil overhang, remove bars from pan. Cut into 16 pieces, dipping knife in very hot water and wiping knife clean and dry between cuts as necessary, before serving.

Storage: 24 hours in refrigerator

Makes 16 bars

Total Time 1½ hours, plus 1½ hours chilling

WHY THIS RECIPE WORKS British banoffee pie (a portmanteau of banana and toffee) combines a thick milk-caramel layer with fresh bananas, all topped with swoops of whipped cream. We put a portable spin on this luscious, sweet, and gooey dessert. It starts with an easy pat-in-the-pan crust, which doubles as the base for a pecan-studded streusel topping. We steep cooked bananas in cream to create a smooth pastry cream filling that bursts with banana flavor. For an airy whipped cream layer that can be sliced neatly, we stabilize the cream with a bit of gelatin. The nutty streusel topping adds crunch and provides a contrast to the sweet caramel that we drizzle over each slice before serving.

BANOFFEE CRUNCH BARS

BANANA FILLING

- 1 tablespoon unsalted butter
- 2 ripe bananas, peeled and sliced ½ inch thick
- 2 cups (462 grams) heavy cream, divided
- 2 teaspoons unflavored gelatin
- 6 tablespoons (74 grams) granulated sugar
- 3 large egg yolks
- 1½ tablespoons all-purpose flour
- ¼ teaspoon table salt
- 1½ teaspoons vanilla extract

CRUST AND STREUSEL

- 1⅓ cups (189 grams) all-purpose flour
- ¼ cup packed (50 grams) brown sugar
- ¼ teaspoon table salt
- 8 tablespoons (114 grams) unsalted butter, melted
- ½ cup (60 grams) pecans, chopped fine
- ¼ teaspoon ground cinnamon

Use all-yellow to lightly spotted, not green-topped or all-brown bananas for this recipe. Peel and slice the bananas just before using to help prevent browning. When straining the banana mixture in step 5, do not press on the bananas or the custard will turn gray as it sits.

1 Adjust oven racks to upper-middle and lower-middle positions and heat oven to 350 degrees. Make foil sling for 8-inch square baking pan by folding 2 long sheets of aluminum foil so each is 8 inches wide. Lay sheets of foil in pan perpendicular to each other, with extra foil hanging over edges of pan. Push foil into corners and up sides of pan, smoothing foil flush to pan. Grease foil.

2 **For the banana filling:** Melt butter in small saucepan over medium-high heat. Add bananas and cook until they begin to soften, about 2 minutes. Stir in 1½ cups (346 grams) heavy cream, bring to simmer, and cook for 30 seconds. Remove from heat, cover, and let sit for 40 minutes.

3 **For the crust and streusel:** While heavy cream mixture cools, whisk flour, sugar, and salt together in bowl. Add melted butter and stir until flour is evenly moistened. Crumble two-thirds of dough evenly over bottom of prepared pan and press firmly into even layer. Bake crust on lower rack until light golden brown and firm to touch, about 20 minutes, rotating pan halfway through baking. Transfer pan to wire rack to cool.

4 Add pecans and cinnamon to remaining dough and mix with your hands or silicone spatula until mixture is texture of coarse meal with pea-size clumps. Spread mixture over parchment paper–lined rimmed baking sheet. Bake on upper rack until golden brown, about 15 minutes. Transfer sheet to wire rack and set aside streusel while making filling.

WHIPPED CREAM

- ¾ teaspoon unflavored gelatin
- 2 tablespoons cold water
- ¾ cup (173 grams) heavy cream, chilled
- 1 teaspoon granulated sugar
- ½ teaspoon vanilla extract

- ¼ cup (80 grams) jarred caramel sauce

5 Sprinkle gelatin over remaining ½ cup (116 grams) heavy cream in small bowl and let sit until gelatin softens, about 5 minutes. Whisk sugar, egg yolks, flour, and salt in medium saucepan until fully combined. Strain cooled banana mixture through fine-mesh strainer into yolk mixture (do not press on bananas) and whisk until incorporated; discard cooked bananas.

6 Cook banana mixture over medium heat, whisking constantly and scraping corners of saucepan, until mixture thickens, bubbles burst across entire surface, and mixture registers 180 degrees in several places, 3 to 5 minutes. Off heat, whisk in vanilla and gelatin mixture until combined. Pour filling into crust (crust needn't be completely cooled) and refrigerate until set, about 1 hour.

7 **For the whipped cream:** Sprinkle gelatin over water in small bowl and let sit until gelatin softens, about 5 minutes. Microwave until mixture is bubbling around edges and gelatin dissolves, about 30 seconds.

8 Using stand mixer fitted with whisk attachment, whip heavy cream, sugar, and vanilla on medium-low speed until foamy, about 1 minute. Increase speed to medium, and whip until whisk begins to leave trail in cream, about 1 minute. Slowly add gelatin mixture, then increase speed to high and continue to beat until stiff peaks form, about 1 minute.

9 Once banana filling is set, spread whipped cream evenly over top, using offset spatula to smooth. Refrigerate until lightly set, about 30 minutes.

10 Before serving, sprinkle streusel evenly over whipped cream, pressing lightly to adhere. Using foil overhang, remove bars from pan. Cut into 16 pieces, dipping knife in very hot water and wiping knife clean and dry between cuts as necessary. Drizzle with caramel sauce.

Storage: 24 hours in refrigerator

Makes 24 bars

Total Time 2 hours, plus 4 hours cooling

WHY THIS RECIPE WORKS These bars—shared with us by chef and food writer Taffy Elrod—turn homey sweet potato pie into a crowd-pleasing big-batch dessert. A supereasy graham-cracker crust provides a sturdy base for the bars, with caramel and spice notes that perfectly complement the sweet potato filling. Roasting whole sweet potatoes (rather than steaming them) intensifies their flavor and bakes off excess moisture, yielding a firmer filling. Citrus (zest in the crumble topping and juice in the filling) and ginger add brightness that cuts through the richness of the dessert, creating a complexity that will keep you coming back for more.

GINGER-CITRUS SWEET POTATO PIE BARS

SWEET POTATOES

- 2 pounds sweet potatoes, unpeeled, each lightly pricked with fork in 3 places

CRUST

- 27 whole graham crackers, broken into 1-inch pieces
- ⅔ cup packed (132 grams) light brown sugar
- ½ teaspoon ground ginger
- ¼ teaspoon ground nutmeg
- 12 tablespoons (171 grams) unsalted butter, melted

CRUMBLE TOPPING

- 1 cup packed (198 grams) light brown sugar
- ½ cup (71 grams) all-purpose flour
- ½ cup (43 grams) rolled oats
- 1 teaspoon grated orange zest
- 1 teaspoon grated lemon zest
- 1 teaspoon ground ginger
- ¼ teaspoon ground nutmeg
- ¼ teaspoon table salt
- 6 tablespoons (86 grams) unsalted butter, melted

FILLING

- 3 large eggs
- ⅔ cup packed (132 grams) light brown sugar
- ⅔ cup (154 grams) heavy cream
- 1 tablespoon orange juice
- 2 teaspoons lemon juice
- 1 teaspoon ground ginger
- 1 teaspoon orange extract
- 1 teaspoon vanilla extract
- ¼ teaspoon table salt

Orange extract deepens the citrus flavor in the filling without changing the texture the way orange zest would. Look for extract made from orange oil for a clear, true orange flavor.

1 For the sweet potatoes: Adjust oven rack to middle position and heat oven to 350 degrees. Arrange potatoes on aluminum foil–lined baking sheet and bake until tip of knife slips easily into potatoes and any released sugars begin to caramelize on sheet, 1 to 1¼ hours. Let cool until just warm, about 1 hour. (Baked, unpeeled potatoes can be refrigerated for up to 3 days.)

2 For the crust: Make foil sling for 13 by 9-inch baking pan by folding 2 long sheets of aluminum foil; first sheet should be 13 inches wide and second sheet should be 9 inches wide. Lay sheets of foil in pan perpendicular to each other, with extra foil hanging over edges of pan. Push foil into corners and up sides of pan, smoothing foil flush to pan. Grease foil.

3 Process cracker pieces in food processor until finely ground, 15 to 30 seconds; reserve 1 cup (4 ounces) cracker crumbs for crumble topping. Add sugar, ginger, and nutmeg to remaining crumbs in processor and pulse to combine, about 3 pulses. Add melted butter and pulse until evenly combined, about 8 pulses. Spread crumb mixture in prepared pan and, using bottom of dry measuring cup, firmly press crumb mixture into even layer. Bake until crust is slightly puffed and fragrant, 12 to 15 minutes, rotating pan halfway through baking. Transfer pan to wire rack while making topping and filling.

4 For the crumble topping: Combine sugar, flour, oats, orange zest, lemon zest, ginger, nutmeg, salt, and reserved 1 cup cracker crumbs in medium bowl. Add melted butter and stir until no dry spots remain; set aside.

5 For the filling: Scoop flesh from cooled potatoes into clean bowl of food processor; discard skins. Process until smooth, about 1 minute, scraping down sides of bowl as needed. Add eggs, sugar, cream, orange juice, lemon juice, ginger, orange extract, vanilla, and salt and process until smooth, 30 to 60 seconds.

6 Pour filling into crust (crust needn't be completely cooled) and use silicone spatula to spread to edges and smooth top. Using your hands, squeeze topping mixture into large clumps, then crumble into rough pea-size pieces over filling in even layer (some topping will be more clumped and some more crumbly). Bake until top is golden and edges of filling puff slightly, 40 to 45 minutes, rotating pan halfway through baking.

7 Let bars cool completely in pan on wire rack, about 3 hours. Using foil overhang, remove bars from pan. Cut into 24 pieces before serving.

Storage: 3 days at room temperature

WHY THIS RECIPE WORKS This indoor version of the iconic campfire treat has all of (and more of) the toasted marshmallow, milk chocolate, and graham crackers of the original in a structurally sound package. In addition to graham crackers, we use some flour for structure, brown sugar for mellow sweetness, and a hefty pinch of salt in the crust to balance the sweet marshmallow and chocolate. We pulse in cold butter with a food processor for a crisp, shortbread-like texture. Once the parbaked crust is cooled, we line it with Hershey's Milk Chocolate bars (their unique taste and soft texture is essential for that classic s'mores flavor). To get the perfect mix of melty goo and campfire-y browning, we top the bars with both marshmallow crème and mini marshmallows and bake them until the mini marshmallows puff and toast.

Makes 16 bars

Total Time 1½ hours, plus 4 hours cooling

S'MORES BARS

- 7 whole graham crackers, broken into rough pieces
- ½ cup (71 grams) all-purpose flour
- ¼ cup packed (50 grams) brown sugar
- ½ teaspoon table salt
- 8 tablespoons (114 grams) unsalted butter, cut into ½-inch pieces and chilled
- 6 (1.55-ounce) Hershey's Milk Chocolate bars, divided
- 1 cup (113 grams) Fluff brand marshmallow crème
- 1½ cups (72 grams) mini marshmallows

Storage: uncut, 2 days at room temperature

Do not cut the bars until you're ready to serve them.

1 Adjust oven rack to middle position and heat oven to 425 degrees. Make foil sling for 8-inch square baking pan by folding 2 long sheets of aluminum foil so each is 8 inches wide. Lay sheets of foil in pan perpendicular to each other, with extra foil hanging over edges of pan. Push foil into corners and up sides of pan, smoothing foil flush to pan. Generously grease foil.

2 Process cracker pieces in food processor until finely ground, about 30 seconds. Add flour, sugar, and salt and pulse to combine, about 5 pulses. Add butter and pulse until mixture is uniform and resembles wet sand, about 20 pulses. Spread crumb mixture in prepared pan and press firmly into even layer. Bake until crust is set and well browned around edges, about 13 minutes. Let cool completely. (Cooled crust can be wrapped in plastic wrap and stored at room temperature for up to 2 days.)

3 Cover crust with 5 chocolate bars, breaking bars as necessary to create even layer (you will have some chocolate left over). Chop remaining chocolate fine and set aside. Spray offset spatula with vegetable oil spray. Using prepared spatula, spread marshmallow crème over chocolate. Sprinkle marshmallows evenly over marshmallow crème.

4 Bake bars until edges are set and marshmallows are puffed and dark brown, about 15 minutes. Transfer pan to wire rack and sprinkle with chopped chocolate. Let bars cool until chocolate is set, about 4 hours.

5 Using foil overhang, lift bars out of pan (marshmallows may stick to foil; use knife to separate, if necessary). Using chef's knife sprayed with oil spray, cut into 16 pieces before serving.

Makes 12 cookies

Total Time 45 minutes, plus 55 minutes chilling and cooling

WHY THIS RECIPE WORKS The texture of a macaroon is as big a key to its appeal as its flavor; with each bite, the crisp exterior gives way to a pleasantly chewy interior with nubby shreds of sweet coconut. This dressed-up version adds milk chocolate chips and toasted slivered almonds for more textural variation. Vanilla and almond extracts provide depth of flavor. We toss the chocolate chips and almonds with the coconut mixture before forming the mixture into uniform mounds and baking them until golden brown.

COCONUT MACAROONS WITH CHOCOLATE CHIPS AND ALMONDS

- 2 large egg whites
- 3 tablespoons sugar
- ½ teaspoon table salt
- ½ teaspoon vanilla extract
- ¼ teaspoon almond extract
- 2⅓ cups (191 grams) sweetened shredded coconut
- ½ cup (64 grams) slivered almonds, toasted
- ⅓ cup (57 grams) milk chocolate chips

We prefer to use a cookie scoop here for more rounded macaroons.

1 Adjust oven rack to middle position and heat oven to 350 degrees. Line rimmed baking sheet with parchment paper and spray lightly with vegetable oil spray.

2 Whisk egg whites, sugar, salt, vanilla, and almond extract in large bowl until foamy, about 30 seconds. Stir in coconut, almonds, and chocolate chips, then cover and refrigerate for 30 minutes.

3 Working with 1½ tablespoons dough at a time, drop 12 mounds of dough onto prepared sheet, spaced evenly apart. Bake until deep golden brown, 25 to 30 minutes, rotating sheet halfway through baking.

4 Let macaroons cool on sheet for 5 minutes, then transfer to wire rack. Let macaroons cool completely before serving.

Storage: 3 days at room temperature

Makes 16 cookies

Total Time 50 minutes, plus 30 minutes cooling

WHY THIS RECIPE WORKS These pillowy, gooey cookies with a hint of lime are inspired by cocadas and besitos de coco, macaroon-adjacent treats enjoyed in Mexico and South America. To sweeten and moisten the dough, we use dulce de leche, the milky caramel beloved in Latin America, which pairs beautifully with coconut. Some flake salt really enlivens these pleasing flavors.

COCONUT DULCE DE LECHE COOKIES

- ½ cup (71 grams) all-purpose flour
- 1 teaspoon table salt
- ½ teaspoon baking soda
- 1 (13.4-ounce) can dulce de leche
- ½ cup (99 grams) sugar
- 6 tablespoons (86 grams) unsalted butter, melted
- 1 large egg
- 2 teaspoons grated lime zest (optional)
- 1 teaspoon vanilla extract
- 4 cups (328 grams) unsweetened shredded coconut
- Flake sea salt

We developed this recipe using Nestlé La Lechera brand of canned dulce de leche. Other brands will work but package sizes vary; you'll need 1 cup plus 2 tablespoons for this recipe.

1 Adjust oven rack to middle position and heat oven to 325 degrees. Line 2 rimmed baking sheets with parchment paper and spray lightly with vegetable oil spray. Whisk flour, salt, and baking soda together in bowl.

2 Using stand mixer fitted with paddle, mix dulce de leche, sugar, and melted butter on low speed until fully combined, about 2 minutes. Add egg; lime zest, if using; and vanilla, then increase speed to medium and beat until combined, about 1 minute. Reduce speed to low; add flour mixture; and mix until combined, about 2 minutes, scraping down sides of bowl halfway through mixing. Add coconut and mix until incorporated, about 2 minutes.

3 Working with 2 tablespoons dough at a time, roll into balls and space evenly on prepared sheets (8 dough balls per sheet). Using your moistened fingertips, press each dough ball to ¾-inch thickness. Sprinkle with sea salt to taste. Bake cookies, 1 sheet at a time, until edges are deep golden and set and centers are puffed, 18 to 20 minutes, rotating sheet halfway through baking.

4 Let cookies cool on sheet for 5 minutes, then transfer to wire rack. Let cookies cool completely before serving.

Storage: 3 days at room temperature

Makes 18 treats

Total Time 1¼ hours, plus 1 hour setting

WHY THIS RECIPE WORKS Huang Fei Hong peanuts, a crunchy, sweet-salty snack that showcases the spiciness of Sichuan chiles and the citric tang and numbing sensation of Sichuan peppercorns, sparked the creation of these delicious cereal treats with an unexpected savory twist. We toss peanuts with a little oil and corn syrup, sprinkle them with spices and salt, roast them, and then chop them fine. A warmed mixture of peanut butter, corn syrup, and sugar binds the peanuts and cereal together. We reinforce the Huang Fei Hong flavor profile by stirring additional Sichuan peppercorns, Sichuan chili flakes, and tiny ribbons of dried facing heaven chiles into the peanut butter mixture.

SICHUAN PEANUT RICE KRISPIE TREATS

SICHUAN SPICY PEANUTS

- 1 cup (142 grams) dry-roasted peanuts
- 1½ teaspoons vegetable oil
- 1 teaspoon light corn syrup
- 1 teaspoon Sichuan chili flakes
- 1 teaspoon Sichuan peppercorns, ground fine
- 1 teaspoon table salt
- ¼ teaspoon white pepper
- ¼ teaspoon monosodium glutamate (optional)

TREATS

- 3½ cups (98 grams) Rice Krispies cereal
- ½ cup (164 grams) light corn syrup
- ½ cup (99 grams) sugar
- 2 tablespoons water
- ¾ cup (196 grams) creamy peanut butter
- 1 teaspoon Sichuan chili flakes
- 1 teaspoon Sichuan peppercorns
- 3 facing heaven chiles, stemmed, halved lengthwise, seeded, and sliced thin crosswise

Look for Sichuan chili flakes and facing heaven chiles at Chinese supermarkets. If they're unavailable, substitute 1 teaspoon gochugaru (Korean chili flakes) for the Sichuan chili flakes in the peanuts and 2 teaspoons (one for the chili flakes and one for the sliced chiles) in the treats. Monosodium glutamate contributes a savory note that recalls the flavor of the Huang Fei Hong peanuts that inspired this recipe, but it can be omitted if desired.

1 For the Sichuan spicy peanuts: Adjust oven rack to middle position and heat oven to 350 degrees. Combine peanuts, oil, and corn syrup in large bowl. Sprinkle with chili flakes; peppercorns; table salt; white pepper; and monosodium glutamate, if using, and toss to coat. Transfer to parchment paper–lined rimmed baking sheet (do not wash bowl) and bake until nuts are fragrant and light golden brown, about 10 minutes, rotating sheet halfway through baking. Transfer sheet to wire rack and let sit until cool enough to handle, about 10 minutes. Chop peanuts fine and return to bowl.

2 For the treats: Grease 8-inch square baking pan. Make parchment sling for pan by folding 2 long sheets of parchment paper so each is 8 inches wide. Lay sheets of parchment in pan perpendicular to each other, with extra parchment hanging over edges of pan. Push parchment into corners and up sides of pan, smoothing parchment flush to pan. Grease parchment.

3 Add cereal to finely chopped peanuts and stir to combine. Combine corn syrup, sugar, and water in medium saucepan. Cook over medium-low heat until sugar is mostly dissolved (mixture will be mostly clear), about 5 minutes, stirring constantly and adjusting heat as needed so that mixture does not come to boil. Stir in peanut butter, chili flakes, peppercorns, and chiles until peanut butter is melted, about 1 minute. Remove from heat.

4 Pour peanut butter mixture over cereal mixture in bowl and stir until fully combined. Transfer cereal mixture to prepared pan and, using greased metal spatula, press firmly into even layer. Let sit for 1 hour until set.

5 Using parchment overhang, remove bars from pan. Cut treats into 3 equal strips. Cut each strip crosswise to create 6 equal rectangles before serving.

Storage: 3 days at room temperature

Makes 8 cookies

Total Time 1 hour, plus 9 hours chilling and cooling

WHY THIS RECIPE WORKS The Chocolate Chip Walnut Cookie from Levain Bakery is huge and chunky, with an exterior that's crisp/crunchy and an interior that is soft, moist, and crammed with walnut nuggets and molten chocolate chips. The cookie's large mass and stout shape mean it takes longer for the oven's heat to penetrate to the center, so you can thoroughly bake the exterior while the interior remains soft and gooey. When making our version of this viral sensation, we dramatically decrease the amount of fat and sugar in our usual cookie formula to decrease the spread—generous amounts of chips and nuts easily compensate for any lost sweetness or richness. Browning the butter makes its flavor more pronounced and removes its water so we can add more butter overall without increasing spread. Chilling the dough portions until they are uniformly solid and then baking them straight from the fridge further limits the spread and produces a crisp, crunchy, well-browned cookie shell encasing a soft, moist, tender interior with gooey chocolate chips.

LEVAIN-STYLE CHOCOLATE CHIP COOKIES

- ⅔ cup packed (132 grams) dark brown sugar
- ½ cup (99 grams) granulated sugar
- 9 tablespoons (128 grams) unsalted butter
- 2¼ cups (320 grams) all-purpose flour
- 1½ teaspoons baking powder
- ½ teaspoon baking soda
- 1 teaspoon table salt
- 2 cups (210 grams) walnut halves, toasted
- 2 large eggs
- 1 tablespoon vanilla extract
- 2 cups (340 grams) semisweet chocolate chips

We strongly recommend using a conventionally sized semisweet chocolate chip such as Nestle Tollhouse Morsels here. Nuts are important for the cookies' texture, so do not omit them, but you can substitute pecans if preferred. These cookies are best when eaten within a few hours of baking. Portions can be refrigerated for up to six days; after 12 hours, transfer to a zipper-lock bag. Alternatively, you can freeze the dough balls for up to one month; defrost them in the refrigerator overnight before baking.

1 Combine brown sugar and granulated sugar in large bowl. Heat butter in 10-inch skillet over medium-high heat until melted, about 2 minutes. Continue to cook, swirling skillet and stirring constantly with silicone spatula, until butter is dark golden brown and has nutty aroma, 1 to 3 minutes longer. Pour over sugar mixture and whisk until combined. Set aside to cool slightly, about 5 minutes.

2 While butter mixture is cooling, whisk flour, baking powder, baking soda, and salt in medium bowl until combined. Pile walnuts on cutting board and crush with heel of your hand to create pieces from ¼ to ½ inch. Set aside.

3 Add eggs and vanilla to butter mixture and whisk until smooth. Using silicone spatula, stir in flour mixture until fully combined. Stir in semisweet chocolate chips and walnuts until evenly distributed.

4 Divide dough into 8 equal portions (about ¾ cup/162 grams each) and form into rough spheres. Space dough spheres about 2 inches apart on parchment paper–lined baking sheet. Refrigerate, uncovered, for at least 8 hours. (Dough portions can be refrigerated for up to 6 days; after 12 hours, transfer to zipper-lock bag.)

5 Adjust oven rack to middle position and heat oven to 350 degrees. Line second rimmed baking sheet with parchment paper. Arrange 4 dough portions on each sheet, leaving about 3 inches between portions.

6 Bake, 1 sheet at a time, until cookies are deep golden brown and edges are set, about 22 minutes, rotating sheet halfway through baking. Transfer sheet to wire rack and let cookies cool on sheet for 1 hour before serving.

Storage: baked, a few hours

Makes 12 sandwich cookies

Total Time 2 hours, plus 20 minutes chilling

WHY THIS RECIPE WORKS Our homemade MoonPies are a delicious construction of marshmallow sandwiched between two graham cookies fully coated in a thin layer of bittersweet chocolate. An even mix of all-purpose and graham flours gives the cookies an appealingly coarse texture and toasty flavor. We spread homemade marshmallow between them, working quickly while the marshmallow is still warm and malleable. Adding a tablespoon of coconut oil to the chocolate helps it maintain a fluid consistency throughout the dipping process. After 20 minutes in the refrigerator, this treat is ready to be devoured.

CHOCOLATE-MARSHMALLOW SANDWICH COOKIES

COOKIES

- 1¼ cups (178 grams) all-purpose flour
- 1 cup plus 2 tablespoons (177 grams) graham flour
- ¾ cup (149 grams) sugar
- 1 teaspoon baking powder
- 1 teaspoon baking soda
- ¾ teaspoon table salt
- ¼ teaspoon ground cinnamon
- 12 tablespoons (171 grams) unsalted butter, melted and cooled
- 5 tablespoons (74 grams) water
- 2 tablespoons molasses
- 1 teaspoon vanilla extract

FILLING

- 6 tablespoons (89 grams) water, divided
- 2 teaspoons unflavored gelatin
- ¼ cup (82 grams) light corn syrup
- ⅔ cup (132 grams) sugar
- ⅛ teaspoon table salt
- 1 teaspoon vanilla extract

CHOCOLATE COATING

- 12 ounces (340 grams) bittersweet chocolate (9 ounces/ 255 grams chopped fine, 3 ounces/85 grams grated)
- 1 tablespoon refined coconut oil

Graham flour, also known as stone-ground whole-wheat flour, is coarser and less processed than conventional whole-wheat flour. The marshmallow filling quickly starts to set after whipping, so have everything ready to assemble the cookies in step 7 before you begin.

1 For the cookies: Adjust oven rack to middle position and heat oven to 350 degrees. Line 2 rimmed baking sheets with parchment paper. Whisk all-purpose flour, graham flour, sugar, baking powder, baking soda, salt, and cinnamon together in bowl of stand mixer. Add melted butter, water, molasses, and vanilla. Using paddle attachment, mix until dough comes together, about 20 seconds.

2 Transfer dough to counter and divide in half. Roll 1 piece of dough (cover remaining piece with plastic wrap) into 12-inch circle, ⅛ inch thick, between 2 large sheets of parchment. Remove top piece of parchment. Using 3-inch round cookie cutter, cut dough into 8 rounds; carefully transfer rounds to 1 prepared sheet, spacing ½ inch apart. Gently reroll scraps into 8-inch circle, ⅛ inch thick, then cut into 4 rounds and transfer to sheet. Repeat with remaining piece of dough (12 rounds per sheet).

3 Bake cookies, 1 sheet at a time, until edges are set, about 10 minutes, rotating sheet halfway through baking. Transfer sheet to wire rack and let cookies cool completely. (Cookies can be stored in airtight container for up to 1 day.)

••• CONTINUED •••

4 **For the filling:** Whisk 3 tablespoons water and gelatin together in clean, dry bowl of stand mixer fitted with whisk attachment. Let sit until very firm, about 5 minutes.

5 Meanwhile, combine corn syrup and remaining 3 tablespoons water in small saucepan. Pour sugar and salt into center of saucepan (do not let sugar hit saucepan sides). Bring to boil over medium-high heat and cook, gently swirling saucepan, until sugar has dissolved completely and mixture registers 240 degrees, 4 to 6 minutes.

6 Turn mixer speed to low and carefully pour hot syrup into gelatin mixture, avoiding whisk and sides of bowl. Gradually increase speed to high and whip until mixture is very thick and stiff and coats whisk, about 7 minutes, scraping down bowl as needed. Add vanilla and mix until incorporated, about 15 seconds.

7 To assemble, place 12 cookies upside down on counter. Place 2 tablespoons marshmallow filling in center of 1 cookie and spread evenly with back of spoon. Place second cookie on top of filling, right side up, and gently press and twist until filling is even with edges of cookies. Repeat with remaining cookies; let sit for 15 minutes until filling is set.

8 **For the chocolate coating:** Line baking sheet with clean sheet of parchment. Microwave chopped chocolate in medium bowl at 50 percent power, stirring often, until about two-thirds melted, 2 to 4 minutes. (Melted chocolate should not be much warmer than body temperature; check by holding bowl in palm of your hand.) Add grated chocolate and coconut oil and stir until smooth, returning to microwave for no more than 5 seconds at a time to finish melting if necessary.

9 Rotate filling-exposed side of 1 sandwich cookie in chocolate until filling and cookie edges are fully covered. Place sandwich cookie in chocolate and, using 2 forks, gently flip to fully coat all sides. Lift cookie out of chocolate with fork. Using offset spatula, spread chocolate on top of cookie into thin, even layer, allowing excess to run off sides. Tap fork against edge of bowl, then wipe underside of fork on edge of bowl to remove excess chocolate from bottom of cookie. Use second fork to slide sandwich cookie onto prepared sheet. Repeat with remaining sandwich cookies, returning chocolate to microwave for no more than 5 seconds at a time if it becomes too firm.

10 Refrigerate sandwich cookies until chocolate is set, about 20 minutes, before serving.

Storage: 2 days at room temperature

COATING THE COOKIES

1. Rotate filling-exposed side of 1 sandwich cookie in chocolate until marshmallow and cookie edges are fully covered.

2. Place sandwich cookie in chocolate and, using 2 forks, gently flip to fully coat all sides.

3. Lift cookie out of chocolate with fork. Using offset spatula, spread chocolate on top of moon pie into thin, even layer, allowing excess to run off sides.

4. Tap fork against edge of bowl, then wipe underside of fork on edge of bowl to remove excess chocolate from bottom of cookie. Use second fork to slide cookie onto prepared sheet.

1

2

3

4

Makes 32 cookies

Total Time 1¾ hours, plus 1 hour 20 minutes chilling and cooling

WHY THIS RECIPE WORKS The dough for these sweet, golden filled-and-rolled cookies popular in Jewish bakeries around the world is supple and easy to roll out, with a mellow, buttery sweetness that's enriched with the mild tang of cream cheese. Chocolate rugelach is a favorite but Nutella is perfect for spreading on the dough as is and introduces appealing nuttiness. We roll the dough flat into circles, spread on some Nutella, and then use a pizza wheel to cut the circle into wedges, rolling up the wedges to create adorable little croissant-shaped cookies.

NUTELLA RUGELACH

- 1½ cups (213 grams) all-purpose flour
- ¼ cup (50 grams) granulated sugar
- ¼ teaspoon table salt
- 6 ounces (170 grams) cream cheese, cut into 3 pieces and chilled
- 10 tablespoons (143 grams) unsalted butter, cut into ½-inch pieces and chilled
- ¼ cup (59 grams) sour cream
- ⅔ cup (196 grams) Nutella, divided
- 1 large egg, beaten with 1 tablespoon water
- 1 tablespoon demerara sugar (optional)

Storage: 3 days at room temperature

To ensure that the demerara sugar sticks to the rugelach, brush only a few cookies at a time with the egg wash before sprinkling with the demerara sugar.

1 Process flour, granulated sugar, and salt in food processor until combined, about 3 seconds. Add cream cheese and pulse until large, irregularly sized chunks of cream cheese form with some small pieces interspersed throughout, about 5 pulses. Scatter butter over top and pulse until butter is size of large peas, 5 to 7 pulses.

2 Add sour cream and process until dough forms little clumps that hold together when pinched with your fingers (dough will look crumbly), about 10 seconds.

3 Transfer dough to clean counter and knead briefly until dough just comes together, about 3 turns. Divide dough in half and form each piece into 4-inch disk. Wrap disks individually with plastic wrap and refrigerate for at least 1 hour or up to 2 days.

4 Adjust oven rack to middle position and heat oven to 375 degrees. Roll 1 dough disk into 12-inch circle on lightly floured counter. Using offset spatula, spread ⅓ cup (98 grams) Nutella evenly over entire surface of circle. Using pizza wheel or chef's knife, cut through center of circle to form 16 equal wedges. Starting at wide edge of each wedge, roll dough toward point and transfer to parchment paper–lined rimmed baking sheet, seam side down.

5 Wipe counter clean, dust counter with additional flour, and repeat with remaining dough disk and remaining ⅓ cup (98 grams) Nutella. Arrange rugelach in 8 rows of four on sheet.

6 Working with few rugelach at a time, brush tops with egg wash, then sprinkle with demerara sugar, if using. Bake until golden brown, 30 to 35 minutes. Let cookies cool completely on sheet before serving.

Chapter 6

RICH AND SQUIDGY

ATK CLASSIC

Makes 24 brownies

Total Time 1 hour, plus 2 hours cooling

We think these everyday brownies are the ideal for most brownie lovers—delicately chewy, nicely fudgy, and as simple to make as they are deeply chocolaty. We didn't want a cakey brownie, but we also didn't want a dense, greasy one. With plenty of fat coming from chocolate in the recipe, we use a modest amount of butter so the squares don't make your fingers slick. And we include just enough baking powder to lighten the crumb a bit without turning the brownies to cake. Chocolate choice is simple here: Unsweetened chocolate provides richness and unadulterated chocolate flavor with fruity dimension. We mix the ingredients together by hand—a stand mixer incorporates too much air. And we bake them in a moderate 325-degree oven so the brownies' edges don't dry out and the center doesn't easily overbake.

FUDGY BROWNIES

- 1¼ cups (178 grams) all-purpose flour
- ¾ teaspoon baking powder
- ½ teaspoon table salt
- 6 ounces (170 grams) unsweetened chocolate, chopped fine
- 12 tablespoons (171 grams) unsalted butter, cut into 6 pieces
- 2¼ cups (446 grams) sugar
- 1 tablespoon vanilla extract
- 4 large eggs
- 1 cup (119 grams) pecans or walnuts, toasted and chopped coarse (optional)

1 Adjust oven rack to middle position and heat oven to 325 degrees. Make foil sling for 13 by 9-inch baking pan by folding 2 long sheets of aluminum foil; first sheet should be 13 inches wide and second sheet should be 9 inches wide. Lay sheets of foil in pan perpendicular to each other, with extra foil hanging over edges of pan. Push foil into corners and up sides of pan, smoothing foil flush to pan. Grease foil.

2 Whisk flour, baking powder, and salt together in bowl. Microwave chocolate and butter in second bowl, stirring occasionally, until melted, 2 to 4 minutes. Whisk in sugar and vanilla until well combined. Whisk in eggs until smooth. Stir in flour mixture until no dry flour remains.

3 Transfer batter to prepared pan and spread into even layer. Sprinkle with pecans, if using. Bake until toothpick inserted in center of brownies comes out with few moist crumbs attached, 30 to 35 minutes, rotating pan halfway through baking. Let brownies cool completely in pan on wire rack, about 2 hours. Using foil overhang, remove brownies from pan. Cut into 24 pieces before serving.

Storage: 3 days at room temperature

Creative *Fudgy Brownie* Takes

- **Make melty pockets** For little pockets of chocolate within the rich crumb, stir in chocolate chips or chunks, or M&M's or other chopped-up candies.
- **Sprinkle with nuts** If you choose to add nuts, sprinkle them on top so they don't steam and go soft within the batter.
- **Turn into dessert** Top the brownies with fruit, ice cream, and/or whipped cream.
- **Repurpose them** Crumble past-their-prime brownies over ice cream or yogurt.

How We Achieve *Rich, Chocolaty* Fudgy Brownies

- **Moderate the butter** Using enough butter to enrich the brownies without turning them greasy results in the most satisfying bars.
- **Simplify the chocolate** Unsweetened chocolate alone provides richness and great flavor.
- **Go with granulated sugar** White sugar gives a neutral flavor that doesn't detract from the chocolate.

Makes 16 brownies

Total Time 50 minutes, plus 2 hours cooling

WHY THIS RECIPE WORKS Classic brownies get a sophisticated—and surprising—update with the addition of soft licorice candies. Licorice adds an unexpected background note that harmonizes with the chocolate, similarly to how coffee might add appealing dimension to a chocolate cake. The unique flavor of the licorice is perfectly balanced by both the bitter dark chocolate and sweet white chocolate chips in these brownies. The licorice flavor is present enough for lovers of it to grin, while gentle enough to convert skeptics.

LICORICE-WHITE CHOCOLATE BROWNIES

- ¾ cup (107 grams) all-purpose flour
- ½ teaspoon table salt
- ¼ teaspoon baking powder
- ½ cup (85 grams) white chocolate chips
- 2½ ounces (71 grams) soft black licorice, pieces quartered lengthwise and sliced crosswise ⅛ inch thick (½ cup)
- 8 tablespoons (114 grams) unsalted butter
- 4 ounces (113 grams) bittersweet chocolate, chopped fine
- ½ cup (99 grams) granulated sugar
- ½ cup packed (99 grams) dark brown sugar
- 1 teaspoon vanilla extract
- 2 large eggs

This recipe was developed using soft black licorice, not salted licorice, which can be more intense in flavor. We liked Wiley Wallaby brand, but any high-quality soft black licorice will work.

1 Adjust oven rack to middle position and heat oven to 350 degrees. Make foil sling for 8-inch square baking pan by folding 2 long sheets of aluminum foil so each is 8 inches wide. Lay sheets of foil in pan perpendicular to each other, with extra foil hanging over edges of pan. Push foil into corners and up sides of pan, smoothing foil flush to pan. Grease foil.

2 Whisk flour, salt, and baking powder together in bowl. Combine white chocolate chips and licorice in second bowl. Microwave butter and chocolate in large bowl at 50 percent power, stirring occasionally, until melted, 2 to 4 minutes. Whisk in granulated sugar, brown sugar, and vanilla until well combined. Whisk in eggs until fully combined and smooth. Stir in flour mixture until just incorporated, then stir in white chocolate mixture until evenly distributed. Transfer batter to prepared pan and spread into even layer.

3 Bake until toothpick inserted in center of brownies comes out with few moist crumbs attached, 30 to 35 minutes, rotating pan halfway through baking. Let brownies cool completely in pan on wire rack, about 2 hours. Using foil overhang, remove brownies from pan. Cut into 16 pieces before serving.

Storage: 3 days at room temperature

Makes 18 brownies

Total Time 1 hour, plus 3 hours cooling and setting

WHY THIS RECIPE WORKS There are fudgy brownies, and then there are these: extra fudgy, supremely chocolaty, and so dark they're almost black. This is an indulgent, adult brownie, with no flour to mute the darkest chocolate flavor (and so, as a bonus, it satisfies our gluten-free friends). Flourless brownies can taste like undercooked batter, however. To create a baked good, not a confection, we add just 3 tablespoons of cornstarch; it binds the ingredients, resulting in brownies with a melt-in-your-mouth center and a crispy, chewy edge. For dark chocolate flavor with dimension, we include a mix of chocolate—bittersweet, unsweetened, and a generous ¼ cup of black cocoa powder that makes our brownies deeper and darker than your average. The cocoa powder also works, along with the cornstarch, to prevent our brownies from being pasty or wet. Finally, we achieve a shiny, sleek, obsidian-like finish with an unadulteratedly chocolate water ganache, made from bittersweet chocolate and more black cocoa powder, that gently drips down the sides.

DEEPEST, DARKEST, FUDGIEST FLOURLESS BROWNIES

BROWNIES

- ¼ cup (21 grams) black cocoa powder
- 3 tablespoons cornstarch
- ½ teaspoon table salt
- 8 tablespoons (114 grams) unsalted butter, cut into 8 pieces
- 4 ounces (113 grams) bittersweet chocolate, chopped
- 2 ounces (57 grams) unsweetened chocolate, chopped
- 1¼ cups (248 grams) sugar
- 2 teaspoons vanilla extract
- 1 teaspoon instant espresso powder
- 3 large eggs

GANACHE

- 5 tablespoons (74 grams) water
- 1 tablespoon black cocoa powder
- 1 teaspoon corn syrup
- 4 ounces (113 grams) bittersweet chocolate, chopped fine

We prefer black cocoa powder in this recipe. You can substitute regular Dutch-processed cocoa powder for the black cocoa, but the brownies will not be as dark and the ganache will turn out thicker.

1 Adjust oven rack to lower-middle position and heat oven to 325 degrees. Make foil sling for 8-inch square baking pan by folding 2 long sheets of aluminum foil so each is 8 inches wide. Lay sheets of foil in pan perpendicular to each other, with extra foil hanging over edges of pan. Push foil into corners and up sides of pan, smoothing foil flush to pan. Grease foil.

2 **For the brownies:** Whisk cocoa, cornstarch, and salt together in bowl. Microwave butter, bittersweet chocolate, and unsweetened chocolate in large bowl at 50 percent power, stirring occasionally, until melted, 2 to 4 minutes. Whisk in sugar, vanilla, and espresso powder until well combined. Whisk in eggs until fully combined and smooth. Stir in cocoa mixture until just incorporated. Transfer batter to prepared pan and smooth top.

3 Bake until toothpick inserted in center comes out with few moist crumbs attached, 33 to 37 minutes, rotating pan halfway through baking. Let brownies cool completely in pan on wire rack, about 2 hours. Using foil overhang, remove brownies from pan.

4 **For the ganache:** Bring water, cocoa, and corn syrup to simmer in small saucepan over medium heat, whisking to dissolve cocoa, then immediately remove from heat. Whisk in chocolate until melted and smooth. Pour ganache over brownies, spreading with offset spatula to cover top (ganache may drip over side but does not have to cover sides). Let sit until ganache is set, about 1 hour. Before serving, using hot knife, cut brownies into 9 squares, then cut each square in half diagonally to create 2 triangles, dipping knife in very hot water and wiping knife clean and dry between each cut.

Storage: 1 week at room temperature

Makes 9 brownies

Total Time 1¼ hours, plus 2 hours cooling

WHY THIS RECIPE WORKS These elegant plated dessert brownies channel the layers of chocolate cake, billowy whipped cream, and tart cherries of Black Forest cake—and leave behind the complicated and long baking method. A rich, tender, chocolaty brownie forms the base for a generous swirl of sweetened tart cherries. Frozen sour cherries give us great flavor, color, and bursts of tender fruit. Thickening the cherries with cornstarch prevents a soggy brownie layer and brings out their vibrant red color, while a touch of almond extract in both the brownies and the cherries heightens their flavor (both almonds and cherries belong to the Prunus genus). We finish the brownies with a spoonful of softly whipped cream, a dollop of the cherry mixture, and a few chocolate curls.

BLACK FOREST BROWNIES

CHERRIES

- 1 pound (454 grams) frozen sour cherries
- 1 tablespoon cornstarch
- 3 tablespoons sugar
- ¼ teaspoon almond extract

BROWNIES

- ½ cup (71 grams) all-purpose flour
- ½ teaspoon baking powder
- ¼ teaspoon table salt
- 6 tablespoons (86 grams) unsalted butter, cut into 6 pieces
- 3 ounces (85 grams) unsweetened chocolate, chopped fine
- 1 cup plus 2 tablespoons (223 grams) sugar
- ½ teaspoon almond extract
- 2 large eggs

- 1 cup (231 grams) heavy cream
- 1 tablespoon sugar
- Bittersweet chocolate curls (optional)

1 Adjust oven rack to middle position and heat oven to 325 degrees. Make foil sling for 8-inch square baking pan by folding 2 long sheets of aluminum foil so each is 8 inches wide. Lay sheets of foil in pan perpendicular to each other, with extra foil hanging over edges of pan. Push foil into corners and up sides of pan, smoothing foil flush to pan. Grease foil.

2 **For the cherries:** Cook frozen cherries in medium saucepan over medium heat, stirring occasionally, until cherries soften and release their juices, 6 to 8 minutes. Strain cherries over bowl, reserving cherries and liquid (you should have at least 7 tablespoons liquid; add water as needed to equal 7 tablespoons).

3 Whisk cornstarch and 1 tablespoon reserved cherry liquid together in small bowl. Whisk remaining 6 tablespoons reserved cherry liquid and sugar together in now-empty saucepan and cook over medium-low heat until sugar dissolves, about 1 minute. Whisk cornstarch mixture into cherry liquid in saucepan and cook until thickened, about 1 minute. Off heat, stir in reserved cherries and almond extract. Set aside. (You should have about 1¼ cups cherry mixture.)

4 **For the brownies:** Whisk flour, baking powder, and salt together in bowl. Microwave butter and chocolate in large bowl at 50 percent power, stirring occasionally, until melted, 2 to 4 minutes. Whisk in sugar and almond extract until well combined. Whisk in eggs until fully combined and smooth. Stir in flour mixture until just incorporated.

5 Measure out and reserve ½ cup brownie batter. Transfer remaining batter to prepared pan and spread into even layer. Using spoon, dollop ½ cup reserved cherry mixture in 9 places over top of batter, then dollop reserved brownie batter in empty spaces. Using chopstick or butter knife, swirl gently together.

6 Bake brownies until toothpick inserted in center (avoiding cherry swirls) comes out with few moist crumbs attached, 35 to 38 minutes, rotating pan halfway through baking. Let brownies cool completely in pan on wire rack, about 2 hours. Using foil overhang, remove brownies from pan. Cut into 9 squares.

7 Just before serving, using stand mixer fitted with whisk attachment, whip cream and sugar on medium-low speed until foamy, about 1 minute. Increase speed to medium-high and whip until just soft peaks form, 1 to 2 minutes. Dollop brownies with whipped cream and spoon remaining cherries over top, then decorate with chocolate curls, if using.

Storage: brownies, 3 days at room temperature; cherries, 3 days in refrigerator

Makes 18 bars

Total Time 1¼ hours, plus 2¾ hours steeping and setting

WHY THIS RECIPE WORKS If you've enjoyed a chicory coffee in New Orleans, these creamy, rich, audaciously flavored three-layered bars will definitely pique your interest. Complex in flavor, with deep notes of coffee and caramelized sugar, and a fragrant woodsy aroma, chicory is a European wildflower related to dandelions that grows a long taproot, which is roasted, ground, and used as a caffeine-free coffee substitute in many countries. While in the United States chicory is most often blended with ground coffee—a practice adopted at times when coffee was scarce—chicory is a worthy star in this coffee-free bar. A fudgy dark brownie base supports a rich, luscious chicory pastry cream. We like some optional cacao nibs in the brownie—they contribute crunch to the soft bars and underscore the bittersweet flavor. In a nod to New Orleans's chicory cafés au lait, we finish the bars with a sleek white chocolate ganache that tempers the bold flavors underneath.

CHICORY CAFÉ AU LAIT CHOCOLATE BARS

BROWNIE LAYER

- ⅔ cup (95 grams) all-purpose flour
- ¼ teaspoon table salt
- 4 ounces (113 grams) bittersweet chocolate, chopped fine
- 3 tablespoons unsalted butter
- 1½ tablespoons Dutch-processed cocoa powder
- ⅔ cup packed (132 grams) dark brown sugar
- 2 teaspoons vanilla extract
- 1 large egg
- 2 tablespoons cacao nibs (optional)

Look for 100 percent ground, roasted chicory, not instant chicory or chicory blended with coffee or other ingredients. We like the way white baking chips (which, unlike white chocolate, do not contain cocoa butter) set up; we used Ghirardelli Classic White Baking Chips. Do not let the chicory filling cool in the saucepan, as it can separate; transfer it immediately to a bowl after it reaches the target temperature. (If the mixture does separate, whisk in 1 to 2 tablespoons cold water until it recombines.)

1 Adjust oven rack to middle position and heat oven to 325 degrees. Make foil sling for 8-inch square baking pan by folding 2 long sheets of aluminum foil so each is 8 inches wide. Lay sheets of foil in pan perpendicular to each other, with extra foil hanging over edges of pan. Push foil into corners and up sides of pan, smoothing foil flush to pan. Grease foil.

2 **For the brownie layer:** Whisk flour and salt together in bowl. Microwave chocolate, butter, and cocoa in bowl at 50 percent power, stirring often, until melted, 2 to 4 minutes. Whisk in sugar, and vanilla until well combined. Whisk in egg until fully combined and smooth. Stir in flour mixture and cacao nibs, if using, until just combined (mixture will be quite thick).

3 Transfer brownie batter to prepared pan and use offset spatula and your dampened hands as needed to spread evenly over bottom and into corners of pan. Bake until edges are just set and toothpick inserted in center comes out with few moist crumbs attached, about 15 minutes, rotating pan halfway through baking. Transfer pan to wire rack and let brownie cool while making chicory filling.

CHICORY FILLING

- 2 cups (462 grams) heavy cream
- 2 tablespoons ground roasted chicory (see note)
- 6 tablespoons (74 grams) granulated sugar
- 3 large egg yolks
- 2 tablespoons all-purpose flour
- ¼ teaspoon table salt

GANACHE

- 1 cup (170 grams) white baking chips
- 3½ tablespoons heavy cream
- 1 teaspoon corn syrup

4 **For the chicory filling:** Bring heavy cream and chicory to simmer in medium saucepan over medium-high heat, then simmer for 30 seconds. Remove from heat, cover, and let sit for 40 minutes. Strain cooled heavy cream mixture through fine-mesh strainer into bowl, pressing on chicory solids to remove as much liquid as possible; discard chicory solids. Measure out and reserve 1 tablespoon chicory cream. Wipe out saucepan.

5 Whisk sugar, egg yolks, flour, and salt together in now-empty saucepan. Whisk in remaining chicory cream, then cook over medium heat, whisking constantly and scraping corners of saucepan, until thickened, bubbles burst across entire surface, and mixture registers 180 degrees in several places, 3 to 5 minutes. Immediately transfer mixture to bowl and let cool for 10 minutes. Pour filling over cooled brownie layer in pan and use clean offset spatula to smooth top. Refrigerate, uncovered, until set, about 1 hour.

6 **For the ganache:** Microwave white baking chips, cream, corn syrup, and reserved 1 tablespoon chicory cream in bowl at 50 percent power, whisking frequently, until melted and smooth, 30 seconds to 1 minute. Pour ganache over chilled chicory filling in pan, using clean offset spatula to smooth top. Refrigerate, uncovered, until set, about 1 hour.

7 Before serving, using foil overhang, remove bars from pan. Using hot knife, cut into 3 equal strips. Cut each strip crosswise to create 6 equal rectangles, dipping knife in very hot water and wiping knife clean and dry between each cut.

Storage: 3 days in refrigerator

WHY THIS RECIPE WORKS Lauretta Jean's is a pie bakery in Portland, Oregon, but when we visited, in addition to the pies, we were enamored by the ganache-filled brownies. They look almost like muffins—squat, chewy little cylinders full of chocolate flavor, with a surprise in the middle: soft, rich chocolate ganache. They remind us of chocolate truffles, and we love the concept of wrapping a brownie around a rich filling. We start our version by making a stir-together brownie batter and dividing it among muffin cups. Once the brownies are baked and cooled, we fill them with the ganache—a simple mixture of melted chocolate and heavy cream. The best way to create a little space for the brownies to receive the ganache is to press the base of a shot glass, lightly greased to minimize sticking, into the just-baked brownies. A sprinkle of flake salt on the top seals the deal on these outsize chocolate truffles.

Makes 12 brownies

Total Time 1¼ hours, plus 5 hours cooling

TRUFFLE BROWNIES

BROWNIES

- 1⅓ cups (189 grams) all-purpose flour
- ¾ teaspoon table salt
- ⅓ cup (57 grams) bittersweet or semisweet chocolate chips
- ⅓ cup (28 grams) Dutch-processed cocoa powder
- ½ cup (118 grams) boiling water
- 2 cups (396 grams) sugar
- ⅔ cup (140 grams) vegetable oil
- 2 large eggs
- 2 teaspoons vanilla extract

GANACHE

- 1⅓ cups (227 grams) bittersweet or semisweet chocolate chips
- ½ cup (116 grams) heavy cream
- 1 teaspoon flake sea salt

We suggest using parchment muffin liners to avoid the brownies sticking to the liners. It is important to press the indentations into the centers of the brownies 15 minutes after they come out of the oven.

1 **For the brownies:** Adjust oven rack to middle position and heat oven to 350 degrees. Line 12-cup muffin tin with parchment liners. Generously spray liners in muffin tin with vegetable oil spray.

2 Whisk flour and salt together in bowl. Place chocolate chips and cocoa in large bowl. Add boiling water and whisk until chocolate chips are fully melted. Whisk in sugar, oil, eggs, and vanilla until combined. Gently whisk in flour mixture until just incorporated.

3 Divide batter evenly among prepared muffin cups (about ¼ cup per cup). Bake until toothpick inserted in center comes out with few moist crumbs attached, 40 to 45 minutes, rotating muffin tin halfway through baking.

4 Transfer muffin tin to wire rack and let brownies cool for 15 minutes. Spray base of 1¼-inch-diameter shot glass (or other object with similar diameter) with vegetable oil spray. With brownies still in muffin tin, press base of glass into center of each brownie, about 1 inch deep, respraying glass as needed. Remove brownies from muffin tin and let cool completely on rack, about 1 hour.

5 **For the ganache:** Microwave chocolate chips and cream in bowl at 50 percent power, stirring occasionally, until melted, 1 to 3 minutes. Distribute ganache evenly among indentations in brownies (about 1 heaping tablespoon per brownie).

6 Let brownies sit until ganache is set, about 4 hours at room temperature or 1½ hours refrigerated (bring to room temperature before serving). Sprinkle ganache evenly with flake sea salt before serving.

Storage: 2 days in refrigerator

Makes 16 brownies

Total Time 45 minutes, plus 2 hours cooling

WHY THIS RECIPE WORKS This crowd-pleasing brownie has swirls of pure, unadulterated peanut butter running throughout a chocolaty base. Simply dolloping large mounds of peanut butter over brownie batter before swirling it in (a common technique) results in unbalanced brownies. Because peanut butter is so thick, some bites are overloaded with sticky peanut butter while others contain no peanut butter at all. We found that several smaller dollops distribute pockets of peanut butter throughout every bite of brownie. If you like a smoother filling, use creamy peanut butter; if you want some crunch, feel free to use chunky.

PEANUT BUTTER SWIRL BROWNIES

- ⅔ cup (95 grams) all-purpose flour
- ½ teaspoon baking powder
- ¼ teaspoon table salt
- 8 tablespoons (114 grams) unsalted butter
- 3 ounces (85 grams) unsweetened chocolate, chopped coarse
- 1 cup (198 grams) sugar
- 1 teaspoon vanilla extract
- 2 large eggs
- ⅓ cup (87 grams) creamy or chunky peanut butter

Room-temperature peanut butter is easier to work with here and if your peanut butter is quite thick (consistency can vary by brand), microwave it for 10 to 20 seconds before dolloping to make swirling easier.

1 Adjust oven rack to middle position and heat oven to 350 degrees. Make foil sling for 8-inch square baking pan by folding 2 long sheets of aluminum foil so each is 8 inches wide. Lay sheets of foil in pan perpendicular to each other, with extra foil hanging over edges of pan. Push foil into corners and up sides of pan, smoothing foil flush to pan. Grease foil.

2 Whisk flour, baking powder, and salt together in bowl. Microwave butter and chocolate in large bowl at 50 percent power, stirring often, until melted, 1 to 3 minutes. Whisk in sugar and vanilla until well combined. Whisk in eggs until fully combined and smooth. Stir in flour mixture until just incorporated. Transfer batter to prepared pan and spread into even layer.

3 Using spoon, dollop 10 small mounds of peanut butter over brownie batter. Using chopstick or butter knife, swirl peanut butter through brownie batter, making marbled pattern and leaving ½-inch border around edges. Bake until toothpick inserted in center comes out with few moist crumbs attached, 22 to 27 minutes, rotating pan halfway through baking.

4 Let brownies cool completely in pan on wire rack, about 2 hours. Using foil overhang, remove brownies from pan. Cut into 16 pieces before serving.

Storage: 2 days at room temperature

WHY THIS RECIPE WORKS A good cream cheese brownie serves up a perfectly matched duet of velvety cheesecake and fudgy brownie, swirled together yet with each maintaining its identity. Knowing that the cream cheese adds plenty of moisture, we start with a slightly cakey brownie so it doesn't become too dense and wet. Adding a half cup of sour cream to the filling provides a refreshing tang that reinforces the flavor of the cream cheese. To compensate for the sour cream's extra moisture, we ditch the egg in our filling and instead stir in a tablespoon of flour to bind. For cream cheese in every bite, we spread most of the brownie batter in the pan and smooth the cream cheese filling over it. Then, we dollop the last bit of brownie batter on top and swirl everything together for a striking marbled effect.

Makes 16 brownies

Total Time 1 hour, plus 2 hours cooling

CREAM CHEESE BROWNIES

CREAM CHEESE FILLING

- 4 ounces (113 grams) cream cheese, cut into 8 pieces
- ½ cup (119 grams) sour cream
- 2 tablespoons sugar
- 1 tablespoon all-purpose flour

BROWNIES

- ⅔ cup (95 grams) all-purpose flour
- ½ teaspoon baking powder
- ½ teaspoon table salt
- 8 tablespoons (114 grams) unsalted butter
- 4 ounces (113 grams) unsweetened chocolate, chopped fine
- 1¼ cups (248 grams) sugar
- 1 teaspoon vanilla extract
- 2 large eggs

To accurately test doneness, be sure to stick the toothpick through part of the brownie and not the cream cheese.

1 Adjust oven rack to middle position and heat oven to 325 degrees. Make foil sling for 8-inch square baking pan by folding 2 long sheets of aluminum foil so each is 8 inches wide. Lay sheets of foil in pan perpendicular to each other, with extra foil hanging over edges of pan. Push foil into corners and up sides of pan, smoothing foil flush to pan. Grease foil.

2 **For the cream cheese filling:** Microwave cream cheese in bowl until soft, 20 to 30 seconds. Whisk in sour cream, sugar, and flour; set aside.

3 **For the brownies:** Whisk flour, baking powder, and salt together in bowl. Microwave butter and chocolate in large bowl at 50 percent power, stirring often, until melted, 1 to 2 minutes. Whisk in sugar and vanilla until well combined. Whisk in eggs until fully combined and smooth. Stir in flour mixture until just incorporated. Transfer all but ½ cup batter to prepared pan and smooth top.

4 Spread cream cheese mixture evenly over top of brownie batter in pan. Microwave reserved ½ cup brownie batter until warm and pourable, 10 to 20 seconds. Using spoon, dollop warmed batter in 6 to 8 places over cream cheese filling. Using chopstick or butter knife, swirl brownie batter through cream cheese topping, making marbled pattern and leaving ½-inch border around edges.

5 Bake brownies until toothpick inserted in center (avoiding cream cheese) comes out with few moist crumbs attached, 35 to 40 minutes, rotating pan halfway through baking.

6 Let brownies cool in pan on wire rack for 1 hour. Using foil overhang, remove brownies from pan. Transfer brownies to wire rack and let cool completely, about 1 hour. Cut into 16 pieces before serving.

Storage: 2 days in refrigerator

WHY THIS RECIPE WORKS Bittersweet chocolate shouldn't have a monopoly on squidgy squares. When stirred into batter and baked, white chocolate infuses these brownie-like bars with a complex, buttery, caramelized flavor that gives dark chocolate brownies a run for their money. These bars are satisfyingly chewy without being heavy. We use just enough white chocolate for a moist, rich-tasting bar but not so much that it's cloyingly sweet. Juicy, bright raspberries are a perfect foil to the sweetness of white chocolate, so we dot these bars with whole fresh berries. Tossing the raspberries with a little sugar before pressing them into the batter encourages them to roast and caramelize. Baking at a slightly higher temperature than most brownie recipes call for—375 degrees instead of 350—results in beautifully browned edges that further enhance the caramel notes of these elegant bars.

Makes 16 brownies

Total Time 50 minutes, plus 2½ hours cooling

RASPBERRY WHITE CHOCOLATE BROWNIES

- 1 cup (142 grams) all-purpose flour
- 1 teaspoon baking powder
- ¼ teaspoon table salt
- 6 ounces (170 grams) white chocolate, cut into ½-inch pieces, divided
- 4 tablespoons (57 grams) unsalted butter, softened
- ½ cup (99 grams) plus 2 teaspoons sugar, divided
- 1 large egg
- 1 teaspoon vanilla extract
- 5 ounces (142 grams/1 cup) raspberries

Storage: 2 days in refrigerator

1 Adjust oven rack to middle position and heat oven to 375 degrees. Make foil sling for 8-inch square baking pan by folding 2 long sheets of aluminum foil so each is 8 inches wide. Lay sheets of foil in pan perpendicular to each other, with extra foil hanging over edges of pan. Push foil into corners and up sides of pan, smoothing foil flush to pan. Grease foil.

2 Whisk flour, baking powder, and salt together in bowl. Microwave 3 ounces (85 grams) chocolate in bowl at 50 percent power, stirring occasionally, until melted, 1 to 3 minutes.

3 Using stand mixer fitted with paddle, beat butter and 1/2 cup sugar on medium-high speed until pale and fluffy, 3 to 5 minutes. Add egg and vanilla and continue to beat until well incorporated, about 1 minute longer. Add melted chocolate and mix until incorporated, about 30 seconds. Reduce speed to low; add flour mixture; and mix until batter is uniform, about 1 minute. Stir in all but 2 tablespoons remaining chopped chocolate.

4 Transfer batter to prepared pan and spread into even layer. Gently toss raspberries with remaining 2 teaspoons sugar, then arrange evenly over top of batter in pan, gently pressing into batter. Bake until edges are puffed and golden and toothpick inserted in center comes out with few moist crumbs attached, 25 to 35 minutes, rotating pan halfway through baking.

5 Let bars cool completely in pan on wire rack, about 2 hours. Using foil overhang, remove bars from pan. Microwave reserved 2 tablespoons chocolate in bowl at 50 percent power, stirring occasionally, until melted, about 45 seconds. Drizzle melted chocolate over bars. Cut into 16 pieces and let chocolate set, about 30 minutes, before serving.

WHY THIS RECIPE WORKS Blondies are baked in a pan and chew like brownies, but their flavor is closer to that of chocolate chip cookies—irresistibly butterscotchy. The ideal blondie is neither too cakey nor too dense, sweet but not cloying, and loaded with nuts and chocolate. As with many of our cookies, a secret to getting the right amount of chew is using melted butter. Light brown sugar, combined with vanilla extract and some salt, gives the bars dimension and the desired butterscotch flavor. A generous amount of pecans brings crunch to the plush bars, and equal amounts of semisweet and white chocolate chips enliven the bars with chocolate punch and buttery sweetness.

Makes 36 blondies

Total Time 40 minutes, plus 2 hours cooling

BLONDIES

- 1½ cups (213 grams) all-purpose flour
- 1 teaspoon baking powder
- ½ teaspoon table salt
- 1½ cups packed (297 grams) light brown sugar
- 12 tablespoons (171 grams) unsalted butter, melted and cooled
- 2 large eggs
- 1½ teaspoons vanilla extract
- 1 cup (119 grams) pecans or walnuts, toasted and chopped coarse
- ½ cup (85 grams) semisweet chocolate chips
- ½ cup (85 grams) white chocolate chips

1 Adjust oven rack to middle position and heat oven to 350 degrees. Make foil sling for 13 by 9-inch baking pan by folding 2 long sheets of aluminum foil; first sheet should be 13 inches wide and second sheet should be 9 inches wide. Lay sheets of foil in pan perpendicular to each other, with extra foil hanging over edges of pan. Push foil into corners and up sides of pan, smoothing foil flush to pan. Grease foil.

2 Whisk flour, baking powder, and salt together in bowl. Whisk sugar and melted butter together in second bowl. Whisk in eggs and vanilla until combined. Stir in flour mixture until just combined, then stir in pecans, semisweet chocolate chips, and white chocolate chips.

3 Transfer batter to prepared pan and spread into even layer. Bake until top is shiny and cracked and feels firm to touch, 22 to 25 minutes, rotating pan halfway through baking. Let blondies cool completely in pan on wire rack, about 2 hours. Using foil overhang, remove blondies from pan. Cut into 36 pieces before serving.

Storage: 3 days at room temperature

Makes 10 blondie bites

Total Time 55 minutes, plus 30 minutes cooling

WHY THIS RECIPE WORKS Tahini's nutty flavor beautifully enriches sweets, and it infuses these chewy bite-size blondies with big sesame flavor. Dolloped with a sticky-sweet jam made from bananas browned in butter, the blondies are bittersweet but balanced and comforting. Tahini is both rich and packed with carbohydrates, so we need only a minimal amount of flour and no additional fat in the batter for just the right chewy-tender texture. Baking in a muffin tin gives the petite treats the ideal ratio of crispy edge to gooey, tender center. Finishing the blondie bites with dark chocolate and sesame seeds adds bold flavor and graphic visual appeal.

TAHINI BLONDIE BITES WITH CARAMELIZED BANANA JAM AND CHOCOLATE

CARAMELIZED BANANA JAM

- 1 tablespoon unsalted butter
- 1 ripe banana, peeled and sliced ½ inch thick
- ¼ cup packed (50 grams) brown sugar
- ⅛ teaspoon table salt

TAHINI BLONDIES

- ⅔ cup (95 grams) all-purpose flour
- 4 teaspoons sesame seeds, toasted, divided
- ½ teaspoon baking powder
- ½ teaspoon table salt
- ¾ cup packed (149 grams) brown sugar
- 1 large egg
- 2 teaspoons vanilla extract
- ½ cup (123 grams) tahini
- 1 ounce bittersweet chocolate, chopped

Make sure that your tahini is well mixed; if the solids are compacted at the bottom of the container, transfer both the oil and the solids to a blender jar and blend for about 30 seconds to re-emulsify. Use a ripe banana that is bright yellow with some light brown speckles. Adding the tahini to the batter last ensures that the tahini is not overmixed, which can stiffen the dough and create a tougher blondie.

1 Adjust oven rack to middle position and heat oven to 350 degrees. Spray 10 cups of 12-cup muffin tin with vegetable oil spray.

2 For the caramelized banana jam: Melt butter in 10-inch skillet over medium-high heat. Add banana and cook, stirring occasionally, until bananas are browned in spots and become soft, 3 to 5 minutes. Stir in sugar and salt and cook, mashing bananas with spatula, until sugar dissolves and mixture is cohesive, about 2 minutes (small bits of banana may remain). Remove from heat and let banana jam cool while making blondies. (You should have about ½ cup banana jam.)

3 For the tahini blondies: Whisk flour, 1 tablespoon sesame seeds, baking powder, and salt together in bowl. Whisk sugar, egg, and vanilla in medium bowl until well combined. Stir flour mixture into sugar mixture until no dry flour remains. Stir in tahini until homogeneous.

4 Divide blondie dough evenly among prepared muffin cups (about 2 tablespoons each), then press dough into bottom of each cup. Dollop about 2 teaspoons banana jam in center of each dough portion, then sprinkle evenly with chocolate and remaining 1 teaspoon sesame seeds.

5 Bake until blondies are golden brown at edges, about 15 minutes, rotating muffin tin halfway through baking. Let blondies cool in muffin tin on wire rack for 10 minutes. Run thin spatula or paring knife around edge of each blondie to loosen, then carefully transfer blondies to rack and let cool completely before serving.

Storage: 3 days at room temperature

Makes 9 blondies

Total Time 1 hour, plus 2 hours cooling

WHY THIS RECIPE WORKS Rich with the taste of nutty browned butter, these chewy blondies earn their fall stripes with a satisfying swirl of spiced pumpkin–cream cheese filling. Incorporating pumpkin this way, instead of stirring it into the batter, prevents the brownies from becoming dense or cakey (moisture-rich pumpkin can have these effects in baked goods). Four different spices—cinnamon, ginger, cloves, and nutmeg—bring fragrant warmth to the filling reminiscent of pumpkin pie. Cream cheese in the mix adds rich tang that's always welcome with pumpkin spice, and an egg yolk binds this mixture for a luxurious texture throughout the satisfying blondie.

PUMPKIN CREAM CHEESE BLONDIES

- 4 ounces (113 grams) cream cheese, cut into 4 pieces and softened
- 1½ cups packed (297 grams) light brown sugar, divided
- ¼ cup (59 grams) canned unsweetened pumpkin puree
- 2 large eggs plus 1 large yolk
- ½ teaspoon ground cinnamon
- ¼ teaspoon ground ginger
- ⅛ teaspoon ground cloves
- ⅛ teaspoon ground nutmeg
- ⅛ teaspoon plus ¾ teaspoon table salt, divided
- 1½ cups (213 grams) all-purpose flour
- ¾ teaspoon baking powder
- 12 tablespoons (171 grams) unsalted butter
- 1½ teaspoons vanilla extract

To accurately test doneness, be sure to stick the toothpick through part of the blondie and not the cream cheese.

1 Adjust oven rack to middle position and heat oven to 350 degrees. Make foil sling for 8-inch square baking pan by folding 2 long sheets of aluminum foil so each is 8 inches wide. Lay sheets of foil in pan perpendicular to each other, with extra foil hanging over edges of pan. Push foil into corners and up sides of pan, smoothing foil flush to pan. Grease foil.

2 Whisk cream cheese, ¼ cup (50 grams) sugar, pumpkin puree, egg yolk, cinnamon, ginger, cloves, nutmeg, and ⅛ teaspoon salt together in bowl. Whisk flour, baking powder, and remaining ¾ teaspoon salt together in second bowl.

3 Melt butter in 10-inch skillet over medium-high heat, about 2 minutes. Continue to cook, swirling skillet and stirring constantly with silicone spatula, until butter is dark golden brown and has nutty aroma, 1 to 3 minutes. Transfer browned butter to large bowl. Whisk in vanilla and remaining 1¼ cups (248 grams) sugar until well combined. Whisk in 2 eggs until fully combined and smooth. Stir in flour mixture until just incorporated, then transfer all but ½ cup blondie batter to prepared pan and spread into even layer.

4 Using spoon, dollop cream cheese mixture and reserved ½ cup batter over top of blondie batter in pan, in 6 to 8 spots each. Using chopstick or butter knife, swirl blondie batter and cream cheese mixture, making marbled pattern and leaving ½-inch border around edges.

5 Bake blondies until edges are light golden and toothpick inserted in center comes out with few moist crumbs attached, 35 to 40 minutes, rotating pan halfway through baking.

6 Let blondies cool in pan on wire rack for 1 hour. Using foil overhang, remove blondies from pan. Transfer blondies to wire rack and let cool completely, about 1 hour. Cut into 9 pieces before serving.

Storage: 3 days in refrigerator

Makes 16 blondies

Total Time 1 hour, plus 2 hours cooling

WHY THIS RECIPE WORKS One of the moment's most popular café drinks has earned a place on the dessert table. The creaminess and the earthy and fruity flavors of a strawberry matcha latte shine in this colorful take on blondies. A traditional blondie batter goes green with the addition of 2 tablespoons of matcha powder (splurge for ceremonial grade for the best flavor and brightest color). To top it off, we simmer a quick cornstarch-thickened strawberry filling made with frozen berries. For the creamy component, we whisk softened cream cheese with a little sugar, milk for fluidity, and flour to bind the mixture during baking. We swirl the three components together for a stunning tricolor marble effect.

STRAWBERRY MATCHA CREAM CHEESE BLONDIES

STRAWBERRY FILLING

- 1 teaspoon cornstarch
- 1 teaspoon water
- 6 ounces (170 grams/1⅓ cups) frozen strawberries
- 3 tablespoons granulated sugar
- ⅛ teaspoon table salt

CREAM CHEESE FILLING

- 4 ounces (113 grams) cream cheese
- 1 tablespoon sugar
- 1 tablespoon milk
- 1 teaspoon all-purpose flour

BLONDIES

- 1 cup (142 grams) all-purpose flour
- 2 tablespoons matcha powder
- ½ teaspoon baking powder
- ¼ teaspoon table salt
- 1 cup packed (198 grams) light brown sugar
- 8 tablespoons (114 grams) unsalted butter, melted
- 1 large egg
- 1 teaspoon vanilla extract

For the best-looking marbling, use restraint when swirling the batters. To preserve your artistry, wipe your knife clean between cuts when slicing the cooled blondies.

1 Adjust oven rack to middle position and heat oven to 350 degrees. Make foil sling for 8-inch square baking pan by folding 2 long sheets of aluminum foil so each is 8 inches wide. Lay sheets of foil in pan perpendicular to each other, with extra foil hanging over edges of pan. Push foil into corners and up sides of pan, smoothing foil flush to pan. Grease foil.

2 For the strawberry filling: Stir cornstarch and water together in small bowl; set aside. Cook frozen strawberries, sugar, and salt in small saucepan over medium heat, stirring occasionally, until strawberries are beginning to soften and juices are bubbling, about 2 minutes. Crush berries with potato masher until mostly broken down and continue to cook until mixture is slightly thickened, 3 to 5 minutes. Stir cornstarch mixture to recombine, then stir into strawberry sauce. Cook until thickened, about 30 seconds. Transfer mixture to bowl and set aside to cool.

3 For the cream cheese filling: Microwave cream cheese until soft, 20 to 30 seconds. Add sugar, milk, and flour and whisk to combine. Set aside.

4 For the blondies: Whisk flour, matcha, baking powder, and salt together in bowl. Whisk brown sugar, melted butter, egg, and vanilla in large bowl until well combined and smooth. Stir in flour mixture until no dry flour remains.

••• CONTINUED •••

5 Measure out and reserve ½ cup blondie batter, then use offset spatula to spread remaining batter into even layer in prepared pan (layer will be quite thin). Dollop cream cheese mixture in 6 to 8 spots over top of batter, then repeat with cooled strawberry filling. Dollops should mostly cover surface of batter. Microwave reserved blondie batter until warm and loosened, 15 to 20 seconds, then dollop into remaining open spaces between strawberry and cream cheese filling, creating rough patchwork. Drag chopstick or butter knife through dollops to create marbled effect.

6 Bake blondies until light golden brown around edges and top of blondie has smooth, shiny crust with some cracks, about 25 minutes, rotating pan halfway through baking. Let blondies cool completely in pan on wire rack. Using foil overhang, remove blondies from pan. Cut into 16 pieces before serving.

Storage: 3 days in refrigerator

MAKING THE BLONDIES

1. Spread blondie batter into even layer in prepared pan (layer will be quite thin).

2. Dollop cream cheese mixture in 6 to 8 spots over top of batter; repeat with cooled strawberry filling.

3. Dollop warmed remaining blondie batter into remaining open spaces between strawberry and cream cheese, creating rough patchwork.

4. Drag chopstick through dollops to create marbled effect.

1

2

3

4

Makes 16 bars

Total Time 1½ hours, plus 2 hours cooling

WHY THIS RECIPE WORKS Hawaiian butter mochi—a custard-like dessert that's cut into bite-size pieces—is known for its irresistibly chewy, dense, bouncy texture. The beloved treat is possibly influenced by the stretchy mochi coming from the island's Japanese population, as well as by the coconutty rice flour dessert bibingka from its Filipino population. Butter mochi is coconut-flavored at its simplest; we inject vibrant berry flavor by blending whole and coconut milks with freeze-dried strawberries for a strawberry milk mixture that makes our bars a colorful pink. The sweet rice flour gives the mochi its signature bounce, while eggs, sugar, and butter ensure tenderness and richness. The bars develop a golden and crisp contrasting surface thanks to a layer of flaked coconut, and it becomes a canvas for stripes of tangy strawberry-lemon glaze.

STRAWBERRY LEMONADE COCONUT MOCHI BARS

MOCHI

- 1 cup (245 grams) whole milk
- 1 cup (233 grams) canned coconut milk
- 3 cups freeze-dried strawberries
- 2 large eggs
- 1½ teaspoons vanilla extract
- 2 cups (312 grams) sweet rice flour
- 1 cup (198 grams) granulated sugar
- 2 teaspoons baking powder
- ½ teaspoon table salt
- 6 tablespoons (86 grams) unsalted butter, melted
- ½ cup (29 grams) unsweetened flaked coconut

GLAZE

- 5 tablespoons freeze-dried strawberries, divided
- ½ cup (57 grams) confectioners' sugar
- 1 tablespoon lemon juice

We used unsweetened coconut here; if using sweetened, toast and sprinkle on after baking. Be sure to use sweet white (glutinous) rice flour, such as Mochiko flour, for this recipe. Plain white rice flour will not create the chewy texture that is essential to this recipe. We prefer to sift the ground strawberries for a smooth consistency in the icing, but you can omit this step if you prefer.

1 **For the mochi:** Adjust oven rack to middle position and heat oven to 350 degrees. Grease 8-inch square baking pan. Make parchment sling by folding 2 long sheets of parchment so each is 8 inches wide. Lay sheets of parchment in pan perpendicular to each other, with extra parchment hanging over edges of pan. Push parchment into corners and up sides of pan, smoothing parchment flush to pan. Grease parchment.

2 Process milk, coconut milk, and strawberries in food processor until mostly smooth, about 30 seconds, scraping down sides of processor as needed. Transfer to large bowl with eggs and vanilla and whisk to combine. Whisk sweet rice flour, sugar, baking powder, and salt together in second bowl. Add flour mixture to milk mixture and fold with silicone spatula until combined. Add melted butter and whisk until smooth.

3 Transfer mixture to prepared pan and smooth top, then sprinkle with coconut. Bake until bars are firm to touch and toothpick inserted in center comes out with few crumbs attached, 1 hour to 1 hour 10 minutes, rotating pan halfway through baking. Let bars cool completely in pan on wire rack, about 2 hours.

4 **For the glaze:** Using parchment overhang, remove bars from pan. Grind 2 tablespoons strawberries in spice grinder until reduced to fine powder. Sift powder through fine-mesh strainer set over medium bowl. Add sugar and lemon juice and whisk until smooth. (Glaze should be used immediately; if it hardens, whisk in ½ to 1 teaspoon water.) Lightly crush remaining 3 tablespoons strawberries and sprinkle attractively over bars, then drizzle bars with glaze and let sit until glaze is firm, about 5 minutes. Cut into 16 pieces before serving.

Storage: 2 days at room temperature (freeze-dried strawberries will soften)

Makes 22 cookies

Total Time 1 hour, plus 30 minutes cooling

WHY THIS RECIPE WORKS Rolled in powdered sugar before baking, chocolate crinkle cookies (often called earthquakes) are made from a deep chocolate cookie dough that erupts through the bright white surface during baking to reveal striking stripes. A combination of Dutch-processed cocoa powder and unsweetened chocolate (boosted with a few teaspoons of espresso powder) gives our cookies intense chocolate flavor, and replacing granulated sugar with brown sugar adds complexity. Three techniques work in tandem to create the cookies' hallmark fissures. First, using both baking soda and baking powder in the dough produces lots of bubbles that quickly rise to the surface and burst during baking. Second, letting the dough sit at room temperature rather than baking the cookies straight from the refrigerator encourages the cookies to spread, leading to cracks in their surface. And finally, rolling the dough in granulated sugar before coating the balls in powdered sugar dries out the surface of the cookies, causing even more fissures to form.

CHOCOLATE CRINKLE COOKIES

- 1 cup (142 grams) all-purpose flour
- ½ cup (43 grams) Dutch-processed cocoa powder
- 1 teaspoon baking powder
- ¼ teaspoon baking soda
- ½ teaspoon table salt
- 4 ounces (113 grams) unsweetened chocolate, chopped
- 4 tablespoons (57 grams) unsalted butter
- 1½ cups packed (297 grams) brown sugar
- 4 teaspoons instant espresso powder (optional)
- 1 teaspoon vanilla extract
- 3 large eggs
- ½ cup (99 grams) granulated sugar for rolling
- ½ cup (57 grams) confectioners' sugar for rolling

1 Adjust oven rack to middle position and heat oven to 325 degrees. Whisk flour, cocoa, baking powder, baking soda, and salt together in bowl.

2 Microwave chocolate and butter in large bowl at 50 percent power, stirring occasionally, until melted, 2 to 4 minutes. Whisk in brown sugar; espresso powder, if using; and vanilla until well combined. Whisk in eggs until fully combined and smooth. Stir in flour mixture until just incorporated, then let dough stand at room temperature for 10 minutes.

3 Place granulated sugar and confectioners' sugar in separate shallow dishes. Working with 2 tablespoons dough at a time, roll into balls, then drop in granulated sugar dish. Roll to coat, then transfer to confectioners' sugar dish. Roll to coat in confectioners' sugar, then space evenly on 2 parchment paper–lined rimmed baking sheets (11 balls per sheet).

4 Bake cookies, 1 sheet at a time, until puffed and cracked and edges have begun to set but centers are still soft (cookies will look raw between cracks and seem underdone), about 12 minutes, rotating sheet halfway through baking. Transfer sheet to wire rack and let cookies cool completely before serving.

Storage: 5 days at room temperature

WHY THIS RECIPE WORKS In a visit to New Orleans Vietnamese bakery Dough Nguyener's, we found a delicious, stunning violet-colored crinkle variation that features Southeast Asian purple yam (known in the West as the Filipino ube) that is increasingly popular worldwide as a flavor for sweets. Ube extract and ube halaya (a Filipino ingredient that is essentially a cooked-down, concentrated jam of sweetened ube) are the most convenient forms for American cooks, and we add both to our crinkles for the strongest flavor. The extract lends our cookies a deep violet color and the earthy, sweet, nutty aroma of the purple yam. The sticky halaya enriches the flavor while giving the cookies dynamic texture: chewy-crisp edges with a dense, soft, fudgy interior.

Makes 24 cookies

Total Time 1 hour, plus 30 minutes cooling

UBE CRINKLE COOKIES

- 2¼ cups (320 grams) all-purpose flour
- 1 teaspoon baking powder
- ½ teaspoon baking soda
- ¾ teaspoon table salt
- 1½ cups (297 grams) granulated sugar, plus ⅓ cup (66 grams) for rolling
- ¼ cup (75 grams) ube jam
- 8 tablespoons (114 grams) unsalted butter, melted
- ¼ cup (53 grams) vegetable oil
- 1 large egg
- 2 teaspoons ube extract
- 1 teaspoon vanilla extract
- ½ cup (57 grams) confectioners' sugar

Ube jam (also known as ube halaya, or ube spread) and ube extract are available in well-stocked Asian markets and online. We developed this recipe with Tropics Ube Halaya (Purple Yam Jam) and McCormick brand ube extract.

1 Adjust oven rack to middle position and heat oven to 350 degrees. Whisk flour, baking powder, baking soda, and salt together in bowl.

2 Whisk 1½ (298 grams) cups granulated sugar and ube jam together in large bowl. Whisk in melted butter, oil, egg, ube extract, and vanilla until smooth. Stir in flour mixture until just incorporated.

3 Spread confectioners' sugar and remaining ⅓ cup (66 grams) granulated sugar in separate shallow dishes. Working with 1½ tablespoons dough at a time, roll into balls, then drop in granulated sugar dish. Roll to coat, then transfer to confectioners' sugar dish. Roll to coat, then space evenly on 2 parchment paper–lined rimmed baking sheets (12 balls per sheet). Using bottom of drinking glass or dry measuring cup, press each ball to ¾-inch thickness. Using fine-mesh strainer, dust tops of cookies evenly with remaining confectioners' sugar from shallow dish (about 2 tablespoons per sheet), using all of sugar.

4 Bake cookies, 1 sheet at a time, until puffed and cracked and edges are just set, 11 to 13 minutes, rotating sheet halfway through baking. Let cookies cool on sheet for 5 minutes, then transfer to wire rack. Let cookies cool completely before serving.

Storage: 4 days at room temperature

Chapter 7

LIGHT AND LOVELY

Makes 40 cookies

Total Time 1¼ hours, plus 1 hour 25 minutes chilling and cooling

WHY THIS RECIPE WORKS Small and delicate, sweet and delightfully lemony, lemon thins had legions of fans in the 70s and 80s, and grocery store shelves, particularly in the South, were crowded with regional versions. We wanted to eat lemon thins . . . today. Lemon thins are lighter than shortbread cookies, so we cut the flour in the recipe with some cornstarch for incredibly tender yet crisp cookies. Though the cookie is delicate, the lemon flavor should be bold. Two tablespoons of juice along with a bit of pure lemon extract gives us bright, pleasantly sour flavor. A light lemon glaze enforces the citrus flavor in these new thins with old-fashioned charm.

LEMON THINS

COOKIES

- 1½ cups (213 grams) all-purpose flour
- 2 tablespoons cornstarch
- ¼ teaspoon table salt
- ¼ teaspoon baking powder
- ⅛ teaspoon baking soda
- 10 tablespoons (143 grams) unsalted butter, softened
- ½ cup (99 grams) granulated sugar
- 2 tablespoons lemon juice
- 1 large egg yolk
- 1½ teaspoons lemon extract

GLAZE

- 1 cup (113 grams) confectioners' sugar
- 1 teaspoon grated lemon zest plus 5 teaspoons juice
- Pinch table salt

1 For the cookies: Whisk flour, cornstarch, salt, baking powder, and baking soda together in bowl. Using stand mixer fitted with paddle, beat butter and sugar on medium speed until pale and fluffy, 3 to 5 minutes, scraping down bowl as needed. Add lemon juice, egg yolk, and lemon extract and continue to beat until well incorporated, about 1 minute longer. Reduce speed to low and add flour mixture until just combined, about 1 minute.

2 Transfer dough to counter and divide in half. Place each piece of dough on sheet of plastic wrap and flatten each into 5-inch disk. Wrap each disk tightly in plastic and refrigerate for at least 1 hour or up to 24 hours.

3 Adjust oven rack to middle position and heat oven to 325 degrees. Line 2 baking sheets with parchment paper. Let 1 chilled dough disk sit on counter to soften slightly, about 10 minutes. Roll dough into ¼-inch-thick circle, about 10 inches wide, on lightly floured counter. Using 2-inch round cutter, cut dough into rounds, gathering scraps and rerolling twice; space cookies evenly over 1 prepared sheet. Repeat with second dough disk (20 cookies per sheet).

4 Bake cookies, 1 sheet at a time, until edges are lightly browned, 16 to 18 minutes, rotating sheet halfway through baking. Let cookies cool on sheet for 5 minutes, then transfer to wire rack and let cool completely.

5 For the glaze: Whisk all ingredients together in bowl. Working with 1 cookie at a time, dip top of cookie into glaze. Lift up from glaze (do not turn upright) and gently shake side to side to allow excess glaze to drip off evenly and back into bowl. Return cookies to wire rack and let sit for 15 minutes before serving.

Storage: unglazed, 2 days at room temperature; 24 hours glazed

WHY THIS RECIPE WORKS Lemon Thins (page 342) beget other citrus thins, and yuzu is a tantalizing twist. "I've recently become a bit obsessed with yuzu juice," says Claudia Catalano, the recipe developer who created this tangy two-bite treat. "I've been whisking it into cheesecakes and shaking it into cocktails—it was only a matter of time before it made it into a cookie!" The Japanese citrus fruit has faintly floral notes and lip-smacking acidity; it tastes like a cross between Meyer lemon, lime, and grapefruit. To drive home the flavor in these buttery cookies, we add some lime zest to the dough. Crunchy black sesame seeds, in the dough and sprinkled onto the glaze, complement the bright yuzu with their earthiness, and they provide lots of visual appeal.

Makes 40 cookies

Total Time 1½ hours, plus 1 hour chilling

YUZU AND BLACK SESAME THINS

COOKIES

- 1½ cups (213 grams) all-purpose flour
- 2 tablespoons cornstarch
- ½ teaspoon table salt
- ¼ teaspoon baking powder
- ⅛ teaspoon baking soda
- 10 tablespoons (143 grams) unsalted butter, softened
- ½ cup (99 grams) sugar
- 2 tablespoons yuzu juice
- 1 large egg yolk
- 2 tablespoons black sesame seeds
- 1 teaspoon grated lime zest

GLAZE

- 1 cup (113 grams) confectioners' sugar
- 5 teaspoons yuzu juice
- Pinch table salt
- Black sesame seeds

Storage: unglazed, 2 days at room temperature; 24 hours glazed

Be sure to use 100 percent yuzu juice for this recipe. Yuzu juice is available at Asian markets and online. If you can't find it, you can substitute a mixture of equal parts lemon, lime, and grapefruit juice.

1 For the cookies: Whisk flour, cornstarch, salt, baking powder, and baking soda together in bowl. Using stand mixer fitted with paddle, beat butter and sugar on medium speed until pale and fluffy, 3 to 5 minutes. Add yuzu juice, egg yolk, sesame seeds, and lime zest and beat until well incorporated, about 1 minute longer. Reduce speed to low; add flour mixture; and mix until dough is uniform, about 1 minute.

2 Transfer dough to counter and divide in half. Place each piece of dough on sheet of plastic wrap and flatten into 5-inch disk. Wrap each disk tightly in plastic and refrigerate for at least 1 hour or up to 24 hours.

3 Adjust oven rack to middle position and heat oven to 325 degrees. Line 2 baking sheets with parchment paper. Let 1 chilled dough disk sit on counter to soften slightly, about 10 minutes. Roll dough into ¼-inch-thick circle, about 10 inches wide, on lightly floured counter. Using 2-inch round cutter, cut dough into rounds, gathering scraps and rerolling twice; space cookies evenly over 1 prepared sheet. Repeat with second dough disk (20 cookies per sheet).

4 Bake cookies, 1 sheet at a time, until edges are lightly browned, 16 to 18 minutes, rotating sheet halfway through baking. Let cookies cool on sheet for 5 minutes, then transfer to wire rack and let cool completely.

5 For the glaze: Whisk all ingredients together in bowl. Working quickly with 1 cookie at a time, dip surface of cookie into glaze. Lift up from glaze (do not turn upright) and gently shake side to side to allow excess glaze to drip off evenly and back into bowl. Return cookies to wire rack and sprinkle tops with sesame seeds. Let cookies sit for 15 minutes before serving.

WHY THIS RECIPE WORKS These two-bite meltaway cookies are literally as cute as a button, and thanks to a generous amount of freeze-dried mangos ground up in the dough, the bright yellow rounds have outsize flavor for their diminutive size. Meltaways are supertender cookies that melt in your mouth. Adding tapioca starch to our dough creates cookies that practically dissolve at first bite. To brighten the fruity flavors, we add some tartness to the glaze in the form of complementary lime juice (plus just a bit of mango powder). A final sprinkling of lime zest adds fresh aroma and color.

Makes 35 cookies

Total Time 1 hour, plus 1½ hours cooling

MANGO-LIME MELTAWAYS

- 2 cups freeze-dried mango
- 1¼ cup (141 grams) confectioners' sugar, divided
- ½ cup (71 grams) all-purpose flour
- 6 tablespoons (43 grams) tapioca starch
- 1½ teaspoons grated lime zest, plus extra for sprinkling, plus 7 teaspoons juice, divided
- ¼ teaspoon table salt
- 8 tablespoons (114 grams) unsalted butter, cut into ½-inch pieces and chilled

1 Pulse mango in food processor until broken down into ¼- to ½-inch pieces, 5 to 7 pulses, then process until finely ground, about 1 minute (you should have⅓ cup mango powder). Measure out and reserve 1 tablespoon mango powder. Add ¼ cup (28 grams) sugar, flour, tapioca starch, lime zest, and salt to mango powder in processor bowl, then process until well combined, about 15 seconds.

2 Sprinkle 1 teaspoon lime juice and chilled butter pieces over flour mixture, then process until cohesive ball forms, about 30 seconds. Transfer dough to lightly floured counter and roll into 9-inch log. Wrap log tightly in plastic wrap and twist ends tightly to seal; refrigerate for at least 1 hour or up to 3 days.

3 Adjust oven rack to middle position and heat oven to 350 degrees. Trim ends of dough log, then slice into ¼-inch-thick rounds, rotating dough log as you slice to prevent any flat edges from forming. Space dough rounds 1 inch apart on parchment paper–lined baking sheet.

4 Bake cookies until just beginning to brown at edges, 12 to 14 minutes. Let cookies cool on sheet for 10 minutes, then transfer to wire rack. Let cool completely.

5 Whisk remaining 1 cup (113 grams) sugar, remaining 2 tablespoons lime juice, and reserved 1 tablespoon mango powder until smooth. (Glaze should be thick and pourable. Add water, drop by drop, if needed, to achieve desired consistency.) Spoon glaze evenly over cooled cookies. Sprinkle with extra lime zest, then let glaze set for 15 minutes before serving.

Storage: 2 days at room temperature

GUAVA-STRAWBERRY SANDWICH COOKIES

Makes 24 sandwich cookies

Total Time 1½ hours, plus 1 hour chilling

WHY THIS RECIPE WORKS These unique sandwich cookies feature two meltingly tender vanilla cookies and a standout creamy guava and strawberry filling. The harmonious floral-berry pairing comes from two special fruit-based ingredients. Guava paste, a solidified conserve made from guava pulp and sugar, makes up the backbone of our filling. We whip it with butter, cream cheese, heavy cream, confectioners' sugar, and just a touch of lime juice for balance. Freeze-dried strawberries, ground into a powder, add bright berry flavor without the added moisture or texture of fresh berries. To give the cookies a very tender texture that gently yields to the filling, we cut the flour with cornstarch: not just a couple tablespoons but a whopping 1⅓ cups. Lots of butter and three tenderizing egg yolks also contribute to the unique texture.

COOKIES

- 1½ cups (213 grams) all-purpose flour
- 1⅓ cups (151 grams) cornstarch
- 1 teaspoon baking powder
- ¼ teaspoon table salt
- 16 tablespoons (228 grams) unsalted butter, softened
- ½ cup (99 grams) granulated sugar
- 3 large egg yolks
- 1 teaspoon vanilla extract

FILLING

- ⅓ cup freeze-dried strawberries
- 4 ounces (113 grams) guava paste, cut into ½-inch pieces
- 2 tablespoons unsalted butter, softened
- ¼ cup (28 grams) confectioner's sugar
- 1½ teaspoons heavy cream
- 1 teaspoon lime juice
- 2 ounces (57 grams) cream cheese, cut into 4 pieces and softened

Confectioners' sugar

Storage: 2 days in refrigerator

Guava paste can be found in well-stocked grocery stores and online; we developed this recipe with Goya brand. We used a 2-inch fluted round cutter; you can use any shape cookie cutter, though you may get a different number of cookies. For a colorful topping, whisk together 2 teaspoons finely ground freeze-dried strawberries and 3 tablespoons confectioners' sugar; dust the cookies with all pink sugar or a combination of pink and confectioners' sugar before serving (for more information, see page 8). If you do not have 3 baking sheets, reuse first sheet, bringing to room temperature before baking.

1 **For the cookies:** Whisk flour, cornstarch, baking powder, and salt together in bowl. Using stand mixer fitted with paddle, beat butter and granulated sugar on medium speed until pale and fluffy, 3 to 5 minutes. Add egg yolks and vanilla and continue to beat until well incorporated, about 1 minute longer. Reduce speed to low; add flour mixture; and mix until dough is uniform, about 1 minute.

2 Transfer dough to counter and divide in half. Place 1 piece of dough in center of large sheet of parchment paper and press with your hands to ½-inch thickness. Place second large sheet of parchment over top and roll dough to ¼-inch thickness. Transfer dough with parchment to rimmed baking sheet. Repeat pressing and rolling second piece of dough, then stack on top of first piece on sheet. Freeze until dough is firm, 20 to 30 minutes.

3 Adjust oven rack to upper-middle position and heat oven to 350 degrees. Line 2 baking sheets with parchment paper. Transfer 1 piece of dough to counter. Peel off top layer of parchment and, using 2-inch cutter, cut dough into 24 cookies, gathering leftover dough scraps and rerolling and chilling once; space cookies evenly over 1 prepared sheet. Repeat with second piece of dough and second prepared sheet.

4 Bake, 1 sheet at a time, until tops are set but still pale and bottoms are light golden, 12 to 14 minutes. Let cookies cool on sheet for 5 minutes, then transfer to wire rack. Let cookies cool completely.

5 **For the filling:** Pulse freeze-dried strawberries in spice grinder until reduced to fine powder, about five 5-second pulses. Using clean mixer bowl fitted with whisk attachment, whip guava paste on high speed until cohesive, sticky paste forms, 10 to 15 seconds. Reduce speed to low; add butter, freeze-dried strawberry powder, and sugar; and whip until sugar is mostly moistened, about 15 seconds. Scrape down bowl, then increase speed to medium and whip until smooth, about 30 seconds. Add heavy cream and lime juice and whip until combined, about 15 seconds. With mixer running, add cream cheese 1 piece at a time, mixing after each addition until well-blended, about 1 minute.

6 Spread about 2 teaspoons filling over flat side of 1 cookie, then place second cookie on top; gently press to adhere. Repeat with remaining cookies and filling. Dust cookies with confectioners' sugar before serving.

Makes 48 cookies

Total Time 1¼ hours, plus 20 minutes cooling

SNOWBALLS

WHY THIS RECIPE WORKS The cookie underneath the snowy coating of confectioners' sugar on these little treats is delicate and crumbly with deeply nutty flavor. Also known by a number of other names, like Mexican wedding cookies and Russian tea cakes, these cookies have an uncertain lineage, while their long-lasting popularity is undeniable. In order to really reinforce the nut flavor, we found it necessary to use an equal amount of nuts (we like pecans or walnuts) and flour. But all of those chopped nuts make a dough that's difficult to hold together. Eggs would make the cookies too cakey; instead, we grind a portion of the nuts very fine, which releases their natural oil and binds the dough. For the snowiest coating of confectioners' sugar, we roll the cookies in sugar twice to ensure thorough coverage.

- 2 cups (238 grams) pecans or walnuts, divided
- 2 cups (284 grams) all-purpose flour
- ¾ teaspoon table salt
- 16 tablespoons (228 grams) unsalted butter, softened
- ⅓ cup (66 grams) superfine sugar
- 1½ teaspoons vanilla extract
- 1½ cups (170 grams) confectioners' sugar

If you can't find superfine sugar, you can process an equal amount of granulated sugar in a food processor for about 20 seconds. You may want to reroll the cookies in confectioners' sugar before serving if you are making these ahead.

1 Adjust oven racks to upper-middle and lower-middle positions and heat oven to 325 degrees. Process 1 cup (113 grams) pecans in food processor until texture of coarse cornmeal, 10 to 15 seconds; transfer to bowl. Process remaining 1 cup (113 grams) pecans in now-empty food processor until coarsely chopped, about 5 seconds; transfer to bowl with ground pecans. Stir in flour and salt.

2 Using stand mixer fitted with paddle, beat butter and superfine sugar on medium speed until pale and fluffy, 3 to 5 minutes, scraping down bowl as needed. Beat in vanilla. Reduce speed to low; add nut mixture; and mix until dough is uniform, about 1 minute.

3 Working with 1 tablespoon dough at a time, roll into balls and space them evenly on 2 parchment paper–lined baking sheets (24 balls per sheet). Bake until tops are pale golden and bottoms are just beginning to brown, about 18 minutes, switching and rotating sheets halfway through baking. Let cookies cool on sheets for 5 minutes, then transfer to wire rack. Let cookies cool completely.

4 Spread confectioners' sugar in shallow dish. Working with several cooled cookies at a time, roll in sugar to coat. Before serving, reroll cookies in confectioners' sugar and gently shake off excess.

Storage: 2 days at room temperature

Makes 32 sandwich cookies

Total Time 1¼ hours, plus 1 hour cooling

BACI DI DAMA

WHY THIS RECIPE WORKS Baci di dama, the tiny chocolate-filled hazelnut cookies with big flavor whose name means "lady's kisses," might just be the world's cutest cookie. They can be a bit fragile, so we sought a workable recipe. Interestingly, leaving bits of skin on the nuts firms up the dough and adds more flavor and color. For fast portioning of the 64 little dough balls, we press the dough into a baking pan, briefly freeze it to firm it up, cut the dough into a "portion grid" of little squares, and roll each square into even balls. Neither ganache nor Nutella firms up enough to fill the cookies. Warm melted chocolate becomes set and snappy but first runs down the side; letting the chocolate cool and thicken before filling the cookies ensures that it doesn't drip off.

- ¾ cup (107 grams) hazelnuts, toasted and partially skinned
- ⅔ cup (95 grams) all-purpose flour
- ⅓ cup (66 grams) sugar
- ⅛ teaspoon table salt
- 6 tablespoons (86 grams) unsalted butter, cut into ½-inch pieces and chilled
- 2 ounces (57 grams) bittersweet chocolate, chopped

Toast the hazelnuts on a rimmed baking sheet in a 325-degree oven until fragrant, 13 to 15 minutes, then gather the warm hazelnuts in a dish towel and rub to remove some of the skins (for more information, see page 39). A square-cornered metal baking pan works best for shaping the dough.

1 Adjust oven rack to middle position and heat oven to 325 degrees. Line bottom of 8-inch square baking pan with parchment paper. Process hazelnuts, flour, sugar, and salt in food processor until hazelnuts are very finely ground, 20 to 25 seconds. Add butter and pulse until dough just comes together, 20 to 25 pulses.

2 Transfer dough to counter, knead briefly to form smooth ball, place in prepared pan, and press into even layer that covers bottom of pan. Freeze for 10 minutes. Run knife or bench scraper between dough and edge of pan to loosen, then transfer dough to counter and discard parchment. Cut dough into 64 squares (8 rows by 8 rows). Roll dough squares into balls and evenly space dough balls on 2 parchment-lined rimmed baking sheets (32 balls per sheet).

3 Bake cookies, 1 sheet at a time, until dry and fragrant (cookies will settle but not spread), about 20 minutes, rotating sheet halfway through baking. Transfer sheet to wire rack and let cookies cool completely on sheet.

4 Microwave chocolate in small bowl at 50 percent power, stirring every 20 seconds, until melted, 1 to 2 minutes. Let chocolate cool at room temperature until slightly thickened and registers 80 degrees, about 10 minutes. Invert half of cookies on each sheet. Using ¼-teaspoon measure, spoon chocolate onto flat surfaces of all inverted cookies. Top with remaining cookies, pressing lightly to adhere. Let chocolate set for at least 15 minutes before serving.

Storage: 10 days at room temperature

WHY THIS RECIPE WORKS Buttery and beautiful, with a golden swirled shape, light, crisp spritz cookies often appear around the holidays. To give them special occasion–worthy richness, we use a generous 16 tablespoons of butter. Spritz cookies get their ridges from the dough being pushed through a cookie press or, in the case of our accessible recipe, a piping bag. Adding a little heavy cream makes the dough workable. Some recipes for spritz cookies call for whole eggs, while others use just yolks or even no eggs at all. We found that cookies made without eggs are too tender and crumbly, with an ill-defined shape. A whole egg makes for chewy, tough cookies. Using just one yolk makes spritz that are tender and crisp yet sturdy.

Makes 72 cookies

Total Time 1¼ hours, plus 20 minutes cooling

SPRITZ COOKIES

- 1 large egg yolk
- 2 tablespoons heavy cream
- 1 teaspoon vanilla extract
- 2 cups (284 grams) all-purpose flour
- ¼ teaspoon table salt
- 16 tablespoons (228 grams) unsalted butter, softened
- ⅔ cup (132 grams) sugar

This recipe calls for a pastry bag to form the cookies, but you can use a cookie press if you have one; follow the manufacturer's instructions.

1 Adjust oven rack to middle position and heat oven to 375 degrees. Whisk egg yolk, cream, and vanilla together in small bowl. Whisk flour and salt together in separate bowl.

2 Using stand mixer fitted with paddle, beat butter and sugar on medium speed until pale and fluffy, 3 to 5 minutes, scraping down bowl as needed. Add egg yolk mixture and continue to beat until well incorporated, about 1 minute longer. Reduce speed to low; add flour mixture; and mix until dough is uniform, about 1 minute.

3 Fill pastry bag fitted with ½-inch star tip with half of dough. Push dough down toward tip until fully compressed and twist top of bag tightly to seal. Holding bag at base of twist and holding tip at 90-degree angle, pipe cookies 1½ inches apart onto 2 parchment paper–lined baking sheets. Refill pastry bag with remaining dough as needed.

4 Bake cookies, 1 sheet at a time, until light golden, 10 to 12 minutes, rotating sheet halfway through baking. Let cookies cool on sheet for 10 minutes, then transfer to wire rack. Let cool completely before serving.

Storage: 1 week at room temperature

PIPING DIFFERENT SPRITZ SHAPES

Using a piping bag gives you some shaping options. Try the standard star or have fun with the following elegant shapes. For stars, a ½- to ⅝-inch tip (measure the diameter of the tip at the smallest point) works best. For rosettes and S shapes, use a ⅜-inch tip. If you make an error while piping, the dough can be scraped off the baking sheet and re-piped.

TO CREATE STARS: Hold pastry bag at 90-degree angle to baking sheet and pipe dough straight down, until it is about 1 inch in diameter.

TO CREATE ROSETTES: Pipe dough while moving bag in circular motion, ending at center; rosettes should be about 1¼ inches in diameter.

TO CREATE S SHAPES: Pipe dough following curves of compact S; they should be about 2 inches long and 1 inch wide.

Makes 36 cookies

Total Time 55 minutes, plus 50 minutes chilling and cooling

WHY THIS RECIPE WORKS These striking cookies with a candy window look intricate, yet they're actually quite easy to make. We start with a workable butter-filled cookie dough that bakes up with the structure needed for the "window frames." The "glass" seems to come together through magic, but all it takes is filling the empty spaces with crushed candies such as Jolly Ranchers. We add the candy halfway through baking so it doesn't bubble over the cookie edges after it melts. Once cooled, the candy resolidifies into a smooth pane of glass.

STAINED GLASS WINDOW COOKIES

- 2½ cups (355 grams) all-purpose flour
- ¾ cup (149 grams) superfine sugar
- ¼ teaspoon table salt
- 16 tablespoons (228 grams) unsalted butter, cut into 16 pieces and softened
- 1 ounce cream cheese, softened
- 2 teaspoons vanilla extract
- 20 hard candies, assorted colors, separated by color and crushed fine

Storage: 5 days at room temperature

If you can't find superfine sugar, you can process an equal weight of granulated sugar in a food processor for about 20 seconds. We used a 2½-inch star cutter; you can use any shape cookie cutter, though you may get a different number of cookies. To crush candies, place in zipper lock bag, seal bag, then smash with a rolling pin until candies are crushed fine.

1 Using stand mixer fitted with paddle, mix flour, sugar, and salt on low speed until combined. Add butter, 1 piece at a time, and mix until dough looks crumbly and slightly wet, 1 to 2 minutes. Add cream cheese and vanilla and beat until dough just begins to form large clumps, about 30 seconds.

2 Transfer dough to counter and knead just until it forms cohesive mass. Divide dough in half. Place each piece of dough on sheet of plastic wrap and flatten each into 4-inch disk. Wrap each disk tightly in plastic and refrigerate for at least 30 minutes or up to 2 days.

3 Adjust oven rack to middle position and heat oven to 375 degrees. Place 1 disk of dough between 2 large sheets of parchment paper and roll to ⅛-inch thickness. Slide dough, still between parchment, onto rimmed baking sheet. Repeat with second piece of dough; refrigerate until firm, about 10 minutes.

4 Remove top sheet of parchment from 1 sheet of dough and line baking sheet. Using 2½-inch cutter, cut out 18 cookies. Using smaller cutter, cut out centers of dough to form windowpane shape. Gather scraps and gently reroll once. Space cookies 2 inches apart on prepared sheet. Repeat with second sheet of dough and second baking sheet.

5 Bake cookies, 1 sheet at a time, for 5 minutes. Sprinkle even layer of crushed candies in center of each cookie, mixing or alternating colors as desired. Rotate sheet and bake until edges are light golden brown and candies have melted, 4 to 5 minutes. Let cookies cool on sheet for 10 minutes, then transfer to wire rack and let cool completely before serving.

Makes 60 cookies

Total Time 45 minutes, plus 20 minutes cooling

WHY THIS RECIPE WORKS With no eggs, no leavener, and batter spread paper-thin on a rimless baking sheet, fairy gingerbread is unlike any ordinary gingerbread: Crisp and wafer-like, it melts in the mouth, and it's spicy-sweet. The century-plus-old recipe was popularly made in Boston and is found in seminal cookbooks such as Jessup Whitehead's 1893 *Cooking for Profit* and Fannie Merritt Farmer's 1896 *Boston Cooking-School Cook Book*. To make the flavor of these ultrathin cookies as bold as any other, we increase the ground ginger called for in most recipes and also toast it. Fresh grated ginger adds another layer of spice. While these old-fashioned cookies traditionally lack leavener, a little baking soda helps them retain their airy crispness after baking.

FAIRY GINGERBREAD

- 1½ teaspoons ground ginger
- ¾ cup plus 2 tablespoons (124 grams) all-purpose flour
- ½ teaspoon baking soda
- ¼ teaspoon table salt
- 5 tablespoons (71 grams) unsalted butter, softened
- 9 tablespoons packed (111 grams) light brown sugar
- 4 teaspoons grated fresh ginger
- ¾ teaspoon vanilla extract
- ¼ cup (61 grams) whole milk, room temperature

If you have a 15 by 12-inch silicone baking mat, use it here in place of the parchment paper and vegetable oil spray. If you do not have a rimless baking sheet, use an overturned rimmed baking sheet. Don't be disconcerted by the scant amount of batter: You really are spreading the batter very thin. Use the edges of the parchment paper as your guide, covering the entire surface thinly and evenly.

1 Adjust oven racks to upper-middle and lower-middle positions and heat oven to 325 degrees. Spray 2 rimless baking sheets with vegetable oil spray and cover each with 15 by 12-inch sheet parchment paper. Heat ground ginger in small skillet over medium heat until fragrant, about 1 minute. Whisk flour, baking soda, salt, and toasted ginger together in bowl.

2 Using stand mixer fitted with paddle, beat butter and sugar on medium speed until pale and fluffy, 3 to 5 minutes, scraping down bowl as needed. Add fresh ginger and vanilla and continue to beat until incorporated, about 1 minute longer. Reduce speed to low and add flour mixture in 3 additions, alternating with milk in 2 additions; scrape down bowl as needed.

3 Using offset spatula, evenly spread ¾ cup batter to cover parchment on each prepared sheet (batter will be very thin). Bake until deep golden brown, 16 to 20 minutes, switching and rotating sheets halfway through baking. Immediately score cookies into 3 by 2-inch rectangles. Let cool completely. Using tip of paring knife, separate cookies along score marks before serving.

Storage: 3 days at room temperature

WHY THIS RECIPE WORKS Thin and crisp but almost cake-like, and fragrant with anise, Italian pizzelle are a centuries-old cookie, with gorgeously filigreed modern versions tracing to the Abruzzo region of Italy (while some food historians trace more primitive recipes to the Roman Empire). The cookie base is a batter, aerated by whipped whole eggs and sugar and enriched with butter. The satiny batter gets spread on a pizzelle maker, a plated iron griddle. This version has a gorgeous perfume from anise seeds, vanilla extract, and orange zest. We love the extra sweetness and playfulness a dusting of confectioners' sugar on the cooled cookies adds, but you can also eat them plain. Pizzelle are perfect for dipping into good coffee or espresso, and also pair well with gelato or berries.

Makes 24 cookies

Total Time 45 minutes

PIZZELLE

- 2 cups (284 grams) all-purpose flour
- ¼ teaspoon table salt
- 3 large eggs
- 1 cup (198 grams) granulated sugar
- 10 tablespoons (143 grams) unsalted butter, melted and cooled
- 2 teaspoons grated orange zest plus ¼ cup (59 grams) juice
- 1½ teaspoons anise seeds
- 1½ teaspoons vanilla extract
- Confectioners' sugar (optional)

1 Whisk flour and salt together in bowl. Using stand mixer fitted with paddle, beat eggs and granulated sugar on medium speed until pale and fluffy, 3 to 5 minutes, scraping down sides of bowl as needed. Slowly add melted butter and beat until incorporated, about 1 minute. Add orange zest and juice, anise seeds, and vanilla and beat until incorporated, about 1 minute.

2 Reduce speed to low; add flour mixture; and mix until just combined, about 1 minute. Increase speed to medium and beat until dough is satiny and smooth, 3 to 5 minutes. (It will look broken at first but will come together to form cohesive dough that is slightly sticky.)

3 Preheat pizzelle maker according to manufacturer's instructions. Spray iron with vegetable oil spray. Drop 1½-tablespoon portions of batter into center of each pizzelle mold. Close cover and cook until golden, 30 to 60 seconds. Using heatproof spatula, gently slide cookies off of iron and transfer to wire rack. Let sit until cool and crisp, about 10 minutes. Repeat with remaining batter, spraying iron with additional vegetable oil spray if pizzelle begin to stick. Dust pizzelle with confectioners' sugar, if using, before serving.

Storage: 1 week at room temperature

ATK CLASSIC

Makes about 40 meringues

Total Time 3 hours, plus 1½ hours cooling

These delicate, crisp, bright white meringues dissolve in your mouth while also providing a little something more to chew on: We embellish them with the flavors and textures of a nostalgic candy bar, Almond Joy. The "joyful" interplay of chocolate, almond, and coconut makes these little kisses irresistible. We use a French-style meringue here—one made by whipping raw egg whites and sugar to stiff peaks. This style bakes up a little coarser than Swiss meringue (see page 367) and Italian meringue, both of which heat the sugar to dissolve. The more open texture makes a cookie that dries out nicely and that's delicate and melts in your mouth. Cornstarch can help meringue hold its shape while baking; we use some confectioners' sugar in this recipe, which takes care of the starch component. Nutty flavor comes in the form of almond extract, which is whipped right into the egg whites before we pipe the meringue into petite peaked kisses. Once the cookies are fully baked and dry, we dip the bottoms in melted chocolate and coat them in toasted coconut.

ALMOND JOY MERINGUE KISSES

- 2 large egg whites
- ¼ teaspoon almond extract
- ⅛ teaspoon table salt
- ⅓ cup (66 grams) granulated sugar
- ⅓ cup (38 grams) confectioners' sugar
- ½ cup (85 grams) bittersweet chocolate chips
- 1 cup (82 grams) unsweetened shredded coconut, toasted

Storage: 2 weeks at room temperature

We found that finely shredded unsweetened coconut adheres more evenly to these cookies; we used Bob's Red Mill during development. Sifting the confectioners' sugar over the egg whites in the mixer bowl helps to prevent the egg whites from deflating and ensures that no clumps of sugar remain. Store the finished cookies with silica packets so that they stay dry and crisp.

1 Adjust oven racks to upper-middle and lower-middle positions and heat oven to 200 degrees. Using stand mixer fitted with whisk attachment, whip egg whites, almond extract, and salt on high speed until very soft peaks form (peaks should slowly lose their shape when whisk is removed), 20 to 30 seconds.

2 Reduce speed to medium and slowly add granulated sugar in steady stream. Once sugar is fully incorporated, stop mixer and scrape down sides and bottom of mixer bowl. Increase speed to high and whip until glossy, just-stiff peaks have formed, 20 to 30 seconds.

3 Remove bowl from mixer, then sift confectioners' sugar into bowl over whipped egg whites. Fold sugar into egg whites until well combined. Working quickly, transfer meringue to large pastry bag fitted with ½-inch round tip. Pipe small amount of meringue onto each corner of 2 baking sheets. Line sheets with parchment paper, pressing on corners to secure. Pipe meringue into 1¼-inch mounds, about 1 inch high.

4 Bake meringues until exteriors feel dry, about 1½ hours, switching and rotating sheets halfway through baking. Turn off oven, prop door open with wooden spoon, and let meringues cool in oven for about 1 hour. Transfer sheets to wire rack and let kisses cool completely on sheets.

5 Microwave chocolate chips in bowl at 50 percent power, stirring occasionally, until melted, 2 to 4 minutes. Place toasted coconut on plate. Working with 1 meringue at a time, dip bottom of meringue in melted chocolate so chocolate comes about ⅛ inch up sides of meringue. Use fork to remove meringue from chocolate (tips of kisses are very fragile and will break if used as handle), then place in coconut,coating chocolate completely in coconut. Use second fork to lift meringue from coconut and return to sheet. Let meringues sit until chocolate is set, about 30 minutes, before serving.

Sugar's Role in Meringues

Sugar flavors meringue, but the addition is necessary for other reasons. While the egg whites whip, the sugar dissolves in the water from the whites to form a viscous liquid. As a meringue bakes, its moisture slowly evaporates, weakening its structure. At the same time, the egg white protein ovalbumin is becoming stronger by bonding with other proteins, providing additional structure for the foam. Because sugar has a tendency to hold on to water molecules, if there is not enough sugar in the meringue, the water evaporates too quickly, causing the cookies to collapse before the ovalbumin has time to strengthen.

Achieving Perfect Peaks

It's important to whip egg whites for meringue exactly to stiff peaks. If whipped shy of that, the protein network will be too weak to provide structure and hold the cookies' trademark peaks.

Soft peaks (top)
Stiff peaks (bottom)

Piping Meringue Kisses

1 Working quickly, transfer meringue to large pastry bag fitted with ½-inch round tip.

2 Pipe meringue into 1¼-inch mounds, about 1 inch high, spaced 1 inch apart over prepared sheets.

Makes 16 meringues

Total Time 2 hours, plus 2¼ hours chilling and cooling

WHY THIS RECIPE WORKS These big, whimsical meringues, full of fanciful swoops and vibrant whirlpools of passion fruit curd, aren't just mesmerizing to look at: Each bite is an enticing experience of contrasting textures and flavors that keeps you coming back for just a bit(e) more. The exterior of the meringue bakes up dry and crisp (thanks to a generous amount of granulated sugar), but it encases a soft marshmallow center, with just a bit of chew where the two meet. This is thanks in part to adding vinegar while whipping the meringue, which lowers the pH, making the foam less apt to collapse. Cornstarch assists in drying out the mixture. We use a Swiss meringue method—one in which egg white and sugar are heated together—because it most reliably creates an inflated, very smooth-textured meringue here. Swirling a striking homemade tart passion fruit curd—our favorite out of many options tested—into the whipped egg whites before baking tames the meringue's sweetness and also gives you something rich and unctuous to sink your teeth into.

PASSION FRUIT MERINGUE SWIRLS

PASSION FRUIT CURD

- ½ cup (122 grams) unsweetened passion fruit puree
- ⅓ cup (66 grams) sugar
- 4 large egg yolks
- 2½ teaspoons cornstarch
- Pinch table salt
- 3 tablespoons unsalted butter, cut into 3 pieces and chilled

MERINGUES

- 1½ cups (297 grams) sugar
- ¾ cup (168 grams) egg whites (5 to 7 large eggs)
- 1½ teaspoons distilled white vinegar
- 1½ teaspoons cornstarch
- 1 teaspoon vanilla extract

Because eggs can vary in size, measuring the egg whites by weight or volume for the meringues is essential to ensure that you are working with the correct ratio of egg whites to sugar. You can find unsweetened passion fruit puree (also labeled passion fruit pulp) in the freezer section. Open the oven door as infrequently as possible while the meringues are inside. We recommend storing these meringues with silica gel packets to extend their shelf life.

1 For the passion fruit curd: Whisk passion fruit puree, sugar, egg yolks, cornstarch, and salt in small saucepan until combined. Cook over medium-low heat, stirring constantly, until mixture thickens and registers 170 to 175 degrees, 4 to 6 minutes. Off heat, whisk in butter until smooth. Strain curd through fine-mesh strainer into bowl. Press greased parchment paper onto surface of curd and refrigerate until chilled, at least 30 minutes or up to 1 week.

2 For the meringues: Adjust oven racks to upper-middle and lower-middle positions and heat oven to 225 degrees. Combine sugar and egg whites in bowl of stand mixer; place bowl over saucepan filled with ½ inch barely simmering water, making sure that water does not touch bottom of bowl. Whisking gently but constantly, heat until sugar is dissolved and mixture registers 160 degrees, 3 to 5 minutes.

••• CONTINUED •••

3 Fit stand mixer with whisk attachment and whip egg mixture on high speed until meringue forms stiff peaks, is smooth and creamy, and is bright white with sheen, 2 to 4 minutes (bowl may still be slightly warm to touch). Stop mixer and scrape down bowl with spatula. Add vinegar, cornstarch, and vanilla and whip on high speed until combined, about 10 seconds.

4 Spoon about ¼ teaspoon meringue onto each corner of 2 rimmed baking sheets. Line sheets with parchment paper, pressing on corners to secure. Spoon ⅓ cup meringue into 8 evenly spaced piles on each sheet. Using back of small spoon, make 1-inch-wide and ½-inch-deep indentation in center of each meringue. Add 2 teaspoons passion fruit curd to indentation, then use chopstick or skewer to gently swirl curd into meringue using figure-eight and spiral motions (do not overswirl).

5 Bake meringues until exteriors are dry to the touch and meringues release cleanly from parchment around edges when gently lifted with thin metal spatula, 1½ to 2 hours. Meringues should be quite pale (a hint of creamy color is OK). Turn off oven, prop door open with wooden spoon, and let meringues cool in oven for 1½ hours. Remove from oven and let cool completely before serving.

Storage: 4 days at room temperature

1

2

3

FORMING THE MERINGUES

1. Using back of small spoon, make 1-inch-wide and ½-inch-deep indentation in center of each meringue.

2. Add 2 teaspoons passion fruit curd to indentation.

3. Use chopstick or skewer to gently swirl curd into meringue using figure-eight and spiral motions.

Makes 18 cookies

Total Time 2 hours 20 minutes

COOKIES

- ⅓ cup (94 grams) seedless raspberry jam
- 1 teaspoon lemon juice
- 1 cup (142 grams) all-purpose flour
- ¼ teaspoon table salt
- ¼ teaspoon baking soda
- ⅛ teaspoon baking powder
- 6 tablespoons (86 grams) unsalted butter, softened
- ⅓ cup (66 grams) sugar
- 2 ounces (57 grams) cream cheese, softened
- ¾ teaspoon vanilla extract

MARSHMALLOW

- 5 teaspoons unflavored gelatin
- ½ cup (118 grams) water, divided
- ¾ cup (149 grams) sugar
- ½ cup (164 grams) light corn syrup
- ¼ teaspoon table salt
- 1 tablespoon grated orange zest
- Orange water-based gel food coloring (optional)

CHOCOLATE

- 2 cups (340 grams) white chocolate chips
- 2 tablespoons refined coconut oil
- Yellow oil-based gel food coloring (optional)

WHY THIS RECIPE WORKS A cookie topped with marshmallow and coated in a thin chocolate shell (known as Mallomars in the United States) is a popular concept the world over. Instead of featuring the typical vanilla marshmallow and semisweet chocolate, our creation awakens the palate, topping a raspberry jam thumbprint with a citrusy orange marshmallow and coating it all with white chocolate, which we color with optional yellow dye. Making your own marshmallow allows you to add flavor and color, and the texture is unbelievably light, fluffy, and springy. This project can easily be broken into three steps: baking the cookie, making the marshmallow, and coating the cookies in chocolate, making it easy to take breaks in between each step. It's al worth it for the most beautiful marshmallow cookie you've ever seen, with an ombré-like sunrise effect from the layers of red, orange, and yellow.

SUNRISE MARSHMALLOW COOKIES

You'll need two types of food coloring for this recipe. Use water-based food coloring in the marshmallow; oil-based will make the mixture break. Use oil-based food coloring in the chocolate; water-based will make it seize.

1 For the cookies: Adjust oven rack to middle position and heat oven to 350 degrees. Stir jam and lemon juice together in small bowl; set aside. Whisk flour, salt, baking soda, and baking powder together in bowl. Using stand mixer fitted with paddle, beat butter and sugar on medium speed until pale and fluffy, 3 to 5 minutes, scraping down bowl as needed. Add cream cheese and vanilla and continue to beat until well incorporated, about 1 minute longer. Reduce speed to low; add flour mixture; and mix until dough is uniform, about 1 minute.

2 Working with 1 tablespoon dough at a time, roll into balls and space evenly on parchment paper–lined baking sheet. Using greased rounded 1-teaspoon measure, make indentation in center of each dough ball.

3 Bake cookies until just set, about 7 minutes, rotating sheet halfway through baking. Transfer sheet to wire rack (do not turn off oven) and immediately use back of rounded teaspoon measure to reinforce indentation in center of each cookie. Spoon ½ teaspoon jam mixture into indent of each cookie, then return sheet to oven and bake until cookies are beginning to turn golden at edges, about 7 minutes, rotating sheet halfway through baking. Let cookies cool on sheet for 5 minutes, then transfer to wire rack. Let cool completely before topping with marshmallow.

••• CONTINUED •••

ASSEMBLING THE COOKIES

1. Pipe peak of marshmallow about 1 inch high onto each cooled cookie. Freeze cookies, uncovered, until marshmallow is firm.

2. Hold cookie base and dip marshmallow into chocolate to coat marshmallow completely, letting excess chocolate drip back into bowl.

4 **For the marshmallow:** Sprinkle gelatin over ¼ cup water in clean, dry stand mixer bowl and let sit until gelatin is very firm, about 5 minutes.

5 Meanwhile, combine remaining ¼ cup water, sugar, corn syrup, and salt in medium saucepan. Bring to boil over medium-high heat and cook, gently swirling saucepan occasionally, until sugar has dissolved completely and mixture registers 240 degrees, 6 to 8 minutes.

6 Fit mixer with whisk attachment and whip gelatin mixture on low speed while carefully pouring in hot sugar syrup, avoiding whisk and sides of bowl. Once all sugar syrup has been incorporated, increase speed to high and whip until mixture is just warm to touch and is very thick and stiff, about 10 minutes. Add orange zest and food coloring, if using, and mix until incorporated, about 1 minute, scraping down bowl once halfway through.

7 Transfer marshmallow to piping bag, then cut off tip to create 1-inch-wide hole. Pipe peak of marshmallow about 1 inch high onto each cooled cookie. Freeze cookies, uncovered, until marshmallow is firm, about 30 minutes.

8 **For the chocolate:** Microwave chocolate chips and coconut oil in 4-cup liquid measuring cup at 50 percent power, stirring occasionally, until melted, 2 to 4 minutes. Stir in food coloring, if using. Working quickly with 1 cookie at a time, hold cookie base and dip marshmallow into chocolate to coat marshmallow completely, letting excess chocolate drip back into bowl. Return cookie to wire rack, marshmallow side up, and let sit until chocolate is set, about 15 minutes, before serving.

Storage: 3 days at room temperature

Chapter 8

SOFT AND CAKEY

ATK CLASSIC

Makes 6 sandwich cookies

Total Time 40 minutes, plus 1 hour cooling and chilling

Made up of two cookie-like cakes and stuffed to the gills with fluffy marshmallow filling, the whoopie pie is a sweet handheld indulgence. A big difference between these cakier cookies and others in the book is the addition of liquid, which turns to steam during baking and boosts lift. We draw inspiration from devil's food cake, first creaming butter with sugar and then adding eggs and buttermilk for tenderness, and we use all-purpose flour for the right amount of structure. Baking soda reacts with the acidic buttermilk to open the fluffy crumb. We prefer the darker color and flavor that Dutch-processed cocoa provides. Replacing the granulated sugar with brown sugar deepens the flavor and adds moisture. For the filling, we eschew the traditional sugar and lard in favor of marshmallow crème, which we enrich with butter for a mixture that's fluffy yet firm.

CHOCOLATE WHOOPIE PIES

CAKES

- 2 cups (284 grams) all-purpose flour
- ½ cup (43 grams) Dutch-processed cocoa powder
- 1 teaspoon baking soda
- ½ teaspoon table salt
- 8 tablespoons (114 grams) unsalted butter, softened
- 1 cup packed (198 grams) light brown sugar
- 1 large egg, room temperature
- 1 teaspoon vanilla extract
- 1 cup (245 grams) buttermilk

FILLING

- 12 tablespoons (171 grams) unsalted butter, softened
- 1¼ cups (141 grams) confectioners' sugar
- 1½ teaspoons vanilla extract
- ⅛ teaspoon table salt
- 2½ cups (283 grams) Fluff brand marshmallow crème

Don't be tempted to bake all the cakes on one baking sheet; the batter needs room to spread while it bakes.

1 For the cakes: Adjust oven racks to upper-middle and lower-middle positions and heat oven to 350 degrees. Whisk flour, cocoa, baking soda, and salt together in bowl.

2 Using stand mixer fitted with paddle, beat butter and sugar on medium speed until pale and fluffy, 3 to 5 minutes, scraping down bowl as needed. Add egg and vanilla and continue to beat until well incorporated, about 1 minute longer. Reduce speed to low and add flour mixture in 3 additions, alternating with buttermilk in 2 additions.

3 Using ⅓-cup measure to scoop batter, drop 12 mounds evenly apart onto 2 parchment paper–lined baking sheets (6 mounds per sheet). Bake until centers spring back when lightly pressed, 15 to 18 minutes, switching and rotating sheets halfway through baking. Transfer sheets to wire rack and let cakes cool completely on sheets before filling.

4 For the filling: Using stand mixer fitted with paddle, beat butter and sugar on medium speed until fluffy, about 3 minutes. Beat in vanilla and salt. Add marshmallow crème and mix until combined, about 2 minutes. Refrigerate until slightly firm, about 30 minutes. Before serving, place ⅓ cup filling on bottom of 6 cooled cakes, then top with remaining cakes, pressing to spread filling to edge.

Storage: 3 days in refrigerator

For *Tender* Chocolate Whoopie Pies

- **Cream the butter and sugar** This gives the cookies cakey lift. (Many older recipes use lard, which can weigh down the crumb.)
- **Use buttermilk for the liquid** Acidic buttermilk inhibits some gluten development.
- **Leaven with baking soda** Baking soda reacts with both the buttermilk and the brown sugar in the recipe to lighten the cakes.

WHY THIS RECIPE WORKS These small, warm-spiced pumpkin sandwich cookies are easy enough to make for everyday occasions and delicious and cute enough to put on a holiday table. Whoopie pies typically tip the cookie scales, and we liked the idea of a smaller version with an alternative flavor profile. Pumpkin can be challenging to incorporate into a chewy cookie, as its moisture can make it cakey, so whoopie pies are the perfect place for its properties to shine. Rather than reduce the moisture in the pumpkin puree, we add it straight from the can and skip using another liquid ingredient. Departing from the marshmallow crème filling used in chocolate versions (see page 376), we take a cue from our favorite spice cakes and stuff these sandwiches with cream cheese frosting. The tangy frosting is a welcome contrast to the moist, warm-spiced cake.

Makes about 24 sandwich cookies

Total Time 50 minutes, plus 30 minutes cooling

MINI PUMPKIN WHOOPIE PIES

- 1 cup (142 grams) all-purpose flour
- 1½ teaspoons pumpkin pie spice
- 1 teaspoon baking soda
- ¾ teaspoon salt
- 2 large eggs
- ¾ cup (149 grams) granulated sugar
- 1 cup (237 grams) canned unsweetened pumpkin puree
- 6 tablespoons (86 grams) unsalted butter, melted and cooled, plus 4 tablespoons (57 grams) softened
- 1 cup (113 grams) confectioners' sugar, plus extra for dusting (optional)
- 4 ounces (113 grams) cream cheese, cut into 4 pieces and softened

A pastry bag makes quick work of forming even cakes, but the batter can be dropped with a spoon instead if you like.

1 Adjust oven racks to upper-middle and lower-middle positions and heat oven to 350 degrees.

2 Whisk flour, pumpkin pie spice, baking soda, and salt together in medium bowl. Using stand mixer fitted with whisk, whip eggs and granulated sugar on medium-high speed until pale and fluffy, about 3 minutes. Reduce speed to low, add pumpkin and melted butter, and mix until incorporated. Slowly add flour mixture and mix until just combined, about 30 seconds.

3 Using pastry bag, pipe 1-tablespoon mounds of batter onto 2 parchment paper–lined baking sheets, spacing them about 1 inch apart. Bake until cakes are set, 10 to 12 minutes, switching and rotating sheets halfway through baking. Let cakes cool on sheets for 5 minutes, then transfer to wire rack and let cool completely.

4 Using clean, dry bowl and whisk attachment, whip softened butter and confectioners' sugar on medium-high speed until pale and fluffy, about 2 minutes. Add cream cheese, 1 piece at a time, and mix until no lumps remain. Spread scant tablespoon filling over bottom of half of cakes, then top with remaining cakes, pressing lightly to adhere. Dust with confectioners' sugar, if using, before serving.

Storage: 3 days in refrigerator

WHY THIS RECIPE WORKS We drew inspiration for this gigantic chocolate-raspberry color-blocked cookie from the iconic New York City deli favorite, the black and white. Black and white cookies first appeared in bakeries in New York in the early 20th century. They rose in popularity because of their unique soft, cake-like texture and beautiful contrasting icings. Milk enriches our glaze just enough to give it flavor, while a touch of corn syrup makes it thick enough to set on top of the cookies instead of sinking in and disappearing. Our white side becomes pink with the addition of freeze-dried raspberry powder that really levels up the classic with a tart, berry-forward flavor explosion, while the chocolate side remains classically rich and fudgy, and colored with black cocoa.

Makes 12 cookies

Total Time 1 hour, plus 2¼ hours cooling and setting

BLACK AND PINK COOKIES

COOKIES

- 1¾ cups (249 grams) all-purpose flour
- ½ teaspoon baking powder
- ¼ teaspoon baking soda
- ⅛ teaspoon table salt
- 10 tablespoons (143 grams) unsalted butter, softened
- 1 cup (198 grams) granulated sugar
- 1 large egg
- 2 teaspoons vanilla extract
- ⅓ cup (79 grams) sour cream

GLAZES

- ¾ cup freeze-dried raspberries
- 5 cups (565 grams) confectioners' sugar
- ½ cup (123 grams) whole milk
- 2 tablespoons corn syrup
- 1 teaspoon vanilla extract
- ½ teaspoon table salt
- 3 tablespoons black cocoa powder

This recipe provides a little extra glaze, just in case.

1 For the cookies: Adjust oven racks to upper-middle and lower-middle positions and heat oven to 350 degrees. Whisk flour, baking powder, baking soda, and salt together in bowl.

2 Using stand mixer fitted with paddle, beat butter and sugar on medium speed until pale and fluffy, 3 to 5 minutes, scraping down bowl as needed. Add egg and vanilla and continue to beat until well incorporated, about 1 minute longer. Reduce speed to low and add flour mixture in 3 additions, alternating with sour cream in 2 additions.

3 Using greased ¼-cup measure, scoop dough and space evenly on 2 parchment paper-lined rimmed baking sheets (6 portions per sheet). Bake until edges are lightly browned, 15 to 18 minutes, switching and rotating sheets halfway through baking. Let cookies cool on sheets for 5 minutes, then transfer to wire rack. Let cookies cool completely before glazing.

4 For the glazes: Pulse freeze-dried raspberries in spice grinder until reduced to fine powder, about ten 5-second pulses. Sift powder through fine-mesh strainer to remove any seeds; discard seeds. Whisk sugar, milk, corn syrup, vanilla, and salt together in bowl until smooth. Transfer 1 cup glaze to small bowl, then whisk in sifted raspberry powder until smooth to create pink glaze. Whisk cocoa into remaining glaze until smooth to create black glaze.

5 Working with 1 cookie at a time, spread 1 tablespoon raspberry glaze over half of flat side of cookie. Refrigerate cookies until glaze is set, about 15 minutes. Spread 1 tablespoon chocolate glaze over unglazed half of flat side of cookie. Let sit until glaze is set, about 1 hour, before serving.

Storage: 2 days at room temperature

WHY THIS RECIPE WORKS This delightful cookie imagines a slice of soft banana bread, a rich chocolate cookie, and a streusel-crowned muffin top all teaming up. You'll fall in love with the tender-as-cake center, the slightly crunchy edges, and the nutty topping. You'll swoon over the triple dose of bittersweet chocolate (thanks to cocoa powder, melted chocolate, and chocolate chunks), which complements the fruitiness of the bananas. And you'll be more than thrilled to use up any languishing bananas in something other than smoothies and banana bread. We use ¾ cup of the mashed fruit to add flavor and moisture to these cookies, and they bind the batter without the need for eggs.

Makes 16 cookies

Total Time 1¼ hours, plus 30 minutes cooling

CHOCOLATE BANANA STREUSEL COOKIES

STREUSEL

- ½ cup (71 grams) all-purpose flour
- ¼ cup packed (50 grams) brown sugar
- ¼ teaspoon table salt
- 3 tablespoons unsalted butter, melted
- ⅓ cup (35 grams) walnuts, chopped

COOKIES

- 1½ cups (213 grams) all-purpose flour
- ¼ cup (21 grams) unsweetened cocoa powder
- 1 teaspoon baking powder
- ¼ teaspoon baking soda
- ¾ teaspoon table salt
- 8 ounces (227 grams) bittersweet chocolate, chopped, divided
- 4 tablespoons (57 grams) unsalted butter
- 1 cup (198 grams) sugar, plus ⅓ cup (66 grams) for rolling
- ¾ cup (182 grams) mashed ripe bananas (about 2 bananas)
- 1 tablespoon vanilla extract

Use very ripe, heavily speckled bananas in this recipe. The dough is a bit soft and sticky; allowing it to rest for 10 minutes makes it a bit easier to roll and coat with sugar. A cookie scoop makes for even more mess-free portioning.

1 For the streusel: Adjust oven rack to middle position and heat oven to 350 degrees. Whisk flour, sugar, and salt together in bowl. Add melted butter and stir until flour is evenly moistened. Add walnuts and mix until dough is texture of coarse meal with pea-size clumps; set aside.

2 For the cookies: Whisk flour, cocoa, baking powder, baking soda, and salt together in bowl. Microwave 4 ounces chocolate and butter in large bowl at 50 percent power, stirring occasionally, until melted, 2 to 4 minutes.

3 Whisk 1 cup (198 grams) sugar, mashed bananas, and vanilla into chocolate mixture until uniform. Stir in flour mixture and remaining 4 ounces chopped chocolate until uniform. Let dough sit for 10 minutes.

4 Spread remaining ⅓ cup (66 grams) granulated sugar in shallow dish. Working with 3 tablespoons dough at a time, roll into balls, dropping a few balls at a time directly into granulated sugar and rolling to coat. Space dough balls evenly on 2 parchment paper–lined baking sheets (8 balls per sheet).

5 Using bottom of dry measuring cup or drinking glass, flatten dough balls into 2½-inch-wide disks and top each cookie with about 1 tablespoon streusel. (If cookie dough sticks to bottom of measuring cup, dip in sugar before continuing to press.) Bake, 1 sheet at a time, until cookies are puffed, edges are just set, and streusel is light golden, 14 to 16 minutes, rotating sheet halfway through baking. Let cookies cool completely on sheet before serving.

Storage: 3 days at room temperature

WHY THIS RECIPE WORKS We love modeling cookies after more complicated desserts, and this recipe is everything you love about carrot cake—warm spices, sweet raisins, toasted walnuts, and bright orange carrots—in miniature form. The cookies have a satisfying carrot-cakey crumb with enough structure and chew that you can pick them up. Using melted butter instead of the oil traditionally called for in carrot cake helps achieve this more sturdy texture. Granulated sugar, rather than brown, produces crisp edges and prevents the cookies from being too soft. A full 2 cups of shredded carrots provide plenty of flavor but also add moisture that can throw off the recipe's ratios. To extract their excess liquid, we salt and sugar the carrots—a test kitchen trick that draws water out of vegetables—and then wring them out before adding them to the dough. Of course, a thick layer of sweet-tangy cream cheese frosting is a must.

Makes 24 cookies

Total Time 55 minutes, plus 1 hour sitting and cooking

CARROT CAKE COOKIES

COOKIES

- 12 ounces (340 grams) carrots, peeled and shredded
- 1 teaspoon granulated sugar, plus ½ cup (99 grams), divided
- 1 teaspoon table salt, divided
- 2 cups (284 grams) all-purpose flour
- 1 teaspoon ground cinnamon
- ½ teaspoon baking soda
- ½ teaspoon ground nutmeg
- 1 cup packed (198 grams) light brown sugar
- 12 tablespoons (170 grams) unsalted butter, melted and cooled
- 1 large egg plus 1 large yolk
- 2 teaspoons vanilla extract
- 1¾ cups (184 grams) walnuts, toasted and chopped coarse, divided
- ¾ cup (107 grams) golden raisins

FROSTING

- 6 tablespoons (86 grams) unsalted butter, softened
- 1½ cups (170 grams) confectioners' sugar
- 6 ounces (170 grams) cream cheese, cut into 4 pieces and softened
- 1 teaspoon vanilla extract

1 **For the cookies:** Adjust oven racks to upper-middle and lower-middle positions and heat oven to 350 degrees. Combine carrots, 1 teaspoon granulated sugar, and ½ teaspoon salt in bowl and let sit for 30 minutes. Place carrots in center of clean dish towel, gather ends of towel to form bundle, and twist to remove as much moisture from carrots as possible (you should squeeze off about ¼ cup liquid).

2 Whisk flour, cinnamon, baking soda, nutmeg, and remaining ½ teaspoon salt together in bowl. Whisk brown sugar, melted butter, egg and yolk, vanilla, and remaining ½ cup granulated sugar in separate large bowl until fully combined. Stir in flour mixture until just combined, then stir in carrots, 1 cup walnuts, and raisins.

3 Working with 2 tablespoons dough at a time, roll into balls and space evenly on 2 parchment paper–lined baking sheets (12 balls per sheet). Using your fingers, press cookies to ¾-inch thickness. Bake cookies until edges are set and beginning to brown, 16 to 20 minutes, switching and rotating sheets halfway through baking. Let cookies cool on sheets for 5 minutes, then transfer to wire rack and let cool completely before frosting.

4 **For the frosting:** Using stand mixer fitted with paddle, beat butter and sugar on medium speed until light and fluffy, about 2 minutes. Add cream cheese, 1 piece at a time, beating after each addition, until fully incorporated. Add vanilla and mix until no lumps remain.

5 Spread about 1 tablespoon frosting over each cooled cookie and sprinkle cookies with remaining ¾ cup walnuts before serving.

Storage: 2 days at room temperature

Makes 24 cookies

Total Time 55 minutes, plus 45 minutes cooling and setting

WHY THIS RECIPE WORKS In supermarkets across the United States, you can spot clamshells of retro ultrasoft sugar cookies made by Lofthouse Foods. Our version captures their nostalgia, and demystifies the ingredients behind their unique characteristics. To achieve their fine crumb and delicate structure, we use bleached cake flour and a surprising ingredient, margarine. Margarine is an emulsion of water and vegetable oil; its stable suspension of unsaturated fat particles yields a uniformly smooth cookie (butter creates cracks and adds a distracting flavor). Vanilla and almond extracts deliver the charming "boxed-good" flavor. Finally, the bright frosting lives between royal icing and buttercream, forms a subtle crust, and is near-identical to the prototype.

FROSTED SOFT SUGAR COOKIES

COOKIES

- 3¼ cups (369 grams) bleached cake flour
- 1 teaspoon baking powder
- 12 tablespoons (171 grams) margarine, softened
- 1½ cups (170 grams) confectioners' sugar
- 1 large egg
- 1 tablespoon vanilla extract
- ½ teaspoon almond extract (optional)
- 2 tablespoons water

FROSTING

- 2½ cups (283 grams) confectioners' sugar
- ¼ cup (58 grams) heavy cream
- 1 teaspoon vanilla extract
- 2 tablespoons margarine, softened
- Gel food coloring (optional)

- ¼ cup sprinkles (optional)

We recommend using margarine sticks, with up to 50 percent vegetable oil content, instead of spreadable margarine; using margarine with a higher percentage of vegetable oil may yield cookies that taste drier. We developed this recipe with Imperial brand margarine. You can substitute an equal amount of softened unsalted butter for the margarine in the cookies and the frosting, but the cookies will be slightly more coarse and crumbly. If using butter, add ½ teaspoon table salt to the cookie ingredients in step 1 and increase the water to ¼ cup; add ¼ teaspoon table salt to the frosting with the sugar, cream, and vanilla in step 4. You can customize the cookies with any number of colors and toppings for different holidays and occasions.

1 **For the cookies:** Adjust oven rack to middle position and heat oven to 350 degrees. Whisk flour and baking powder together in bowl. Using stand mixer fitted with paddle, beat margarine and sugar on medium speed until pale and fluffy, 3 to 5 minutes. Add egg; vanilla; and almond extract, if using, and continue to beat until well incorporated, about 1 minute longer (mixture may appear slightly curdled; this is OK). Reduce speed to low; add flour mixture; and mix until just combined and no dry flour remains, about 30 seconds. Add water and beat until mixture is smooth and well combined, about 30 seconds.

2 Working with 1½ tablespoons dough at a time, roll into balls and space them evenly on 2 parchment paper–lined baking sheets (12 balls per sheet). Using your dampened fingertips, press dough balls to ¼-inch thickness, patting to smooth edges if necessary.

3 Bake cookies, 1 sheet at a time, until slightly puffed and dough is just firm to touch, 7 to 8 minutes, rotating sheet halfway through baking. Let cookies cool on sheet for 5 minutes, then transfer to wire rack. Let cookies cool completely before frosting.

4 **For the frosting:** Using stand mixer fitted with whisk attachment, mix sugar, cream, and vanilla on low speed until sugar is moistened. Increase speed to medium-high and whip until mixture begins to form large clumps, about 1 minute. With mixer running, add margarine and whip until mixture is smooth and fluffy, about 1 minute, scraping down bowl as needed. Add food coloring, if using, and mix until homogeneous in color, about 1 minute.

5 Working with 1 cookie at a time, place 2 scant teaspoons of frosting in center of cookie. Using small offset spatula, spread frosting evenly over top, leaving ½-inch unfrosted border around outer rim of cookie. Immediately sprinkle with ½ teaspoon sprinkles, if using. Let cookies sit until frosting begins to form a crust, about 15 minutes, before serving.

Storage: 3 days at room temperature

Makes 24 cookies

Total Time 50 minutes, plus 30 minutes cooling

WHY THIS RECIPE WORKS We think snickerdoodles' simple sweet profile makes them a match for more than just cinnamon, and these soft treats are made extra aromatic from a roll in the warming, sweet-savory Iranian spice blend advieh. In Iran, advieh (which means "spice" in Persian) seasons everything from rice dishes to soups, stews, meats, and even sweets. Blends vary from region to region and family to family, but also by purpose: For our cookies, we make advieh by grinding whole coriander seeds, green cardamom pods, and black peppercorns and then pulsing in dried rosebuds until the petals become soft, confetti-like flecks. Cinnamon, flaky sea salt, and coarse turbinado sugar round out the coating, adding familiar warmth and a hint of crunch. This spiced, floral crust perfumes the dough as it bakes for a cookie that looks so familiar but tastes entirely new.

ADVIEH SNICKERDOODLES

- 4 teaspoons coriander seeds
- 1 teaspoon green cardamom pods
- ½ teaspoon black peppercorns
- ⅓ cup (14 grams) dried rosebuds, stems removed
- 2 tablespoons turbinado sugar, for rolling
- ½ teaspoon ground cinnamon
- ½ teaspoon flake sea salt
- 2½ cups (355 grams) all-purpose flour
- 2 teaspoons cream of tartar
- 1 teaspoon baking soda
- ½ teaspoon table salt
- 8 tablespoons (114 grams) unsalted butter, softened
- 8 tablespoons (88 grams) vegetable shortening
- 1½ cups (297 grams) granulated sugar
- 2 large eggs

Be sure to use food-grade dried rosebuds. The final dough will be slightly softer than most cookie doughs. You can substitute granulated or brown sugar for the turbinado but the coating will not have the same crunchy texture.

1 Pulse coriander, cardamom, and peppercorns in spice grinder until coarsely ground, about 5 pulses. Add rosebuds and pulse until coarsely ground and pieces of petal are no larger than ¼ inch, about 3 pulses. Transfer to small bowl and stir in turbinado sugar, cinnamon, and flake sea salt. Set aside.

2 Adjust oven rack to middle position and heat oven to 375 degrees. Whisk flour, cream of tartar, baking soda, and table salt together in bowl.

3 Using stand mixer fitted with paddle, beat butter, shortening, and granulated sugar on medium speed until pale and fluffy, 3 to 5 minutes, scraping down bowl as needed. Add eggs and continue to beat until well incorporated, about 1 minute longer. Reduce speed to low; add flour mixture; and mix until dough is uniform, about 1 minute.

4 Working with 2½ tablespoons dough at a time, roll into balls, then roll in reserved spice mixture to coat; space them evenly on 3 parchment paper–lined baking sheets (8 balls per sheet). (If you do not have 3 baking sheets, reuse first sheet once it's cooled to room temperature.)

5 Bake cookies, 1 sheet at a time, until edges are just set and beginning to brown but centers are still soft, puffy, and cracked (cookies will look raw between cracks and seem underdone), 9 to 12 minutes, rotating sheet halfway through baking. Let cookies cool on sheet for 5 minutes, then transfer to wire rack. Let cookies cool completely before serving.

Storage: 3 days at room temperature

WHY THIS RECIPE WORKS Angeletti, also known as anisette cookies, are a Sicilian specialty and a staple at any big Italian American celebration. Cakey, with a little heft, the anise-scented cookies share similarities with a scone or a biscuit. To achieve their unique texture, we use shortening in addition to butter. The shortening gives the cookies a lighter texture and an appealing crisp edge, while the butter contributes plenty of flavor. Lemon zest and juice complement the refreshing hit of anise. To ensure that the anise flavor fully permeates our cookies, we use extract in both the dough and the glaze. These cookies are traditionally decorated with cheery multicolored nonpareils after their bright white glaze is applied.

Makes 32 cookies

Total Time 45 minutes, plus 1 hour cooling and setting

ANGELETTI

- 2 cups (284 grams) all-purpose flour
- ½ cup (99 grams) granulated sugar
- 2 teaspoons baking powder
- ½ teaspoon table salt
- 4 tablespoons (57 grams) unsalted butter, cut into ½-inch pieces and chilled
- 4 tablespoons (44 grams) vegetable shortening, cut into ½-inch pieces and chilled
- 2 large eggs
- 1¼ teaspoons anise extract, divided
- 1 teaspoon vanilla extract
- 1 teaspoon grated lemon zest plus 2 tablespoons juice
- 1½ cups (170 grams) confectioners' sugar
- Multicolored nonpareils (optional)

Feel free to use any sprinkles you like; just be sure to glaze and decorate only a few cookies at a time so the sprinkles stick before the glaze dries. Anise extract provides the classic licorice flavor, but you can substitute vanilla extract if you prefer it.

1 Adjust oven racks to upper-middle and lower-middle positions and heat oven to 375 degrees. Process flour, granulated sugar, baking powder, and salt in food processor until combined, about 5 seconds. Scatter butter and shortening over top and pulse until mixture appears sandy, 10 to 12 pulses. Add eggs, 1 teaspoon anise extract, vanilla, and lemon zest and process until dough forms, 20 to 30 seconds.

2 Working with 1 tablespoon dough at a time, roll into balls and space them evenly on 2 parchment paper–lined baking sheets. Bake until tops of cookies have puffed and cracked and bottoms are light golden brown, 14 to 16 minutes, switching and rotating sheets halfway through baking. Let cookies cool on sheets for 5 minutes, then transfer to wire rack. Let cookies cool completely before glazing.

3 Whisk confectioners' sugar, lemon juice, and remaining ¼ teaspoon anise extract in bowl until smooth. Working with a few cookies at a time, spread cookies with glaze and decorate with nonpareils, if using. Let glaze set for at least 30 minutes before serving.

Storage: unglazed, 24 hours at room temperature; 3 days glazed

WHY THIS RECIPE WORKS Inspired by Italian ricotta cookies, which are usually flavored with just a little lemon, we wanted a soft, cakey cookie with a new profile: Delicate rose water called to us, as it's used extensively in Sicily thanks to the region's Arab influence. We use it in the glaze so its flavor isn't lost—just ¼ teaspoon is enough to perfume the sweet glaze without being overpowering. Cardamom adds a subtle, warm aroma to our cookies that complements the rose water. These cookies get their moisture and lightness from ricotta but also a pleasant sandy texture from semolina flour. A sprinkling of chopped pistachios and crumbled dried rose petals makes these tender treats irresistible to the eye (and the taste buds). These little cake drops look like they came from the finest bakeshop, but they are so very simple to make.

Makes 24 cookies

Total Time 50 minutes, plus 1½ hours cooling and setting

RICOTTA ROSE COOKIES

COOKIES

- 1¼ cups (177 grams) all-purpose flour
- ¾ cup (106 grams) semolina flour
- ½ teaspoon baking soda
- ½ teaspoon table salt
- ½ teaspoon ground cardamom
- 8 tablespoons (114 grams) unsalted butter, softened
- 1 cup (198 grams) granulated sugar
- 1 large egg plus 1 large yolk
- 1 teaspoon vanilla extract
- 8 ounces (227 grams) whole-milk ricotta cheese

GLAZE AND TOPPING

- 2 tablespoons whole milk
- 1 tablespoon cream cheese, softened
- ¼ teaspoon rose water
- 1½ cups (170 grams) confectioners' sugar
- 2 tablespoons chopped shelled pistachios
- 2 tablespoons crumbled dried rose petals (optional)

Some ricotta brands add starches and stabilizers to their ricotta. In our testing we preferred the shape and texture of cookies made with natural, additive-free whole-milk ricotta. This recipe was developed using Bob's Red Mill semolina flour, which has a slightly coarse texture similar to fine cornmeal. Be sure to use food-grade dried rosebuds.

1 For the cookies: Adjust oven racks to upper-middle and lower-middle positions and heat oven to 350 degrees. Whisk all-purpose flour, semolina flour, baking soda, salt, and cardamom together in bowl; set aside.

2 Using stand mixer fitted with paddle, beat butter and sugar on medium speed until pale and fluffy, 3 to 5 minutes, scraping down bowl as needed. Add egg and yolk and vanilla and continue to beat until well incorporated, about 1 minute longer. Reduce speed to low and add flour mixture in 3 additions, alternating with ricotta in 2 additions, mixing until dough is uniform, about 1 minute.

3 Working with 1 heaping tablespoon of dough at a time, roll into balls and space them evenly on 2 parchment paper–lined baking sheets (12 balls per sheet). Bake until tops of cookies have puffed and bottoms are light golden brown, 13 to 15 minutes, switching and rotating sheets halfway through baking. Let cookies cool on sheets for 5 minutes, then transfer to wire rack. Let cookies cool completely before glazing.

4 For the glaze and topping: Whisk milk, cream cheese, and rose water in medium bowl until no lumps remain. Add sugar and whisk until smooth. Spoon 1 teaspoon glaze onto center of each cookie (glaze should drip down sides but not run off entirely), then sprinkle with pistachios and rose petals. Let glaze set for about 1 hour before serving.

Storage: unglazed, 24 hours at room temperature; 2 days glazed

Makes 16 cookies

Total Time 55 minutes, plus 30 minutes cooling

WHY THIS RECIPE WORKS When summer berries are at their ripest, we love a tender and flaky biscuit piled high with billowy whipped cream and juicy strawberries. We decided to capture the essence of strawberry shortcake in a handheld cookie format, no matter the season. The results are remarkably reminiscent of the original. To achieve a light, not-too-sweet cookie base, we make a scone-like dough by cutting butter into flour and bringing it together with heavy cream. We roll the dough thin and cut it into rounds. For strawberries and cream with enough stability to top a cookie, we turn to American buttercream and freeze-dried strawberries. The tart, dehydrated fruit packs a punch and infuses the butter and sugar with intense berry flavor (without wetness).

STRAWBERRY SHORTCOOKIES

SHORTCAKES

- 2 cups (284 grams) all-purpose flour
- 1 tablespoon baking powder
- ¼ cup (50 grams) granulated sugar, divided
- ½ teaspoon table salt
- 6 tablespoons (86 grams) unsalted butter, cut into ¼-inch pieces and chilled
- 1 cup (231 grams) plus 1 tablespoon heavy cream, divided

FROSTING

- 10 tablespoons (143 grams) unsalted butter, softened
- 1¼ cups (141 grams) confectioners' sugar
- Pinch table salt
- 1 tablespoon heavy cream
- ½ teaspoon vanilla extract
- ½ cup freeze-dried strawberries

- 6 ounces (170 grams) strawberries, hulled and cut into ¼-inch pieces (optional)
- 1 tablespoon chopped fresh mint (optional)
- Freeze-dried strawberries, crushed, for garnishing (optional)
- Sprinkles (optional)

When it comes to decorating, you have a lot of choices. If you're planning on eating the cookies right away, chopped fresh strawberries tossed with fresh mint make a wonderful topping. To eat later and for easier transport, opt for crumbled freeze-dried strawberries and/or sprinkles for garnish.

1 For the shortcakes: Adjust oven racks to upper-middle and lower-middle positions and heat oven to 425 degrees. Process flour, baking powder, 3 tablespoons sugar, and salt in food processor until combined, about 5 seconds. Scatter butter over top and pulse until mixture resembles coarse crumbs with visible pea-size pieces, about 12 pulses. Add 1 cup (231 grams) cream and pulse until mixture begins to clump together, about 10 pulses, scraping down sides of bowl once halfway through.

2 Transfer dough to lightly floured surface and gently press together until dough is mostly smooth; pat into 6 by 4-inch rectangle. Roll dough into 14 by 12-inch oval, about ¼ inch thick. Using 3-inch round scalloped cutter, cut dough into 14 rounds, gently pressing together and re-rolling scraps once to cut out 2 more rounds.

3 Space rounds evenly on 2 parchment paper–lined baking sheets, then brush tops of shortcakes with remaining 1 tablespoon cream and sprinkle with remaining 1 tablespoon sugar. Bake until edges are light golden brown, about 10 minutes, switching and rotating sheets halfway through baking. Let cookies cool on sheets for 5 minutes, then transfer to wire rack. Let cool completely before frosting.

4 For the frosting: Using stand mixer fitted with paddle, beat butter at medium-high speed until smooth, about 30 seconds. Add sugar and salt and beat at medium-low speed until most of sugar is moistened, about 45 seconds. Scrape down sides of bowl and beat at medium speed until mixture is fully combined, about 15 seconds longer; scrape down bowl. Add heavy cream and vanilla and beat at medium speed until incorporated, 10 to 30 seconds. Increase speed to medium high and beat until light and fluffy, 4 to 5 minutes, scraping down bowl once or twice during mixing.

5 Pulse freeze-dried strawberries in spice grinder until reduced to fine powder, about ten 5-second pulses. Add powder to buttercream and beat on medium speed until fully incorporated, about 30 seconds. Before serving, spread 1 heaping tablespoon frosting evenly on each cookie, leaving ½-inch border around rim of each cookie. If using, toss chopped strawberries with mint in bowl before sprinkling over frosted cookies, or sprinkle frosted cookies with extra crushed freeze-dried strawberries and/or sprinkles.

Storage: unfrosted, 24 hours at room temperature

WHY THIS RECIPE WORKS These moist, oval-shaped Greek cookies are soaked in a floral honey syrup, and are made without egg for a sturdy, biscuit-like texture that softens just enough (without falling apart) in their honey dip. The dough combines bright orange juice and zest with the warm spice of cinnamon and cloves for a comfortingly familiar flavor combination typical of many Greek sweets. Another Mediterranean ingredient that makes these cookies unique: olive oil, which we simply blend with sugar in the food processor before mixing in the remaining dry ingredients by hand—no cutting, creaming, or melting of butter required. After carefully submerging the egg-shaped cookies in honey syrup so they're fully soaked—but not soggy—we give them a decorative finish of chopped toasted walnuts, which we mix with some soaking syrup to help them stay put.

Makes about 36 cookies

Total Time 45 minutes, plus 30 minutes cooling

MELOMAKARONA

- 2¼ cups (320 grams) all-purpose flour
- ¾ teaspoon baking soda
- ¾ teaspoon ground cinnamon, divided
- ½ teaspoon table salt
- ¼ teaspoon ground cloves
- 1½ cups (297 grams) sugar, divided
- 1 tablespoon grated orange zest plus ½ cup (118 grams) juice
- ¾ cup (158 grams) extra-virgin olive oil
- ¾ cup (177 grams) water
- ½ cup (167 grams) honey
- ½ cup (53 grams) walnuts, toasted and chopped fine

1 Adjust oven racks to upper-middle and lower-middle positions and heat oven to 350 degrees. Whisk flour, baking soda, ½ teaspoon cinnamon, salt, and cloves together in large bowl.

2 Process ½ cup (99 grams) sugar and orange zest in food processor until moist and fragrant, about 30 seconds. Add oil and orange juice and process until slightly thickened, about 45 seconds. Stir sugar mixture into flour mixture until dough forms.

3 Working with 1 tablespoon dough at a time, roll into ovals and space them evenly on 2 parchment paper–lined baking sheets. Bake until light golden brown, 16 to 18 minutes, switching and rotating sheets halfway through baking. Let cookies cool on sheets for 5 minutes.

4 Meanwhile, bring water, honey, and remaining 1 cup (198 grams) sugar to boil in medium saucepan over medium-high heat, stirring frequently to dissolve sugar. Remove saucepan from heat and let syrup cool slightly.

5 Combine walnuts, 3 tablespoons syrup, and remaining ¼ teaspoon cinnamon in small bowl. Working in batches, drop cookies into warm syrup in saucepan for about 1 minute, gently flipping them halfway through soaking. Transfer cookies to wire rack and top each with ½ teaspoon walnut mixture. Let cookies cool completely before serving.

Storage: 2 days at room temperature

Makes 20 cookies

Total Time 45 minutes, plus 40 minutes cooling

WHY THIS RECIPE WORKS These diminutive sandwich cookies pack considerable flavor in their petite package. For a bit of flavor intrigue, the soft, deeply chocolaty cookies are spiced (and spiked) up with coffee liqueur and cayenne pepper. An exterior coating of ground almonds gives the cookies some texture and complementary nutty flavor. Dulce de leche is the perfect glue to hold the cookies together—the gooey, thick caramel adds sweetness and more depth to the bold little cookies.

SPICY MOCHA SANDWICH COOKIES WITH DULCE DE LECHE

- ⅓ cup (52 grams) blanched almonds
- 1½ cups (213 grams) all-purpose flour
- ¼ cup (21 grams) Dutch-processed cocoa powder
- ½ teaspoon table salt
- ¼ teaspoon cayenne pepper
- 4 ounces (113 grams) bittersweet chocolate, melted and cooled
- 12 tablespoons (171 grams) unsalted butter, softened
- ⅔ cup (132 grams) sugar
- 2 large egg yolks
- 2 tablespoons coffee liqueur
- 1 teaspoon vanilla extract
- ¼ cup dulce de leche

Use either Kahlúa or Tia Maria for the coffee liqueur.

1 Adjust oven racks to upper-middle and lower-middle positions and heat oven to 350 degrees. Line 2 baking sheets with parchment paper. Process almonds in food processor until finely ground, about 30 seconds. Combine flour, cocoa, salt, and cayenne in bowl.

2 Microwave chocolate in bowl at 50 percent power, stirring occasionally, until melted, 2 to 4 minutes. Using stand mixer fitted with paddle, beat butter and sugar on medium-high speed until pale and fluffy, about 2 minutes. Add melted chocolate, egg yolks, liqueur, and vanilla and beat until incorporated. Reduce speed to low, add flour mixture in 3 additions, and mix until just combined, scraping down bowl as needed.

3 Working with 2-teaspoon portions at a time, roll into balls and space them 1 inch apart on prepared sheets. Sprinkle ground almonds on top, pressing lightly to adhere. Bake cookies until edges appear dry, 8 to 10 minutes, switching and rotating sheets halfway through baking. Let cookies cool on sheets for 5 minutes, then transfer to wire rack and let cool completely, about 40 minutes.

4 Spread ½ teaspoon dulce de leche over bottom of half of cookies, then top with remaining cookies, pressing gently to adhere.

Storage: 3 days at room temperature

Makes 12 madeleines

Total Time 40 minutes, plus 1 hour chilling and cooling

WHY THIS RECIPE WORKS Madeleines are light and airy sponge cakes in cookie form, with a beautiful ridged exterior formed by the shell-shaped tins in which they're baked. The elegant vanilla cakes may prompt a Proustian memory, but we wanted to tell a new story with these nutty-tasting browned butter madeleines, gently scented with cardamom. A half teaspoon of baking powder lifts the madeleines and creates the signature hump in the center of each cookie. Egg yolks impart a nice custardy flavor, and using a generous amount of sugar produces golden brown, lightly caramelized edges. These new madeleines are, as ever, perfect with coffee or tea.

BROWNED BUTTER CARDAMOM MADELEINES

- 4 tablespoons (57 grams) unsalted butter
- 6 tablespoons (53 grams) all-purpose flour
- ½ teaspoon baking powder
- ¼ teaspoon table salt
- ¼ teaspoon ground cardamom
- ¼ cup (50 grams) granulated sugar
- 3 tablespoons whole milk, room temperature
- 2 large egg yolks, room temperature
- 1 teaspoon vanilla extract
- Confectioners' sugar, for dusting

The batter emulsifies best with room-temperature ingredients. Letting the madeleines cool in the pan for 10 minutes before unmolding helps preserve their ridged edges. There is no need to spread the batter out in the molds as it will spread during baking. We had the best success using a noncoated aluminum madeleine pan. If using a nonstick madeleine pan, reduce the baking time to about 6 minutes; the cookies will be slightly darker.

1 Heat butter in 8-inch skillet over medium-high heat until melted, about 2 minutes. Continue to cook, swirling skillet and stirring constantly with silicone spatula, until butter is dark golden brown and has nutty aroma, 1 to 3 minutes. Transfer browned butter to small heatproof bowl, being sure to scrape any milk solids at bottom of skillet into bowl.

2 Whisk flour, baking powder, salt, and cardamom together in bowl. Whisk granulated sugar, milk, egg yolks, and vanilla together in separate medium bowl until smooth. Stir flour mixture into egg mixture until thoroughly combined, then fold in browned butter until batter is homogeneous. Cover and refrigerate for at least 30 minutes or up to 12 hours.

3 Adjust oven rack to lowest position and heat oven to 375 degrees. Spray 12-cup madeleine pan with baking spray with flour. Divide batter evenly among prepared cups (about 1 tablespoon per cup), then bake until madeleines are golden and spring back when pressed lightly, 7 to 9 minutes, rotating pan halfway through baking.

4 Let madeleines cool in pan for 10 minutes. Using offset spatula or butter knife, loosen edges of madeleines, then transfer to wire rack, shell pattern side down. Let madeleines cool completely, then dust with confectioners' sugar before serving.

Storage: 2 days at room temperature

Makes 24 cookies

Total Time 40 minutes, plus 1½ hours cooling and setting

WHY THIS RECIPE WORKS Financiers are delicate little cakes made with ground nuts (usually almonds), aromatic browned butter, egg whites, and sugar. One bite reveals the moist, nubby interiors and crisp edges—it's these contrasting textures that are the hallmark of this French treat. For a variation, we lean into classic flavors of the American South: bourbon and pecans. The caramel-like notes of the toasted nuts are echoed in a boozy glaze, transporting this treat from the Champs-Élysées to Charleston.

BOURBON PECAN FINANCIERS

FINANCIERS

- ¾ cup (89 grams) pecans, toasted
- 2 tablespoons all-purpose flour
- 5 tablespoons (71 grams) unsalted butter
- ½ cup plus 1 tablespoon (111 grams) granulated sugar
- ⅛ teaspoon table salt
- ⅓ cup (85 grams) egg whites (3 to 4 large eggs)

GLAZE

- 1 tablespoon cream cheese, softened
- 1 tablespoon milk
- 1 tablespoon bourbon
- 1½ cups (170 grams) confectioners' sugar

You'll need a 24-cup mini-muffin tin for this recipe. Because egg whites can vary in size, measuring the whites by weight or volume is essential. Baking spray with flour ensures that the cakes bake up with appropriately flat tops; we don't recommend substituting vegetable oil spray in this recipe.

1 For the financiers: Adjust oven rack to middle position and heat oven to 375 degrees. Generously spray 24-cup mini-muffin tin with baking spray with flour. Process pecans and flour in food processor until finely ground, about 1 minute, scraping down sides of bowl twice during processing.

2 Heat butter in 10-inch skillet over medium-high heat until melted, about 2 minutes. Continue to cook, swirling skillet and stirring constantly with silicone spatula, until butter is dark golden brown and has nutty aroma, 1 to 3 minutes. Transfer browned butter to small heatproof bowl, being sure to scrape any milk solids at bottom of skillet into bowl.

3 Whisk pecan mixture, sugar, and salt together in second bowl. Add egg whites and whisk until combined, then stir in butter until incorporated. Distribute batter evenly among prepared muffin cups.

4 Bake until edges are well browned and tops are golden, about 14 minutes, rotating tin halfway through baking. Remove tin from oven and immediately invert wire rack on top of tin. Invert rack and tin, then carefully remove tin. Turn cakes right side up and let cool completely before glazing.

5 For the glaze: Whisk cream cheese, milk, and bourbon in medium bowl until no lumps remain. Add confectioners' sugar and whisk until smooth. Dip sides of cooled financiers halfway into glaze, spooning glaze to coat as needed. Transfer glazed financiers to wire rack set in baking sheet and let sit until glaze is set, about 1 hour, before serving.

Storage: 3 days at room temperature

Nutritional Information for Our Recipes

We calculated the nutritional values of our recipes per cookie or bar. We entered all the ingredients, using weights where it's important. We also used our preferred brands in these analyses. We did not include additional salt for cookies that are finished with flake sea salt.

	Cal	Total Fat (g)	Sat Fat (g)	Chol (mg)	Sodium (mg)	Carbs (g)	Fiber (g)	Total Sugar (g)	Protein (g)
Chapter 1. Chewy and Gooey									
Chewy Chocolate Chip Cookies	270	14	9	50	190	35	1	22	3
Buckwheat Chocolate Chunk Cookies	280	15	9	50	230	35	1	23	4
Salted Malted Milk Chocolate Chunk Cookies	390	19	11	60	380	50	1	34	5
Vegan Peanut Butter Chocolate Chip Cookies	270	14	9	0	200	35	2	23	4
Spiced Almond Chip Skillet Cookie	560	29	15	95	560	69	2	43	8
Chewy Sugar Cookies	150	7	3	20	85	21	0	13	2
Olive Oil, Anise, and Orange Sugar Cookies	150	7	3	20	85	22	0	13	2
Matcha and Black Sesame Sugar Cookies	170	8	3	20	85	23	0	13	2
Dragon Fruit Mochi-Stuffed Lime Cookies	380	18	5	25	190	48	1	23	7
Lemon Cookie Bars	200	7	3	25	90	32	0	22	2
Brown Sugar Cookies	170	7	4.5	35	80	25	0	16	2
Brown Sugar Milk Tea Cookies	280	12	7	50	130	41	0	29	3
Maple Sugar Cookies	180	7	4	35	130	27	0	17	2
Garam Masala Molasses Cookies	160	6	4	25	115	23	0	12	2

	Cal	Total Fat (g)	Sat Fat (g)	Chol (mg)	Sodium (mg)	Carbs (g)	Fiber (g)	Total Sugar (g)	Protein (g)
Chapter 1. Chewy and Gooey (Continued)									
Pumpkin Spice Hermits	180	5	3	30	100	32	0	20	2
Triple Citrus Gingerbread with White Chocolate	200	9	6	15	80	27	0	16	2
Sticky Toffee Date Cookies	300	12	7	55	230	47	1	34	3
Hojicha Pistachio Cookies	270	15	7	45	200	31	1	19	5
Chewy Oatmeal Cookies	190	7	2.5	25	125	28	1	15	3
Oat Guava Cookies	240	10	6	35	85	36	1	22	3
Oatmeal Creme Pies	470	21	8	55	330	67	2	40	5
Classic Peanut Butter Cookies	190	9	2.5	20	150	23	1	14	5
Browned Coconut Butter Cookies	300	17	16	0	200	32	3	17	3
No-Bake Cherry-Amaretto Balls	130	4.5	3	0	70	20	0	18	1
Chapter 2. Fully Loaded									
Loaded White Chocolate–Macadamia Cookies	360	20	9	50	230	41	1	27	4
Peanut Butter Candy and Bacon Cookies	370	20	11	55	350	41	0	28	7
Cookies and Cream Cookies	320	14	8	50	270	45	1	27	4
Browned Butter Halva Crunch Cookies	410	23	9	50	230	48	1	32	7
S'mores Cookies	290	12	7	45	230	42	1	22	3
Chocolate–Orange Twist Cookies	270	12	5	25	160	39	0	23	3
Chewy, Gooey Biscoff Butter Cookies	360	19	7	45	210	42	1	23	5
Molten Toasted Marshmallow Peanut Butter Cookies	220	10	3	20	170	29	1	19	5
Chocolate Chunk Oatmeal Cookies with Pecans and Dried Cherries	320	17	7	35	120	42	2	26	3
Texas Trail Cookies	330	18	9	45	135	39	2	25	4
Triple Chocolate–Cherry Cookies	190	8	4.5	25	75	27	0	20	3
Crunchy Salty Snack Cookies with Caramel Frosting	190	10	5	20	35	24	0	15	1
Blueberry Jam Breakfast Cookies	300	16	5	30	180	37	2	21	5
Oatmeal-Date Bars with Whipped Labneh	440	21	5	35	200	60	4	40	9

	Cal	Total Fat (g)	Sat Fat (g)	Chol (mg)	Sodium (mg)	Carbs (g)	Fiber (g)	Total Sugar (g)	Protein (g)
Chapter 2. Fully Loaded (Continued)									
Peanut Butter–Stuffed Chocolate Cookies	300	14	4.5	25	240	43	1	28	5
Stuffed Red Velvet Cookies	560	29	16	90	400	68	2	38	7
Ultimate Brookies	400	21	10	70	230	53	2	34	5
M&M's Fudge Ripple Ice Cream Sandwiches	420	20	12	80	260	56	1	38	5
Butterscotch Coffee Ice Cream Sandwiches	380	18	12	80	260	48	0	26	5
Chapter 3. Crispy and Crunchy									
Thin and Crispy Chocolate Chip Cookies	160	9	5	35	135	20	1	13	1
Thin and Crispy Rosemary Toffee Cookies	150	6	3.5	40	130	22	0	15	1
Thai Tea Crisps	210	7	4	40	140	37	0	29	1
Speculoos with Almonds	80	3.5	2	15	55	11	0	5	1
Coconut Oatmeal Cookies	180	9	6	25	95	22	1	13	2
Iced Espresso Oatmeal Crunchies	70	2.5	1.5	10	45	11	0	7	1
Chocolate-Dipped Almond Cookies	160	11	5	20	55	13	1	4	3
Double Gingersnaps	50	2	1	10	45	8	0	5	1
Florentine Lace Cookies	150	11	4.5	15	25	11	1	5	3
Chocolate-Vanilla Crème Sandwich Cookies	60	2.5	1	10	25	8	0	5	1
PB&J Sandwich Cookies	250	13	3.5	15	170	29	1	22	6
Double Chocolate Tim Tams	250	13	10	15	90	30	0	20	2
Thin Chocolate-Mint Cookies	60	3	2	5	20	8	1	5	1
Black Cherry and Chocolate Linzer Cookies	210	9	5	30	55	31	1	19	2
Blackberry-Thyme Linzer Cookies	140	6	3	20	65	20	0	12	2
Almond Biscotti	140	6	1.5	20	70	17	1	9	3
Pink Peppercorn–Pistachio Biscotti with White Chocolate	170	7	3	20	120	22	1	12	4
Chocolate-Hazelnut Biscotti	150	9	2	20	80	17	2	9	3

	Cal	Total Fat (g)	Sat Fat (g)	Chol (mg)	Sodium (mg)	Carbs (g)	Fiber (g)	Total Sugar (g)	Protein (g)
Chapter 4. Butter Makes It Better									
Raspberry-Dipped Shortbread	140	10	7	15	40	14	0	6	1
Chocolate Shortbread	190	12	7	30	75	19	1	4	2
Browned Butter Shortbread	80	4	2.5	10	60	9	0	5	1
Sparkling Blueberry-Lavender Shortbread Cookies	200	11	6	25	75	26	1	11	2
Millionaire's Shortbread	200	10	6	25	90	26	0	16	2
Sablés	50	3	2	10	15	6	0	2	1
Chocolate Sablés	50	3	2	10	15	6	0	2	1
Saffron Sablés with Pistachios	60	3.5	2	15	35	6	0	2	1
Salted Egg Yolk Shortbread Sandwiches	170	9	5	75	340	15	0	7	3
Simplest Raspberry-Cinnamon Slice-and-Bakes	70	4	2.5	15	25	7	0	3	1
Peppermint Checkerboards	50	2.5	1.5	10	15	6	0	3	1
Easiest-Ever Marbled Butter Cookies	60	3.5	2	15	20	8	0	4	1
Ma'amoul	160	7	4	15	40	20	1	8	2
New Mexican Biscochitos	90	4.5	2	10	30	10	0	5	1
Coconut Alfajores	270	13	8	50	110	35	1	22	3
Raspberry-Lemon Sweetheart Thumbprints	120	5	3	25	80	17	0	10	2
Coconut Thumbprints with Tamarind Caramel	110	5	3.5	15	80	15	0	10	1
Chocolate-Pistachio Thumbprints	190	9	4.5	25	95	24	1	14	3
Gingerbread Eggnog Thumbprints	200	9	5	40	110	23	1	15	3
Apricot-Cardamom Diagonals	130	6	3.5	15	40	19	0	9	1
Hamantaschen with Poppy Seed Filling	150	8	4	25	75	18	1	8	2
Cape Breton Oatcakes	110	5	3	10	125	16	1	6	2

	Cal	Total Fat (g)	Sat Fat (g)	Chol (mg)	Sodium (mg)	Carbs (g)	Fiber (g)	Total Sugar (g)	Protein (g)
Chapter 5. Sink Your Teeth In									
Cherry Streusel Bars	170	4	2	10	55	32	1	17	2
Chocolate Raspberry Streusel Bars	200	9	5	20	75	29	1	17	2
Cranberry-Rosemary Corn Streusel Bars	250	10	6	25	120	40	2	22	2
Salted Caramel Apple Crumb Bars	310	12	8	30	450	49	0	29	2
Lemon Bars	260	13	8	125	170	32	0	21	4
Meyer Lemon–Blueberry Reflection Bars	210	7	4	60	90	36	1	28	2
Ultranutty Pecan Bars	280	20	6	20	105	24	2	12	3
Caramel Pistachio Bars with Cacao Nibs	330	20	10	40	230	35	2	24	4
Giant Coconut-Caramel Shortbread Cookie	530	32	22	45	370	58	3	26	6
Miso Magic Bars	340	19	10	20	250	39	1	34	5
Turtle Bars	350	21	10	35	210	40	2	27	3
Strawberry Cheesecake Bars	270	17	11	80	160	25	0	19	4
Mango Lassi Bars	190	11	7	30	70	19	0	15	3
Banoffee Crunch Bars	320	25	14	100	95	22	0	11	4
Ginger-Citrus Sweet Potato Pie Bars	410	15	8	70	260	66	2	37	5
S'mores Bars	200	11	7	20	105	26	0	20	2
Coconut Macaroons with Chocolate Chips and Almonds	150	10	6	0	150	14	1	12	2
Coconut Dulce de Leche Cookies	260	17	13	30	280	27	2	20	3
Sichuan Peanut Rice Krispie Treats	190	10	1.5	0	220	22	2	11	5
Levain-Style Chocolate Chip Cookies	780	47	20	80	490	84	6	46	14
Chocolate-Marshmallow Sandwich Cookies	490	24	15	30	310	69	4	32	6
Nutella Rugelach	120	8	5	15	40	11	1	5	1

	Cal	Total Fat (g)	Sat Fat (g)	Chol (mg)	Sodium (mg)	Carbs (g)	Fiber (g)	Total Sugar (g)	Protein (g)
Chapter 6. Rich and Squidgy									
Fudgy Brownies	210	10	6	45	75	26	1	19	3
Licorice-White Chocolate Brownies	200	10	6	40	95	28	0	20	2
Deepest, Darkest, Fudgiest Flourless Chocolate Brownies	200	12	7	45	100	24	1	17	3
Black Forest Brownies	410	23	14	90	115	46	3	35	5
Chicory Café au Lait Chocolate Bars	280	18	12	80	85	25	0	18	3
Truffle Brownies	470	27	10	45	350	58	2	43	5
Peanut Butter Swirl Brownies	190	12	6	40	85	19	1	13	3
Cream Cheese Brownies	230	14	8	50	130	25	1	18	3
Raspberry White Chocolate Brownies	150	7	4	20	80	20	1	13	2
Blondies	130	8	3.5	20	50	16	0	11	2
Tahini Blondie Bites with Caramelized Banana Jam and Chocolate	230	10	2.5	20	180	33	1	21	4
Pumpkin Cream Cheese Blondies	410	21	13	115	320	51	0	33	5
Strawberry Matcha Cream Cheese Blondies	180	8	5	35	100	23	0	16	3
Strawberry Lemonade Coconut Mochi Bars	220	7	4.5	35	140	38	1	19	3
Chocolate Crinkle Cookies	170	6	3.5	30	100	27	1	20	3
Ube Crinkle Cookies	170	6	3	20	120	28	0	15	2
Chapter 7. Light and Lovely									
Lemon Thins	70	3	2	10	25	10	0	5	1
Yuzu and Black Sesame Thins	70	3.5	2	15	35	10	0	5	1
Mango-Lime Meltaways	60	2.5	1.5	5	20	8	0	5	0
Guava-Strawberry Sandwich Cookies	180	10	6	50	50	21	0	9	1
Snowballs	100	7	2.5	10	35	10	0	5	1

	Cal	Total Fat (g)	Sat Fat (g)	Chol (mg)	Sodium (mg)	Carbs (g)	Fiber (g)	Total Sugar (g)	Protein (g)
Chapter 7. Light and Lovely (Continued)									
Baci di Dama	60	4.5	2	5	10	6	0	2	1
Spritz Cookies	45	2.5	1.5	10	10	5	0	2	0
Stained Glass Window Cookies	110	5	3.5	15	20	15	0	6	1
Fairy Gingerbread	25	1	0.5	5	20	4	0	2	0
Pizzelle	80	0.5	0	25	35	17	0	9	2
Almond Joy Meringue Kisses	25	1	1	0	10	4	0	3	0
Passion Fruit Meringue Swirls	130	3	1.5	45	30	25	0	24	2
Sunrise Marshmallow Cookies	280	12	8	15	120	40	0	34	3
Chapter 8. Soft and Cakey									
Chocolate Whoopie Pies	900	39	25	135	510	129	0	77	9
Mini Pumpkin Whoopie Pies	130	7	4	35	150	16	0	11	2
Black and Pink Cookies	450	11	7	45	190	85	0	67	4
Chocolate Banana Streusel Cookies	270	12	7	15	170	39	1	17	3
Carrot Cake Cookies	300	17	7	45	160	35	1	24	4
Frosted Soft Sugar Cookies	200	8	2	10	65	31	0	19	2
Advieh Snickerdoodles	180	8	3.5	25	170	25	0	14	2
Angeletti	130	4.5	2	20	90	20	0	11	2
Ricotta Rose Cookies	160	6	3.5	30	90	25	0	15	3
Strawberry Shortcookies	270	17	11	50	200	26	0	12	2
Melomakarona	130	6	1	0	60	19	0	12	1
Spicy Mocha Sandwich Cookies with Dulce de Leche	190	11	6	40	70	22	0	12	3
Browned Butter Cardamom Madeleines	80	5	3	45	70	8	0	4	1
Bourbon Pecan Financiers	100	5	2	5	20	13	0	12	1

CONVERSIONS + EQUIVALENTS

Some say baking is a science and an art. We would say that geography has a hand in it too. Flours and sugars manufactured in the United Kingdom and elsewhere will feel and taste different from those manufactured in the United States. So we cannot promise that the cookies you bake in Canada or England will taste the same as a batch baked in the States, but we can offer guidelines for converting measures and temperatures. You should also rely on your instincts and refer to the visual cues in the recipes. We use standard volume measures following U.S. government guidelines.

Volume Conversions

U.S.	Metric
1 teaspoon	5 milliliters
2 teaspoons	10 milliliters
1 tablespoon	15 milliliters
2 tablespoons	30 milliliters
¼ cup	59 milliliters
⅓ cup	79 milliliters
½ cup	118 milliliters
¾ cup	177 milliliters
1 cup	237 milliliters
1¼ cups	296 milliliters
1½ cups	355 milliliters
2 cups (1 pint)	473 milliliters
2½ cups	591 milliliters
3 cups	710 milliliters
4 cups (1 quart)	0.946 liter
1.06 quarts	1 liter
4 quarts (1 gallon)	3.8 liters

Oven Temperature

Fahrenheit	Celsius	Gas Mark
225	105	¼
250	120	½
275	135	1
300	150	2
325	165	3
350	180	4
375	190	5
400	200	6
425	220	7
450	230	8
475	245	9

Converting Temperatures from an Instant-Read Thermometer

We include doneness temperatures in many of the recipes in this book. We recommend an instant-read thermometer for the job. Refer to the table above to convert Fahrenheit degrees to Celsius. Or, for temperatures not represented in the chart, use this simple formula:

Subtract 32 degrees from the Fahrenheit reading, then divide the result by 1.8 to find the Celsius reading.

Example

"Cook caramel until it registers 234 degrees."

To convert

234°F – 32 = 202°
202° ÷ 1.8 = 112.22°C, rounded down to 112°C

INDEX

Note: Page references in *italics* indicate photographs.

D

E

L

M

U

V

W

Y